The Singer of Tales in Performance

Voices in Performance and Text

John Miles Foley, General Editor

*

THE SINGER OF TALES
IN PERFORMANCE

JOHN MILES FOLEY

INDIANA UNIVERSITY PRESS

Bloomington and Indianapolis

The paper used in this publication meets the minimum requirements of American
National Standard for Information Sciences—Permanence of Paper for Printed
Library Materials, ANSI Z39.48-1984.

Manufactured in the United States of America

Library of Congress Cataloging-in-Publication Data
Foley, John Miles
The singer of tales in performance / John Miles Foley.
p. cm.—(Voices in performance and text)
Includes bibliographical references and index.
ISBN 0-253-32225-1 (cl).—ISBN 0-253-20931-5 (pa)
1. Folklore—Performance. 2. Oral tradition. 3. Oral-formulaic analysis
I. Title. II. Series
GR72.3.F65   1995
398'.01—dc20   94-17638
1   2   3   4   5   00   99   98   97   96   95

This book is for
Isaac Michael Foley, joyful image of his etymon
Albert Bates Lord, ἀοιδὸς περικλυτός
Walter J. Ong, wordsmith

The word
was born in the blood,
grew in the dark body, beating,
and took flight through the lips and mouth. . . .
Later on, the word fills with meaning.
Always with child, it filled up with lives.

from Pablo Neruda, "The Word"

CONTENTS

PREFACE

Words are always situated; they cannot naturally occur but in context, and they cannot naturally recur without reference to prior occurrences and prior contexts. Such truisms occasion no argument in their application to literary forms such as the novel, since the involved fields of reference for highly literary and textual forms of verbal art have been familiarly delineated by a grid of approved and customary organizing principles, among them author, text, genre, and (literary) tradition.[1] We think we know how words in novels are situated, or how they situate themselves. Indeed, even in an age learning to prize "intertextuality," we can observe that the very etymology of that critical term denominates two or more formally bounded, complete items that interact—so that their separate contexts are more or less sharply defined, and the individual text maintains an absolute status uniquely its own. Even though the field of interpretation is enlarged and deepened, textual heuristics tacitly demands that we privilege the individual document above all else.

But what if the familiar grid were to prove at least in part unhelpful? What if, by insisting on a text-centered perspective, it obscured more than it illuminated? Questions such as these arise whenever one considers either those forms of verbal art that arise and flourish wholly within an oral tradition or, perhaps less obviously, those related forms that, although they may survive only as texts, have roots planted firmly in an oral tradition. In either case, contexts that lie outside the received version or text are most certainly active and crucially important, both for the performer/writer and for the audience, and interpretation requires consideration of those engaged contexts. To put it aphoristically, such oral traditional forms are situated in part within a set of associations and expectations *formally extrinsic* but *metonymically intrinsic* to their experience as works of verbal art. To ignore the immanent context is to force situated words out of their natural significative settings—obviously a crippling and artistically violent reorientation; the result might well parallel the dysfunction occasioned

1. Here I intentionally refer to work based on "standard," even old-fashioned literary-historical, categories rather than the current polyphony of critical voices that seek to refine and reshape them, on the grounds that these earlier categories—rather than their contemporary modulations and redefinitions—have historically constituted the literary model to which scholars have often sought to assimilate oral traditional works. It has been the outmoded or old-fashioned critical perspective on literary art, in other words, that has blocked the way to an appreciation of traditional oral works on their own (nonliterary) terms. And while many newer methods certainly hold great promise for less parochial and predetermined viewpoints on all types of verbal art (e.g., Bakhtin 1981 on "dialogism"; for critical studies, see esp. Briggs 1988, Tedlock 1983, Tyler 1987; also Foley 1991: chap. 2), by definition they are not part of the historical problem, whose roots go far back in time and which is perhaps epitomized in the hypertextuality that is the hallmark of New Criticism and Formalism (cf. Ong 1982: 160–64).

by forcing a novel into another generic category, or into another unrelated literary tradition, for the purpose of (mis)reading its situated signals.[2]

In an effort to release traditional oral works from the straitjacket of literary assumption, to let them speak in their own tongue(s), I have developed a three-part strategy. The initial move entailed demonstrating, hopefully with some precision, the levels of structure in a generically unified sample of extended narratives; this philological underpinning, the subject of *Traditional Oral Epic* (Foley 1990a), was intended both as an end in itself and as an exordium to responsible investigation of the art of ancient Greek, Old English, and South Slavic epic.[3] Then, as the title implies, *Immanent Art* (1991) went on to examine the trajectory from structure to meaning, illustrating the metonymic, associative enrichment of simple forms by institutionalized reference to an ever-impinging tradition. In short, the first book attempted to establish the nature and dynamics of the "words" that constitute traditional oral epic, while the second asked not just *what* but *how* these words mean.

In both of these discussions it was in fact that elusive quality of "tradition" that underlay the investigation, in the one case accounting for the shape and texture of the specialized "words" and in the other imbuing them with a specialized signification. As Dan Ben-Amos (1984) has shown so memorably, however, this is not a concept that admits of a single, simple definition,[4] and my own usage certainly weaves together at least three of his "seven strands" of tradition, namely, "as canon," "as process," and "as performance." In these two earlier studies and this sequel, let me acknowledge explicitly that I have assumed tradition to be a dynamic, multivalent body of meaning that preserves much that a group has invented and transmitted but which also includes as necessary, defining features both an inherent indeterminacy and a predisposition to various kinds of changes or modifications. I assume, in short, a living and vital entity with synchronic and diachronic aspects that over time and space will experience (and partially constitute) a unified variety of receptions.

With this notion of tradition in mind, I had originally thought that these two

2. Thus it is that Richard Bauman and Charles Briggs argue strenuously that a better understanding of performance requires us "to recognize the historical and cultural specificity of Western thinking about language and society and to explore a broader range of alternatives" (1990: 60). Complementarily, Stephen Tyler characterizes the reality of writing (as opposed to performance and oral traditional communication) as follows (1987: 20): "Writing invents its own origin in the disjunction of signifier and signified and sets itself the problem of overcoming the self-inflicted amputation which was its own parthenogenesis."

3. At the time this book is being written, the various nationalities that constituted the former Yugoslavia are in a state of civil war, and we can no longer speak of a Yugoslav state without severe qualification. Throughout this volume I use the term *South Slavic* to designate genres of verbal art that supersede ethnic boundaries, that can occur, for example, among either ethnic Serbs or ethnic Croats, albeit in distinctive forms. The adjective *Serbian* is applied to the *bajanje* or "charms" collected by our fieldwork team strictly in the southern Serbian region of Šumadija.

4. On the problematics of this term and concept, see also Finnegan 1991 and the collection of articles on "The Invention of Tradition" in Hobsbawm and Ranger 1983. Hymes (1975b: 359) speaks for many when he encourages the following view: "Let us root the notion [of tradition] not in time, but in social life. Let us postulate that the traditional is a functional prerequisite of social life. Let us consider the notion, not simply as naming objects, traditions, but also, and more fundamentally, as naming a process."

parts—*Traditional Oral Epic* and *Immanent Art*—would make up the whole, that the methodology could be grounded and explicated within the compass of these two studies. But that first approximation proved naive, for reasons that are best explained, perhaps not unexpectedly, in a story.[5]

*   *   *

In the midst of finishing up Immanent Art, *I was contacted by David Greetham, a scholar who has written engagingly on matters as seemingly diverse as editorial methods and Derridean deconstruction. David announced that he was assembling a volume on textual editing for the Modern Language Association, and asked whether I would be willing to write the chapter on "folk literature." This project seemed appealing in two ways: it had obvious inherent importance, and my knowledge of the subject was limited enough that I would be forced to read rather widely—and learn a good deal in the process—in order to carry it off.*

Reviewing the history of editing "folk literature" proved a revelation: from the Grimms onward, prospective editors had resorted to a wide variety of (at best partially) successful techniques for reducing performed events to textual cenotaphs.[6] The ongoing task of intersemiotic translation from experience to text was addressed in many ways, and none of them was entirely satisfactory. It would be more to the point to say that none of them could *be entirely satisfactory.*

In the process of writing this brief history and adding a few modest suggestions for the future, I found it organizationally convenient to denominate as most promising a few of the more recent approaches to folklore and editing folklore events/texts. Among these were the Oral-Formulaic Theory associated with Milman Parry and Albert Lord, and the Performance/Ethnography of Speaking/Ethnopoetics school linked closely with Roger Abrahams, Keith Basso, Richard Bauman, Dan Ben-Amos, Charles Briggs, Robert Georges, Dell Hymes, Barbara Kirshenblatt-Gimblett, Dennis Tedlock, Barre Toelken, and many others.[7] Pressed

5. This inserted story, told in a less discursive idiom and drawing to a modest extent on traditional storytelling techniques, in effect represents an (artificial) "breakthrough into performance" such as those reported and analyzed by Hymes (esp. 1975a), who calls such a shift a "metaphrasis," or "interpretive transformation of genre."

6. Many of the core issues are conveniently focused by a series of position papers published in *Western Folklore:* Jones 1979a, Ben-Amos 1979, Jones 1979b, Georges 1980, Zan 1982, Georges 1986, and Bronner 1988; of prime importance as precursors to this debate are Ben-Amos 1971 and Wilgus 1973; cf. also Joyner 1975. See esp. Georges (1980: 37), who neatly observes of the textual artifact that "it is a record of, and not the same thing as, the behavior complex it is created to represent." To state my own perspective succinctly, I cannot agree with Jones's assertion (1979b: 53) that "when compared to the folklore itself, the debris of daily life and the chaff of context are like so much dust in the winnowing wind of tradition," but would nonetheless heartily second the very next (and for Jones presumably the logically consequent) sentence: "Thus tradition is, and will remain, an essential part of the definition of folklore." The distinction I would draw that rationalizes these apparently disparate reactions to his two sentences is as follows: tradition must be conceived of as a dynamic and processual force, a full partner in the performance context—and not as a static and unreactive monolith. To encapsulate in an interpretive proverb to which we shall return below, *Tradition is the enabling referent, performance the enabling event.*

7. Since the relevant bibliography is much too voluminous to cite, let me simply refer to Bauman and Briggs 1990 (also Hanks 1989: esp. 111–13), and highlight a few of the contributions that are particularly significant to the theoretical connection broached in this volume: Abrahams 1977, 1983; Arewa and Dundes 1964; K. Basso 1984, 1988; Bauman 1977, 1986; Bauman and Sherzer 1989; Ben-Amos 1971; Ben-Amos and Goldstein 1975; Briggs 1988, 1990; Caraveli 1982; Fox 1988b; Georges 1969; Hymes 1981, 1989a; Kirshenblatt-Gimblett 1975; Sherzer 1983; Tedlock 1983; Toelken

to examine just what it was that made these two approaches so appealing and promising, I found a single answer for both: their attention to verbal art as a situated, experienced event in traditional context.

It then became obvious that these connections, once perceived on an abstract, descriptive level, should be pursued more rigorously and thoroughly in order to draw out their significance. If the performance-centered approach could be tied theoretically to the oral-formulaic approach, both methodologies stood to profit. If in the process the sometimes forbidding gap between what we call folklore and what we call literature could be reevaluated (at least in this one area) as a spectrum of differences rather than a two-part typology, so much the better. Perhaps best of all, my admittedly personal preference for interpretations or perspectives that can be reached by more than one avenue—an outright bias to which I gladly confess—might be fulfilled.

*   *   *

This volume really amounts to the working out of that story in an overtly discursive, critical idiom, that is, of recontextualizing the basic insights associated with writing the textual editing essay in the new medium of an extended analytical discussion.[8] Likewise, to emphasize the common ground underlying the oral-formulaic and performance-centered approaches, I have chosen as its title *The Singer of Tales in Performance*. Paying sincere homage to both the late Albert Bates Lord's pathbreaking comparative study, *The Singer of Tales*, and Richard Bauman's liberating analytical exposition, *Verbal Art as Performance*, this book seeks to place both experienced oral traditions and texts with roots in oral tradition within an empowering network viewed from different perspectives by Lord and Bauman. Because the situated verbal art of the works examined in this volume depends on a specialized idiom that is both traditional and individual, we can speak of a singer of tales. Because that art depends for its expressive force on its emergence within a specialized context, we can speak of a realm of performance. Even when the discussion turns to texts, and even when those texts are not transcriptions but lettered works in the traditional idiom, rhetorically the singer persists and the performance goes on.

In order to make the connections between the oral-formulaic and performance-centered theories as plain and as logically independent of either perspective as possible, I have coined the term *word-power* to signal the special dynamics of meaning identified by both approaches. In the present context *word-power* will name that particular mode of meaning possible only by virtue of the enabling event of performance and the enabling referent of tradition. It should be emphasized that this focus does not constitute an attempt to formulate a single, grand, overarching theory that would entirely rationalize these sister approaches, but rather an effort to reinforce and validate each method by analogy to a second perspective. It is hoped that this strategy will deepen our

1969, 1987; Toelken and Scott 1981; and Urban 1986. For brief discussions of Performance and the Ethnography of Speaking in historical context, see Bronner 1986: 119–25 and Zumwalt 1988: 138–40.

8. Cf. the issues involved in "entextualization" and "decontextualization" (Bauman and Briggs 1990: 72–78).

understanding of both methods and, most important, offer a clear view of the nature and possibilities of verbal art in oral tradition.

Toward these ends, the first three chapters present the theoretical basis for word-power, from the discovery of common ground among the Ethnography of Speaking, Ethnopoetics, and Oral-Formulaic Theory (chapter 1), through a Receptionalist study of the dimensions of performance arena, register, and communicative economy (chapter 2), and on to a consideration of traditional oral works that survive only as written texts. The applications that follow are intentionally focused on genres or works that have received relatively little attention in the past, with the idea that some knowledge of their existence and dynamics will help to fill out our understanding of the South Slavic, ancient Greek, and Anglo-Saxon repertoires. The fourth chapter thus treats the living tradition of South Slavic *bajanje* or charms, a genre that our fieldwork team experienced firsthand in the village of Orašac in central Serbia. The Homeric Hymns, particularly that devoted to the goddess Demeter, form the subject of chapter 5, as we move from living to textualized traditions. The final chapter addresses the problematic Old English verse hagiography *Andreas,* whose poet has employed the traditional oral idiom to translate a story that can stem only from a Latin or Greek source.

I have used the Oxford standard editions of the *Iliad* and *Odyssey* and the Allen-Halliday-Sikes (1980) edition of the Homeric Hymns; the *ASPR* (*Anglo-Saxon Poetic Records*) edition of Old English poetry, with the exception of the Klaeber (1950) edition of *Beowulf* and the Brooks (1961) edition of *Andreas,* citing Old English poems according to the system of abbreviation set forth in Bessinger and Smith 1978; and the *SCHS* (*Serbo-Croatian Heroic Songs*) editions of the Parry Collection epics. Much of the South Slavic epic material is, however, drawn from my own editing of the unpublished Parry Collection songs from the region of Stolac in central Hercegovina; the charms are without exception those collected by Barbara Kerewsky-Halpern and me in and around the village of Orašac in southern Serbia.

Parts of chapter 1, now completely revised and substantially augmented, were previously published in the *Journal of American Folklore* (105 [1992]: 275–301). I am grateful to *JAF* and its editor, Burt Feintuch, for permission to reprint those sections.

This volume inaugurates the new Indiana University Press series Voices in Performance and Text.

Among the many people whose writings or personal discussion (or both) have substantially improved this book are Mark Amodio, Samuel Armistead, Egbert Bakker, Richard Bauman, Dan Ben-Amos, Charles Briggs, Robert Creed, Michael Cusick, A. N. Doane, Alan Dundes, Mark Edwards, Ruth Finnegan, Paul Goetsch, Joel Halpern, Lee Haring, Joseph Harris, Lauri Harvilahti, Bonnie Irwin, Richard Janko, Barbara Kirshenblatt-Gimblett, Svetozar Koljević, Anne Lebeck (*in memoriam*), John McDowell, Elizabeth McNulty, Nada Milošević-Djordjević, Michael Nagler, Gregory Nagy, Joseph Nagy, John Niles, Emmanuel Obiechina, Ward Parks, Svetozar Petrović, Catherine Quick, Steve Reece,

Karl Reichl, Alain Renoir, Bruce Rosenberg, Joseph Russo, Ursula Schaefer, Joel Sherzer, Dennis Tedlock, and Barre Toelken. Thanks are also due three institutions at the University of Missouri–Columbia: Ellis Library, whose physical resources and expert reference librarians made my job much easier and more pleasant; the Center for Studies in Oral Tradition, with continuing support from Deans Larry Clark and Theodore Tarkow and Provost Gerald Brouder; and the Classical Studies department, *neos oikos*. Both the various incarnations of courses in Classical Studies and English (Oral Tradition, Homeric Poetry, the Greek epic seminar, and the *Beowulf* seminar) at Missouri and a succession of National Endowment for the Humanities Summer Seminars (especially those in 1991 and 1992) have also contributed much to my understanding of the issues addressed herein. I offer special thanks to Dell Hymes, Jenny Strauss Clay, and an anonymous reviewer, who read sections of the manuscript at various stages and provided invaluable commentary; to Jug Stojančić, who critiqued the translations from South Slavic from a native speaker's perspective; to Anastasios Daskalopoulos, who assisted me in reading proof; to Barbara Kerewsky-Halpern, my teacher and partner in fieldwork and subsequent analysis; to the people of Orašac, who proudly shared their rich cultural heritage with us; and to Albert Bates Lord (*in memoriam*) and Walter J. Ong, two of the dedicatees for this volume, whose influence on my understanding of oral tradition reaches far beyond their published works to their personal intellectual generosity.

The third dedicatee, Isaac Foley, can read this when he grows up; for now, baseball is much more to the point. Let me also thank the other steadfast ones: my late aunt Frances Foley Kelly, the *glaukôpis* thespian Elizabeth, and especially Anne-Marie, inveterate reader of large books.

The Singer of Tales in Performance

I

COMMON GROUND
ORAL-FORMULAIC THEORY AND
THE ETHNOGRAPHY OF SPEAKING

Yet after all that has been said about *oral* composition
as a technique of line and song construction, it seems
that the term of greater significance is *traditional.*
Oral tells us "how," but traditional tells us "what,"
and even more, "of what kind" and "of what force."

Lord 1960: 220

To claim that researchers must choose among the analyses
of poetic patterns, social interaction, or larger social
and cultural contexts is to reify each of these elements
and to forestall an adequate analysis of any.

Bauman and Briggs 1990: 69

The Singer of Tales in Performance is first a book about *word-power,* that is,
about how words engage contexts and mediate communication in verbal art
from oral tradition. It is also, and crucially, about the enabling event—*performance*—and the enabling referent—*tradition*—that give meaning to word-
power. Like the coinage created to bear this metonymic burden, the investigation
has two interlocking primary responsibilities: the problem of defining what a
"word" is in this communicative medium, and the coordinate task of locating
and explaining its peculiar "power."[1] On the way to our initial goal of building
a bridge between Oral-Formulaic Theory and Immanent Art on the one hand
and the Ethnography of Speaking and Ethnopoetics on the other, then, we must
first traverse the more familiar territory of structure and implication, of the
nature of contexted words and their ability to convey meaning.

The journey actually begins in two different places—hopefully to be seen as
at least contiguous in the topography of narrative theory by the end of this

1. As we shall see, *word-power* is not only the subject or focus of this study, but also, and more
radically, a verbal trope that names the fundamental expressive strategy employed by the singer of
tales in performance.

chapter. In pursuing the identity of the "word" and its power, we shall turn first to a modified version of the Oral-Formulaic Theory of Milman Parry and Albert Lord, inquiring what that approach has to say about the levels of structure and involved meanings in traditional oral narrative. Part of this section will treat the issue of metonymic referentiality associated with the structural integers (formula, theme, story-pattern) perceived as constituents of such works. The second beginning will query the Ethnography of Speaking approach for its explanation of word-power, asking in particular what the perspective from performance and ethnopoetics can offer to the colloquy. From this series of questionings it will emerge that, while developed from quite disparate points of view and across different sets of disciplines, the Oral-Formulaic and Ethnography of Speaking approaches share a surprising array of core concerns and attitudes. This common ground, largely unnoticed until now, will provide a foundation for the next chapter's project: construction of a composite theory that can translate "ways of speaking" to "ways of meaning" with new fidelity.

Oral-Formulaic Theory: Songs and "The Song"

Absolutely critical to the Parry-Lord theory as originally construed was a radical explanation of the apparently iterative quality of traditional oral narrative.[2] Whether dealing with Parry's original discussion of formulaic structure in Homeric phraseology, Lord's pioneering characterization of narrative themes or typical scenes in South Slavic narrative and elsewhere, or any of the research that has followed and built upon their first principles, the root perception underlying all such studies of units may be traced to the idea of a traditional *multiform*. As the term implies, multiforms take various shapes—in the case of some formulas, for instance, always the same shape—depending on the particular phraseological or narrative context in which they appear.

One useful index of the "word-by-word" texture of traditional narrative poetry is, as explained more fully elsewhere,[3] the singer's own conception of the "word." Time and again the South Slavic *guslari* questioned by Parry and Lord characterized a word not as a lexeme or a chirographically distinct item, but rather as a unit of utterance in performance. The minimal "atom" in their compositional idiom was the poetic line, a ten-syllable increment whose integrity or wholeness is reinforced by recurrent vocal and instrumental melodies of the same length. They also spoke of a combination of lines, of a speech, of a scene, and of a whole song as a *reč* or "word," using the same term employed by contemporary linguists to denote something very different. It is striking that both Homer and the Anglo-Saxon poets also seem to conceive of the same kind

---

2. Throughout this volume I have intentionally kept bibliographical references to Oral-Formulaic Theory to a minimum. For an introduction, cf. Foley 1988; for bibliography and a selection of historically important essays, cf., respectively, Foley 1985 (with updates in *Oral Tradition*) and 1990b.
3. Cf. Foley 1990a: 48–50.

of quantum, with Greek *epos* and Old English *word* both frequently employed to name units of utterance rather than the linguist's or the printer's conventions.[4]

Underlying the recurrency observed at all levels of traditional oral narrative, and understood as its major cause, was the criterion of utility. Composing rapidly under the ever-present pressure of oral performance, so goes the Oral Theory, the tradition had to evolve a means of narrating fluently and continuously. Multiformity, as expressed in formulas, themes, and story-patterns, provided the synchronic solution to the ongoing challenge of performance.

This approach led to the discovery of elaborate "grammars" of phraseology and narrative pattern that subtended the languages of traditional oral poetry. It became a tour de force to "count the formulas" or to map the themes in given versions of given songs, and thus to begin to glimpse the traditional multiformity that was available as a communicative medium. But for all of the progress that was made in various traditions at the structural level, correspondingly little attention was paid to the possibilities of these units as meaning-bearing entities. The formulaic phrases were said to reduce to metrically apposite "essential ideas," the import of "grey-eyed Athena" (γλαυκῶπις Ἀθήνη) and "Hektor of the glancing helm" (κορυθαίολος Ἕκτωρ) being simply "Athena" and "Hektor," respectively.[5] With the poet understood as primarily involved with maintaining compositional fluency, there seemed little room for conscious artistic contribution, that is, for assimilation of multiformity to the familiar Western literary model.

Numerous scholars, especially Homerists, have found this portrait of the traditional oral bard less than satisfactory, viewing the Oral-Formulaic explanation as mechanistic and reductive of Homer's, and other poets', art. In an effort to restore these poets to their proper position, in effect to put the performer back in charge of the performance, they have often argued for a deemphasis of real or supposed differences between "oral" and "literate" composition and have not seldom posited a poet so masterfully in control of his or her tradition that the envisioned process of artistic creation closely

4. The situation is clearest in speech introductions, where a singular *epos* or *word* references an entire speech. Cf. the Homeric verse formula *cheiri te min katerexen, epos t' ephat', ek t' onomadze* ("and stroked him with [his/her] hand, and spoke a word, and called him by name," *Iliad* 1.361, 5.372, 6.485, 24.127; *Odyssey* 4.610, 5.181; with fully 37 additional occurrences of the second-hemistich phrase over the two poems). The Old English *word,* being a neuter noun with zero inflection in nominative and accusative plural cases, does not present so clear a picture morphologically; but the unambiguously singular usages in the formulaic phrase *ond þæt word acwæð* ("and spoke that word," *Beowulf* 654b, 2046b) argue strongly that those ambiguously marked occurrences of *word* in the same or a similar formulaic phrase and performing the same function of speech introduction are also in the singular (315b, 341b, 390b). The argument for this idiomatic verse as a traditional usage gains strength from the 28 additional instances of some version of *ðæt word acwæð/gecwæð* that occur throughout the Old English poetic corpus (*Gen* 639a, 1110b; *And* 896a, 1172b, 1299b, 1361b, 1400b, 1663a; *Ele* 338a, 344a, 440b, 748b, 938a, 1071b, 1190b; *Chr* 316b, 714b; *Glc* 1347b; *Phx* 551b; *Jln* 45a, 143b, 631b, 640b; *Ptg* 4a; *Jud* 82b, 151b, 283a; *Mld* 168b; evidence of plural word in this phrase at *Dan* 282b; *Ele* 748b; *Aza* 4b; *Wan* 91b). Cf. a similar notion of a quantum unit of utterance among the Kuna (Sherzer 1987: 136), and see further "Ethnopoetic Words: The Shape of Integers in Context," below.

5. Parry's original definition of the formula (1971 [1930]: 272) was "a group of words which is regularly employed under the same metrical conditions to express a given essential idea."

resembled the written, post-traditional activity with which Western cultures are both more familiar and more comfortable. One then imagines the poet of the *Iliad,* or the *Chanson de Roland,* or *Beowulf* as an individual who has superseded the constraints of the oral traditional method, and who can therefore compose in a virtually literary way.

Such a reaction to nascent Parry-Lord theory might have been predicted. More to the point, these negative reactions foreground a number of crippling problems with the Oral Theory as originally conceived and applied, the most significant and far-reaching of which is the false dichotomy set up between structure and aesthetic meaning. If one accepts the alternatives as framed—that is, if the choice must be made between an explanation of structure and an understanding of verbal art—then the impasse is real and both of the (mutually exclusive) options are untenable. But any approach as successful as the Oral Theory has been in demonstrating the lineaments of structure in dozens of oral narrative traditions must have more to offer than a morphology of multiforms that finally reduce only to hackneyed "essential ideas" and stock narrative scenes. There must be more to this grammar of conventions than convenience and base-level compositional fluency.

From a historical perspective there is considerable irony in the road that led to this impasse. Parry's first move, after all, was to rediscover not the oral but the *traditional* nature of Homer's epics: his 1928 doctoral theses were primarily concerned with proving Homeric diction to be an ages-old medium employed by a long succession of poets, the latest and presumably finest of whom was the mythical Homer. With his 1930 and 1932 "Studies" essays, however, the relative emphasis was redistributed—permanently—to the *oral* origins of the *Iliad* and *Odyssey.* Parry argued, in other words, from traditional character to oral provenance, on the basis of formulaic diction, comparative studies, and the necessity of rapid composition in performance. Once the "oral" term had superseded the "traditional" term in the equation, the *Oral* Theory, as it is customarily referred to, never looked back; although Lord was to speak eloquently in *The Singer of Tales* and elsewhere about the central importance of tradition,[6] in fact the theory focused on orality as the central distinguishing feature of this "different" kind of "literature."

Associated with that distinctive emphasis on orality was its celebrated litmus test—the idea that density of formulaic phraseology, itself understood as generated in response to the demands of performance, could stand as an unambiguous measure of whether a given ancient or medieval text was orally composed. In other words, the textual libretto became the source for ascertaining the pretextual nature of a work, as scholars searched for visual, document-specific evidence of oral provenance. Submerged in this interpretive program were concerns about the necessary reduction of performance to text, not to mention the estimable problems associated with the variety of traditions, genres, and docu-

---

6. In addition to the first epigraph to this chapter, cf., for example, Lord 1970 on "Tradition and the Oral Poet," and, in general, the recent collection of his essays, *Epic Singers and Oral Tradition* (1991).

ments addressed by the theory. From Parry's original focus on a traditional diction, an idiom that by definition far outstripped the parameters of any single performance/work, the theory now sought to explain each text on the basis of whether its "oral" structures were repeated in that or another text.

If the impetus of the Parry-Lord research veered off from its initial target, it would be well to specify as precisely as possible what it left behind. The most important casualty, as mentioned above, was the poetic tradition. Instead of appealing actively to the traditional context for an explanation of how and what the recurrent structures mean, the textual parallax induced by focusing on visual evidence in this or that work blinded scholars to the possibility of anything more than generic meanings such as "Athena" or "Hektor." Since the full literal, semantic force of "grey-eyed Athena" or "Hektor of the glancing helm" was not textually appropriate to every particular occurrence, generic signification seemed the single possible route. The only other avenue—unacceptable to or-alists—was to resort to then-conventional literary criticism.

But what if the *traditional* character of these structures was given more than lip service? What if traditional came actively to indicate extratextual? What if it came to refer to a reality larger even than the entire individual performance, or group of performances? Clearly, such a rebalancing of the Parry-Lord equation would entail demoting metrical utility to the status of a superficial or morphological feature of the idiom, akin to the "surface structure" described by transformational linguistics, but, just as clearly, it would also mandate engaging worlds of signification inherently larger and more complex than isolated usages, texts, or performances. Under the aegis of such a reconception, "grey-eyed Athena" would serve as an approved traditional channel or pathway for summoning the Athena not just of this or that particular moment, but rather of all moments in the experience of audience and poet.[7] In the same way, Hektor could be well and economically summoned to narrative present by employing one of his traditionally designated forms of address. In these cases, and in so many others, the semantic value of the epithet—"grey-eyed" or "of the glancing helm"—would serve as a nominal detail standing metonymically, or pars pro toto, for the character in all of his or her traditional complexity. Neither reducible to generic metrical fillers nor (by default) equivalent to literary, textual ways of naming, these formulas would be *situated in the tradition*.[8]

7. Cf. Paul Zumthor's (1990: 89) characterization of this idiom: "Rather than as a type of organization, the formulaic style can be described as a discursive and intertextual strategy: it inserts and integrates into the unfolding discourse linguistic and rhythmic fragments borrowed from other preexisting messages that in principle belong to the same genre, sending the listener back to a familiar semantic universe by making the fragments functional within their exposition."

8. On the metonymic, pars pro toto nature of Rotinese ritual language, cf. Fox (1988a: 188–89): "Any chant can, and often does, relate to a variety of other chants—sometimes by the briefest of passing allusions (the change of a single word, for example, to imitate another chanter's style) and, at other times, by taking up a theme and elaborating on it. All of this is part of a dense web of oral intercommunication, much of which is so specific that it is difficult to recover outside the immediate context of a particular performance." Similarly, in respect to Eastern Sumbanese ritual language, Forth (1988: 154) demonstrates that "paired terms, regardless of their apparent logical connection, can in context further be regarded as complementary components of a single semantic unity.

The argument proceeds similarly for the vast array of traditional structures outside the noun-epithet formulas, and beyond even the larger category of the phraseology as a whole. That is, the traditional phrase or scene or story-pattern has an indexical meaning vis-à-vis the immanent tradition; each integer reaches beyond the confines of the individual performance or oral-derived text to a set of traditional ideas much larger and richer than any single performance or text. To varying degrees that are best understood as representing a spectrum of signification, phraseology and narrative patterns, long studied as compositional units in the narrowest sense, encode metonymic realities in a highly connotative, pars pro toto idiom. The specifics of the surface description in various multi-forms—the grey eyes of Athena, the rosy fingers of dawn, the particular foodways of the Homeric feast, the funeral rites of fallen heroes, and so forth—provide the in-text or in-performance vehicle for the uniquely economical communication of traditional ideas. These specifics must of course harmonize with the immediate geography of the narrative surface, else the illusion on which the communication is based will collapse, but their lexical force is otherwise nominal.[9] To search this nominal code per se for all of the solutions to interpretive problems will necessarily be to search in vain; only when we realize that the structural integers necessarily, even institutionally, convey worlds more than the semantic sum of their parts will we begin to glimpse the depths of such works.[10]

Partnered to this set of traditional signals, which are deployed by an individual poet with his or her own artistic agenda, is a necessary indeterminacy in the performance or text. As Receptionalist critics have emphasized, any work of art lacking opportunities for the perceiver to contribute from his or her own prior experience to the fashioning of a coherent present apprehension will appear over-determined and expressively pallid. It is precisely the ongoing challenge to fill these

Therefore, by virtue of this latter kind of relation—which of course derives from the fact that ritual language pairings are fixed by tradition—by receiving one element it would be possible to understand by it the whole of which it forms a part." In relation to Kalapalo oral narrative, E. Basso remarks (1985: 7) that "it is through the many metonymic chains of sensory detail that mental apparitions are created in the minds of listeners." Cf. Caraveli (1982: 130) on Greek folksong: "It is the degree of the song's dependency on a world outside of it and the ensuing interaction between song and community, present and past, that define the song and render the system of folk aesthetics a communicative process by which an 'incomplete' song is 'completed' by the meaning found in the forces surrounding it." Cf. also Richman 1991: 16 on the dynamics of metonymy in the pluralization of the *Ramayana*.

9. On what amounts to the artistic "illusion" fostered by traditional forms, see Foley 1991: 48–53, and chap. 2 below. Exclusive concentration on specific, nominal details at the expense of the referents to which they advert results from the (textual) insistence on stripping a phrase down to its "essential," mechanistic, functional identity, thus admitting the minimum signification possible and severely foreshortening the horizon of poetic expression. Determining the maximum referentiality of the phrase or scene requires not the location of a "lowest common denominator" among its instances, but rather the extratextual, value-added, metonymic signification that will (re)invigorate the text or performance with a more than textual meaning.

10. Cf. K. Basso's compelling discussion of Apache place-names that take on story-based signification for those who know the tradition (1990 [1984]: 129): "In the world that the Western Apache have constituted for themselves, features of the landscape have become symbols of and for this way of living, the symbols of a culture and the enduring moral character of its people." An Apache consultant, Barrie Greenby, put the matter this way (K. Basso 1990 [1988]: 138): "while some aspects of the landscape are clearly external to both our bodies and our minds, what each of us actually experiences is selected, shaped, and colored by what we know."

"gaps of indeterminacy" that activates prior experience, and in the case of the traditional oral (or oral-derived) performance or text, the audience (later the readership) will depend on their working knowledge of traditional implications. Both individual poet and individual audience member or reader thus draw from a spectrum of responses selected by the unifying—but explicitly extraperformance and extratextual—context of tradition.[11] It is of course equally important to understand that any reception is by nature a process that admits of heterogeneity, and that the sign-to-meaning relationship involved in traditional verbal art will certainly not be of the one-to-one allegorical sort. Nonetheless, the fact that the signs are received in performance, the enabling event, and in the context of tradition, the enabling referent, will help to focus individual perception.

This, then, was the direction in which *Immanent Art* (Foley 1991) took Parry-Lord theory: from utilitarian structure and compositional exigency to metonymic meaning and what is finally an artistic imperative. For the record, immanence may be defined as *the set of metonymic, associative meanings institutionally delivered and received through a dedicated idiom or register either during or on the authority of traditional oral performance.* The grammars of "words" at various levels—the formulaic phraseology, the typical narrative scenes, and the story-pattern as a whole—are understood as highly focused, densely encoded systems of integers that open onto implicit and ever-impinging worlds of signification. Structure and tectonics are full partners in this special taletelling idiom, but they do not entail the constraint upon expressivity that rightly exercised so many scholars in various fields; rather, they set the program, constitute the palette, demarcate the cognitive categories with which the individual poet then manages meaning and art.[12] In this way, I came to believe, we could understand how verbal art was made, not in spite of the communicative medium, but in the most fundamental sense through its singular agency.

Performance and Ethnopoetics: Songs in Truer Context

The concept of immanent meaning as the institutionalized partner to oral-formulaic structure dovetails with the concept of performance understood as an

---

11. On the "implied audience," an extension of Wolfgang Iser's (esp. 1974) "implied reader" from textual into traditional oral works, see Foley 1991: 42–45, and n. 15 and chap. 2 below.

12. See esp. the discussion of the metonyms *niz Markovac* kleti ("below *accursed* Markovac") from the Parry-Lord Moslem epics and physizoos *aialgê* physizoos ("*life-producing* earth") from Homer, in Foley 1991: 243–52, in both of which cases the epithet is shown to cue not a denotative but a metonymic referent. Cf. Mitchell (1988: 81) on the significative dynamics of Sumbanese ritual language: "the couplets derive their power from their capacity to condense subtle abstractions into concrete examples, to remind us, by the immediacy of their images, of what is at the heart of the matter"; further (86), "[the parallel form] gives to a statement a cast of unique authority, identifying it as part of a body of traditional wisdom passed down from ancient times, and distinguishes it from the passing and changeable thoughts of common men." On this special economy of metonymic language, cf. E. Basso (1985: 7), who contends that "Kalapalo storytelling should be approached as an extremely efficient means of communication, compressing a great amount of information, interpretation, speculation, and imaginative play."

enabling event. For initial justification of this theoretical bridge, let me adduce early statements by two of the leading figures in the Ethnography of Speaking and Ethnopoetics approaches.[13] In his landmark *Verbal Art as Performance,* Richard Bauman (1977: 9) observes that

> performance represents a transformation of the basic referential . . . uses of language. In other words, in artistic performance of this kind, there is something going on in the communicative interchange which says to the auditor, "interpret what I say in some special sense; do not take it to mean what the words alone, taken literally, would convey." This may lead to the further suggestion that performance sets up, or represents, an interpretive frame within which the messages being communicated are to be understood, and that this frame contrasts with at least one other frame, the literal.

What Bauman refers to in this passage as an "interpretive frame" I prefer to call the *performance arena,* understanding by that term the locus in which some specialized form of communication is uniquely licensed to take place. In such an arena the linguistic integers—in the case of traditional oral narrative, the various "words" or units of utterance that constitute the idiom—no longer defer simply to the literal meanings of the everyday language extrinsic to performance but rather are charged with associative values particular to the event taking place.[14] In this way the situated "words" encode a set of different, highly focused meanings in order that they may convey—with communicative economy—a message indexed by other than textual strategies.[15]

13. Although for the purpose of a clear exposition the approaches are treated separately in this chapter, I heartily agree with Hymes that "the roots of 'performance theory' and 'ethnography of speaking,' and also 'ethnopoetics,' are intertwined" (personal communication, 30 January 1992). Indeed, a major thrust of this study is to demonstrate a further natural relationship among these approaches and the theory of Immanent Art.

14. Thus E. Basso (1985: 15) understands "the telling of a Kalapalo story [as] an event in which the speaker engages in a special relationship with the listeners and ordinary speech and social conventions are suspended, with important consequences for both teller and listener." One of the more interesting corroborations of the performance-centered perspective is Rosaldo's demonstration for Ilingot discourse that even an approach as putatively universal as speech-act theory is essentially an ethnography of speaking of a particular group (1982: 228–29): "One reason to attend to some of the ways in which Ilingot notions of linguistic action differ from the select Western notions documented by Searle is thus that certain of our culturally shaped ideas about how human beings act have limited our grasp of speech behavior, leading us to celebrate the individual who acts without attending to contextual constraints or meaning." We must be concerned with more than a speaker's intent, then, "because, as Ilingots themselves are well aware, the 'force' of acts of speech depends on things participants expect; and then again, because, as our comparison makes clear, such expectations are themselves the products of particular forms of sociocultural being." Cf. K. Basso 1990 (1988): 159 on the special nature of the performance arena in Western Apache narrative, a situation that consultants describe as "socially 'taut' (*ndoh*) and 'heavy' (*ndaaz*)," and outside of which they use different, unmarked forms for place-names.

15. For a full exposition of the concepts of *performance arena, register,* and *communicative economy* in the context of a composite theory of traditional oral art, see chap. 2 below. As K. Basso shows in relation to Western Apache narratives, one side of this economy is the tremendous density of ideational content that can be delivered with a very few words (1990 [1988]: 170): "By virtue of their role as spatial anchors in traditional Apache narratives, placenames can be made to represent the narratives themselves, summarizing them, as it were, and condensing into compact form their essential moral truths. As a result, narratives and truths alike can be swiftly 'activated,' foregrounded and

In similar fashion, Dell Hymes issued this early statement on the interplay and relationship between linguistic items and their contexts (1962: 19):

> Contexts have a cognitive significance that can be summarized in this way. The use of a linguistic form identifies a range of meanings. A context can support a range of meanings. When a form is used in a context, it eliminates the meanings possible to that context other than those that form can signal; the context eliminates from consideration the meanings possible to the form other than those the context can support. The effective meaning depends on the interaction of the two.

Transferring to the performance arena of traditional oral and oral-derived poetry, we could observe that the interaction of item and context mutes the denotative force of traditional units of utterance and foregrounds the special metonymic, performance-based meaning selected by the situated "words."[16] A prime corollary of Hymes's theorem is that, given the originative importance of context in such a selection, it is incumbent upon the reader or audience receiving the communication to be as aware as possible of what is, by performance fiat, immanent to the linguistic items.[17] This in turn means making every effort to understand whatever can be understood of context, whether as a member of

brought into focused awareness through the use of placenames alone." On the other hand, he also notes that the "texts" of their contributions to the discourse are by nature incomplete (152): "According to consultants from Cibecue, the depictions offered by Western Apache speakers are invariably incomplete. . . . Consequently, Apache hearers must always 'add on' (*'inágoda'aah'*) to depictions made available to them in conversation, augmenting and supplementing these spoken images with pictures they fashion for themselves." Of course, the very incompleteness of these utterances constitutes the performative invitation to participation in the discourse; to strive to "fill out" in literal fashion the highly metonymic string of linguistic integers would be to violate the expressive rules of the involved register, and to indulge in a prolix, overdetermined, and aesthetically unsuccessful verbal act (cf. Basso's complementary conclusions, 153). On indeterminacy and the audience's interpretive responsibility, see further Foley 1991: 53–60 and chap. 2 below.

16. Cf. Hymes 1981 (1965): 61: "Formal structure . . . is as necessary as grammar and dictionary to the recognition of the verbal meaning of the original, for it is intrinsic to what in fact happens in the poem, to what there is to be felt in the verbal meaning. In its ritual-like function, a pattern of repetition is a pattern of insistence." On the yield of ethnopoetic structure in North American Indian narrative, he notes (1987a: 49, emphasis mine): "There is a grouping, or segmentation, internal to the tradition not only of lines but also of groups of lines, sometimes at a series of levels. In addition to a segmentation and an architecture, there is also an arc, or series of arcs, to the story, *governed by conventional understandings as to the logic or rhetorical form of enacted action.*" Cf. Woodbury 1985: 153 on the four functions of what he calls the "rhetorical structure" of Central Alaskan Yupik Eskimo discourse: "organization of information, expression of affective meaning, indexing of genre, and regulation of dialogic interaction."

17. Audiences, co-participants in implicitly dialogized speech acts, will of course vary even for a highly focused traditional genre such as the folk epic, and the role of the individual—the single performer or single members of the audience—must always be considered. Cf. Kirshenblatt-Gimblett (1975: 130), who shows that "the significance of a parable is not in the story itself—the narrative is not an autonomous entity which encapsulates one kernel of wisdom or a single 'moral'—but in the particular and variable meaning which the participants give it in specific social contexts"; also Bauman, who offers this balanced view (1982: 14): "Tradition, the collective, the communal, the conventional, are not forsaken here; rather, the individual and the creative are brought up to parity with tradition, in a dialectic that is played out within the context of situated action, viewed as a kind of praxis." Cf. also the Receptionalist perspective on interpretation of oral traditional performance as described in Foley 1991: 38–60.

the participatory group present at a performance or as a latter-day, far-removed reader construing texts related in various significant ways to oral tradition.[18]

In light of Bauman's and Hymes's emphasis on the special channel opened by the combination of signal and context, it is easy to see how interpretation of traditional oral narrative could go awry, particularly when subliminal literary modes of cognition block the way to appreciation of performed verbal art on its own terms. Thus the generations of scholars hastily trying to cover Homer's tracks, convinced that there must be some explanation for his "nodding" when in fact it was the critics themselves who were dozing by applying irrelevant, impertinent interpretive criteria.[19] Thus the negative reaction against the introduction into the comparative picture of the South Slavic *guslari,* who have so often been "evaluated" according to false premises, specifically without taking into account that transformation of referential values that the special nature of the performance arena necessarily and institutionally entails. Homer, the *guslari,* and not a few other verbal artists have in effect been deprived of their "words" in favor of ours; we have substituted our literary, textual categories for their untextual, unliterary cognitive categories. Worse yet, when the inevitable discrepancy has reared its ugly head, we have not seldom chastised them for expressive malfeasance.

But the approach through the Ethnography of Speaking and Ethnopoetics has helped greatly to set the enabling event of performance, and its linguistic vehicle, in proper perspective. As Hymes puts it in his well-known "Breakthrough" article (1981 [1975a]: 86), "especially in an oral tradition performance is a mode of existence and realization that is partly *constitutive* of what the tradition is."[20] The word-power that is the natural concomitant of verbal art in an oral tradition, in other words, stems directly from performance, indeed depends upon that empowering event. Without the event, the special art that requires its contextualization is in effect disabled, or at least thoroughly changed.

We shall have more to say in chapter 3 about the less straightforward—but for many fields exceedingly important—cases in which the performance arena, and all that it implies, is rhetorically summoned through textual signals encoded in oral-derived traditional forms. But staying for the moment with actual performed narrative, the next step in our overall inquiry is to relate the Oral-For-

18. Cf. the role of the "implied audience" as described in Foley 1991: chap. 2 (esp. 42–45), which attempts a translation of Receptionalist theory (particularly of the interpretive program of Wolfgang Iser [1974, 1978, 1989]) into a form appropriate for application to oral traditional works.

19. Parry had argued similarly in his first "Studies" paper (1930); although setting the terms of the problem in an absolutist dichotomy of "oral" versus "written" that most scholars would no longer endorse, he observed (1971: 269) that "this failure to see the difference between written and oral verse was the greatest single obstacle to our understanding of Homer," and that, as a result of having realigned our expectations by placing the ancient Greek poems in their originative context of oral tradition, "we shall cease to be puzzled by much, we shall no longer look for much that Homer would never have thought of saying, and above all, we shall find that many, if not most of the questions we were asking, were not the right ones to ask." Cf. the concept of "traditional referentiality" as sketched in Foley 1991: 6–8 and passim.

20. Cf. his terse comment on "The Sun's Myth" and related works (1975b: 359): "To comprehend the structure of myth, content (referential function) is not enough; expression (stylistic function) is necessary too."

mulaic Theory and the Ethnography of Speaking on the important issue of "keying performance," that is, of marking or cueing the discourse as a communication to be received in a particular way. For this purpose let us consider Bauman's list of such characteristics—special codes, figurative language, parallelism, special paralinguistic features, special formulae, appeal to tradition, and disclaimer of performance[21]—applying them to South Slavic Moslem epic, the living tradition on which Parry and Lord based their comparative research and scholarship.

Keying Performance in South Slavic Moslem Epic

Most of these features are manifest in the Moslem subgenre of South Slavic epic, the particular form that Parry and Lord sought for comparison with the Homeric poems.[22] Bauman chooses to illustrate *special codes,* for example, with the phenomenon of linguistic archaisms, which occur with considerable frequency in the Moslem epic, as both lexical and morphological fossilizations. The most obvious and frequent kind of archaism in vocabulary is the Turkicism, the lexical heritage of the Ottoman Empire; these words tend to name aspects of either heroic action or material culture, and occur quite often in a second-hemistich formulaic pattern involving the verb *učiniti,* "to do or make." Examples include *(h)izmet* "service," *zulum* "violence," *timar* "grooming (of a horse)," *juriš* "attack," and *haber* "news."[23] One of the most common morphological archaisms is the anachronistic usage of the aorist tense, a feature that has long since dropped out of contemporary spoken and written language but which retains its currency in the Moslem epic idiom on the basis of fossilization in traditional diction, not seldom in a proverbial phrase with leonine rhyme:[24]

21. Bauman straightforwardly acknowledges (1977: 22) the "limited utility" of such a list, since "the essential task in the ethnography of performance is to determine the culture-specific constellations of communicative means that serve to key performance in particular communities" (italics deleted). Nonetheless, this general sampling of features does characterize a number of different traditional genres, and will serve as a representative selection for the purposes of illustration in this initial part of the discussion. Cf. the principles of comparative investigation (differentiation by tradition, by genre, and by "document") advocated in Foley 1990a (esp. chaps. 1–2).

22. For explanation see Foley 1991: 62–64, and illustration in chaps. 3–4.

23. Cf. further Škaljić 1979 and, on this particular pattern, Foley 1990a: 192–94. All quotations from South Slavic epic, unless otherwise noted, are taken from the unpublished songs collected by Parry and Lord from *guslari* from the region of Stolac in central Hercegovina, which I am in the process of editing for the *SCHS* series. The designation 1868 indicates a text dictated by the singer Mujo Kukuruzović and given the title *Ropstvo Alagić Alije* (*The Captivity of Alagić Alija,* with the original-language title reflecting the *guslar*'s compositional habit of inflecting only the final element of a noun-epithet formula under the six-syllable colonic constraint); 1287a indicates a second dictated text by the same singer, given the title *Ropstvo Ograšćić Alije* (*The Captivity of Ograšćić Alija*). For further information on Kukuruzović and his songs, see Foley 1990a, esp. 48–51, 178–88. Translations, unless otherwise noted, are my own.

24. Many times the "selection" of the archaic aorist form seems to have been a response to *traditional rules* for the generation of traditional phraseology (see Foley 1990a, esp. chap. 5): *mlidijaše,* an augmented inflection of *mliti/mniti,* for example, fills out the four-syllable first colon in a way that simple past inflections of the same verb (*mlijo, je mlijo,* e.g.) cannot. Once "coined," such a special form—with its special function—retains a compositional and metonymic vigor that long outlives its

Mlidijaše, niko ne *čujaše,*

[Thus] he *thought,* no one *heard,*

Kukuruzović, 1868.714, etc.

To *bijaše* [Djulić bajraktare / ličanine Tale / Ograšćić hadžija]

This *was* [Djulić the standard-bearer / Tale of the Lika / pilgrim Ograšćić]

Kukuruzović, 1287a.746, etc.

When one considers that these archaic forms help to mark the language of the *guslar* as a traditional oral phraseology, it is telling that Parry (1932) had also remarked the same feature in the Homeric poems, pointing to the artificial *Kunstsprache*—a puzzling mixture of Ionian, Aeolic, and Arcado-Cyprian dialects with deep diachronic roots—as a sign of oral traditional composition.[25]

Figurative language is likewise quite common in the South Slavic epic, as, for example, in the memorable description of horses racing across a plain in Avdo Medjedović's *The Wedding of Smailagić Meho* and elsewhere (*SCHS* III: 108):

The foam fell on their rounded rumps and from the rumps it fell to the plain; one would say that lambs were being born. From their nostrils flames emerged and set fire to the mesh on their forelocks. Clouds of smoke billowed before them as if Venetian rifles were being fired whose smoke was poisoned. Like hares they crossed the level plain; like wolves they took to the mountains. All day long until nightfall, like two fiery dragons on phantom steeds, they crossed the ranges.

Oral Theory has long identified such figures as prime examples of the richness of a formulaic repertoire, and in many narrative traditions proverbial and figurative language contributes some of the most highly patterned phrases.[26]

One finds *parallelism* everywhere in the Moslem epos, from the basic structure of the line itself through pleonasm or terracing between and among units, and on to additive sequences of grammatical forms.[27] The ubiquitous traditional verse quoted above as an example of the aorist verb inflection, *Mlidijaše, niko ne čujaše,* illustrates a common type of balancing within the line, with the two-part syntactic figure harmonizing with both the two-colon metrical struc-

vernacular currency, and may as in this instance strengthen its place in the traditional idiom, and in a singer's repertoire, by participating in the oral/aural resonance provided by morphological leonine rhyme in *-aše.* Many such archaic usages thus become embedded in traditional phraseology as parts of "larger words," or, as explained above, what the singers call *reči.*

25. This epic register also contains, and is marked by, a heterogeneous concatenation of older and newer dialect forms selected according to compositional rather than geographical logic (i.e., on the basis of metrical word-type; see Foley 1990a, esp. chap. 5).

26. With reference to fields deeply influenced by Oral Theory, one need look no further for examples than Homer's "rosy-fingered dawn" (*rhododaktylos êôs;* 5 times in the *Iliad,* 22 times in the *Odyssey*) or the Old English poets' characterization of a ship as "most like a bird" (*fug[o]le gelicost; Beowulf* 218b, *Andreas* 497b).

27. It is important to recognize that parallelism, like other features of the traditional idiom of Moslem epic, takes shape on the foundation of traditional rules (Foley 1990a: chap. 5). The particular relationship between cola in the example of pleonasm below, for example, is governed by the symbiosis of phraseology and metrical structure, from a diachronic as well as a synchronic point of view.

ture and the semantic parallelism between the verbs ("thought/heard"). Interline pleonasm is if anything more frequent, with the most common version consisting of a partial, reduced repetition of the second colon of one line in the first colon of the next:

> Pomiri se *s mojom pobratimom,*
> *S pobratimom* begom od Ribnika.

> Reconcile yourself *with my bloodbrother,*
> *With bloodbrother* beg of Ribnik.
>
> Kukuruzović, 1287a.1215–16

Longer additive sequences, which occur somewhat less often, can take many forms; one of them is illustrated by the following vow spoken by the hero Mujo to his brother Halil:

> O tako mi mača i junaštva,
> O tako mi mojega bjelana,
> O tako mi četirnaest godina,

> Oh by my sword and heroism,
> Oh by my white horse,
> Oh by my fourteen years,
>
> Bajgorić, *6699*.542–44[28]

Parry-Lord theory has dealt with this feature of parallelism at great length, understanding the paratactic, additive impulse as a primary pattern in oral tradition.[29] As a compositional figure, it underlies the formation and maintenance of the idiom at the level of both generalized structure and specific sequences. From the point of view of metonymic referentiality, each occurrence of any traditional structure would constitute a figure of anaphora,[30] and thus a kind of parallelism, since it would have primary reference not to spatially or temporally contiguous occurrences but to the immanent meaning keyed in performance.

Formulas are of course legion in Moslem epic, but few have been designated by Oral Theory as *special formulae,* simply because the emphasis has been on a compositional rather than an artistic, meaning-bearing imperative. Bauman's example of "Once upon a time" (1977: 21) well illustrates the resonant, keying function such a phrase can perform, and we may cite parallels from South Slavic narrative. A song beginning with the simple phrase *Turčin cmili tri bijela dana*

---

28. *6699* designates a sung and acoustically recorded performance of *Ženidba Bećirbega Mustajbegova (The Wedding of Mustajbeg's Son Bećirbeg)*, collected in the Stolac region by Parry and Lord from the *guslar* Halil Bajgorić (on whom, cf. Foley 1990a, esp. 45–48, 188–96). (*Note:* The Parry Collection convention is to use italic numerals for accoustically recorded performances and numbers in roman type for dictated texts.)

29. This is an aspect with a relatively long history in the scholarship. Of particular interest is Lord 1960: 57–59 on parallelism, as well as Notopoulos's early discussion of parataxis in Homer (1949) and Austerlitz's (1958) and Watkins's (1976) studies of terracing and responsion in Ostyak, Vogul, and Hebrew narrative.

30. Cf. Foley 1991, esp. 9–10.

("The Turk cried out for three white days"), for example, would set the narrative table for a very particular type of story—a Return Song, or basically a South Slavic *Odyssey;* likewise, a character who terms his or her weapon a *sablja okovana* ("forged saber") will be wielding a sword with a significant history or future (or both), one that will either figure dramatically in what follows or simply accord its bearer a unique measure of heroic prestige.[31] From the perspective of Immanent Art and special formulas, I would further contend that this value-added, indexical meaning is to an extent a characteristic of all formulas in this genre of South Slavic Moslem epic, even of a "new" or "nonce" formula that follows traditional rules for phraseological structure and, at minimum, assists in establishing or maintaining the informing context of the performance arena merely by virtue of that structure.[32]

There is also no question that the *guslar* issues frequent *appeals to tradition,* perhaps most obviously in the highly conventional *pripjev* or proem that begins the poem. Here is an example drawn from a performance of *Halil Rescues Bojičić Alija* by Halil Bajgorić (6703.1–9).[33]

> Gusle moje, gusle javorove,
> Zaguslite sada ja ikada,
> Zaguslite tanko, glasovito—
> Meni gusle a vama gudalo.
> Ja ću pjevat' pjesmu od istine,
> Što sam čuo ja [od] babe moga
> Na hiljadu devete stotine
> I dvanaeste po broju godine,
> Jednu pjesmu od ovog junaka.

> Oh my gusle, maplewood gusle,
> Speak now and ever,
> Speak softly, loudly—
> The gusle is mine and it's played for you.
> I will sing a song of truth,
> Which I heard from my father
> In one thousand nine hundred
> And twelve by count,
> A song about a certain hero.

31. Cf. Foley 1991: 107–108.

32. For examples of the metonymic referentiality of formulaic phraseology in South Slavic, ancient Greek, and Old English epic, see Foley 1991: 17–33.

33. 6703 denotes a text dictated by Bajgorić (see n. 28), entitled *Halil izbavlja Bojičić Aliju* (*Halil Rescues Bojičić Alija,* again with the colonic form of the name). I have suggested the additional *od* ("from") in line 6 partly on the basis of sense and syntax (*babe moga* has otherwise no reason for its genitive inflection), but most importantly because all other instances of this common type of proem include the preposition. Since with a dictated text there is obviously no way to recover the actual performed line, we must leave open the possibility that the *guslar* rather than the amanuensis omitted the *od* and spoke the line in its unemended form. On the metonymic function of the *pripjev,* see Foley 1991: 68–75.

In addition to other examples of the *pripjev,* we should also note such subsidiary keying items as the proem-like lines that a singer can use to restart the narrative after a pause for rest (e.g., "Where were we, where did we leave / The little song of times long past?"); the mid-narrative marker phrases such as "But you should have seen [character X]" that customarily serve to introduce a major character in the next narrative increment; and ritualistic addresses to the audience such as "O my brothers."[34] Parry-Lord theory, as extended to Immanent Art, complementarily understands such appeals as implicit references to the body of traditional phrases and scenes that constitute the singer's idiom, as in-progress citations of the enabling event of performance. And although this particular genre of South Slavic epic does not normally include *disclaimers of performance* in its expressive repertoire, such keys can occur in the conversations that not occasionally envelop breakthroughs into epic performance in the Parry-Lord songs collected from this tradition.

Granted that Oral Theory and the Ethnography of Speaking point to many of the same poetic features as central to the keying of performance, and with the important caveat that these features are to a considerable extent dependent on the particular tradition and genre one is examining, let us venture a step further and ask how each approach understands the dynamic function of performance and the resultant yield of meaning.

In order to accomplish this comparison as expeditiously as possible, I introduce the useful concept of *register* employed by many linguists, prominently in Ethnopoetics by Hymes, who makes the following distinction (1989a: 440): "major speech styles associated with social groups can be termed *variants,* and major speech styles associated with recurrent types of situations can be termed *registers.*"[35] By this latter term, then, I will be referring to an idiomatic version of the language that qualifies as a more or less self-contained system of signification specifically because it is the designated and sole vehicle for communication in the act of traditional oral performance. Any culture or social group will have a variety of registers on which its members draw as they transact the business of verbal art (as well as other, less poetic discourses) as activities

34. The original-language form of the first subsidiary appeal to tradition is *Dje li bismo, dje li ostavismo / Malku pjesmu o' duga zemana?* (Bašić, *291b*.961–62, etc.), which also illustrates both archaism (aorist tense) and parallelism. The second is *Pa da vidiš X,* which occurs extremely frequently in the performances of all singers of Moslem epic and customarily acts as a boundary line (Foley 1990a: 286–87, 295–96) between thematic patterns, conferring a traditional unity on narrative progress. Although deprecated by some commentators as a simple filler phrase (in much the same way as some half-lines in Old English poetry are called "fillers" because they are perceived as inessential to the ongoing action), the third phrase, *moje brate* ("O my brothers"), keys performance by acknowledging the audience and the nature of the enabling event.

35. Halliday et al. (1964: 90–93) argued that a register is distinguished according to the field of discourse ("the area of operation of the language activity," 90), the mode of discourse (spoken or written), and the style of discourse ("the relations among the participants," 92); see also Halliday 1976: 7ff. and 1978: 31–35, 111. For a fuller treatment of register in traditional oral art, see chap. 2 below.

situated in daily life.[36] As Joel Sherzer (1983) has shown with great thoroughness, peoples such as the Kuna may have many traditional registers, marked by different morphologies, lexicons, expressive contexts, paralinguistic gestures, and the like; some of these will be, from the point of view of the relatively unmarked "standard" variety of nonpoetic language, highly focused and demanding, while others will be less so.[37]

As a general principle, we might observe that the more "dedicated" a register is to a particular function (and here my analogy is to the world of "dedicated" word-processors that perform a single task with great speed and efficiency born of that very "limitation"), the more economically it can convey meaning.[38] Another way to say the same thing is to speak of the density of associative, metonymic meaning accruing to and implied by linguistic integers, or of the complexity and richness of the allusive world summoned by the simple forms or "words" that constitute the "way of speaking."[39] For this reason John McDowell (1983: 41) describes the Kamsá ritual language as "an expressive and communicative medium which has surrendered the broad referential capacity of the ordinary speech variety in order to obtain an especially intense and evocative hold on a bounded referential universe." The reverse is of course also true: as one leaves behind the more generic register for the more "dedicated" idiom, one also reduces the variety of objects, ideas, and actions that can be appropriately summoned.[40] Thus the performance arena becomes ever

36. Halliday, the originator of the term, notes (1976: 7): "It is obvious that the social functioning of language determines the pattern of language *varieties,* in the sense of diatypic varieties, or registers; the register range, or verbal repertoire, of a community or an individual derives from the range of social uses of language in the context of the particular culture." Cf. also Halliday 1964: 90–93 and 1978: 111, 186.

37. Cf. the Kuna speech acts associated with politics, curing and magic, and puberty rites (chaps. 3–5) as compared with the discourse of everyday life (chap. 6). Of related interest is Gossen's (1971) discussion of Chamula genres of verbal behavior; cf. further his 1974 book on Chamula oral tradition.

38. Another analogy from word-processing, suggested to me by Barbara Kirshenblatt-Gimblett, would compare the pars pro toto nature of metonymic signification with the keyboard macro, the specially encoded single keystroke that economically accesses a whole series of operations by deferral to a previously programmed referent. The difference, of course, is that the indeterminacy and natural heterogeneity of response that we would associate with the use of a linguistic register are impossible (and highly undesirable) in the lockstep function of a keyboard macro.

39. Cf. Friedrich (1986: 33), who observes of formulaic phrases in oral tradition, specifically in Homer, that such "culturally specialized variants of poetic language" as "'barren' and 'wine-dark' exhaust what you can attribute to the sea with an adjective"; from the perspective of immanent signification, I would maintain that they exhaust what can be metonymically encoded in a (nominal) adjective. The dynamic by which this resource of meaning is keyed is well expressed in Friedrich's comment on the relationship between the sound system (language music) and mythic context of poetry (39): "To create felt consubstantiality between language music and myth *is* the master trope of poetry—'master' because it is superordinate to and in control over such lesser figures as image, metaphor, and paradox." On the complicating parameters of the singer's idiolect, the regional dialect, and the pantraditional language as levels or subsets of the performance register, cf. Foley 1990a, esp. chaps. 5, 8; note that these distinctions constitute morphological, not metonymic, differences.

40. On the limitation and resultant focus of "signs" in the performative repertoires of five South American Indian tribes, Urban (1986: 379) observes that "all dialogues share in common the fact that they limit the range of variation in pragmatic expressive devices. They are in this sense 'marked speech styles,' the restrictions serving to highlight the ceremonial dialogue as sign vehicle and also the associated linguistic interaction itself." Likewise, McDowell (1983: 33) speaks of significative economy (and its price) in this way: "The generic character of these expressions allows them to

more carefully mapped out and charged with expectation and the communicative medium concomitantly increasingly economical, while the circumference of the arena necessarily shrinks, as one moves from a less to a more highly focused register.

Ethnopoetic Words: The Shape of Integers in Context

Of what are such registers actually composed? Attempting a general answer to this question, to be taken up in detail in the next chapter, and with specific applications to various areas in chapters 4–6, will bring into the foreground one final aspect of the common ground shared by Performance Theory and Ethnopoetics on the one hand, and Oral-Formulaic Theory and Immanent Art on the other.

Over the past twenty years it has been particularly the work of two scholars, Dennis Tedlock and Dell Hymes, that has moved toward a realistic, nonparochial answer to this question from the perspective of Ethnopoetics. Each has tried to encounter the traditional oral performance on its own terms—with special respect for the idiosyncratically poetic nature of the orally enacted event and its reception, as well as for the special characteristics of the language and form in which the event occurs. Although sharing these and other concerns, with particular reference to Native American verbal art, Tedlock and Hymes have by no means agreed on either the detailed texture of the experience or how best to facilitate study of its implications. In addressing some of the core issues of their joint work and ongoing debate, I hope to highlight some features of the Ethnopoetics approach that coalesce meaningfully with the perspective from Oral-Formulaic Theory and Immanent Art.

Although the movement toward an ethnopoetically informed process of edition, translation, and analysis can be discerned somewhat earlier,[41] two particular articles by Tedlock (1971) and Hymes (1977) stand out as seminal documents in the establishment of this area of inquiry within the Ethnography of Speaking. For his part, Tedlock proposed a radical revision of the criteria for translation—and therefore for representation and analysis—to take full account of the purely performance-based aspects that historically have been edited out when even the most sympathetic and meticulous scholar reduces the process of an oral experience to the product of an objective text. For Tedlock it is precisely the "'oral' or 'paralinguistic' features," in addition to the simple referential content and the "'linguistic' features of style" (45), that must be

circulate within a certain subset of the entire corpus, but simultaneously deprives them of the capacity to encode very much information concerning the species of the genre, that is, the accidental features rendering each greeting encounter or each wedding ceremony in some sense unique."

41. E.g., Hymes 1965 (1981). For histories of text-making that reveal the influence of successive schools of folkloristics and cultural anthropology, see Fine 1984 and Foley in press. Tedlock (1990, esp. 139–43) offers a thoughtful exposition of the problems associated with textual representation, particularly on the topics of chronology versus topology, multivocal texts, and what he refers to as the "uncertainty principle" of language itself.

attended to; without representation of these essential paralinguistic characteristics, any translation, or edition, only reifies those facets of the performance
that can be assimilated to the textual model privileged by Western literary norms.
One thus finds oneself stymied by a libretto that is not merely incomplete but
actively misleading.[42]

In an effort to escape what amounts to a monocultural dead-end, and con-
currently to present Zuni verbal art in its full poetic voice, he formulates and
illustrates a charter for at least partial recovery or echo of oral traditional
narration in ethnopoetic context. Among linguistic features typical in their use
or frequency of the storytelling register, he identifies phonological "distortions,"
grammatical differences (length of sentences), lexical items and formulaic
phrases, archaisms, and onomatopoetic words, for some of which he also suggests modes of typographical representation.[43] But Tedlock's major focus remains on those paralinguistic factors of "oral style"—chiefly voice quality,
volume control, and pausing—heretofore virtually completely ignored by editors
and translators but crucially important to the understanding of the performance
as an event.

Perhaps the most radical suggestions in this groundbreaking proposal stem
from the third of his principal concerns, *pausing,* which has naturally proved
the first casualty of intersemiotic translation from sounded, experienced event
to silent, extruded object. On the basis of a hierarchy of pauses prescribed by
temporal duration, he lineates the performance, determining the extent of a
poetic line not by recourse to the more familiar criteria of syllable, stress, or
colon, but purely on the basis of interposed silences. When the narrator pauses,
the line as a unit of utterance is over and the next one begins; that next one may
end within a few syllables or it may reach two or three times across a normal
printed page, depending on when the next pause occurs.[44] What Tedlock achieves
as a result of this attention to pauses in performance is a cadence that exactly
reflects the vocal presentation by the storyteller, just as the tale was spoken in
the original units of time and utterance rather than the received quanta of
Western poetic measurement.

Similarly, working initially with Chinookan narrative, Hymes speaks of "measured verse" in order to emphasize that the compositional and performance units
of his material do not depend on syllabic, stress-based, syntactic, or other
parameters commonly associated with meter and prosody in Western literature.
Rather, these narratives must be approached on their own terms, with regard

42. As he puts it toward the end of this essay (54): "The apparent flatness of many past translations
is not a reflection but a distortion of the originals, caused by the dictation process, the notion that
content and form are independent, a pervasive deafness to oral qualities, and a fixed notion of the
boundary between poetry and prose."

43. Cf. his translation-edition of Zuni narratives, *Finding the Center* (1972a); and his programmatic
commitment (1977: 516): "Just as the critical act in oral poetry begins where a performance begins,
rather than waiting until it is over, so the critical act in an oral poetics begins where the establishment
of a critical text (in the philologist's sense) or translation begins, rather than taking that act for
granted."

44. In the introduction to *Finding the Center* (1972a: xx), he reports the length of the Zuni poetic
line at "from one syllable to more than seventy."

for the special poetic features on which they are based. But although he too seeks to discover the verbal art that heterodox edition and translation have eliminated, Hymes's program varies from Tedlock's in at least two major ways. First, he proposes a more systematized grid of poetic units (1981 [1977]: 309):

> The narratives of the Chinookan peoples of Oregon and Washington can be shown to be organized in terms of lines, verses, stanzas, scenes, and what one may call acts. A set of discourse features differentiates narratives into verses. Within these verses, lines are differentiated, commonly by distinct verbs. . . . The verses themselves are grouped, commonly in threes and fives. These groupings constitute "stanzas" and, where elaboration of stanzas is such as to require a distinction, "scenes." In extended narratives, scenes themselves are organized in a series of "acts."[45]

Verses, the most fundamental unit, are marked by recurrence of initial elements such as "now," "then," and "now again,"[46] and are segmented into lines on the basis of the verbs involved. Stanzas, scenes, and acts represent formal features at a higher, less technically determined level. It should be explicitly noted that Hymes understands these aspects of structure as recurring traditional principles of poetic form, and as distinct from the features associated with what he terms "vocal realization."[47]

The second major difference between Tedlock's and Hymes's programs lies in the latter's willingness and even commitment to apply his discovery of "measured verse" to dictated texts for which no acoustic record exists, scoring these silent witnesses on the basis of discovering their linguistic and narrative structure.

---

45. For illustration and further discussion of this program, see "Discovery of Verse and Line," 318–20. Cf. also Tedlock's rebuttal (1983 [1971]: 56–61) to Hymes's rearrangement of his own libretti. An updating of the system to seven levels, adding the macro-unit of "part" and the micro-unit of "versicle" (a small grouping of lines within a verse), may be found in Hymes 1987b: 20–32, with an example of analysis and interpretation at 45–56. See further Hymes 1983, wherein the system of rhetorical analysis and representation is shown to support interpretation.

46. Cf. Sherzer's four criteria for lineation in Kuna oral discourse: (1) initial and final words, particles, and affixes; (2) semantic and syntactic parallelism; (3) intonation patterns; and (4) co-participant (back-channel) structures (1987: 105). It is striking that the South Slavic and, to a lesser extent, the ancient Greek epic lines answer a similar structural definition, with proclitic particles—of more prosodic than semantic importance—often occurring at the beginning of (conventionally Western) metered lines and line-parts; for discussion, see Foley 1990a: 89–103. In these other poetries the initial particles answer the traditional rule of "right justification," the tendency for metrically heavier and more extensive words and word units to seek the end of prosodic units, leaving the metrically lighter and less extensive units at or near the onset of such units. On right justification, ostensibly a property of Indo-European traditional oral versification, see Foley 1990a, esp. 96–106, 178–96; for an example of the lack of right justification in a poetry defined by a stress-based meter, see the discussion of the Old English alliterative line at 106–19.

47. By this latter term he means (321): "direct quotation, rather than reported speech; the taking of the voices of those who speak, differentiating them; onomatopoeic precision, giving the words that define characteristic sounds (Chinookan has a rich taxonomy of kinds of sound); expressive interactional detail, through particles initial in a quoted statement (or statement from the point of view of the narrator) that define the attitude taken, for example, assent, pain, lament, pondering, expectation; recurrent audience response with such elements, ranging from *ã* at ordinary detail to *adí* and *aná* at moments of high drama; lengthening of vowels for emphasis; interchange of consonants (according to a regular pattern) to express augmentation and diminution."

Although this is more properly a subject for extended consideration in the third chapter, where problems associated with textual witnesses to oral traditions are taken up in depth,[48] we may remark in passing the originally diametrically opposed positions taken by these two proponents of ethnopoetics. While in his early work Tedlock wishes to dismiss from primary consideration for editing and translation any performance not available in audible form, Hymes specifically argues for application of what is learned from acoustic records to dictated texts.[49] Once again, the contrast rests on the perception of a poetic principle, understood as informing all instances of a traditional process, versus an insistence on treating and interpreting only those actual paralinguistic features that are vocally realized by the individual narrator in a given performance.

In a broader sense, it is this same core distinction that lies at the root of the disparity between the still closely related ethnopoetic approaches advocated by these two scholars. Tedlock has been courageous and forward-thinking enough to throw over many of the deeply ingrained visual and textual biases that condition our perception of verbal art at the deepest levels, locating poetry not in the printed icon of metrically regular line length and the like but rather in the alternation of sound and silence that can be phenomenologically realized only in performance (and in experience of that performance). Toward this end he wishes to substitute for "literary" criteria a set of standards that promotes the understanding of traditional oral narrative as an event, emergent in its initial occurrence and, if appropriately edited and translated, reflectively emergent as well in its re-creation by the reader.[50] All of his iconoclastic discussion of the nature of poetry, not to mention the elaborate typographical scheme he develops to convey paralinguistic features, is directed toward the admirable and important goal of giving this species of verbal art a "fair hearing." With this uncompromising commitment to the apotheosis of the spoken word, he in effect *must* conclude that (1983 [1971]: 61):

> In seeking exhibition space in the galleries of literature, Hymes specifically addresses the jury that requires lines of poetry to show measurement when he argues

48. For illustration of how these notions apply to actual works that survive only in textual form (and in which writing may well have played a compositional as well as transmissional role), see below the discussion of the *Homeric Hymn to Demeter* (chap. 5) and the Old English *Andreas* (chap. 6).

49. E.g., Tedlock observes (1972b: 238) that "nearly all of the published [Native American] narratives were collected by the dictation method, which distorts narrative flow and results in the total loss of paralinguistic features. Our most valuable resource, far more valuable than the phonetically transcribed texts so cherished in the past, will be our tape recordings of actual performances," while Hymes counters (1981 [1977]: 337–38): "If one must use only tape-recorded material, most of what is recorded in Native North American tradition must be forgotten"; further, "the best dictated texts are not in fact wholly without indication of the features in question." On the notion of putting older texts in their "true form" as a kind of "repatriation," see Hymes 1991. Cf. Woodbury (1987: 187), who argues that "no one line-and-verse representation can be wholly adequate, given the many competing dimensions of meaningful form present in a single narrative performance"; cf. also his explicit comparative evaluation of Hymes's and Tedlock's systems of analysis and representation (1985: 165–70). Bright (1979: 119) has attempted to show how the two systems "coincide 90% of the time in their identification of basic units."

50. Whom he naturally advises to read aloud (1972a: xii).

that his analysis of American Indian narratives "makes it possible, indeed essential, to regard such texts as works of literary art." But I take the word "poetry" to cover much more than "verse," if by verse is meant discourse that scans by meter or by measure; in so doing, I must appeal to juries that are both more arcane and more modern than this one.

But while for Tedlock the imputation of literary qualities amounts to an abrogation of ethnopoetic responsibility for representation and interpretation of traditional oral narratives on their own terms, for Hymes the designation "literary," far from being pejorative or impertinent, licenses their acceptance and treatment as a worthy form of verbal art—certainly not a form limply assimilable to the Western textual model for canonical literature, but nonetheless a form that even in its idiosyncrasies shares the reality of a complex and responsive poetics. Indeed, it is because such poetic structures exist as traditional principles, informing not just the single performance but all performances, that Hymes can extend his method of analysis and presentation from the inimitable acoustic event to the admittedly denatured textual remnant of that experience. The crucial difference between the two systems, then, at least as originally conceived, lies in Tedlock's virtually exclusive focus on what can be gleaned from the individual's oral narrative performance per se and Hymes's insistence on poetic principles as instanced in the individual performance *because* resident in the overarching tradition.

More recently, each scholar's approach has deepened and gained in complexity, with the result that the central issues they address are even clearer than before. Hymes is able to cite analyses of the kind of poetic structures he describes in some thirty Native American traditions (1987b: 18–19) and to relate verse and stanza structure to the given culture's "pattern numbers."[51] Both new directions reinforce the traditional nature of the poetic patterning he and his colleagues discover, emphasizing that it must be understood not as a property of one or more performances or of one or more narrators, but rather as a culture-wide (and even intercultural) web of significative structure. The demonstration of such patterning from one performance to the next within a single culture and, with appropriate variations, across a number of cultures not only increases the likelihood that "measured verse" and attendant features constitute a real, verifiable dimension of Native American verbal art; it also calls ever more insistently for taking line, versicle, verse, stanza, scene, act, and part into account as meaning-bearing, rhetorical signals in their own right.

Tedlock has likewise widened his perspective, in his case to include a textual witness to an oral traditional event, the Mayan *Popol Vuh*. The specific text with which he works is the Quiché alphabetic version, and the specific goal for which

---

51. See also Tedlock 1990: 154, n. 5. Cf. Hymes 1987b: 22: "The grouping of lines into verses, and of verses into stanzas, tends to follow, but not exclusively, the pattern numbers of the culture . . . , depending on pairs and sets of pairs in cultures in which the pattern number is four, and upon threes and fives in cultures in which the pattern number is five."

he aims is an ethnopoetically grounded translation.[52] In order to escape the limitations of intratextual and other written evidence, he advocates "becom[ing] an ethnopaleographer, taking the Popol Vuh text back to those who continue to speak the language in which it was written" (1987: 143). This new science of ethnopaleography operates not on comparison with everyday conversational Quiché, but in effect on a rough match of registers, with the fieldworker "seeking after contemporary speeches, prayers, songs, and narratives, looking for patterns in the wording that have analogs in the ancient text and noting the ways in which such patterns are actualized in performance."[53] The careful denomination of cola, periods, and lines—demarcated by analogy with actual witnessed performance—then allows the construction of a performance-based libretto for the alphabetic *Popol Vuh.*

It should be noted that while he proceeds as before according to paralinguistic features, on two other scores Tedlock's work with the *Popol Vuh* moves his approach closer to that of Hymes. First, he has evolved a way to establish continuity between the spoken and heard voice of contemporary Native American verbal art and its frozen, deracinated textual avatar.[54] Second, the very assumption that the performance of contemporary poetic genres can inform the performance of an ancient text bespeaks a conviction that the paralinguistic features are traditional. Only if there were some direct, genetic relationship between, say, the pausing associated with the genre of prayer as enacted in modern Quiché society and the pausing one hypothesizes for the orally performed *Popol Vuh* would ethnopaleography make sense; moreover, the only vehicle that could account for such a relationship would be tradition.

*   *   *

We are now in a position to inquire what effect this ethnopoetic focus might have on the overall convergence that is one of the principal subjects of this volume. Does the exchange over paralinguistic features versus "literary" principles bear at all on the common ground shared by the Ethnography of Speaking and Ethnopoetics on the one hand and Oral Theory, as extended to Immanent Art, on the other?

Setting aside the specifics of the Tedlock-Hymes debate for the moment, let us take a wider comparative view of the problem. In those cases in which the opportunity presents itself to experience actual performances, or at one remove

52. In addition to the background information provided in this article (1987), see Tedlock's translation itself (1985). Of related interest are his most recent comments on the problems associated with edition and translation (1990).

53. 1987: 147. He also observes (143) that "the work of the ethnopaleographer will have more resemblance to research in oral history, folklore, sociolinguistics, and cultural anthropology than to plain linguistics."

54. Tedlock also has aspirations for ethnopaleography beyond this case of comparative elucidation (1987: 173): "If sound recordings can help us hear a voice in the Popol Vuh, a Quiché Maya text that first took alphabetic form more than four hundred years ago, they can help us with the vast corpus of ancient texts from other Mesoamerican languages, to say nothing of North American texts taken down in dictation not so long ago. Ethnopaleographic enterprises are properly part of a larger reshaping of anthropological and linguistic field research along dialogical, collaborative lines, only in this case even the dead will be heard from."

their acoustic or video recordings, it would seem imperative to learn from Ethnopoetics the necessity of coding performance features into any textual representation. There can now be little argument that failing to do so condemns all who consult the second-generation record to a distorted reexperiencing of the event, familiarly like the textual art to which we are accustomed but all the more unreal for that manufactured affinity.

Ethnopoetics also puts a sharper focus on the oral traditional "word" as a unit of utterance. Whether viewing a register from Tedlock's or Hymes's point of view, we have dramatic cross-cultural confirmation of the South Slavic *guslar's* notion of the *reč* as an integer defined by pertinent prosodic and narrative (rather than impertinent lexical) criteria. In addition, the ethnopoetic perspective illustrates graphically how the "word," as an integer in a specialized discourse, cannot be delineated textually as a visually apprehended "repetition," as the formula defined by Oral Theory often has been. Rather, each culture and language and genre will establish its poetic "lexicon" of integers more or less differently, and a given idiom's rules for the formation of phraseology may or may not result in numerous recurrent lines or line-parts, depending upon compositional parameters. A corollary to this theorem, especially important because most of the major principles underlying Oral Theory were developed via reasoning that was rooted in a closely related coterie of European languages and only then extended outward,[55] is that the definition of poetic "words" can vary widely across traditions and genres, particularly as one moves between Western and non-Western language traditions.

A tougher challenge arises when we ask—for each tradition on its own terms—the following question: To what extent do the paralinguistic features that we acoustically perceive function as expressive habits restricted to the individual or the individual performance, and to what extent do they amount to shared traditional strategies? If they are primarily idiosyncratic, that quality will affect their word-power or metonymic meaning, since they will demarcate connotative fields largely the province of the individual narrator, and available in full resonance only to the audience that understands their specialized import. Many if not most of Tedlock's parameters—among them volume control, pausing, and the like—have obvious, potentially universal import in their gross application, but they certainly must gain additional signification from usage within an individual's narrative register. Another aspect of the individuality of paralinguistic features is their situation-specific deployment: a narrator may choose to raise the volume at a particularly dramatic moment in one telling of a story,

55. It has been observed that the Parry-Lord basis in ancient Greek and South Slavic epic was in some ways fortunate and in other ways misleading. Because these two registers operated under similar (but hardly identical) phraseological rules, the comparison between them encouraged the idea of a universal category of "formula" independent of linguistic variables. While this relative congruence offered a *pied à terre* for the fledgling theory as a comparative instrument, it also falsely predicted that other traditional phraseologies would turn out just as closely congruent to the original model. Discrepancies in medieval vernacular poetries, for example, were often taken as evidence of "nonorality" (whatever that might mean with relation to a text) rather than as an incentive to a more complex, less doctrinaire theory. Cf. on these issues Foley 1990a: chap. 6.

and yet not modulate as much, or at all, at the same moment in another telling. To some extent this kind of variation among versions is cognate to Lord's proverbial distinction that "the song we are listening to is 'the song'; for each performance is more than a performance; it is a re-creation" (1960: 101), in that it tracks the multiformity among occurrences of a theme, for example, or instances of a formulaic system, or even tellings and retellings of the "same song." As mentioned above, Tedlock's more recent ethnopaleographic research implicitly presupposes a traditional dimension to paralinguistic features, a continuity underlying at least the general repertoire, but his own emphasis on variation and uniqueness in performance demands that we accord a full measure of attention to the individual narrator or performance.

And there is an additional complication as comparison closes in on specific parallels. For some traditions, among them South Slavic epic,[56] the repertoire of paralinguistic features is relatively slim because traditional poetic principles in many cases clearly and unambiguously supervene the development of individual expressive traits: the *guslar* uses a handful of common and recurrent tunes to sing his narrative, without discernible correlation between tune and action; the volume of his delivery varies only with degree of fatigue; pauses are of regular placement and duration at the synchronized ends of poetic lines and musical phrases, and do not coincide with the dramatic presentation of the story;[57] and so forth. As for line length in this poetry, the *epski deseterac* (or epic decasyllable) appears to be based not on pause as such, but diachronically on Indo-European metrical prototypes (not all of which were syllabic) and synchronically on grammar and syntax, with secondary support from phonological features such as sound-patterning.[58]

One could say that many of the avenues of paralinguistic expression apparently open to personal and situation-specific manipulation by the Zuni narrator, for example, are in the South Slavic songs the province of traditional regulation via inherent poetic principles.[59] I hasten to add that the balance

56. The specific stylistic features discussed below relate to what is historically the mainstream South Slavic epic form, the decasyllabic epic, that form on which the research of Parry and Lord is exclusively based; on the other chief narrative form, the *bugarštica,* see esp. Stolz 1969 and Miletich 1990.

57. It is interesting that Hymes (1981 [1977]: 339–40, n. 10), responding to Tedlock's pioneering study of pause as a prosodic boundary in Zuni narrative, cites the word break between syllables four and five in the South Slavic epic decasyllable as an example of a prosodic boundary entailing no temporal pause. That the same is likely true of the various caesurae and diaereses in the Homeric hexameter, according to the writings of ancient scholars, has long been known (cf. esp. Bassett 1919). But the South Slavic line also reveals an example of the co-occurrence of prosodic word break and temporal pause—at line-end. Most of the Parry-Lord *guslari* follow the practice, apparently institutionalized and traditional, of pausing for the temporal equivalent of two syllables at the end of the verse, during which period the singer continues to play the instrument (*gusle*) and after which vocal rest the next line starts. On the epic decasyllable, cf. further Foley 1990a: 85–106.

58. On the possible origin and history, as well as the dynamics, of this line, see Jakobson 1952, Vigorita 1976, and Foley 1990a: chaps. 3, 5.

59. Here I must acknowledge the contribution made by a series of students in the University of Missouri–Columbia course on oral tradition, who asked the very sensible question of why the presentation of South Slavic epic (samples of which they heard in the original recordings) lacked the paralinguistic qualities of dramatic expression that we (only too parochially) associate with storytelling traditions in general. In responding to what amounts to a problem in multiculturalism,

being tipped toward the traditional and away from the idiosyncratic in regard to this aspect does not indicate that the South Slavic epic is either poorer or richer in its presentation; such a shift of balance, opposite to the Zuni at this particular point, merely argues for a differently configured mode of signification, with the import of features such as those invoked by Tedlock more a matter of what can be traditionally as opposed to idiosyncratically coded, and the opportunities for personal and situation-specific contributions shifted to other expressive channels.[60]

From a comparative point of view, we have seen that genres from different traditions may focus or determine the range of individual control over pause and other paralinguistic features quite variously, over a spectrum that theoretically would extend from an individually regulated situation (closer to the Zuni) to an intensely traditional situation (closer to the South Slavic). It perhaps goes without saying that traditional implication and individual manipulation make themselves felt in other than purely paralinguistic channels, as when the Zuni narrator has recourse to highly resonant formulas for greeting, or when the *guslar* shows great individual skill in the composition of elaborate versions of arming for combat and even the "invention" of formulaic phraseology.[61] One could of course not claim viability for any theory of verbal art that did not allow for the cultural variables that I have elsewhere labeled "tradition-dependence" and "genre-dependence," and without stipulating a central, seminal role for the individual performer.[62]

we found ourselves coming to grips with the variety of expressive strategies across the rich and complex spectrum of traditional oral forms; that is, we learned to inquire first not *what* but rather *how* a performance means.

60. Hymes makes a similar structural distinction when he contends (1981 [1977]: 339): "Yet even if pause is basic to poetry, there remains the problem of differentiating pause that is motivated, that heightens the organization of lines, from pause that is inherent in the spoken medium. There remains the problem of detecting the invariants of cultural genres and the characteristics of personal styles."

61. See Foley 1991: chaps. 3–4 for the spectrum of traditional and individual signification in thematic patterns as illustrated in the Moslem and Christian songs in South Slavic. As for phraseology, the term *invention* finally proves oblique: since all diction forms (or is formed by an individual) in accordance with poetic principles that I have elsewhere denominated "traditional rules" (1990a: chaps. 4, 5, 6 for ancient Greek, South Slavic, and Anglo-Saxon, respectively), the matter of sheer frequency of occurrence of a given phrase cannot constitute a measure of "tradition" versus "invention." In effect, all phraseology used in accordance with these rules is by definition traditional, and the indexes of frequency and formulaic density amount in the end to textual (and thus impertinent) criteria.

62. On tradition- and genre-dependence, cf. Foley 1990a: 8–9 and passim. It is perhaps impossible—at minimum it would be artificial and misleading—to segregate individual and traditional contributions to a work of verbal art in performance, since even the most highly traditional ideas or strategies must after all be communicated by an individual, and since each individual must employ the traditional (register-specific) means in order to achieve intelligibility. As Hendricks (1990: 25) observes of a Shuar storyteller, "Tukup's narrative is a unique composite of the personal experience story, the multi-episodic characteristics of myth narrations, and the poetic form of all formal Shuar discourse. Tukup' structured the narrative by drawing on the resources available to him in order to construct a form of discourse appropriate to a novel situation." Cf. Sherzer (1987: 135–36) on the Kuna: "At the same time and against this background of shared tradition, the diversity of linguistic-poetic devices—grammatical, semantic, lexical, intonation, musical, and social-interactional—provides a set of resources that are drawn on in different ways by performers who are thus able to produce line and verse patterns, meanings, and metaphors which, while steeped in the traditions of Kuna verbal art, are also their own unique and personal creation"; also Sherzer and Wicks 1982, esp. 163.

Hymes's grid of poetic structures—line, versicle, verse, stanza, act, scene, and part—show some resemblance to, and predictably some variance from, the poetic principles underlying South Slavic epic performances. Although the individual decasyllabic lines are often marked by initial particles, there are numerous other linguistic factors involved in their definition,[63] and one should not overestimate their functional congruence with the units described in the Chinookan and other Native American material. Multiples of lines constituting stanzas or strophes have been described in the performances of certain *guslari*,[64] but this seems to be more of an individual and singer-dependent rather than a traditional poetic feature in South Slavic narrative. Scenes and acts find a rough counterpart in the theme or typical scene discerned by Oral-Formulaic Theory, with both the Native American and the Slavic units providing an institutionalized, suprapersonal pattern that nonetheless offers the opportunity for individual artistic design. In general, Hymes's special concern with poetic principles that inform the composition and reception of verbal art over the traditional spectrum of many performances and many individual narrators seems to coalesce more closely with Oral-Formulaic Theory than does Tedlock's program, chiefly because the Parry-Lord approach has historically privileged the traditional over the immediate features of performance.

It would seem most productive, then, to pay close attention to both Tedlock's and Hymes's foundational contributions from Ethnopoetics, and at the same time to be clear that they approach poetic structure from two different directions. Tedlock has scored his libretto to reflect the performance of a single narrator in a single time and place, to re-present an event that by definition cannot be duplicated in the original or any other medium. With respect to the Zuni stories, he has paid exclusive attention to the singular performance, and has forgone any attempt at connection with a tradition, except insofar as the features he analyzes are universal or generalizable after the fact; his later ethnopaleographic analysis assumes a traditional continuity that in effect enables his imaginative use of contemporary Mayan genres to "hear a voice in an ancient text." Hymes, on the other hand, has concentrated on laying bare recurrent poetic structures, at the expectable and reasonable expense of forgoing exclusive concentration on the individual performance; his libretto implicitly links the event he is textualizing to other events in the tradition and encourages their apprehension according to shared principles. The one set of characteristics prescribes as its starting point a narrator's personal, conferred assignment of meaning, the other begins from a tradition's inherent set of associations.[65] Making lines from pauses and making lines from initial particles and verbs are not the same thing, at least on the

---

63. Cf. Foley 1990a: chap. 4.
64. Cf. David Bynum's analysis of stanza, strophe, pause, and melody in the Parry-Lord songs collected in and around Bihać ("The Singing," *SCHS*, XIV: 14–43).
65. The latter are of course also amenable to individual artistic manipulation; cf. esp. the discussion of the Old English *Andreas* in chap. 6 below, and of the Christian narratives from South Slavic in Foley 1991: chap. 4.

surface,[66] but each opens up enormous new areas for investigation, and taken together they constitute a well-balanced poetics that looks toward both immediate and traditional contexts.

In terms of the convergences we have been developing in this chapter, such a dual conception squares with the principle of "performance as the enabling event, tradition as the enabling referent." How individual or institutionalized a given paralinguistic or other feature may be will turn on the nature of the tradition itself: as we have seen, the avenues for individual expressivity are not universally the same, but may involve a range of possibilities; likewise, different traditions will designate different linguistic and paralinguistic sites or channels for institutionalized, metonymic signification. Within the web of compositional and receptional units and strategies, different poetries will naturally configure their registers of structural integers differently, the one offering an individual the feature of pause with which to inscribe his or her personal signature on the palimpsest of oral traditional performance, the other mandating pause as an invariable feature of the poetic idiom at large. The ethnopoetic challenge is to appreciate, and not to singlemindedly reduce, this wondrous complexity of "words" (in the *guslar's* sense of "units of utterance"); our most basic charge must be to begin by recognizing that a poetics consists of both immediate and traditional features, and then to sort out which are recurring principles shared by a number of narrators and performances and which are specific to one narrator or one performance. Although the answer will of course vary, just as the role of various linguistic and paralinguistic aspects of the Zuni and South Slavic narratives has been shown to vary, both types of features are indeed crucial to the significative force—the word-power—of any register, and therefore to the (re)creation of the performance arena and the special kind of communicative economy so fundamentally a part of verbal art in oral tradition.

Word-Power: Event and Referent

In summary, then, I have attempted in this brief format to sketch out some basic correspondences between two important and wide-ranging approaches to the study of verbal art in oral tradition: on the one hand the Oral Theory developed initially by Milman Parry and Albert Lord and more recently extended to the theory of Immanent Art, and on the other hand the Ethnography of Speaking/Ethnopoetics emphasis that has been the work of many scholars, prominent among them Richard Bauman, Dell Hymes, and Dennis Tedlock. My major contention is that both theories seek to open up more faithful understanding of certain species of verbal art by attention to their "untextuality,"

---

66. Once again, since Tedlock's ethnopaleography implicitly posits a traditional continuity—and also because one would expect that paralinguistic features to at least some extent would depend on a shared, suprapersonal repertoire in any case—there may be a closer relationship between Tedlock's and Hymes's systems than is readily apparent. Cf. further the correspondence in their lineations as described by Bright (1979).

that is, to their richly contexted array of meanings that can be communicated only through the special, "dedicated" set of channels that constitute the multi-valent experience of performance, and that, as we shall see in chapter 3, can be accessed in diminished but still resonant form through the augmented rhetoric of the oral-derived traditional text. Both approaches appeal to what lies beyond any collection of linguistic integers by insisting on the value-added signification of these integers as perceived by an audience suitably equipped to accord them their special valences. Such is the challenge issued—and the reward promised—by the singer of tales in performance.

To reconstrue formulaically, as it were, I would see the common basis of these approaches to word-power as consisting of mutual attention to *performance as the enabling event* and *tradition as the enabling referent*. Empowerment of the communicative act results from the keying of performance—whether in the first instance by an actual experienced event or in the textual instance by its rhetorical vestige—and from the shared immersion in traditional context that is the performer's and audience's experiential heritage. To be situated within the performance arena is to be alive to the metonymic referentiality that the given register institutionally encodes: to be so situated means that, among other things, the special formulae and linguistic archaisms of South Slavic epic will help create the extratextual mythos that both outstrips and contextualizes the individual story.[67] At their core, both approaches foreground what is irretrievably lost when we reduce experiences to texts, and both create programs for interpreting verbal art as a richly textured event that takes place in the fecund context of tradition.

Having forged this linkage at the general level of structure and implication, let us now sharpen the focus by considering the narrative and significative antics of two unusual and memorable characters—the Zuni bungler Pelt Kid and the iconoclastic Tale of Orašac from South Slavic epic—and by examining more closely three concepts that lie at the foundation of the composite theory of word-power: performance arena, register, and communicative economy.

67. As we shall see in the following chapters, the perspective from word-power will allow generalization of metonymic meaning to any stylistic feature realized in performance as a compositional and receptional unit.

II

WAYS OF SPEAKING, WAYS OF MEANING

"The stories told to me were like arrows. Elsewhere,
hearing that mountain's name, I see it. Its name is like
a picture. Stories go to work on you like arrows.
Stories make you live right. Stories make you replace yourself."

Apache storyteller Benson Lewis,
quoted in K. Basso 1990 (1984): 100

"Mora da se rekne"

"It has to be said like that"

Halil Bajgorić, *guslar*

With the mapping of common ground shared by Oral-Formulaic Theory and
Immanent Art on the one hand and the Ethnography of Speaking and
Ethnopoetics on the other as a guide, the present chapter seeks to deepen our
understanding of the singer of tales in performance. The aim is to integrate these
approaches further and to move toward a composite theory that will meld the
phenomenon of metonymic meaning with the act of keying performance in an
ethnopoetic context. To put the same matter another way, we will be exploring
the extent to which *word-power* speaks to its partners—*performance* and *tradition*—and how word-power itself constitutes a trope that images a way of
speaking and, complementarily, a way of hearing. "Words," understood as
signals that within the special domain of performance institutionally engage
enormous spheres of traditional reference, will again be our subject, but this
time the focus narrows to three particular and interactive phenomena briefly
introduced in the last chapter: *performance arena, register,* and *communicative
economy.* As the theoretical underpinning of the investigation, and the context
that rationalizes both the various approaches and these three phenomena, we
will be invoking Receptionalism, a critical perspective concerned with the operation of interpretive signals and natural gaps of indeterminacy within a work's

"horizons of expectation."[1] Toward these ends we begin with consideration of two unlikely characters, the comically inept Pelt Kid of Zuni narrative and that redoubtably unheroic hero Tale of Orašac of South Slavic epic song.

A "Literal Failure": The Case of Pelt Kid

The seventh story in Dennis Tedlock's collection of retellings, *Finding the Center,* memorably illustrates the radical integration, or situatedness, of verbal art in cultural context. In "Pelt Kid and His Grandmother," narrated by the Zuni storyteller Walter Sanchez,[2] the named protagonist blunders his way through a stunning series of misapprehensions, leaving even the unindoctrinated, readerly audience wondering, in great amusement, how any reasonable person could go so wrong so often. What is more, the tasks he tackles are not Herculean labors in any sense: they constitute merely the basic human and social repertoire that would logically be available to anyone of Pelt Kid's culture, or even his species. Indeed, that striking discrepancy between reasonable expectation and mystifyingly dysfunctional behavior may be one of the chief points of the story.

The narrator's suppressed laughter a few lines into the performance signals the traditional background against which he will be performing, perhaps more tellingly than his subsequent explicit verbal notation of Pelt Kid's cultural illiteracy: "he just didn't know anything" (193). The depth of his character's lack of knowledge soon becomes apparent, as the grandmother's tutorial on the less than overwhelming assignment of felling a tree and gathering firewood leads to a result she could not have imagined (194):[3]

> Before he left, his grandmother
> had told him:
> "Grandson, when you
> gather wood, when the tree
> falls
> you must run away from it," that's what his grandmother had told him.
> "Well then
> I'll try to do that," he had said.
> He went on until
> he came to where a dried-up tree stood, and he started to cut it down.
> He laid his thongs aside and started cutting.
> Finally the TREE STARTED FALLING and he RAN AWAY, ALL
>   THE WAY BACK TO HIS GRANDMOTHER.

On his unexpectedly empty-handed return, the grandmother finds herself in as

---

1. As a companion to the discussion below, see Foley 1991: chap. 2; as well as Iser 1974, 1978, 1989 and Jauss 1982, 1985.

2. For the ethnopoetically scored libretto, see Tedlock 1972a: 191–213.

3. I quote here from Tedlock's scored text; for an explanation of his system of representation, see Tedlock 1972a: xi–xxxv.

much of a quandary over this behavior as does the reader, since from her (and our) point of view her grandson has followed only the letter and not the spirit of her directions and, consequently, his actions are hilariously illogical.

Things get no better for Pelt Kid as his voice grows hoarse, marking the advent of his maturity and his assumption of sexual status within his society. His voice, and all that it betokens, does not go unnoticed by two girls, each of whom finds him "cute 'n silly" and invites him to her home in what amounts to a coded suggestion of sexual activity and a possible conjugal relationship. But although he has been warned beforehand by his grandmother that the Middle Place will be peopled by members of the opposite sex, his only response to the girls is confusion and a promise to ask his grandmother whether he can accede to their (for him opaquely) coded invitations to "go up to my house."[4] In fact, his major reason for hesitating lies once again in a comically overliteral apprehension of what is said to him: "I'm so bashful I can't just go right into a person's house" (197). No one misses the point quite like Pelt Kid.

In the interim between this and his next escapade, his grandmother makes explicit what should have been but clearly was not implicit beforehand: generally, that Pelt Kid may meet a girl with whom he wishes to live, and specifically, that in the presence of her and her family he must keep his wrist and attached bow-guard near his eyes while he eats, as a symbolic gesture of respect and politeness.[5] After a day of hunting, the young man does indeed happen upon a girl who invites him home, and, recalling his grandmother's advice, he proceeds to remove the bow-guard from his wrist and to gaze through the disattached item while he eats. Having inadvertently (but by now predictably) confuted this ritual of showing respect, he soon flees their laughter, once again running back to his grandmother. Her scolding corrective at once reacts to Pelt Kid's latest cultural/human transgression and indexes the source of his chronic troubles (203): "that's the way the SAYING goes," she tries to explain.

The remaining episodes reveal a cognate sensibility at work, as Pelt Kid first mistakes a girl's father's request to "put away our child's animal" (205, 206) as a command to relinquish the animal skin worn around his waist, when all the man is asking about is some already butchered meat to roast. From this point on he runs away from a potential partner after discovering the existence of her breasts and diagnosing them as a terminal disease for which he might well be blamed and punished; then fractures his grandmother's sex-education allegory about "looking for the hills" and "sticking his peeny in" by scouring the actual landscape for a geographically steamy place; and finally decides that his potential wife has suffered a terrible injury in the genital area (211): "someone must've hit you with / an axe, you're badly wounded." In short, from wood-gathering

---

4. Tedlock observes (1972a: 213) that "Zuni newlyweds normally take up residence with the family of the wife. Today, as in the story, the act of getting married consists of little more than a man's moving in with his wife's family."

5. Tedlock (1972a: 213) reports Joseph Peynetsa's explanation of this custom: "'When you get married you're supposed to be bashful and eat like this,' and he shaded his eyes with his left wrist, where a bow-guard would be worn. It would be impolite not to act bashful."

through culture-specific social behavior to human sexuality, Pelt Kid shows a remarkable talent for consistently botching problems and encounters that have easy, even instinctual, solutions for any member of the Zuni culture or, in some cases, for any member of the human species.

Aside from being the most important, because determining, feature of Pelt Kid's character, this surpassing gift for reduction from contextualized message to skeletal literalism may also serve as a metaphor for what takes place when the "message" of verbal art is denied its word-power and condemned to a dysfunctional literalism. To isolate the dynamic linguistic integers of a work by fossilizing them artificially in a text—for example, stripping away the features of loudness, pause, and so on that Tedlock has rightly argued are fully part of the work[6]—is to imitate Pelt Kid, who strives mightily but in the end futilely to understand what is spoken, since he labors under the handicap of a complete lack of access to the institutionalized context necessary to that hermeneutic task. From the ethnopoetic perspective adopted by Hymes, Pelt Kid's transgressions can be seen as analogous to failing to discover the line, versicle, verse, stanza, scene, act, and part that provide the cognitive, "literary" grid for the composition and reception of a given work.[7] By blinding ourselves to the ethnopoetic context from which the tale derives, we automatically eliminate from consideration anything but the distortion inherent in Pelt Kid's foreshortened point of view.

The analogy holds for the perspective from performance and immanence as well. Understanding that, as his grandmother said, "that's the way the SAYING goes" translates to constituting an audience that can recognize—and credit—the keying of performance. She might as well be tutoring her grandson to, in Bauman's words (1977: 9), "interpret what I say in some special sense; do not take it to mean what the words alone, taken literally, would convey." Alas, Pelt Kid does precisely the opposite, and with great and dependable consistency. Likewise, his actions can be metaphorically construed as depicting the separation of traditional integer and metonymic meaning, with a heavy, resistant wedge of textualism driven between the signal and its signification. The nourishing vessel that maintains the circulation between the grandmother's words and their immanent meaning—that associative, more-than-lexical definition that empowers them to serve their most basic communicative function—has been severed. The result in either case is a "reading" disqualified by a virtually textual parallax, induced either by failure to recognize the keying of performance or, to put the same matter in another way, by divorcing the linguistic integer from its traditional ambience.

"Primus inter impares": The Case of Tale of Orašac

Behaviorally a close cousin to Pelt Kid, Tale of Orašac from the Moslem epic tradition in South Slavic also illustrates, again in an almost allegorical way, the

---

6. See esp. 1977, 1990.
7. See chap. 1 above for a discussion of Hymes's structural categories.

necessary and more than semantic connection between a traditional oral word and its peculiar expressive power. In Tale's case, however, it is not at all a pattern of cultural or human ineptitude that causes him to stand out from the narrative background, but rather another kind of (equally dramatic) discrepancy. The central paradox of his epic existence is that, no matter how egregiously unheroic his actions, dress, or retinue, the Moslem force assembled for either of the great group efforts in this storytelling tradition—a battle or a wedding—simply is not considered complete, or even viable, without Tale's participation. No matter how lamentable he may seem when "read" against the heroic ideals to which all others must conform, we hear again and again that "there can be no journey there without him."[8]

Because he represents a traditional figure par excellence, with so much implied (rather than explicitly reconveyed) in his every appearance, and because both the songs in question and the figure himself have been little commented upon in published sources, it is difficult to hint at the full measure of Tale's character with a few excerpts. But perhaps an account of his unique personality and curious activities in performances by two Parry-Lord Moslem singers will provide some outline of how eccentric and, in our special sense, *power*ful a presence he is.

Turning first to an unpublished source, the Stolac singer Halil Bajgorić's *Ženidba Bećirbega Mustajbegova* (*The Wedding of Mustajbeg's Son Bećirbeg*, no. *6699*),[9] let us consider how Mustajbeg, the groom's father and the greatest hero of the Lika borderland, reacts after all but Tale have answered his summons to join the wedding party, and just what that reaction leads to (405–78):

All the company was there, except for Tale,	405
Except for that dragon, Fool Tale.[10]	
Then Mustajbeg of the Lika shouted:	
"Go, son, Djulić Nuhan,	
Go down to his tower in Orašac,	
To Ibro's tower in Orašac,	410
And summon Fool Tale to me.	
There can be no journey there without him."	
Djulić leaped to his light feet.	
Then he mounted the stout hare,	
The young man went to accursed Orašac.	415
Then he yelled for Fool Tale,	
But Tale's mother responded from the porch:	
"My son Ibro is not at home.	
He left for the stream over there,	
And he bore with him a forged sword,	420
And he led twelve horsemen,	

8. Parry-Lord *6699*.412, e.g.: "Tamo *prez* njeg' hoda ne*ji*made."

9. On Bajgorić, the Stolac regional tradition, and this and other related songs, see Foley 1990a, esp. 45–48, 188–96.

10. "Fool" is Lord's translation of *budaline* (e.g., *The Wedding of Smailagić Meho, SCHS* IV: 254, line 7206; *SCHS* III: 175). As for the name Tale itself, he observes (III: 268, n. 154): "Tale is a short form for Tahir, which comes from the Arabic word *tahir,* meaning 'pure.'"

To put the sword to the whetstone."
And when Djulić Nuhan heard this,
Toward the stream he continued his journey.
When he found Fool Tale,   425
He was holding the saber to the whetstone,
And the twelve horsemen were turning the whetstone.
Then in the stream Tale scolded them:
"O horsemen, deftly turn it,
And leave it to me to strike with the blade."   430
Djulić Nuhan shouted:
"Brother Ibro from accursed Orašac,
The beg sends you his greetings
And asks that you come immediately to Grbava,
To Grbava to the beg of the Lika,   435
That you lead twelve horsemen."
Then Fool Ibro shouted:
"I will come, go tell the beg."
Then Djulić returned to Grbava—
The young man went, dancing his horse,   440
Dancing it, singing all the way.
And when he came down to the wide Lika,
Then he spoke to Mustajbeg of the Lika.
And they slaughtered cattle and oxen,
Hey! The cooks put up kettles to boil,   445
And the gypsy women gathered up meats.
The tumult went on for four days.
All was ready, except for Tale.
Until there he was, Fool Tale,
On his shaggy, dun-colored horse—   450
And he reined it with a striped string,
And on it was no saddle at all,
But he threw only a shepherd's coat over it,
And he pulled it with a striped string,
And on it he hung knapsacks,   455
And in them flour meal.
And yet they said this was the hero Ibro,
And behind him were twelve horsemen,
All in sterling silver and pure gold.

[*Singer's break and instrumental reentry*]

And behind Tale were twelve horsemen,   460
All in sterling silver and pure gold.
How Tale drove his dun horse;
So much did Tale infuriate him
That he was grazing along the road,
The good dun horse, on both sides of the way.   465
When Tale reached the wedding party,
When indeed he reached them, he shouted foully:

> "Beg Mustajbeg, may someone take your mother,[11]
> O Turk, powerful Osmanbeg,
> Have you come to do some digging, beg,   470
> To do some digging or start a household?
> But as for us we're men for a wedding party—
> Short days, magical gorges[12]—
> If we stay here, we will arrive late;
> If we start to move, we will arrive sometime.   475
> Let's begin the journey now!"
> And beg Mustajbeg shouted:
> "Indeed, let's go, Fool Tale!"

This brief passage contains traces of much of Tale's traditional presence. First, although all of the heroes of the Lika have arrived in a prior muster-list not unlike the Iliadic Catalogue of Ships in structure and narrative function, the nonappearance of Tale, or Ibro as he is often called, causes serious enough concern that Mustajbeg immediately dispatches his servant Djulić to invite him personally.[13] Arriving in Orašac, Djulić learns from the mother with whom Tale traditionally feuds that the object of his master's summons is not at home (he almost never is), but has gone to a nearby stream to sharpen his sword! The much-sought-after hero leaves off quarreling with his own horsemen long enough to assert, with typically disrespectful terseness, that he will indeed answer the beg's call, and Djulić returns to an encampment in the midst of preparations for a journey.

Soon Tale makes his appearance, and what an appearance it (always) turns out to be. Whereas other heroes ride prized mounts into the assembly—some of them sleek and black, others with nostrils blazing—our most unheroic of champions arrives on a shaggy, dull brown horse that by immanent implication also suffers from being swaybacked and harried by swarms of flies. And whereas other heroes' steeds boast rich and ornate caparisoning, as does the horse ridden by Djerdelez Alija, the main hero of this song, which earlier required some thirty-two lines of elaborate description (18–49) to cover the grooming process, the careful application of saddleblanket, pommeled saddle, girths, bit, reins, bridle, and a lyrical warm-up, Tale's mount cannot boast even the homeliest of saddles. Worse yet, he directs the poor animal with a single striped string, weighs it down with knapsacks full of flour meal, and grazes it only when convenient, along the side of the road. This beast of burden represents the antithesis of the high-strung heroic steed that is the valued possession of the typical Moslem epic hero, the kind of war-charger that so proudly resists

11. A euphemism: *jebiti* is the coarse word for "copulate with."
12. An uncertain translation of "*h*aloviti klanci" as "magical gorges."
13. At line 413, we hear that "Skoči Djulić na noge lagane" ("Djulić leaped up to his light feet"), an unassuming phrase that seems to describe a simple preparatory act but which metonymically connotes "a heroic or honorable response to an unexpected or threatening turn of events that demands the principal's immediate attention" (Foley 1991: 84). The word-power associated with this line thus emphasizes the critical nature of the situation, and initiates an action that will soon lead to the appearance of Tale himself.

the efforts of anyone but its owner to ride it and that many times prances about a courtyard or undertakes a journey without any physical guidance whatsoever.[14] On the basis of what the tradition teaches us about heroes' horses, Tale's seems a sorry arrangement indeed.

And how does our paragon of heroic virtue behave once he has reached the beg who summoned him for this honorable occasion? Instead of the expected verbal obeisance that marks the traditional meeting of heroes, even when the principals are miserable prisoners in an enemy jail,[15] virtually the first words out of his mouth are a vulgar cursing of his host's mother. Not only that, but this tardiest—and on the face of it, hardly most promising—of arrivals has the gall to upbraid Mustajbeg for not getting the expedition underway sooner: derisively asking whether the beg had perhaps assembled the great host for the mundane tasks of digging or building, specifically domestic and unmartial enterprises, he reminds him that this is a wedding party charged with an obvious duty (ritual bride-capture). Mustajbeg accedes without any negative reaction whatsoever to Tale's intemperate demand, and the gathered force is immediately set in motion toward its goal.

A similar episode—similar, that is, in its performance-specific shape and its performance-implicit meaning—occurs in Avdo Medjedović's famed 1935 version of *Ženidba Smailagina sina* (*The Wedding of Smailagić Meho*).[16] Once again a wedding party is being assembled, this time by the regent Smail for both a marriage and a great battle; in keeping with Medjedović's penchant for elaborate, even effusive, description, the catalogue is much longer and fuller than that of Bajgorić referred to above, but the thrust is the same.[17] Also the same is the coda to the lengthy series of letters of invitation; Smail observes (7149–55):

> "I have invited all I knew, but I have not invited him who is the best of all, Lički Tale of Orašac. If I write that kind of letter to Tale, since Tale will not pay any

14. Such preternatural cooperation between a hero and his (equally heroic) mount is a staple of both Moslem and Christian epic. Kraljević Marko's horse, Šarac, for example, often takes the initiative in leading his master to a person or place Marko cannot himself locate, and we occasionally see the two companions actually conversing or sharing red wine. This relationship—both the specific bond between the two and the general pattern of horse-master cooperation—makes Marko's slaughtering of Šarac, done to prevent his faithful friend's falling into enemy hands, that much more poignant; see further Foley 1991: 124–33.

15. In Parry-Lord song *6597*, "Alagić Alija and Velagić Selim" by Ibro Bašić, for example, the two imprisoned heroes—the long-incarcerated champion Velagić Selim and the new arrival (and former comrade) Alagić Alija—exchange what may under the circumstances seem a perfunctory greeting (68): "They asked after each other's heroic health" ("Za junačko ispitujem zdravlje"). Clearly "each other's heroic health," especially that of the long-time prisoner Velagić Selim, is not optimal. As with other metonymic phrases, however, the traditional integer draws its meaning not exclusively or even primarily from the particular, immediate situation, but rather from the larger, much more resonant context of the entire performance tradition. In effect, the pars pro toto referentiality of this phrase makes such a singular, highly unusual embedding that much more striking, emphasizing as it does the discrepancy between the more customary narrative embedding and this particular instance.

16. For the original-language transcription, cf. *SCHS* IV; for Lord's English translation rendered in prose, *SCHS* III. All quotations are taken from these two sources.

17. On Medjedović's singular talents, cf. Lord 1991 [1956]: 62–71. Many forms or subgenres such as the catalogue have a traditional identity and metonymic force of their own; cf. the highly stylized *pripjev* (proem) and negative comparison (Foley 1991: 68–75 and 75–83, 111–15, respectively).

heed to the warriors anyway, he will not leave his house or even listen to you. You know how Tale is accustomed to act."[18]

Apparently those listening certainly do know how Tale is accustomed to act, since the messenger Husein asks for an alternate assignment, *any* alternate errand, citing the justifiable fear that he may lose his head in delivering the invitation in person.

Smail does persuade Husein to undertake the mission, however, and the courier finds Tale and family in great poverty and squalor, with the object of his quest predictably sharpening his sword (as he has been doing for three months, we are told!). Speaking to his sword, the "necessary hero" is mourning the glory days now gone by, when on various adventures he could beg money and goods of his companions, in part to furnish his mad sister Aziza with clothes to prevent her running naked.[19] As Tale rails on, lamenting Aziza's unmarriageable status and other anomalies he takes as signs of the cultural decay so prevalent in the contemporary world, Husein realizes that the golden ducats Smail had suggested as a bribe may well prove the key to Tale's mercurial acquiescence.[20] After one further complication—the unbelievable discovery that Tale had been seeking to make the bride in question his own betrothed—Husein, not least because of the promise of riches, secures this eccentric champion's crucial participation in Smail's wedding party/army.

A comic portrait not unlike that in the Bajgorić performance then ensues in Medjedović's song. Notwithstanding the riches and enormous martial power assembled in answer to Smail's letter, we hear, quite expectably, that "the best of our comrades is not yet here, even Tale Ličanin from Orašac."[21] Not long after that observation, the missing (and necessary) comrade rides in, looking only too typically deplorable and antiheroic. In place of the fine clothing and

18. *SCHS* III: 174; IV: 252–53:
   "Što sam znao, sve sam ti pozvao.
   Nijesam ti zvao najboljega,   7150
   Ličkog Tala od Orašca grada.
   Da za Tala 'naku knjigu šaram!
   A Tale ti z delijama neće,
   Ni' će poći, ni' će te slušati.
   Ti znaš šta je naučijo Tale."

19. Lord notes (*SCHS* III: 267, n. 149) "the strange characters by whom Tale is surrounded—a mad sister, a standard-bearer whose name is woe, and a scolding wife with naked and hungry children, to say nothing of the hodža Šuvajlija!" On this final figure, see below. By no stretch of the imagination does such a curious familial and extrafamilial group resemble in any fashion the kind of retinue one would expect of a Moslem epic hero, especially one who is apparently so crucial a participant in all such causes.

20. The poetic tradition would gloss this realization with at least two immanent episodes from the implied mythos associated with Tale. One would be his customary fond recollection of begging alms from companions on earlier adventures, and another would be the common and related ruse by which Tale—alone of the august wedding party—sees through the disguise of another pseudo-mendicant and merrily appropriates his accumulated proceeds.

21. Lines 9032–33: "No nam nema najboljega druga, / Sa Orašca Ličanina Tala" (*SCHS* IV: 295). One explanation for such special status is given by Sejdić Pasha of Travnik immediately after this assertion: namely, that Tale has many saints and "mighty powers" (*krupni adaleti*) on his side (9047–48).

armor worn by all other Turkish stalwarts, the leading light from Orašac—and, lest we forget, putative rival suitor for Meho's betrothed Fatima—has bedecked himself in goat- and donkey-skin garments, boots with holes at the toe, threadbare breeches and jacket, and a belt of reeds!

If we are an informed traditional audience, we know that scenes describing heroic dress are customarily partnered with scenes devoted to (sometimes equally ornate) descriptions of the hero's horse, and, structurally at least, our traditional expectations are not disappointed (9113–44):

> And this is how he had decked his mouse-gray horse. The reins were reeds from the river bank. There was neither proper saddle nor pack-carrier on the mouse-gray horse, but only the blanket from a smelly goat. Over the blanket hung a broken-down saddle of sorts. The boards that were next to the pommel were so cursed old that they were broken and patched with a metal plate. . . . There were no stirrups on the saddle but only two slings of reeds, and they were both broken away from the saddle frame and hung loosely down the mouse-gray horse's flank. The reins of reed had broken against the mouse-gray horse's teeth. Tale's legs hung free, and the cursed mouse-gray horse frequently trotted a bit and often grazed on the grass at the side of the road. Tale tried to kick the horse with his feet, but there were no stirrup slings, and his two legs dangled free and his boots struck against the stones, which nicked his boots.

When compared to the horses and equine fineries sported by earlier-arriving heroes—silver-footed dapple-grays and spotted whites equipped with all manner of accouterments, befitting both the heroes astride them and the errand they are on—Tale's "charger" seems sorry indeed, an unlikely mount for an unlikely champion.

The final section of Medjedović's traditional vignette on the man from Orašac treats his reception among the larger group and his two closest comrades-in-arms. To the general complaint that such a disgracefully clothed hero and shamefully caparisoned horse would engender only mocking laughter, thus making things difficult for the army as a whole, the ubiquitous Mustajbeg warns his fellows that while Tale conventionally "does not bedeck himself either for war or for weddings,"[22] he is essential to the success of any martial escapade. Their fears allayed, the comrades then ask, understandably, about the two who accompany Tale: the priest (*hodža Šuvajlija*) who defiles himself with dust and is overfond of the forbidden flask, and the standard-bearer (*bajraktar*) who holds the standard upside down, rides backwards on his unshod mare, and is a bastard, a matricide, and a sevenfold patricide! Mustajbeg explains that both are "accompanied by saints"[23] and, recounting the standard-bearer's remarkable history, observes that his very name is Woe or Misfortune (*Belaj*) and that so far the ill luck has been visited only upon Tale's enemies.

In both of these narratives, as in all others, Tale does indeed prove to be the linchpin in the action—undertaking assaults that no one else would dare, for-

22. 9174: "Ni' s' oprema u rat ni u svate. . . ."
23. 9204: "Sa obadva ima ćirameta."

mulating battle plans that the rest adopt and implement without question or hesitation, and generally serving as the absolutely necessary figure that the various proverbial phrases maintain he is. Still, despite his predictable role and equally predictable success, we must wonder at the apparent illogic of the actions traditionally assigned to his character. How can such a crude, ignoble, unheroic, self-absorbed, often mad figure command the heroic prestige accorded him in Moslem epic?

One answer to this question would lie in recognizing how Tale, with his Zuni counterpart Pelt Kid, in fact serves to encode a panoply of positive and admirable values, but through a dramatic and precisely calibrated indirection. Both characters conduct themselves in a manner that contradicts convention at every turn, that completely denies the accepted and honorable in favor of the unacceptable and disgraceful. Such a discrepancy not only triggers amusement—in Pelt Kid's case the laughter of those who experience his befuddled behavior and his narrator's continuing attempt to muffle his own laughter, and in Tale's case the outright entertainment he provides for his comrades as well as for his various listening or reading audiences—but also suggests by implication the right and proper behavior that is the basis of the mockery. Were such cultural and heroic illiteracy, respectively, not so diametrically opposed to what is understood as the baseline knowledge and practice in these storytelling traditions, then Pelt Kid and Tale would amuse neither their most immediate audiences nor their latter-day readers. To put it another way, only because these two figures rhetorically engage the very actions and values that they appear to confute can they be humorous and, perhaps more important for the present purposes, memorable and resonant.

Furthermore, just as Pelt Kid allegorized the mistaken interpretive practice of demanding literalism in a nonliteral, metonymic medium, so his colleague from Moslem epic images another aspect of the dynamics of expression and perception associated with word-power and the singer of tales in performance. For it is a matter not just of reversal at the surface of a character or action, but also of the nature of the significative bond between that surface and its implied depths. In everything that he does (and does not do)—from his devil-may-care flaunting of authority through his almost slapstick dress and "regalia" and on to his uniquely heroic (and superficially unexpectable) performance on the battlefield—Tale of Orašac illustrates the institutionalized relationship between a traditional, performance-centered metonym and its implied field of meaning. The observed as well as proverbial fact that such an unlikely figure proves so crucial to an army otherwise composed of the conventionally great heroes of the Lika, the necessary truth that one who seems far the least of his company proves its most important member and its sole salvation during the darkest hours, mirrors in tangible narrative form the central trope of word-power: metonymic signification, the nominal part standing institutionally for the untextualized and untextualizable whole, as based on the enabling event of performance and the enabling referent of tradition.

One moment in Medjedović's *Smailagić Meho,* a scene briefly alluded to above,

particularly well captures the institutionalized relationship between the singu-
larly discrepant figure Tale and the equally singular heroics of which he is
capable and for which he is in fact renowned. In rebuttal to his (straightforwardly
heroic) peers' abject complaint about the moth-eaten "champion" on the mouse-
gray horse, Mustajbeg cautions (9169–94):

> "I pray you, as personages of great power amongst us, not to deceive yourselves,
> and not to mock or laugh at him. Such is Tale's nature. He does not bedeck himself
> especially either for war or for weddings. Were an imperial firman to come now
> and summon him to appear in council before the sultan, he would approach the
> sultan even as he is now." The pashas marveled at this, and again the bey spoke:
> "O pashas, do you see Tale? In battle up and down the empire, along the imperial
> border and in Hungary, where there are most strongholds, where platforms have
> been excavated in the trenches and great cannon placed upon the platforms, there
> it falls to the lot of none to attack the cannon and the breastworks but to Tale
> alone and his three hundred men of Orašac. He cuts off heads and reads prayers
> over them, and he seizes strongholds from the Germans. If today, as seems likely,
> there is a battle beneath Buda, you will see what Tale is like."[24]

Despite his appearance, Mustajbeg of the Lika is saying, Tale can accomplish
things no one else—including both himself and those proud warriors he is
addressing—can accomplish. The fact that it is *lički Mustajbeg* who offers this
gloss confers on it a certain rhetorical force, since he is customarily the *primus
inter pares* when heroes gather in Moslem epic.[25]

If this conversation reflects in miniature the way in which word-power melds
metonym and meaning into an indissoluble whole perceptible once performance
is keyed and tradition is engaged, then we might complement Mustajbeg's
"despite" with our own "precisely because." In other words, the nominal shape
of Tale's description in this or that performance, memorably resonant in its
reversals of standard heroic values, serves as a sign vehicle not simply for the
wonderfully contrary figure it summons to narrative present but also, and
perhaps more importantly, for the litany of heroic accomplishment that it
directly and unequivocally implies. To concentrate only on Tale's superficial
features, as do the pashas, is in essence to textualize a character who lives beyond
the boundaries of one or a hundred texts; they fear his participation because,
like Pelt Kid, they understand only the literal dimension of his identity. With
the enormously richer field of vision made possible by traditional context in a

24. The reference to "Germans" may be an instance of a contemporary detail inserted into an
otherwise traditional account, a detail in this case attributable to Medjedović's own war experience
(see, e.g., *SCHS* III: 43). One could compare the modulations reported by Matija Murko for South
Slavic epic (1929/1990: 124), in which the tsar anachronistically uses the telephone to contact
Enverbeg; or by Elizabeth Gunner (1986) for Zulu praise poetry, in which she illustrates the
"re-interpretation of tradition to fit a contemporary situation" (186).

25. For example, he often heads up the party of suitors vying for an imprisoned hero's wife or
fiancée in a Return Song, the South Slavic equivalent of the *Odyssey* (Foley 1990a: chap. 10).
Consonant with this Antinoos-like position (but not only in this particular role), Mustajbeg is also
by nature a dangerous, duplicitous person, the very one who in the heat of battle closes the city gates
on a countryman and permits his capture by the enemy. Cf. further Foley 1991: 18–19.

performance situation, Mustajbeg can remove their literalist bias by reference to what really matters, both on the present adventure and more generally in matters of understanding verbal art; he remakes Tale in his immanent wholeness, allaying fears based on textual literalism with wisdom derived from performance and tradition. From our external point of view, we can then go even further: the beggar clad in donkey-skin and perched on the mouse-gray horse uniquely and directly *means* inimitable courage and actions in battle that can be achieved by no one else; the metonym—no matter what its nominal denotation—uniquely commands a "dedicated" field of reference that can be activated only through its agency.

Such a relationship between Tale and what he portends has many parallels in the word-power associated with traditional oral narrative and related forms. One thinks, for example, of the much-studied noun-epithet combinations so common in South Slavic and other epic traditions. As has been demonstrated elsewhere,[26] each of these "words" amounts to a kind of mytheme, with the nominal parts ("Tale of Orašac," "swift-footed Achilleus," "Beowulf, son of Ecgtheow") standing for wholes that cannot be reduced to suit only the confines of any one textual situation. Even in cases when there is more than one phraseological avenue to the same immanent characterization, differences in deployment of metonyms are not always, or even chiefly, to be sought in authorial adaptation to immediate context; typically, two or more noun-epithet phrases simply mark morphologically variant nominal pathways to the same traditional reality. In accordance with the central trope of such verbal art, word-power derives from the contractual signification of an extratextual whole by an integer dedicated solely to that function.

So it is that Mustajbeg encourages his pashas to bypass the nominal content of Tale's character—the superficial details of that presence nonetheless memorably etched on the traditional idiom by their very incongruity—and to credit the integer with its true meaning. In urging this displacement from the literal into the immanent, Mustajbeg, like the audience who laughs at the inane misconceptions of Pelt Kid, becomes a Receptionalist critic,[27] an interpreter who activates a "text" by conquering its textual inertia and transforming it into an experience. It is to this process of experience we now turn, as we attempt to delineate the hybrid theory of word-power from the perspective of Receptionalism and in terms of three interdependent principles: performance arena, register, and communicative economy.[28]

---

26. Cf. esp. Foley 1991: 18–22 (South Slavic epic), 22–28, 139–50 (Homeric epic), 195–210 (Old English narrative).

27. Cf. the seer and Receptionalist critic Theoklymenos, who interprets the strange and disturbing blood-feast of the suitors in Book 20 of the *Odyssey* against the traditional background of the hero's immanent return; cf. Foley 1987: 199–207.

28. As noted in the Preface, the focus on word-power does not constitute an attempt to hatch a grand, overarching theory that would comprise Oral-Formulaic Theory and the performance-centered approach, but rather an effort to point out their common ground and to validate each method by referral to a second perspective.

Receptionalism and Word-Power

"You know how Tale is accustomed to act" (7155), says Hasan Pasha Tiro
to the assembled nobles and scribes; "Such is Tale's nature" (9173), announces
Mustajbeg to the complaining pashas.[29] Both of these statements, arguably
species of special pleading that strive to exculpate the "odd man out" by transferring judgment on his appearance and actions to another interpretive venue,
assume, as we have seen, an implicit knowledge on the part of the audience or
reader. If we are a competent audience, in short, such virtually proverbial
nuggets activate networks of immanent meaning to which they are linked by
performance fiat and traditional practice,[30] and as co-creators of the action
before us we invest Hasan Pasha Tiro's and Mustajbeg's shorthand observations
with the resonance they metonymically command.

Such encoded signals, whether at the level of phrase, character, scene, or
whatever, are the primary object of the Receptionalist approach to verbal art,
which was formulated, it should be admitted at the start, specifically and strictly
for literary texts. Seeking to free the act of reading from the straitjacket of
empirical analysis, wherein the work is too often understood as coextensive with
the concrete textual object, Receptionalists such as Hans-Robert Jauss and
Wolfgang Iser[31] have placed great emphasis on the potential activity of a text,
the dynamic contribution of the reader, and the experience occasioned when
text and reader interact. They not seldom speak of the ways in which a text can
"teach" its reader to read, locating the "work" midway between subject (the
individual reader) and object (the textual artifact), and under the absolute
control or determination of neither (Iser 1974: 279): "The literary text activates
our faculties, enabling us to recreate the world it presents. The product of this
creative activity is what we might call the virtual dimension of the text, which
endows it with its reality. This virtual dimension is not the text itself, nor is it
the imagination of the reader: it is the coming together of text and imagination."

Corollaries to the general theory of Receptionalism treat, for example, what
Jauss calls the "horizons of expectation" (1974: 16–17, e.g.), the set of expressive
and perceptual contexts brought into play by textual strategies of all sorts. Texts
are received within the latitude circumscribed by these horizons, and interpretations must consequently be endemically heterogeneous; no two readers will
react to the text's coded messages in exactly the same way, and so the works
realized by cooperation between a plurality of readers and a single text must
vary accordingly. The variation over time, as different ages react to a given text,

29. "Ti znaš šta je naučijo Tale" (7155); "Onaki su tabijati Talu" (9173).

30. In serving as a node for a network of references, the proverb and metonym function similarly.
Thus, for example, Emmanuel Obiechina's (1992) characterizing as a "narrative proverb" the kind of
story that an author takes from oral tradition and insets into the African novel; by recalling—in this
case into a decidedly textual arena—the world and mythos of an ever-implicit oral tradition, such
inset stories function metonymically.

31. Esp. Iser 1974, 1978, 1989; Jauss 1982, 1985. See Foley 1991: chap. 2 for an extended discussion
of Receptionalism and traditional oral art.

will constitute a history of receptions, and will represent the viability of the work in various historical and cultural milieux. Receptionalists also observe, however, that interpretation is hardly so willy-nilly a process as this model might initially lead one to suspect, for there are natural brakes or controls placed on variability by the coherence of the set of signals that make up the expressive code. Relative consistency of reception thus amounts to evidence of aesthetic coherence, and even a highly original text will not suffer for lack of contextualization within accepted horizons; as Jauss puts it (1974: 16), "A literary work, even if it seems new, does not appear as something absolutely new in an informational vacuum, but predisposes its readers to a very definite type of reception by textual strategies, overt and covert signals, familiar characteristics or implicit allusions."

For Iser the text's tutorial extends to creating an "implied reader," brought into being by the text's requirement that it be translated into an experience rather than left a libretto only, and yet limited by the fact that the work must take shape within certain horizons of expectation. The implied reader's role is what the individual reader, according to his or her lights and the coherence of the text, must accept in order to co-create the work of art.[32] And here Iser provides an insight that is striking in its simplicity and programmatic force: he maintains that the reader equipped to respond to textual signals must also be ready to bridge the gaps of indeterminacy that exist in all works of fiction. In other words, it is not only the reception of positive, content-laden signals that constitutes the reader's interpretive charge, but also the "emendation" of apparent lacunae that the author has left in the textual map as a natural and necessary part of the script for performance of the work.[33] Filling such gaps, a process he calls "consistency-building" because the solutions to such problems must harmonize with the rest of the co-created work, is a major part of the Receptionalist program.

In explaining how the textual map marshals reception and directs (but does not wholly predetermine) aesthetic response, Iser turns to an examination of Tobias Smollett's novel *Humphry Clinker* from the vantage point of genre. He argues that three distinct generic patterns, each with its own identity in the overall history and contemporary varia of the novel, are complicit in Smollett's libretto: the epistolary form associated first with Samuel Richardson, the travel book form so popular during the eighteenth century, and the picaresque substrate that figures in the evolution of the novel from its beginnings.[34] Each of

32. Elsewhere I have described this process as follows (Foley 1991: 40–41): "Even in a world of literary texts precipitated out into a convenient array of standard editions, each text complete with its own canonical history and critical heritage, Receptionalism reminds us that we cannot settle for the distortion of dynamic activity into stasis, of ever-contingent reception into known and appropriated fact, of the implied reader's continuing responsibility into the kind of textual archaeology that converts our living literary tradition into a museum filled with dusty artifacts."

33. As Iser puts it (1974: 287), "by reading we uncover the unformulated part of the text, and this very indeterminacy is the force that drives us to work out a configurative meaning while at the same time giving us the necessary degree of freedom to do so."

34. On the evolution of the novel and the picaresque form, with special reference to the works of Charles Dickens, see A.-M. Foley 1992.

these subgeneric matrices prescribes certain avenues for the reader's interpretive activity, and "the combination of the three forms transforms them into channels of perception through which reality is to be seen" (1974: 70). Iser understands this blending of three familiar perspectives into a composite technique as an important moment in the history of the novel and in some ways an anticipation of nineteenth-century developments, yet he stresses that it is because each of the generic forms has its ready context, replete with prior associations, that the "new" synthesis they constitute has such force.[35]

The concept of the implied reader "designates a network of response-inviting structures, which impel the reader to grasp the text" (Iser 1978: 34), and thus entails an individual who strives, on the basis of his or her cultural and individual preparation, to make sense of a text composed of, on the one hand, decipherable signals—whether they be generic patterns or other sorts of content-laden features—and gaps of indeterminacy. In *Immanent Art* I offered the analogy of pictorial representation to explain how the perceiver navigates a route partially prescribed by the object "text" he or she confronts, and partially undetermined and therefore open to the involvement that is a condition of experience. Using Ernst Gombrich's theories of interpretation in the plastic arts, as most succinctly documented in his classic *Art and Illusion* (1972a), I argued that the link between signal and message is at the same time arbitrary and institutionalized. Gombrich expresses this idea in terms of the *illusion* created by the artificial and individually unlikely colors and schemes of nineteenth-century British landscape painting, for example, pointing out that an artist such as John Constable made no attempt at a one-to-one representational scheme, but communicated in an idiom that, by appeal to the ongoing tradition of this mode of painting, dependably evoked certain responses within the viewer. To parse his selection of colors and shapes according to photographic realism or another impertinent syntax would be to shatter the illusion and destroy the linkage between (illusionary) signal and (institutionalized) meaning.

This analogy suggests that textual signals likewise engage cognitive categories of perception and expression, bringing into play resources based not upon their literal denotation but rather upon their idiomatic usage, their connotative dimensions. That is, it emphasizes the finally artificial nature of the language of communication, whether pictorial or linguistic,[36] and the kind of significative

35. Iser 1974: 80: "Letter, travel book, picaresque novel and humors are the elements of the eighteenth-century novel which form the link with what the reader is accustomed to. Their interplay makes him see these familiar forms in a new combination, thus opening his eyes to new possibilities of human experience."

36. Cf. the notion of "linguistic relativity" suggested by Tedlock in reference to the representation and interpretation of a performance (1990: 139): "The more we attend to the chronology of the performance, the progress of its phonemes and syntax, the unfolding of its argument or plot, the less we can apprehend its topology, the depths of its resonances and breadths of its references, the contours of its contents and characters. And the more we attend to topology, the more chronology escapes us. ... Our proffered representation and the world it projects will undergo apparent changes of movement and shape each time we change the perspective or vector of our interpretation. What we are up against is a principle internal to language use itself. It is our very own *uncertainty principle,* and that is what we might as well call it."

dynamics that fosters the artistic illusion—what Receptionalists would call the "work" as distinguished from the "text." It also illuminates what it means to engage in "consistency-building," since the tone, movement, and overall impression of the painting will be as much dependent on the viewer's internally consistent extrapolation from conventional signals as on the literal force of the signals themselves. In Gombrich's terms (1972b: 17), "we tend to project life and expression onto the arrested image and supplement from our experience what is not actually present." Thus the gaps of indeterminacy are filled in accordance with what the text, by virtue of its map of idiomatic features, teaches us. Both signals and gaps are necessary parts of the "script": without the former there would be no basis for coherent perception and expression, and without the latter the textual or pictorial object would foreclose upon the interpreter's participation and never modulate from libretto to experience.

In applying this set of observations to the singer of tales in performance, we must make certain modifications in Receptionalist theory, but the broad outlines will remain quite recognizable. For example, the implied reader must become the *implied audience,* with a number of consequent complications: instead of the single text as libretto, we may have many performances of the "same work," all of them formally equivalent as situated events in the social life of a given group;[37] and instead of the single reader, we must deal with a plurality of audience members, a constituency that multiplies as one moves from performance to performance, synchronically and diachronically, in a given tradition.[38] At first sight, then, Receptionalist theory's focus upon the idiosyncratic receiver—on the singularity of his or her preparation and individual activity in the perceptual process—might seem to diversify the interpretation of traditional oral narrative beyond an acceptable level. If we have not one but many different individuals constituting many audiences over time, and thus a multiplicity of "readers" charged with the translation of signals and the filling of gaps of indeterminacy—and this is to say nothing of the variability among performance "texts" themselves—will the series of co-creations of the work not be so incongruous as to defy any meaningful rationalization?

The answer to this reasonable query can be found in the unifying roles of performance, the event that frames the communicative exchange, and tradition, the body of immanent meaning that always impinges upon the linguistic integers of the metonymic idiom. The single performance of a traditional oral work is both something unique, a thing in itself, and the realization of patterns, characters, and situations that are known to the audience through prior acquaintance with other performances. The performer will surely contribute importantly to this or that instance or event, making the single occurrence in many ways unparalleled, and

37. As Lord (1960: 101) put it so elegantly: "Each performance is the specific song, and at the same time it is the generic song. The song we are listening to is 'the song'; for each performance is more than a performance; it is a re-creation. . . . In a sense each performance is 'an' original, if not 'the' original."

38. On the complex web of performances, texts, and audiences, with special attention to the medieval situation, see Parks 1989, 1991.

we should most certainly not make the mistake of assuming that originality is only a rare feature of traditional oral art.[39] Nonetheless, the performer of such a work depends much more heavily upon the encoded, immanent meaning of his or her idiomatic language than does a highly literary artist.[40]

It is in effect the word-power associated with a performance tradition that rationalizes the heterogeneity of reception among audiences and individual audience members, not only by tuning the resonance of the linguistic and paralinguistic signals that make up the presentational fabric of the performance but also by providing implicit connotations that assist in filling the performance's gaps of indeterminacy. In terms of Gombrich's controlling metaphor, it is in fact the illusion fostered by the event of performance and the referent of tradition that makes possible the experience of verbal art in oral tradition. As long as there exists an audience able to bring to such performances—whether oral or oral-derived—the knowledge of the cognitive categories in and through which they are enacted, the entire experience will retain at least a measure of its integrity, continuity, and fullness.[41]

A Receptionalist approach to word-power thus entails a full consideration of the dynamics of performance and tradition. Instead of the text we have the performance, instead of the implied reader the implied audience. Signals and gaps in the libretto are still the focus of the methodology, but the signals have metonymic, immanent meaning, and the negotiation of gaps depends not only on a given audience member's individual preparation but on strategies in place under the interpretive contract of the performance tradition. With these qualifications, or accommodations, the central tenets of Reception still hold: the performance and audience member co-create the "work," and that experience is set in motion by the recognition of and response to cues that constitute the "text." To echo what was observed above in relation to the analog of pictorial

39. Such a lack of originality, or individuality, has been only too readily imputed in the past by those applying a strictly constructionist version of the Oral-Formulaic Theory. Concerned at all costs to explain the apparently repetitive idiom as the poet's hedge against the pressure of composition in performance, this narrowed version of the theory cannot afford to credit the performer with much independence of the medium. From the perspective of Immanent Art and word-power, however, what was viewed as a compositional imperative becomes an expressive and artistic imperative, and adherence to the traditional idiom only opens up the referential dynamics while also leaving room for a singular contribution to the ongoing performance.

40. Compare the highly traditional pictorial artist, who relies especially heavily on a stylized, "limited" vocabulary of (intensely coded) expressive items (cf. Gombrich 1972a: 73–75, 128). Feld describes the dynamic linkage between Kaluli performer and audience as follows (1982: 131, my emphasis): "When Kaluli compose and perform songs, they assume that their audiences will be prepared to listen to them in a reflective and nostalgic way. They consciously utilize this assumption to construct texts that will make their audiences attend to and think about imagery *in an amplified manner.*"

41. In the next chapter we will consider what happens when the traditional oral idiom first enters a textual form (at a point when audiences can still credit it with its extratextual, metonymic referentiality), eventually moving toward a more self-sufficient textuality without an audience that can receive the traditional, performance-centered signals on their own terms. It should also be emphasized that the very rationalization provided by performance and tradition creates the background for—and therefore makes meaningful—individual, performance-specific aspects of traditional oral art.

representation, parsing such verbal art according to a strictly literary, post-traditional syntax amounts to precluding its faithful, perhaps even coherent, reception. With reference to the two examples cited earlier in this chapter, we must be able to appreciate the deep and functional incongruity of Pelt Kid and Tale of Orašac, to place these curious figures in a context that explains and justifies their undeniable eccentricity. In short, Receptionalism will demand that we understand the work on its own terms, not only by perceiving its structural lineaments of phraseology and narrative scene, but also, and crucially, by hearing the immanent resonance of these integers—in short, by sensing their word-power.

Performance Arena

In simplest terms, the *performance arena* designates the locus where the event of performance takes place, where words are invested with their special power. I favor this spatial metaphor, together with its geographical and ritualistic overtones, because it implies a recurrent forum dedicated to a specific kind of activity, a defined and defining site in which enactment can occur again and again without devolution into a repetitive, solely chronological series. For, as argued elsewhere at some length,[42] the "repetition" that many have ascribed to traditional verbal art has better characterized the mindset of the contemporary analyst than the actual phenomenon examined; only when one views the instances of a performance tradition through a textual lens does the staccato emergence of individual events fold neatly into a matched set of facsimiles, best construed as a linear sequence. When each event is understood as speaking first to an ambient tradition that is the chief source of its word-power, then the question of linearity is merely a secondary imposition upon the phenomenon, a heuristic that allows a modern investigator, highly conditioned by textuality, to interpret by assimilation to the familiar, canonical model. For events that are not repeated but *re-created,* the performance arena describes the place one goes to perform them and the place the audience goes to experience them.[43]

In terms of the Ethnography of Speaking, this arena names a site (or sites) distinct from the locales in which other kinds of discourse are transacted. It marks the special area in which performance of a certain kind is keyed—by the speaker and for the participating audience—and in which the way of speaking is focused and made coherent as an idiom redolent with preselected, emergent kinds of meaning. Within this situating frame the performer and audience adopt a language and behavior uniquely suited (because specifically dedicated) to a

42. Cf. Parks 1991, esp. 47; Foley 1991: 56–68.
43. The independence of the performance arena from any geographically or temporally defined place—the fact that the term names an experience rather than a designated place or moment—can be well illustrated, for instance, by the pageant-wagon employed in the presentation of medieval English drama. By means of this mobile stage, participants were in effect able to move the arena, and all that it implied, from one community to another.

certain channel of communication.[44] To take the example of the spectrum of
South Slavic verbal arts in oral tradition, one would therefore speak of the events
collectively constituting genres as taking place in a series of different performance arenas. Because Moslem epic, Christian lyric (or women's songs), Serbian
charms, and the various regional forms of graveside lament all command different fields of reference, they each play themselves out within definable and
distinct frames. Because the performer and the audience (both implied and
tangible) experience these events according to their recurrence in the appropriate
arena, crediting each act or verbal transaction with the context they have learned
to provide, the performance is intelligible on its own terms.

The perspective from Immanent Art offers a complementary and very similar
set of insights. Here the notion of performance arena conveniently designates
the place wherein the expansion of nominal metonymic integer to ambient
traditional meaning is not only a possible but a prescribed mode of interpretation. The discrete verbal sign, that which in and of itself has over the ages of
Homeric criticism, for instance, proven inadequate to the task of construing the
work,[45] can bloom into its full, pars pro toto signification only within the
performance arena. Attending the event of traditional oral narrative in the
"wrong" arena means, necessarily, misunderstanding that event; the rules, frame,
all that constitutes the infelicitous context will prove impertinent and misleading
as the reader or audience tries to fashion coherency on the basis of disparate
codes.[46] To appreciate the work on its own terms, one must attend the event in

44. Thus Bauman observes (1977: 11) that "performance as a mode of spoken verbal
communication consists in the assumption of responsibility to an audience for a display of
communicative competence." Cf. Hanks 1989: 103–13 on the boundaries of text, "centering" of text
within an interpretive matrix, and related issues. Complementarily, we could observe that any
performance/version is fundamentally a "tale within a tale," with the avenues of implication
necessarily running both ways. The present tale both enriches and is enriched by the larger, implied
tale—itself unperformed (and unperformable) but metonymically present to the performer and
audience.

45. One of the most glaring examples of failure to construe traditional integers is the long-standing
disagreement over the significance of Homer's "winged words" phrase (*epea pteroenta*); cf., for
example, Calhoun 1935, Parry 1937, Fournier 1946, Combellack 1950, Vivante 1975 and 1982.
Although this phrase per se actually fails to qualify as a classically defined formula (Foley 1990a:
129–37), the larger point is that the variance of opinion over its meaning has resulted from insistence
that it either mesh situationally with its most immediate surroundings or serve merely as a metrical
convenience.

46. It is an attempt to counter this sort of interpretive malfeasance, institutionalized by
contemporary Western culture's privileging of the document over the experience from which it has
been reduced, that is at the root of Tedlock's revolutionary work in ethnopoetics and
ethnopaleography (e.g., 1971, 1983, 1985), as well as of Henry Glassie's equally brilliant methodology
for re-creation of experiential context (e.g., 1982). Cf. Pond 1990: 217 on songs of protest from the
Niua Islands: "Thus, textual analysis alone does not reveal the full import of these songs; that can
only be revealed by the social context of the poem's composition and empathy with the poet's
perspective." On a personal level, I can attest to the hilarity I often incited among Serbian academic
colleagues as a fieldworker equipped with a decent knowledge of the traditional epic register but
without a mastery of more informal, contemporary, conversational registers. Once, when asked where
a child's toy might be located, I resorted to the only "formula" I knew for "on the porch": *na čardaku.*
It turns out that while the Turkicism *čardak* well describes a sultan's or pasha's royal (and quite
magnificent) veranda in decasyllabic verse, it does not equally well name the modern, modest-sized,
quite un-epic concrete platform where the toy happened to have been left.

the proper arena, the same place (within certain limits)[47] in which it has always been performed and received; in other words, one must engage the work of verbal art in the context in which both tradition and the individuals involved have located it. Only then can metonym modulate into extratextual meaning, only then will the empowering cognitive categories come into play.

In Receptionalist terms the performance arena is coterminous with the horizons of expectation within which the text or performance becomes the work. Precisely because the audience recognizes the surroundings from attending previous events, it is in a position to decode the signals that constitute this particular event. What is more, the familiarity of the performance arena—all that it prescribes about the present transaction in terms of earlier transactions—places the audience in a position to bridge the gaps of indeterminacy that are the natural partners to the (now recognizable) meaning-laden signals. Outside this forum for exchange, the signals will lack their implied content, and will necessarily be "read" according to a code other than that employed by the performer in generating them. Outside the dedicated forum such an unaugmented discourse will founder as well on unmanageable instances (and a collective surplus) of indeterminacy, as the audience seeks to fill logical lacunae without the special knowledge available only with admission to the performance arena. The Receptionalist viewpoint makes the two-way nature of word-power especially evident: if the focused way of speaking is also to become a focused way of meaning, then both performer and audience must equally and together enter the performance arena. For only there, and only with the cooperation of both parties, can the text or performance become fully an experienced event.

Register

Once they have entered the designated place in which the desired transaction can uniquely be accomplished, just what passes between the suitably prepared performer and the suitably prepared audience? In what language do they communicate, or, more exactly, to what sort of language do they resort in order to carry on the project of co-creating the work that is the social and artistic imperative behind their attendance at the given event?[48]

Continuing with our Receptionalist perspective on word-power, we can observe as a first principle that, however the system of signs is constituted, its primary burden is to stimulate the audience to an experience of a particular sort, based on the syntax of the event situated in a performance tradition. To invoke Gombrich's theory of artistic perception, this brand or usage of language must

47. Such limits are set by the extent to which replicability of an event is possible (historical and individual variation being rationalized by word-power, as explained above), or, in the case of oral-derived texts, by the singularity of the textual medium (cf. further chap. 3).

48. As will become especially apparent in the study of Serbian charms in chap. 4, the notion of register, though conceived originally as an exclusively linguistic category, must include for our purposes all expressive dimensions of a performance tradition, whether formally linguistic or not.

be able to create the sought-after illusion unambiguously and coherently, though that responsibility does not in any way necessitate a "denotative" idiom[49] that describes by unremitting, ever more detailed recourse to conventional types of signification. In fact, as discussed briefly in the opening chapter, the languages of traditional oral expression are special languages, made up of systems of elements that—under the prescribed transactional conditions of a performance tradition—stand in arbitrary but institutionalized relationships to their referents, with those referents being much larger and more complex than those to which the usual modes of textualization have access.

Such special languages were termed *registers* in chapter 1, in Hymes's sense (1989a: 440) of "major speech styles associated with recurrent types of situations." This distinction stems ultimately from the linguistic theories of M. A. K. Halliday, who conceived of register in terms of three controlling variables: *field of discourse* ("the area of operation of the language activity" [1964: 90]), *mode of discourse* (spoken or written, with many more layers of taxonomy possible), and *style or tenor of discourse* ("the relations among the participants" [1964: 92]). Although the present study analyzes the sociolinguistic setting into a slightly different and fuller array of variables, Halliday's core distinctions are still applicable, emphasizing as they do the special semantic realm that is uniquely the referent of the dedicated language variety (1978: 111, emphasis mine):

> A register can be defined as the configuration of semantic resources that the member of a culture typically associates with a situation type. . . . Since these [semantic] options are realized in the form of grammar and vocabulary, the register is recognizable as a particular selection of words and structures. But *it is defined in terms of meanings;* it is not an aggregate of conventional forms of expression superposed on some underlying content by "social factors" of one kind or another. It is the selection of meanings that constitutes the variety to which a text belongs.

While the linguistic integers constitute the expressive code, in other words, they are merely the dedicated, agreed-upon, contextually appropriate signals for institutionalized meanings. We focus strictly on that code—formulaic phraseology per se, for example—at the exorbitant price of neglecting that which it is uniquely licensed to convey.

A register may consist of a polydialectal *Kunstsprache,* an artificial form of the general language in question that contains a mélange of morphological and lexical variants that would in normal conversation not constitute a coherent expressive code; this is the case, for example, with the language of Homeric

---

49. I use this term advisedly and as a heuristic, rather than as an absolute category, opposing it to "connotative" across a spectrum comprising many different blends of the two types of signification. In no way should the opposition be understood as reifying the Great Divide model of orality versus literacy, since all forms of verbal art engage both expressive dynamics. On this juxtaposition as an analytic entry-point, see Foley 1991: xiv-xv, as well as 8–9 on "inherent" versus "conferred" meaning.

Greek and South Slavic Moslem epic.[50] Or the register may include archaic or obsolescent words or forms, as in the instance of Serbian charms, or unusual because inherently reverberative phrases, as in the Old English riddles.[51] Such a dedicated idiom, pressed into service for a particular communicative purpose as the lingua franca of the given performance arena, may even employ words or forms that stem from or are modeled on words or forms from entirely separate languages. Once again, the Moslem epic, with its heavy dependence on Turkish words for its material culture vocabulary, or the "nonsense" spells in Old English, with a fair share of their "gibberish" so clearly patterned on Latin morphology, offer examples of this phenomenon.[52] Or, as in the case of the Native American performance-texts studied by Hymes, the register may be marked more by rhetorical structures (part, scene, act, etc.) than by nonstandard lexical or morphological features.[53] With Gombrich, we must be aware that the primary duty of the register as a significative instrument is to convey an impression or set of impressions according to the agreed-upon code; the literal identity of its elements—outside the performance arena, after all—may be relevant to investigators who seek to establish an "etymology" or a structural morphology for each integer in the register, but it is the metonymic identity of the items that bears the primary responsibility for creating the illusion that is verbal art.

The instances of archaic language cited in the opening chapter as features that key performance illustrate one possible dimension of the relationship between register and co-creation of the work. To these specific items should be added not only the polydialectalism, inherently contradictory phrases, lexical borrowings, and other specific phenomena mentioned above, but in general any linguistic, rhetorical, or other performance-constituting phenomenon that marks an otherwise inexplicable departure or change in emphasis from the

50. Parry was the first to establish the Homeric *Kunstsprache* as an "artificial" variety of language that was "natural" to the event and process of oral tradition; see esp. his 1932 "Studies" essay. For examples of how such a specialized idiom stems from traditional rules for the composition of phraseology (rules for admission to the performance register), see Foley 1990a: chaps. 4 (ancient Greek), 5 (South Slavic), and 6 (Old English). On the difference between two narrative registers in South Slavic, those associated with the *deseterac* (decasyllable) and *bugarštica* (long line), see Koljević 1992, esp. 349–50.

51. With respect to Serbian charms, cf. chap. 4 below; an example of unusual, highly echoic phraseology in the Old English riddles is the half-line formula *wunderlicul-e wiht*, which names the "wondrous creature" who is the hidden subject of the verbal quest (see Riddles 18 [1a], 20 [1a], 24 [1a], 25 [1a], 87 [1a]; and cf. 29 [1b] and 88 [19a]). Another example is furnished by the archaic codes that support the tradition of Balinese shadow theater (Zurbuchen 1987, esp. 39). Cf. also Tedlock (1972a: xxvii), who observes: "Zuni narratives contain many words, usages, and phrases which would be absent in completely neutral everyday speech, including the formulaic frames that enclose telapnaawe ["tales," regarded as fiction], esoteric terms borrowed from ritual language, highly formal greeting exchanges, and archaic interjections."

52. On Turkish loan-words and traditional phraseology in South Slavic epic, see Foley 1990a: 192–94; on the Old English "nonsense" charms, see Foley 1980a: 81.

53. E.g., Hymes 1975a, 1977, more generally 1981; also 1994 and via personal communication. Cf. McLendon (1981: 303), who comments as follows, with special reference to Eastern Pomo texts: "The rhetorical system of a language, then, is not simply a matter of style or optional choices. It is the communicative principle which organizes discourses, determining sentence boundaries, paragraphs, and episodes. It is the means through which speakers impose a point of view on what they say."

standard language and presentational mode employed for ordinary, unmarked discourse.[54] Thus the displacement from conventional "prose" word order that can take so many forms across different genres and different traditions, and which is governed by the traditional phraseological rules of each genre and tradition, many times signals entry into the performance arena and all that such entry entails for both performer and audience. To take only two examples,[55] we might note the very frequent reversal of normal word order in the second colon of the South Slavic epic decasyllable (e.g., the common phrase *knjiga šarovita,* lit. "book decorated," reversed from the usual sequence), a response to the rule of "shorter before longer" that governs the succession of items in that particular register. A second example would be the concentration of noun-epithet formulas in the latter part of the ancient Greek hexameter (e.g., *glaukôpis Athênê,* "grey-eyed Athena," 51 instances in the *Odyssey,* all at line-end), a generalized feature of Homeric phraseology that locates "words" of substantial metrical extent toward the end of available units. Both of these examples, it turns out, are reflexes of a traditional rule of "right justification" that informs the versification of both epic poetries; but whatever the source of the deflection of standard, unmarked language may be,[56] it serves as a signal within a particular register and accompanying performance arena.

From what may be a more familiar perspective, we might also note the general role of formulaic phraseology, thematic structure, and story-pattern—

54. Sherzer (1983) offers many useful examples of Kuna registers associated with specific genres, as does Gossen for the Chamulas (1974: 46ff., esp. 239–40 on "Style and Cosmos"); cf., more generally, the section "Style and Genre" in Urban and Sherzer 1988 (285–87). As noted in chap. 1, "standard," relatively unmarked language may be the chief vehicle for performances in some traditions, and in those cases it will be paralinguistic or rhetorical or other types of cues that are paramount in keying performance; an interesting case of an alternate kind of cue is the ritual wailing in Amerindian Brazil studied by Urban (1988), who demonstrates that such stylized expression amounts to "indexing a desire for sociability" (393). Whatever the actual signals involved in constituting the formal texture of the register, however, recognition of the special communicative mode invoked is crucial to reception of the utterance. In this regard, cf. Besnier's (1988: 732) caveat, made in the context of Nukulaelae Tuvaluan expressive varieties, that "in our quest for universal cognitive explanations for the difference between spoken and written language, we need to better understand how the communicative norms at play in various spoken and written registers affect the verbal output of the members of particular speech communities."

55. For numerous other examples in ancient Greek, South Slavic, and Old English narrative, see Foley 1990a: chaps. 4–6.

56. As noted above, such deflections may also be paralinguistic (involving features such as loudness, intonation, pitch, etc.) or situational (involving a specified place, ritual event, or type of audience, for example). In the three traditions and various genres under direct examination in this study, the traditional, performance-centered features of the register are often most clearly manifest in its linguistic texture (especially in lexicon, morphology, and word order; but cf. also the study of Serbian charms in chap. 4). In general, however, as with other aspects of traditional oral and oral-derived works, the nature of signals or keys will necessarily vary from one tradition and genre to another. Cf. Hanks 1987: 670: "Viewed as constituent elements in a system of signs, speech genres have value loadings, social distributions, and typical performance styles according to which they are shaped in the course of utterance." With particular reference to Kamsá ritual language, McDowell (1990), examining "the largely unspoken potential for advancing personal goals within the framework of this community-building register," explains that "speeches are composed during performance through recourse to a secondary craft of language, a formulaic system gradually integrated into the adult speaker's competence, allowing for the spontaneous formulation of appropriate phrases" (68).

the cadre of features identified by Oral-Formulaic Theory as constitutive elements of traditional narrative—as symptomatic of a register.[57] For beyond their first approximation as "building blocks" indicative of, because necessary for, "composition-in-performance," these multiform features mark the special nature of an idiom, keying performance and serving individually and collectively as an invitation to enter a focused and reverberative arena. More than a compositional imperative, these aspects of register answer what is finally an expressive and artistic imperative, cooperating in the imbuing of the immediate and concrete with the immanent. In effect, naming Achilleus as "swift-footed Achilleus," or speaking the ritual boast before battle in *Beowulf,* or telling a tale in the Return pattern so common in South Slavic epic—all of these, and myriad more, oral-formulaic signals are "words" in the register devoted exclusively to the (re-)creation of verbal art in oral tradition. They are words, that is, with enormous power.

In short, all linguistic features that make an idiom a dedicated register also comprise its ability to function as a dedicated medium for conveyance of meaning within the performance arena. Maintenance of the illusion of verbal art depends upon fluency—both the compositional fluency of the performer and the receptive fluency of his or her co-creating audience. To step outside that idiom is thus to exit the performance arena and to leave behind the register's unique ability to provide access to implied signification. In terms of the Ethnography of Speaking, it is in such code-switching that the secret of keying performance (as the enabling event) lies; with respect to Immanent Art, it is through such bi- or even multilingualism that metonymic connotations resident in tradition (as the enabling referent) are activated.

Communicative Economy

The third leg of the theoretical tripod, along with performance arena and register, is the particular brand of communicative economy they license.[58] From a Receptionalist point of view, this last dimension of the process is perhaps the most crucial: precisely because both performer and reader/audience enter the same arena and have recourse strictly to the dedicated language and presentational mode of the speech act they are undertaking, signals are decoded and gaps are bridged with extraordinary fluency, that is, economy. While from the

---

57. With the natural variation arising from idiolectal, dialectal, and pantraditional realizations of these features; see further Foley 1990a: chaps. 5, 8.

58. This concept of *communicative* economy should not be confused with the Parry-Lord idea of "thrift" or "economy." For Oral-Formulaic Theory "the thrift of a [formulaic] system lies in the degree in which it is free of phrases which, having the same metrical value and expressing the same idea, could replace one another" (Parry 1971 [1930]: 276). In other words, Parry-Lord economy—itself a tradition-dependent phenomenon (cf., e.g., Foley 1990a: 128, 163–64, 354–55)—is a morphological feature of the register, while the term "communicative economy" speaks to the dedicated, focused relationship between the register and its traditional, performance-centered array of meanings.

perspective of post-traditional, textual communication[59] such verbal signals as "swift-footed Achilleus" might seem cumbersome and unwieldy, sacrificing descriptive accuracy to the necessity to maintain the reusable "building block" of generic connotation, in fact each metonymic integer functions as an index-point or node in a grand, untextualizable network of traditional associations. Activation of any single node brings into play an enormous wellspring of meaning that can be tapped in no other way, no matter how talented or assiduous the performer may be; everything depends upon engaging the cognitive fields linked by institutionalized association to the phrase, scene, paralinguistic gesture, archaism, or whatever signal the performer deploys to key audience reception. Once those signals are deployed, once the nodes are activated, the work issues forth with surpassing communicative economy, as the way of speaking becomes a way of meaning.

This special brand of economy, which must be appreciated on its own terms or fall victim to crippling because impertinent comparisons, underlies, for example, the fascinatingly elaborate techniques of drum language in Sub-Saharan Africa as insightfully analyzed by Walter Ong (1977). As he points out, the talking drums "speak" the Lokele language in an exacting and tightly controlled code, a speech surrogate that imitates the traditional texture of vocal-language phraseology, but that at first encounter might well seem at the furthest possible remove from an "economical" medium of communication (100–101):

> So the "words" on the drums are set into stereotyped contexts or patterns. . . .
> "Moon look toward the earth" is beat out on the drum every time the drummer
> wants to say "moon." And so with the rest of the drum lexicon. For each simple
> word of ordinary speech, the drum language substitutes a much longer expression.
> These expressions moreover are stereotyped, fixed in the drumming tradition, and
> must be learned by each novice drummer: a drummer cannot make up his own
> stereotyped expression at whim.

From the strictly utilitarian view advocated by Parry and Lord, Ong interprets the percussive and tonal formulas as "much longer"—by tacit comparison to vocal speech and especially standard, nonformulaic speech—than they "need" to be. Although he recognizes that these more extensive phrases constitute a specially stylized language, he is still measuring them by their nominal difference from ordinary vocal and nontraditional language, and not by their much more far-reaching difference in significative force.

In the terms we have been developing, the Lokele drum language is patently a register, a variety of "speech" dedicated solely to the single situation of communicating within this medium. As such, it conveys by means of established traditional categories or units, with each integer implying much more than its

59. Elsewhere (1991: 6, n. 12) I have defined *post-traditional* as "the kind of work whose meaning derives chiefly from a single text created by a single author and specifically without active dependence on an oral tradition. In the case of transitional or oral-derived texts one would distinguish between traditional and post-traditional modes of meaning, the former deriving from the work's dependence on its roots and the latter from its textuality."

nominal stylized denotation. Each element of the communication is sent and received against the background of that register and its institutionalized meaning, as Ong himself observes in respect to the "drum names" reported by an earlier investigator, John F. Carrington (Ong 1977: 110):

> Another drum name given to Carrington . . . is both patronymic and event-recording. Knowing that his father, who did not have a drum name of his own, had been a member of a group of folk dancers in England, the drummers designated Carrington as "The European, Son of the European Whom the Villagers Laughed at When he Leaped in the Air." Despite the historic rooting of many if not most names through the many cultures around the globe, few other names carry the load of explicit information often borne by drum names as recorded by Carrington.

To the extent that the highly complex referential system of drum-names functions as a traditional and performance-constituting register, one should add that this concrete designation summons at least as much *implicit,* immanent information in the form of the "mytheme" inherently engaged by the name. Much like the verbal pathways maintained between noun-epithet formulas and complete, extrasituational personalities in ancient Greek or Moslem South Slavic epic, such integers are highly economical in opening a channel for a particular kind of performance and reception.[60] The "length" of the phrase so employed is relevant only when one moves outside the performance arena and disattaches the integer from the register, essentially canceling its indexical function. Nor, within that arena and register, can word-power be measured in terms of the number of syllables or morphemes that make up an expression; without the communicative economy made possible by this focused, dedicated medium, just how many morphs would it take to summon a living character or to (re)create a living situation? Would it even be possible to do so? Communication within a performance tradition is uniquely economical, and cannot be imitated outside it.

Just how sharply the performance arena and register focus composition and reception is adumbrated in Ong's telling observation about the permanence of traditional (oral) communication (116):

> Although sound is ineluctably time-bound, existing only when it is going out of existence, in a certain way the formula, in oral speech or on the drum, gives sound some independence of time. It spreads out the perception of sound, not only beyond the present physical instant, but also beyond the lengthier psychological "present," *la durée* of Henri Bergson. The formula, in this peculiar function, appears as a precocious equivalent of writing. . . .

Because so much of what a register "means" depends crucially on what is understood of its context as brought into play by the event of performance and the referent of tradition, the individual integers can indeed portray a continuing reality. That is, the world to which they provide access is not simply inaugurated ex nihilo with each instance or sounding, but must be understood as ever-present to the

---

60. Cf. the highly resonant Apache place-names, as discussed by K. Basso (1984, 1988).

always vocable code and therefore present to anyone who can use that code properly. Any aspect of a register, not just the formula,[61] commands this reverberation, which, because it is always an echo rather than a sound never heard before, confers a nontextual permanence on the speech act in which performers and audiences are engaged. What greater economy of communication could one imagine than that of a medium that depends not on the perishable spatialization of a text but rather on the imperishable reenactment of a performance, set in a defined and defining arena, expressed through a register dedicated to the purpose, and as a result communicated with an efficiency unknown to (and inimitable by) conventional texts? From a Receptionalist point of view, such a medium inescapably and unambiguously implies its audience in every phrase, scene, gesture, back-channel response, and so forth, and the coherence and permanence of its experience are assured through metonymic implication, the central trope of this kind of verbal art.

Clichés versus Word-Power

With these concepts in mind, let us close this chapter's discussion metonymically, by training the light of the composite approach through word-power on a particularly nettlesome but potentially instructive area in the interpretation of verbal art in oral tradition: the entrenched notion of *cliché*. Under the aegis of a highly textual and text-bound criticism, it has been only too easy to class the recurrent integers of traditional oral narrative as hackneyed fillers, that is, as phraseology, narrative scenes, and story-patterns that are so frequently repeated that they lose their significative "punch." What were once resonant signals degenerate through overuse, so goes the argument, and the result is only a muffled, hollow echo that eventually becomes enervating.

This perception of a diminished ability to bear meaning derives, of course, from the sense of too intimate a familiarity with the offending item, whether that traditional integer be a much-repeated phrase such as "swift-footed Achilleus," a ubiquitous scene such as the South Slavic "Shouting in Prison" theme, or a story-pattern that in its absolute transparency has made a given tale's dénouement uncomfortably inevitable. What the presentation lacks, for the contemporary reader of literary texts, is the textual indeterminacy that invites creative participation: with the gaps closed—indeed filled by clichés that seem to preclude all but a

---

61. As noted above, there may be no formulaic phraseology involved, nor must all of the signals answer a "linguistic" definition; cf. the traditional metonymic force of visual displays in Ponam society (Carrier and Carrier 1990), as well as Jane Hill's (1990: 42) description of the role of weeping in a Mexicano women's narrative: "weeping as a semiotic 'meta-signal' can be extremely complex. In Doña María's narrative, it brackets the crucial moments of thematic development, indexes her sincerity as a narrator, and almost certainly plays a role in her own work of self-coherence." The interweaving of register and myth may be richly complex and many-leveled; Feld (1982: 14) observes that "the Kaluli expressive modalities of weeping, poetics, and song, in their musical and textual structure, are mirror representations of the symbolic code constructed by the myth, 'the boy who became a *muni* bird,'" and that "expressive modalities are culturally constituted by performance codes that both actively communicate deeply felt sentiments and reconfirm mythic principles."

plodding recognition of the "same old story"—where is the audience or reader to find an opportunity for the co-creation that constitutes the Receptionalist imperative of the work of art? Complications only multiply when one turns from the experienced performance (or its nearest dictated kin) first to the textualized transcription, and then to the second removal of a translation.

In considering this set of problems from the vantage point of word-power, we might start by observing that the complaint of cliché can be issued only against the background of a poetics based on assimilation to a literary, textual model. Only if the field of primary reference is unnaturally demarcated by the boundaries of a text, with the most immediate relationship of linguistic integers mandated as involving only those occurrences and recurrences within the spatial limits of the document, can a traditional structure be accused of cliché. Secondarily, within a literary tradition of closely comparable texts understood as integral items genetically related by that tradition, a poet's or school's phraseology or narrative scenery may also be condemned as cliché; one thinks of the "finny tribe" of the British Neoclassicals, for example. Once again the limitation placed upon signification is at root textual, since in this latter case the integer has been emptied of much of its poetic dynamics by perceived overuse within a well-defined, coherent collection of texts—a collection that, from the perspective of literary history, functions as one large text assembled from a group of smaller, finite texts. Could the "author" of this macrotext not sense that "he" or "she" had dipped into the communal well once too often? Could this composite author not have selected a "fresh" phrase or scene that allowed for the play of indeterminacy in the audience or reader's joint construal of the work?

If textuality is the controlling dynamic in the composition and reception of verbal art, then it is clear that any linguistic (or nonlinguistic) integer can become hackneyed and diluted in meaning: the limitations imposed upon field of reference—that is, the finite spatialization that a text or series of texts represents—place severe constraints upon resonance of phrases, scenes, and story-patterns. In terms of the concepts developed in this chapter, the performance arena shrinks from tradition to text (or collection of texts), and the very same items and structures that would be imbued with metonymic signification in the context of oral tradition now must resonate chiefly within the relatively claustrophobic confines of the single work or group of works. Another way to say the same thing is to observe that the mapping of integer to referent is modified dramatically: instead of encoding an untextualizable mythos in a limited number of densely connotative verbal signals, the text-bound situation places primary emphasis on the document and its most immediate context.[62]

---

62. Of course, any text also accrues meaning to itself by reference to the literary tradition of which it is a part—through referral by genre or narrative persona, for example. But I distinguish broadly here between the inherent, automatic field of reference engaged by traditional oral metonyms and the individually driven selection of signals more typical of textual works. Conversely, the traditional referential frame of a performance tradition not only provides the fully fleshed-out characters, the skein of related situations, and the unified field of tale-type context; it also inculcates large and necessary gaps of indeterminacy that the audience or reader is charged with filling.

To take one kind of example, the same phrase that served as a trip-switch for naming a character in all of his or her mythic complexity, the same nominal marker that keyed the introduction of that multivalent personality into the present situation with all of his or her tradition-wide identity intact, now must do its work in a much more closely circumscribed context. And just as the predictable qualities and aspects of that figure were summoned to narrative present to enliven the action with what amounts to traditional characterization, so the unpredictable facets of the same figure also came center-stage, leaving the reader or audience in the classic quandary of co-creating that significant part of the action that the medium naturally leaves undetermined. With the severing of the institutional linkage between metonym and referent, that is, with the foreclosure upon the possibility of word-power as we have been understanding that communicative phenomenon, both the crucially important signals and the equally important gaps disappear. To put it aphoristically, performance arena becomes textual arena, and the recurrent phrase (or other integer)—now denied access to the larger tradition in favor of primary focus on its most immediate and explicit surroundings—becomes cliché.

Likewise, as the arena shifts from performance to text, so the register must take on a different role. With metonymic referents displaced from the compositional and receptional negotiation, what were once merely nominal meanings gain new status: by default, the "swift feet" of Achilleus, once a coded summons for the heroic figure in all of his traditional complexity, must now be worked into the surface of the narrative situation (or damned as a generic filler). The nominal is foregrounded, while that for which it stands pars pro toto recedes into the background; the idiom as a whole undergoes an enormous shift and, in losing the capacity to key performance (to "mean" traditionally), presents a libretto for a very different kind of (re-)enactment. Deprived of the lifeblood of extratextual or extraperformance implication, the register must soon become simply iterative and degenerate to a patina of cliché, the only salvation from which will be the eventual call for fresh, unclichéd ways of signifying. That call for originality will proceed hand in hand with an increasing textuality, a lessening dependence on tradition, and in general a growing awareness of both the opportunities and the limitations of the textual arena.

Another way to describe this same process is to observe that a shift from performance arena to textual arena and a fundamental modulation in the meaning-bearing capacity of the register also portend a major and concomitant change in communicative economy. If this kind of economy depends upon a special arena and dedicated register, and if the spatialization of experience changes the rules of the artistic game, then the mode of communication must also change accordingly. Instead of the complexly coded implications attendant on this or that linguistic integer, implications that of course assume an audience or reader capable of receiving the dedicated signals, the traditional structures will, as noted above, fall back upon the literal meanings that were merely the concrete vehicle for a densely packed, highly economical form of verbal communication. Under such conditions nominal meanings are frozen into an inflated textual prominence, and their function as conveyors of traditional implication is diminished or entirely vitiated. What was a privileged pathway to value-added meaning hardens into the textual cenotaph of cliché, and, among other things, the work (or its putative author) may begin to be understood as fatally constrained by a medium now perceived as merely iterative and, worse yet, unimaginative. This is what happens when the enabling referent of tradition recedes into the background of the performer-audience relationship, when the enabling event of performance no longer places its decisive stamp on the interpretation of verbal art—in short, when metonyms become clichés, the "dead letters" of artistic correspondence.

In the next chapter we shall study the ways in which this shift—only the crude outlines of which could be drawn here—takes place in a variety of contexts, as the signifying strategies endemic to traditional oral art are adapted to textual deployment. In coming to terms with the rhetorical transformation of metonymic cues, or keyings of performance, in texts, we shall be attempting a version of the composite theory of word-power that will help us to hear the resonance of oral tradition—its characteristic register and communicative economy—even within what seems to amount to an indisputably textual arena. To put it aphoristically, how does the singer of tales in performance communicate through texts?

III

THE RHETORICAL PERSISTENCE
OF TRADITIONAL FORMS

> To have the alphabetically written text of an
> ancient performance is one thing, and to hear
> a full voice in that text is another.
>
> Tedlock 1987: 141

> One can believe, I do believe, that about
> the dry bones of print, words heaped up in
> paragraphs, something of the original spirit
> lingers. That spirit need not be lost to com-
> prehension, respect, and appreciation. We are
> not able to revive by singing, or stepping over
> a text five times, but by patient surrender to
> what a text has to say, in the way it has to
> say it, something of life can again become
> incarnate.
>
> Hymes 1991: 11

In this chapter we turn from the comparatively straightforward situation of the
traditional oral performance to the endemically more problematic area of the
oral-derived text, that is, the text with roots in oral tradition.[1]

Assessing the role of the singer of tales in performance as inscribed in the ·
medium of a textual document will require a number of steps. First will be an
overview of the general principles involved as we move from performance to
libretto, with consideration of the wide spectrum of processes actually informing
such transpositions and with specific references to the ancient Greek and early
medieval English texts that will be our focus in chapters 5 and 6. After this initial
sketch of the rhetorical persistence of pretextual, traditional forms, we will
concentrate on delineating that rhetoric via the threefold analytical strategy

---

1. For specific details on the use of the term *oral-derived* as applied to ancient and medieval texts
deriving from oral traditions, see Foley 1990a: chap. 1, esp. 5–8. Implicit in the term, as I use it, is the
additional value of *traditional*. There will be occasion in this chapter to discuss both texts that are
known to be direct transcriptions of oral performances and texts composed in writing but employing
a traditional oral register.

introduced in the last chapter: performance arena, register, and communicative economy. In this second section we will be examining the "fine print" of what may be called the "signifying contract" for oral tradition-become-text: from a Receptionalist point of view, we will be interested in what becomes of the implied audience, for example, as the emergent experience modulates to a textual object. The final segment will offer a brief and simplified "how-to" manual for decoding the rhetorical reflexes of traditional performance features and strategies, as a brief prelude to larger-scale applications to follow. Our aim in the present chapter thus comprises both a theoretical understanding of the ways in which traditional oral-derived texts convey meaning and a practical grasp of how we might more deeply, if still (and inevitably) incompletely, sense their word-power. To put it proverbially, we will be concerned fundamentally with how oral-derived texts continue traditions of reception.

Exordium: From Performance to Libretto

A traditional oral performance, whatever its linguistic or cultural background, is, as both the Oral Theory and the Ethnography of Speaking eloquently testify, an experienced event that becomes a text only at the high price of intersemiotic translation.[2] What, then, do we make of those works of verbal art that took shape in or under the influence of oral tradition, but that now survive—for historical reasons—only as texts? Do the expressive qualities we have been attributing to experienced events also apply, even if in some modified or reduced fashion, to such necessarily and exclusively textual objects?

These questions have, of course, engendered a considerable debate over the status of verbal art from oral tradition that exists only in a manuscript or on the printed page, with some commentators denying admissibility to anything outside the living, experienced event as recorded on acoustic or video tape and contextualized by the fieldworker's direct, engaged participation.[3] Only in this way, they contend, can the performance be understood as an event; only in this way can some facsimile of the full, multi-channel communication be conveyed to the "outsiders" who have been permanently ostracized by lack of direct access. Since texts are already removed from the performance and preserve only a limited and decontextualized record of that performance, they in effect make even the scholar closest to them an "outsider" who can never recover the multifaceted reality that lies behind them.

For a comparatist interested in learning what living oral traditions can tell us about the long-defunct (read: "manuscript-prisoned") verbal art of ancient Greece and medieval England, this issue is indeed a crucial one. Having labored both in the field and in the archive, and having many times wished fervently that

---

2. On the history and implications of making folklore texts, see esp. Fine 1984 and Foley in press.
3. Much of the groundbreaking work in this area has been done by Dennis Tedlock and Dell Hymes. See chap. 1 above for an account of the contribution from Ethnopoetics.

the Codex Marcianus *Iliad* or the unique Cotton Vitellius A. xv. *Beowulf*—or their precursors—could be reinvigorated just long enough to glimpse (or aurally review) the performances that were their ultimate contexts, I have felt the challenge and the frustration of trying to tailor comparison judiciously. The contention that performed, experienced events are not and never can be equivalent to textual cenotaphs cannot be gainsaid; they are not superimposable media, and we cannot pretend that they are. At the same time, however, I question the extreme conclusion that we must therefore forsake comparison, completely segregating the oral traditional performance from the oral traditional text, learning nothing about the textual residue from firsthand acquaintance with enabling events in the same or other traditions.

In this respect I concur with Dell Hymes, who in his 1977 study of ethnopoetic structure in Chinookan tales sought to admit manuscript records to the discussion, noting that (338) "the best dictated texts are not in fact wholly without indication of the features in question."[4] Similarly, in a review of the Dauenhauers' anthology of Tlingit narratives, he compliments the editors' use of works taped from oral tradition and scored for ethnopoetic rhetorical features, nonetheless evenhandedly observing (1989b: 238): "Yet what was written down early in the century is an important part of the heritage as well. Its pauses and intonation contours cannot be recovered (although perhaps sometimes guessed at), but its rhetorical pattern can be inferred and made plain. The absence of oral recordings is not a bar." Notice that Hymes nowhere claims that the dictated text is as faithful a representation of the performed event as an acoustic or video recording, or better yet the fieldworker's personal witness to the contexted experience; he acknowledges the shortfall in medium and the reduced fidelity with which one can represent a living performance in a script or libretto. But he does hold out for the importance of the partial but finite gain—in the case of the tales he studies, the vestige of continuity between the living oral tradition on the one hand and, on the other, texts taken down from dictation before the advent of instruments that allow the encoding of more expressive (and receptional) channels.

The situation is fundamentally the same with ancient Greek and medieval English manuscripts that provide our only windows on oral traditions forever lost to us as performances. We must begin, as Oral Theory has frankly been loath to do, by not only admitting but stipulating and setting a calibration for

---

4. Further (339), "texts dictated without benefit of tape recorder, though deficient for some purposes, are often the only monument of their kind to a heritage. That the texts exist at all in usable form may make them the only avenue to a tradition for descendants of those who dictated them." Cf. now Hymes 1994, which treats the common ground shared by Ethnopoetics and Oral-Formulaic Theory as part of a discussion of editing and oral tradition. See also related contributions to a cluster of essays on the challenge of editing oral traditional works: Doane 1994 on Old English, Niles 1994 on ballads and Old English, Russo 1994 on Homeric epic, and Slyomovics 1994 on Arabic.

the documentary nature of the evidence.[5] We do not have Homer's performances; we have texts of uncertain provenance that first surfaced as whole works almost two millennia after their probable date of composition. And we do not have a performance of *Beowulf;* we have a manuscript, again of uncertain provenance, probably written in the first third of the tenth century, with the encoded version of the poem having been composed, depending on which theory of "origin" one chooses, as long as three hundred years before that copy or much more recently.[6] In its earliest incarnation, Oral Theory saw fit to level these comparanda to a single hypothetical standard, so that acoustically recorded epic from then-Yugoslavia was placed alongside the manuscript sources (although each textual tradition was also itself quite different from the other) without adjustment. This enforced equivalence stemmed, of course, from the theory's overly narrow focus on traditional oral narrative as fundamentally a species of text, that is, as an object or set of objects that could be analyzed and quantitatively measured. With Hymes, then, I would subscribe to the first step in responsible comparison as entailing a recognition of differences, an honest effort at an informed analogical procedure through which one can investigate similarities and differences without demanding absolute congruity or imputing absolute disparity.

To give the picture its full and realistic complication, we should also acknowledge the possibility, in many cases the virtual certainty, that the classical and medieval texts are not always simply dictations from performances. That is, given the presence of at least incipient literacy at the time of their supposed (re-)creation in extant form, as well as the vagaries of transmission during the so-called Dark Ages of Homeric Greece and Anglo-Saxon England, original composition-in-writing *of the surviving documents (or their direct antecedents)* cannot be ruled out. Scholars have labored in vain to demonstrate the "pure orality" of such works[7]—whatever "pure orality" might mean, especially in the complex cultural milieux from which the Homeric epics and *Beowulf* emerge—and tenable theories of composition, transmission, and also reception must now take into account the heretofore heretical hypothesis that these works of verbal art, while drawing on deep roots in oral tradition, were written out by the very wordsmiths responsible for their present form.

5. For a detailed discussion of the manuscript (and probable pretextual) history of the Homeric epics and the Anglo-Saxon *Beowulf,* see Foley 1991: chap. 2. Cf. also Nagy (1990: 53), who posits for ancient Greek *epos* "gradual patterns of fixity in an ongoing process of recomposition in diffusion, and without presupposing that the actual composition of the 'text' required the medium of writing." See further "The Riddle of Incipient Textuality," below.

6. On the linked questions of origin, dating, and transmission, cf. Chase 1981, Foley 1990a: 31–39, and "The Riddle of Incipient Textuality," below.

7. Perhaps the most egregious example of attempting to "prove" the orality of a document was Magoun's (1953) study of the density of formulaic phraseology in Old English poetry. Some responses to this and similar claims for other medieval and ancient works have often been just as categorical in their denial of the possibility or impact of oral traditions behind the received, extant manuscript poems, and thus no more satisfactory as we seek to establish a realistic context for interpretation. Ruth Finnegan's (1970, 1977, 1988) demonstration of the tremendous and natural variety of oral genres worldwide has served as a welcome antidote to the excesses of both extremist positions.

I refer to "wordsmiths" as a lexical avenue to the basic, rationalizing issues subtending the forbidding morass of texts that, while certainly texts, still encode vestiges of oral traditional performance. For, all complications aside, the most fundamental concern of our inquiry must remain the "word-power" wielded by these "wordsmiths." If, in the first instance of complication, we have available only a dictated text as a mute monument to the living performance in all of its multifariousness, then we may seem to have lost the enabling event, the empowering experience that transforms both the expressive and perceptual quality of the message and prescribes a certain mode of reception.[8] To put it more accurately, the enabling event has been (at least in part) submerged into the rhetorical fabric of the text. This means that we lack certain of Bauman's keys to performance, most obviously the vast panoply of signals conveyed through paralinguistic phenomena, and such features will almost certainly remain forever unrecoverable.

But—and here is the crucial point—we have not lost *all* of the keys to performance. If as audience or readers we are prepared to decode the signals that survive intersemiotic translation to the medium of texts, and whose recognition will require some knowledge of the enabling referent of tradition, then performance can still be keyed by these features. What of special codes, for example, as imaged in the archaisms of South Slavic epic and charm? Do these metonymic cues not pepper the texts of Homer and *Beowulf,* serving notice that a particular kind of speech act, taking place within a circumscribed performance arena, is in progress?[9] What of figurative language, parallelism, and special formulae? Are these not equally characteristics of the *Iliad,* the *Odyssey,* and much Old English poetry, and does their presence—in forms as simple as metrical predispositions and phraseological rules[10]—not help to determine the channel through which the communication must be interpreted? In short, are the registers of ancient Greek and Old English traditional oral narrative not at least partly preserved in the admittedly reduced textual record that survives?

If these questions are answered in the affirmative, as I believe they must be, then our responsibility as a reading audience attempting to fashion as meaningful a context as possible for expressive acts is radically affected. No, the manuscripts are not performances, not experiences; but yes, they not only retain the linguistic integers that constituted the meaning-laden idiom of the actual events in oral tradition, but, even more crucially, they hold open the possibility of

8. On the dynamics of this reception, see Foley 1991, esp. chap. 2.

9. For examples, see Foley 1991: chaps. 5 (ancient Greek) and 6 (Old English), and cf. Renoir 1988 on "oral-formulaic context." We may add that even ostensibly unechoic phrases and lines may, by performance convention, bear special meaning. A case in point is the Homeric line *hoi d' ara pantes akên egenonto siôpêi* (literally, "and they were all struck silently to silence"), which, in addition to conveying a simple momentary cessation in the dialogue, certifies the speech that precedes it as "proposing or reporting a radical, usually unexpected action that will give way to stunned silence, followed by a response that immediately or eventually involves substantial qualification if not dismissal of the proposed or reported action"; on this metonymic phrase, cf. Foley 1994.

10. On these rules, which govern the linguistic matrix within which formulaic phraseology takes shape, and which are therefore more fundamental than the formulaic expressions themselves, see Foley 1990a: chaps. 4–6.

access to the implied array of associative, metonymic signification that such a medium or register was uniquely licensed to convey. The "way of speaking," as Hymes has put it, once fashioned as a communicative instrument that promoted highly focused and highly economical interchange, is also a "way of signifying," and its word-power, though necessarily diminished by the shift from performance to text, may survive.

This scenario assumes, as indicated above, an audience or readership sufficiently acquainted with the signals embedded in the register to be able to summon the special, institutionalized meanings that are those signals' reason for being. Without that level of participation, the communicative act is denatured, and it makes little difference whether the act involves a performance or a text. To put the same matter in other words, the scenario assumes an audience who can rhetorically simulate the performance arena—in the absence of the actual enabling event of performance itself—on the basis of textualized cues that engage the enabling referent of tradition. It is, in brief, prior experience with the communicative channel opened by a particular kind of event that will inform the reception of subsequent related events and, to a diminished but still finite degree, of their textual recensions and yet more distantly related descendants.

At a second level of complication, which emerges when we take into active account the possibility or near-certainty that some texts are not simply oral dictations but also at least partly the result of composition-in-writing, it will again be the performance register and its signals that demand interpretation through examination of metonymic meaning, that is, through an understanding of how performance is keyed. Even in the later stages of the medieval period, when authorship is more and more taking on a new phenomenological status and we can begin to speak more meaningfully about "literary" composition,[11] the context provided by immanence and performance will continue to be an important dimension of poetics and verbal art. As long as the communicative medium remains the dedicated register forged for and in performance to convey meanings that institutionally impinge upon the individual event, and with the proviso that there also remains an audience alive to the encoded signals for interpretation, then we must continue to respect that register's significative force, in short its word-power.

Thus it is that, as silent and intersemiotically reduced as the libretti left to us by the Homeric and Anglo-Saxon traditions most certainly are, they cannot be dismissed as simply "literary texts," without qualification, and tacitly assimilated to the familiar textual model. The integers of expression and reception, the cognitive categories that function optimally only within the enabling event of performance, retain in their textual forms a rhetorical vestige of that performance that cannot be ignored. Only now the channels are fewer, the keys more limited, the performance-based significative options more restrictive; in turn, the

11. Cf. Gellrich 1985; Stock 1983, 1990; Amodio 1994. In general, many later medieval works provide an easier assimilation to a modern textual model than do Anglo-Saxon poems, which because of more frequent rhetorical persistence of traditional forms customarily depend more heavily on an extratextual context; see further Renoir 1988, Foley 1991: chap. 6.

path for the development of inherently textual signification broadens. Does this sea change mean that we as readers can no longer "perform" such works, no longer serve as a participating audience in their construal as emergent, evolving experiences? I think a measured response is truest to the issues of poetics and verbal art that lie beneath that question: while we should recognize that we can never wholly resuscitate textual libretti and cause them to live again (or for the first time) as actual performances, we will be derelict in our interpretive duty if we do not reach beyond the parallax induced by their textuality and release the resources of meaning that stem ultimately from the performance and immanence that still inform them. In an effort to understand just how traditional, performance-centered integers can retain word-power even within a textual idiom, let us examine more closely the processes involved in textual transposition.

The Riddle of Incipient Textuality

What becomes of oral traditions committed, in myriad ways, to textual form? How does this textuality—"incipient" in that it represents either a historical culture's initial known attempt at such codification or a relatively rare document adrift in a sea of living oral tradition—deal with and convey the textless world that preceded it or exists alongside it? Another way to put the same question is, as noted above, to ask how and to what extent a given text continues the tradition of reception.

In the early stages of inquiry into oral traditions and texts, whether from the point of view of folklore or of literature, and whether with primary emphasis on living or no longer living traditions, the simplex model of spoken versus written words seemed adequate. A corollary of this Great Divide theory held that oral traditions and texts sorted neatly into separate categories not only within a given culture's repertoire of discourse modes but across the worldwide spectrum of cultural diversity. Such reductionism then led to further excesses of various kinds, such as the Oral Theory's original contention that ancient and medieval *texts* could be proven *oral* by quantitative means,[12] and that, once. proven so, they would necessarily have to be interpreted—all of them—according to one particular code.

Recent years have of course witnessed the problematizing of this initial set of assumptions, as Oral Theory, Ethnopoetics, and the Ethnography of Speaking have all sought to avoid crippling generalizations and to complicate our understanding of verbal art in oral tradition, and of literature with roots in oral tradition.[13] Thus it seems only proper, before moving on to a discussion of the survival of oral traditional strategies as textual rhetoric, to spend a few moments

---

12. But cf. the significant mitigation of this position even by Lord (1986a: 478–81).

13. E.g., Hymes 1985: 395: "One must work out a 'grammar' of the local world of discourse and work out the internal relations of a text in relation to that grammar, before proceeding to analytic comparison and interpretation in terms of relationships found elsewhere." Cf. Foley 1990a, esp. 9, 16–18 on the principle of tradition-dependence.

with one of the most intriguing aspects of this new concern for complication: the linked questions of how, why, and with what implications an oral traditional performance actually becomes a text, and, correlatively, what impact the answers to these questions might have on the nature and interpretability of the text. In what follows, I naturally attempt neither an exhaustive review of all available information nor any grand, overarching principles that rationalize all known cases; either aim, in addition to being foolhardy in itself, would run counter to the very trend of pluralization and distinction I have been trying to describe. What is offered here instead is simply a collection of inherently interesting and hopefully instructive instances of the range of dynamics involved when performances become libretti.

Native American Traditions

Let us begin with Native American traditions and texts, an area that has seen substantial activity over the last two decades as many of the most forward-thinking linguists and folklorists have turned to this body of traditions in attempting to come to grips with the ungraspable phantom of faithful textual representation. As mentioned in the first chapter, the approach often called Ethnopoetics has been at the forefront of this discussion: in particular, Dell Hymes and Dennis Tedlock have pointed the way toward modes of representation that recall the event-centered, oral/aural reality of the works they are examining and making ever more available to others. The common thread connecting their highly individualistic versions of Ethnopoetics is a concern that the endemic expressive structure of the narratives be recovered and made the fundamental basis upon which Native American verbal art is presented and interpreted. Instead of forcing these narratives into an essentially irrelevant form under the patently false premise that western European (and fundamentally Greco-Roman) poetics constitutes a universal set of categories, they have insisted on tradition-dependent identities for the works they study.

Since the core assumptions and theorems of both varieties of Ethnopoetics, as well as the questions of how and why these two investigators make their texts as they do, have already been treated in chapter 1, let us concentrate here on the implications of Tedlock's and Hymes's methods for the transformation of performance to libretto. Tedlock's procedure with the Zuni stories consists of mapping the oral event onto an augmented textual surface designed to bear more and different kinds of meaning than can the conventional printed page. His criteria for this encoding derive entirely from the unique event of performance, and reflect traditional strategies of expression only to the extent that the individual event is representative of the performance tradition. The thrust of his text-making, then, is by usual standards a kind of overdetermination of the reader's activity, a mandate to exit the silence and convention of the usual process and to give (or restore) voice to the "dead letters" of the printed page. What he aims to preserve in this intersemiotic facsimile amounts to the set of cues—partially reflective of Bauman's keys to performance or the metonymic signals that are the stock-in-trade of Immanent Art—that shape the reader's reception of the work, only now with the reader also becoming a listening audience. In short, Tedlock has transformed the heard reality of the oral traditional event into a visual, textual rhetoric, specifically a set of typographic cues, with the express intention of mitigating the displacement caused by textualization of that event, that is, of making the text speak.

Tedlock's subsequent move toward what he calls "ethnopaleography," which consists of "taking the Popol Vuh text back to those who continue to speak the language in which it was written" (1987: 143), illustrates yet more radically the thrust of his overall interpretive program. Instead of attempting an analytical parsing of the textual document, he advocates restoring its voice, breaking the silence to which time and script have condemned it by direct appeal to an ongoing speech tradition. The success of this appeal depends on at least two crucial factors: (1) some degree of continuity between the ancient text and the modern oral traditions that are to be its comparanda, and (2) what we might understand as at least a rough match in performance register: "The fieldworker will be seeking after contemporary speeches, prayers, songs, and narratives, looking for patterns in the wording that have analogs in the ancient text and noting the ways in which such patterns are actualized in performance" (147). At its root, ethnopaleography offers another way to revivify the text, to privilege that which textuality has rendered rhetorical by reduction of experience to object, and to do so by reawakening the voice that makes it an event.

In the same spirit of causing texts to speak, Hymes has concentrated on editing into his editions and translations a set of native poetic features that includes lines, verses, versicles, stanzas, scenes, acts, and parts.[14] All of these interlocking features are derived from, rather than imposed upon, the works he studies, and together they form a rhetoric that is instrumental in their reception. What is more, Hymes views this set of features as both traditional—in their institutionalized identity as rhetorical structures in not just one but all related performances and texts—and individually deployed—in the sense of a single author's license to create within their general purview. For example, in his analysis and presentation of Charles Cultee's "Salmon's Myth," he distinguishes between Tedlock's emphasis on pause and other intonational features on the one hand, and the kinds of performance structures in which he is interested on the other (1985: 395–96, emphasis added):

> Dennis Tedlock's admirable insistence on the vocal realization of texts has given
> rise to the impression in some quarters that pauses alone, not other kinds of
> markers as well, let alone interdependence of signals with content and function,

---

14. Cf. esp. Hymes 1987b, as well as chap. 1 above. See also the rhetorical analyses carried out on Lushootseed (Puget Salish) narrative by Toby C. S. Langen (e.g., 1989–90), who elsewhere remarks of the relationship between individual performance and the larger tradition (1989: 6): "no one version is an isolate, either for the storyteller or the audience, but resounds against the knowledge of the collection held by each person present at the performance; no storyteller ever tells the whole collection, but she always knows more than she tells in any one performance or perhaps in all the performances she ever gives. . . ."

are the foundation of units in a text. . . . But pause or any other feature of sound is *in itself* a physical, not a cultural phenomenon. It becomes an aspect of structure only in terms of the basic principle of "practical structuralism," contrast and repetition, the use of form/meaning covariation to establish what counts as the same and what as different. In a single case, one cannot be sure what features are accidental, what are conventional in the style of one narrator, what are conventional in the community.

Hymes's ethnopoetics is, then, essentially an immanent poetics: strategies and categories for expression constitute aspects of a register that provides for a high degree of communicative economy within a well-defined performance arena. The uniqueness of the narrator's individual realization of a given tale resonates against and within that larger cultural poetics.

With this distinction in mind, it is not difficult to see how Hymes can derive from early dictated texts an ethnopoetically faithful libretto, without necessary recourse to ethnopaleography. If performance rhetoric inheres in works of verbal art as a coherent set of signals that in their dedicated form tap into dedicated channels of meaning, then even the most prosaically configured written record of a tale can be reconfigured and made to speak. Of course it cannot be forced back into the event from which it was extruded; plain common sense must tell us that there are endemic limits on extrapolation from silence. But for Hymes some important aspects of Native American narrative poetics persist as performance modulates to text, and although the intersemiotic translation must make recovery less than complete, recognition of what amounts to a traditional rhetoric opens the now-written work to more faithful interpretation.

South Slavic Traditions into Texts

Although South Slavic oral traditions share with the Native American the temporal accidents of being both living (or in some cases recently living) and much studied over the past few decades, their histories of edition and analysis vary quite dramatically. Insofar as epic narrative is concerned,[15] the Serbian and Croatian traditions were from their first extensive collection and publication closely linked with the western European hegemony established by the Homeric poems and seconded by medieval vernacular works such as the Old French *chansons de geste* and Anglo-Saxon *Beowulf.*[16] For this and other reasons the classic texts, such as those collected, edited, and published by Vuk Stefanović Karadžić in the mid-nineteenth century, have always exhibited standard poetic lineation of their decasyllabic or *bugarštica* verses,[17] but have lacked entirely any

15. For purposes of illustrative expediency, this section is limited to a consideration of the epic genre; for a discussion of *bajanje,* or magical charms, from the Serbian tradition, see chap. 4.

16. Cf. esp. Murko 1929/1990, with its frequent comparisons of South Slavic *narodne pjesme* ("folk [narrative] songs") to Homeric and Old French narrative. For an excellent survey of South Slavic heroic traditions, cf. Coote 1978; on the history of collection in this area, Bynum 1986: 302–10.

17. On the distinction between these two verse forms, see Stolz 1969. On *bugarštica* poetry, cf. esp. the collection and translation by Miletich (1990) and the historical reconstruction by Kekez (1991).

encoding of paralinguistic or rhetorical features such as those highlighted in the text-making of Tedlock and Hymes.

This leveling may have focused attention on those aspects of poetics that happened to have precedent in the western European model, but they just as certainly obscured those features that did not enjoy such precedent. The deca-syllabic line, for instance, an archaic and complex metrical structure, was only too easily misinterpreted as a trochaic pentameter, with the obvious consequence of deflecting analysis from the real nature of the meter-phraseology symbiosis that informed the traditional idiom.[18] For another example, the instrumental and vocal music that accompanied the performance of most Moslem and some Christian epic was in effect "written out" of the textual transcriptions; to date it has never received the attention it deserves as a full partner in the performance event.[19] More generally, the native Serbian and Croatian scholarship, largely laboring under the same typically modern, unexamined predisposition that "oral tradition is usually a book and not a memory" (Parks 1991: 58), has concentrated almost exclusively on the individual artistry of the singers of tales, seeking to discover literary values in their performed narratives and downplaying (if even considering) their traditional resonances.[20]

Karadžić, an ethnographer, linguist, and lexicographer very much ahead of his time,[21] felt the widespread nineteenth-century European urge to lay bare his culture's roots and yet managed to introduce or refine contemporary methods of textual representation. Unlike many scholars of that period, most infamously the Grimms,[22] he interfered little with the received transcriptions of oral perfor-mances during editing, making very few if any changes in the dictated texts. Even when he did intervene to modify, or much more rarely to add, a line or part-line, he consistently turned to patently traditional diction as the source for his emendations.[23] Furthermore, he not seldom included multiple variants or

---

18. Cf. esp. Foley 1990a: 85–106.

19. Among the very few contributions in this area are Herzog 1951; the partial transcription by Béla Bartók of *The Captivity of Djulić Ibrahim* (*SCHS* I: 435–67); Lord 1960: 37–41; and Bynum 1979.

20. Cf. Koljević (1980: viii), perhaps the most evenhanded of native scholars, who complements his acknowledgment of the traditional background with the following statement: "But there are also occasions when [the singer's] spiritual needs make him step beyond history and push through the limits of existing social morality. It is not surprising that in such instances his basic formulas sometimes fail him: his utterance has to be unique, or formulopoeic, not because he cares for originality, but because he has to compel the language to do what it has never done before."

21. For a general biography of Karadžić, cf. Wilson 1970; on his editorial practices, cf. esp. Mladenović 1973 and Foley 1983.

22. Cf. esp. Ellis 1983.

23. Cf. esp. Foley 1983: 192–94. Examples of Karadžić's intervention are the syllabic expansion of *belu* to *belinu* to yield the formally metrical decasyllabic line "Te on seje belinu pšenicu" ("And he sowed white wheat"); and the much rarer kind of substitution represented in the modification of "Mitar skoči, *u planinu podje*" ("Mitar jumped up, he headed for the mountain") to "Mitar skoči *na noge lagane*" ("Mitar jumped up to his light feet"). This latter intervention, constituting the substitution of a phrase more traditional and metonymically resonant than the dictated text reading (cf. the discussion of this and similar phrases in Foley 1991: 83–87), illustrates the sureness of Karadžić's grasp of the register. An interesting comparison is provided by Elias Lönnrot's "editing" of the Finnish *Kalevala*, on which see esp. DuBois 1993.

versions of a given collected narrative, customarily by a different poet from a different geographical area, placing the two (rarely more) contiguously in the volume and labeling the subsequent version(s) "Opet to isto" ("Again the same"). In addition, Karadžić attempted to create natural settings for the poems within individual volumes of his published collection, either by genre (e.g., the "various women's songs" of volume one being separated from the "oldest heroic songs" of its sequel)[24] or by principal characters or events (e.g., groupings centered around the beloved Serbian hero Marko Kraljević or the historically and mythically epochal Battle of Kosovo of 1389). By these latter two strategies Karadžić the editor was able to simulate something of the (extratextual) traditional context, presenting alternate realizations of some songs while encouraging a reception of each poem/performance against a larger, more resonant background. To a remarkable extent, given what other contemporary investigators licensed themselves to do, he demonstrated a respect for these narratives on their own terms and tried to fashion a mode of textual presentation in which at least some of the performance rhetoric was inscribed.

The collection and publication project undertaken by Milman Parry and Albert Lord, from the 1933–35 fieldwork in then-Yugoslavia through the ongoing series *Serbo-Croatian Heroic Songs* (1953-), brought the pragmatics of textual representation of this tradition to a new level. In concert with the theory behind the Parry-Lord field methods, the first two volumes of *SCHS* presented multiple versions of the same tale by the same and different singers from the region of Novi Pazar. Lord described the publication plans for the series as follows:

> In investigating an oral epic tradition, it is necessary to begin with a study of the songs of an individual singer and then to proceed to a consideration of the other singers in the same district. One thus sees the singer both as an individual and in relation to the community of singers to which he belongs. For that reason our selected texts will be published by districts, and within each district the songs of a single singer will be grouped together.[25]

By reading through the different performances of *The Captivity of Djuljić Ibrahim,* for example, one can gain some sense of the multiformity of oral epic tradition. Although this series also has some drawbacks (run-on prose translations, concentration on textual aspects of performance, and so on),[26] it does

24. Karadžić's four original volume titles for his *Srpske narodne pjesme* are: I. *Različne ženske pjesme* (Various Women's Songs); II. *Najstarije pjesme junačke* (The Oldest Heroic Songs); III. *Pjesme junačke srednjijeh vremena* (Heroic Songs of the Middle Ages); and IV. *Pjesme junačke novijih vremena o vojevanju za slobodu* (Heroic Songs of Modern Times about the Fight for Freedom). On the various categories of historical and nonhistorical songs in the South Slavic tradition, see Coote 1978: 260–69.

25. *SCHS* I: 16; cf. the distinctions among idiolect, dialect, and language in the epic register made in Foley 1990a: 178–96, 288–327. Lord also adheres to an editorial policy of absolute noninterference (*SCHS* I: 18): "These volumes will present epic songs as they are sung, by both highly skilled and less highly skilled singers, with all the errors and inconsistencies which result from rapid performance."

26. I have experimented (e.g., 1984) with electronic "hypertext" editions of songs in multiple versions, in order to avoid privileging (in essence textualizing) one version and, complementarily, to deepen the resonance of each variant and multiform.

offer the reader a chance to escape many of the drawbacks of editions that epitomize individual versions at the expense of context.

Ancient and Medieval Traditional Texts

In moving on to ancient and medieval texts that constitute our only entrée to long-extinct oral traditions, with respect to which the complexities associated with the persistence of traditional forms only multiply, it may be well to recall the central goal of this chapter—to ascertain as well as possible *how a given text continues the tradition of reception.* In those simplest of situations where, as is often the case with living traditions, we are confronting a transcription of an oral performance, the question, though demanding, is clear: to what extent does the text contribute meaningfully to the faithful reconstrual of the experience, with all of the implications inherent in an understanding of the work as a performed event? We have considered the opinions and strategies offered by Tedlock and by Hymes for Native American, and by Karadžić and by Parry and Lord for South Slavic, and have noted both advantages and shortcomings in each approach to representation of oral tradition in the textualized format. But now we must consider texts about whose genesis we may know very little. What is more, for ancient and medieval texts we must acknowledge the strong possibility or probability that writing may have been employed at any or all levels of their composition or transmission or both, so that the relatively simpler problem of transcriptions made according to incompletely understood rules and assumptions will not be the only complication. For such transitional documents, passed down through an unrecorded series of rewritings, the picture of compositional identity becomes very murky indeed. Elaborate hypotheses painstakingly formulated to explain the probable act or acts of composition may founder if pressed to account for even this or that small alternative in the chain of composition and transmission.

Among the pitfalls awaiting the classicist or medievalist will be the potentially quite misleading matter of whether or not writing was "available" to the poets and audiences of the so-called Dark Ages of Greece and England. As folklorists have long known, the mere presence of some kind or level of literacy, established perhaps by an inscription on an artifact, means next to nothing as evidence for or against oral or written communication in a given mode or situation. Late-twentieth-century North Americans, many of them deeply engaged in intensely literate pursuits for most of their waking hours, also participate in oral traditions that may never have been textualized.[27] In terms developed in earlier chapters, we will need to keep firmly in mind the fact that verbal activities involve registers of discourse that may or may not be immediately or eventually textualized, according to the demands of the codicils to the sociolinguistic contract in force in a given culture. The past decade has seen awareness of the importance of social function emerge among classicists and medievalists as well, with scholars such as William V. Harris

27. Two among myriad examples are folk preaching (e.g., Rosenberg 1970, 1986; Lawless 1988) and oral narratives such as "tall tales" (e.g., Bauman 1986).

(1989) and Rosalind Thomas (1989) offering realistically complex views of the various uses of oral and written media in the ancient world, and with Franz H. Bäuml (1980, 1984–85), Katherine O'Brien O'Keeffe (1990), and A. N. Doane (1991, 1994), among others, productively complicating our perspective on the false dichotomy of medieval vernacular orality and literacy.

For such reasons it seems best to stipulate that our understanding of the "original composition" of the Homeric epics and *Beowulf*—if indeed that phrase is strictly applicable—is likely to remain uncertain, and to focus instead on what can be inferred about the reception of these works from the persistence of traditional forms as a textual rhetoric. This emphasis entails a reversal of the usual heuristic perspective: instead of trying to gauge how much has been preserved or lost, we need rather to ask what the documents can tell us about how they should be read. Our authority for posing the analytical query in this way rests on the evidence for a prior (and perhaps ongoing) oral tradition accompanying the generation of texts, on comparative evidence from other oral traditions, and not least on the principles of word-power, performance, and tradition as developed in the opening chapters.[28]

Anglo-Saxon Texts

Recent research has done much to demystify the process underlying the textual transmission of Anglo-Saxon poetry, especially to modify what was long perceived as an absolute gap into a complex spectrum of oral-to-textual transmission.[29] Foremost among scholars pursuing a reevaluation of the model for writing and reading manuscripts from this period have been Katherine O'Brien O'Keeffe and A. N. Doane, both of whom have sought to reconcile the textual record presented in Old English poetic manuscripts with the traditional oral environment from which they stem and to which they remain linked in significant ways. Through careful examination of texts that appear in multiple copies, O'Keeffe has concluded that "early readers of Old English verse read by applying oral techniques for the reception of a message to the decoding of a written text" (1990: 191). Her method entails an exacting analysis of poetry as various

28. To amplify this last point, we should recall the aphorism that underlies this study as a whole—that word-power arises from the enabling event of performance and the enabling referent of tradition. By concentrating on the issues associated with performance arena, register, and communicative economy, we can gain insight into the textual coda to the event: the rhetorical transformation of traditional oral signals.

29. In what follows, I make no attempt to reconstrue what is known or hypothesized about the actual transmission or dating of Old English texts; for a summary of relevant scholarship on *Beowulf*, see Foley 1990a: 31–39. The general thrust of what has been called the New Philology points in a complementary direction, away from a collection of hierarchically arranged objects and toward a plurality of witnesses that demand interpretation in social context; as Nichols observes (1990: 8–9), "if we accept the multiple forms in which our artifacts have been transmitted, we may recognize that medieval culture did not simply live with diversity, it cultivated it." Cf. also Spiegel (1990: 85), who advocates "a literary history that begins with a focus on the social logic of the text, . . . incorporates yet modifies existing features of current historical and critical thought," and "preserves the emphasis of cultural history in seeing textuality as both arising from and constitutive of social life, which it seeks to endow with meaning." For a historian's perspective, see Kelly 1990.

as Cædmon's *Hymn, Solomon and Saturn I*, the "Metrical Preface" to Alfred's *Pastoral Care*, and poems from the *Anglo-Saxon Chronicle*, with special attention to the mechanics of copying as an index of the mix of residual orality and literacy not only indicated but also prescribed by the document in question.

O'Keeffe finds not a static but a developing literacy in these texts, and interprets this variance as evidence of differing expressive and perceptual contracts. In distinguishing between our modern, monolithic notion of literacy and this more realistic, situated conception of the various modes of literacy in Anglo-Saxon England, she thus (6–7)

> refer[s] not to the numbers of individuals who might be judged to have been able to read in Anglo-Saxon England, but, more significantly, to the very practice of reading, the decoding strategies of readers, their presuppositions, visual conventions and understanding of space.

She goes on to argue that

> the manuscript records of Old English poetry witness a particular mode of literacy, and examination of significant variants and of developing graphic cues for the presentation of verse (such as mise-en-page, spacing, capitalization and punctuation) provide strong evidence of persisting residual orality in the reading and copying of poetry in Old English.

Even as Anglo-Saxon scribes were writing out their manuscripts, and even as these manuscripts were copied and recopied, it was not our contemporary model of literate behavior that was informing the commission to writing and apprehension by reading. It was rather the expressive and perceptual strategies of oral tradition that would play a major role in "post-oral" reception of the poetry, only now in a form that survived the transformation from performance to text.[30]

Doane's perspective also sheds considerable light on the transition or continuum between oral tradition and text in Anglo-Saxon poetry. As an editor who advocates "making an informed, principled, definitive, and declared decision about a given text's relation to writing and orality" (1991: 76), he posits four kinds of interfaces. The first three are familiar from earlier scholarship: (1) the scribal transcription of a performed event, (2) the oral "autograph" poet who serves as his or her own scribe, and (3) the literate poet who knows the tradition well enough to emulate an oral performance in writing. Interestingly, however, his fourth scenario entails a scribe who may be thought of as composing in the oral traditional manner, an act he calls "reperformance" (80–81):

> Whenever scribes who are part of the oral traditional culture write or copy traditional oral works, they do not merely mechanically hand them down; they rehear them, "mouth" them, "reperform" them in the act of writing in such a way

---

30. Cf. Machan 1991: 237 on Late Middle English texts, who argues "that a variety of the conscious alterations effected by scribes as they 'copied' texts are similar to the changes made by oral poets as they re-create songs—that a model of improvisation can describe the performance qualities of both oral poets and scribes." Cf. also the essays in Amodio 1994.

that the text may change but remain authentic, just as a completely oral poet's text changes from performance to performance without losing authenticity.

While not concurring with O'Keeffe at all points, Doane shares her commitment to dissolving the old typology of text-making as distinct from composition, and in doing so he emphasizes the ways in which the multiformity that is the lifeblood of oral tradition still nourishes the ongoing process of textualization.[31]

These insights obviously have important implications for our discussion of the persistence of traditional oral forms as textual rhetoric. First, a continuity of reception across the supposed gulf between oral traditional performance and manuscript record means that mere commission to writing entails neither the final fossilization nor the wholesale shift in poetics that earlier studies in oral tradition had assumed as matters of course. In the simplest of cases, in which an Anglo-Saxon scribe might, not unlike a nineteenth- or early twentieth-century fieldworker, have taken down an oral poem from a poet's dictation, O'Keeffe's and Doane's conclusions lead us to view the visual spatialization of the utterance as rife with residual orality, as representing the performed event in at least some of its pretextual identity. Do all oral traditional signals survive the transformation? Certainly not, but their theses would hold—in an interesting parallel to Tedlock's ethnopoetic vision of a text being made to encode its performance—that some of the signals do in fact survive, and that they are foregrounded when one has multiple texts of a poem to compare.

But what of the more complicated (and almost certainly much more numerous) cases, those involving Anglo-Saxon poems not simply taken down from dictation but actually composed in writing? This is precisely the distinction made by Larry Benson in his much-discussed but ultimately reductive article "The Literary Character of Anglo-Saxon Formulaic Poetry" (1966), in which he showed that the formulaic content of Old English verse probably composed in writing was approximately equivalent to that of poems that some scholars had assigned to oral tradition, and then went on to hold that the hypothesis of orality was thus untenable.[32] What the new evidence teaches us is that even the "least

31. Cf. Doane's idea of "performative situation" (1991: 78) with the notion of "performance arena" advocated throughout this volume, and note his commitment to understanding "the nature of [scribal] writing in a culture in which speech has not yet lost its primacy and where the role of the scribe is to respond to the voice, obeying as he works many of the same somatic imperatives voice imposes, where text is as much act, event, gesture, as it is thing, with its origins not just in prior texts, but in memory and context" (1994: 420). Another medievalist who shares some of the same convictions as O'Keeffe and Doane is Suzanne Fleischman, who comments as follows in relation to Old French texts (1990: 23): "As a linguistically oriented philologist, I am convinced that many of the disconcerting properties of medieval vernacular texts—their extraordinary parataxis, mystery particles, conspicuous anaphora and repetitions, 'proleptic' topicalizations, and jarring alternations of tenses, to cite but a few—can find more satisfying explanations if we first of all acknowledge the extent to which our texts structure information the way a spoken language does, and then proceed to the linguistic literature that explores the pragmatic underpinning of parallel phenomena in naturally occurring discourse." Cf. also Fleischman 1989.

32. Two major problems with Benson's approach are his failure to take account of the tradition-dependent nature of Old English phraseology (he effectively searches for Homeric formulas in Anglo-Saxon texts) and an exclusive focus, typical of the early period of scholarship, on the product rather than the process of composition.

oral" of links in the chain of composition and transmission—the textual record itself—retains significant traces of a mode of expression and reception associated in its origin with oral tradition. And if this least oral part of the process, what we normally conceive of as an end product or objective fact far removed from the process of oral tradition, can maintain such signals and help to determine its own reception within what was once construed as a medium entirely antithetical to oral tradition, then clearly some reconsideration of the interpretive issues involved in its composition and reception is in order.[33] To put it telegraphically, this new view of textual dynamics at the level of the manuscript representation of Old English poetry dovetails snugly with the investigation of word-power in the form of textual rhetoric.

The Homeric Texts

The theme of supposedly mute texts, heretofore edited into submission, teaching twentieth-century readers to interpret them also finds expression in Homeric studies, especially in the work of Richard Janko and Gregory Nagy.[34] In a 1990 article on editing practices and the text of the *Iliad,* Janko observes (326) that "to delete verses, emend, or postulate multiple authorship is the natural reaction of scholars trained in a literate and literary culture, whether ancient or modern, but it is the wrong response." Instead of "correcting" the received text, an editorial program that in effect forces it into agreement with a mythical standard and in the process deletes all evidence of its true provenance,[35] he advocates an edition that reflects the inherent diversity of the surviving texts, with full attention to the apparent contradictions that especially the Parry-Lord studies have shown are a natural feature of extended oral narrative. By aligning the recently published evidence of early contact between the Greeks and the Near East with his own investigations of ancient Greek poetry from a diachronic point of view,[36] Janko then concludes that the Homeric poems were, in origin, oral dictated texts that can be seen as arising in a "plausible cultural context" sometime during the eighth century B.C. (330).

---

33. Note O'Keeffe's extension of her discovery of evidence indicating the residual orality of manuscript representation to its implications for the making of editions (193): "The challenge is clear: what editorial strategies may we devise to present a multiply attested Old English poem in a form which both reflects its existence as a complex of realized texts and represents the subtle visual information contained in its graphic arrays?"

34. For summaries of what is known about the history and transmission of the Homeric poems, see Foley 1990a: 20–31 and Janko 1992: 20–38.

35. For example, he comments as follows on the vexed question of repeated passages in Homer (1990: 332): "Surely an oral poet would not necessarily repeat [such passages] word for word? The answer is that we do not always know whether he did, because the editorial pressure for conformity between one passage and another was clearly very great. This is reflected to an extreme degree in the Oxford Classical Text, which is the standard modern text of the *Iliad,* and on which nearly all twentieth-century scholarship is founded. . . . Unfortunately this is, for many reasons, the worst text of the *Iliad* in print." Nor was this standardization understood as only a modern phenomenon; Janko contends (331) that Aristarchus, the greatest of the Alexandrian librarians, "emended away many of the minor oddities that seemed to antiquity to be cases of 'Homer nodding off,' but that in fact are pointers toward an oral dictated text." For detailed information on Aristarchus's activities and their influence on an envisioned oral-dictated text, cf. Janko 1992: 25–29.

36. 330; cf. Janko 1982.

For Janko the thesis of oral dictation offers a waystation on the road from an entirely unlettered oral tradition to the textual heterogeneity that exists in the extant manuscripts. The importance of his argument reaches beyond an explanation of the surviving evidence, however, to the core of our attempt to come to grips with the Homeric texts as libretti. For if Janko is correct, the texts themselves present a picture not unlike that described by O'Keeffe and Doane for the Old English manuscripts: a group of residually oral (or oral-derived) documents that in effect preserve the multiformity that amounts to the tradition's bequest to a now-written or -textualized poetry. If this is a realistic assessment of the texts as they stand, then we are not only licensed but also required to confront the implications of their multiformity. That responsibility will mandate, among other things, an attention to the specialized Homeric register, together with the performance arena it helps to create and the communicative economy it inherently fosters.

Nagy envisions a quite different cultural context for the fixation of the Homeric poems, one that expressly does not involve writing as the crucial dynamic. Rather he nominates the phenomenon of Panhellenism—a nationalistic and normalizing sociohistorical reality that shaped the *polis* and the Olympic Games, for instance—as the leveling factor that proved most important in streamlining a diverse set of Homeric traditions to an epitomized, unified tradition.[37] Through the increased social mobility of the poet, who as *dêmiourgos* ("artisan in the community") could more and more move from one locale to another and experience the tradition in its multiformity, the variety inherent in a collection of insular situations gradually started to lessen and a more uniform single situation began to gain ascendancy. Eventually this process would lead to rhapsodes, performers who do not themselves compose, and a fixed text would be created without the primary impetus of writing technology.

The fundamental textuality behind the conventional (literary) ideas of "canon" and "author" is called into question by Nagy's reconstrual of the evolution of ancient Greek poetry. Canon comes to name not that which critics have sifted out of documents with clear individual pedigrees, but rather that which the internally driven process of fixation has presented as poetic epitomes. The composer also becomes an idealized figure, as the Panhellenic process erodes or eliminates opportunities for both recomposition in performance and self-identification of the poet.[38] For such reasons Nagy contends (84) that

37. That is, "Panhellenic poetry would have been the product of an evolutionary synthesis of traditions, so that the tradition it represents concentrates on traditions that tend to be common to most locales and peculiar to none" (1990: 54).

38. Cf. esp. his three stages of fixation (80), wherein the identity of the poet gradually becomes effaced, with only the generic aspects being preserved: "the Panhellenic tradition of oral poetry appropriates the poet, potentially transforming even historical figures into generic ones who represent the traditional functions of their poetry. The wider the diffusion and the longer the chain of recomposition, the more remote the identity of the composer becomes. Extreme cases are Homer and Hesiod." Cf. Segal (1992: 28): "The Homeric bard presents himself as more attuned to his audience than to the situation of composition or creation. His chief concern, one could say, is pragmatics, not poetics (which is not to say that he lacks a poetics). His Muses are the repositories of social memory rather than principles of creativity per se."

the evolution of an ancient Greek canon in both poetry and song need not be attributed primarily to the factor of writing. Granted, writing would have been essential for the ultimate preservation of any canon once the traditions of performance were becoming obsolete; still I argue that the key to the actual evolution of a canon must be sought in the social context of performance itself.

This emphasis on performance brings us back to the question of the interrelationship of event and text. Whereas Janko relates the two by interposing an oral dictated text, a written document that preserves Homeric multiformity and deserves to be understood for that very lack of uniformity, Nagy constructs a model that avoids this initial quantum leap to another medium and proposes instead a different kind of fixation—in essence an incipient textuality without texts. Drawing from the work of J. L. Austin (1962) and Barbara Johnson (1980), Nagy explains that he views composition and performance as inextricably linked (9):

> If indeed performance "takes on meaning only by referring to the instance of its utterance," then this instance, this occasion, must be the basis for the intent of the utterance, for its rhetoric. If, further, the occasion should ever be lost or removed, then the intent of the utterance is destabilized. We may say that the very notion of genre serves as a compensation for the lost occasion.

In the terms that we have been developing throughout this chapter and earlier, he is providing a rationale for the textual rhetoric that persists in an oral-derived traditional text (whether actually written or fixed without writing through Panhellenization). The destabilization he envisages as "compensated for" by the idea of genre can be extended to apply to the reduction of a performance to the cenotaph of a manuscript: in this case it is not only the genre but all of its associated rhetorical strategies that assume the expressive responsibility. To make possible reentry of the performance arena and to reengender some vestige of the communicative economy that was the natural yield of that situation, textual artifacts must counteract the destabilizing influence of the lost occasion by recourse—institutionalized and traditional recourse—to the submerged rules of genre and rhetoric that now bear the responsibility for keying performance.[39]

Transformation(s)

The range of opinions and perspectives on the nature of oral traditional works that survive in textual form is, as we have seen, quite various. Each tradition or

39. Cf. the oral-dictated text theory advanced by Barry Powell (1991), who argues that the scribe who cooperated with Homer in fashioning the massive *Iliad* and *Odyssey* was also the person who adapted Phoenician letter-forms and invented the Greek alphabet (232–33): "Once we accept that the adapter and the man who wrote down Homer are one and the same man, we will loosen the exasperating tangle of contradictions that has puzzled generations of Homeric scholars. According to my hypothesis, there was originally a single text of the *Iliad* and the *Odyssey*, the adapter's. At first only he could read them. Copies of the poems, or parts of the poems, first circulated among the Euboians, who may have carried them even to Italy. With the poems were disseminated the rules of alphabetic writing."

genre encounters textualization differently, and theories of how that process proceeds even within the same tradition and genre themselves vary.[40] We can, however, locate at least two common emphases in recent scholarship having to do with this question.

First, the old model of the Great Divide between orality and literacy has given way in most quarters, pointing toward the accompanying demise of the absolutist dichotomy of performance versus document. One of the preconditions for this shift from a model of contrasts to one of spectra has been the exposure of writing and literacy as complex technologies that are certainly neither monolithic nor deserving of unqualifed reduction across cultures, but which, as generalized abstractions, harbor virtually innumerable differences according to tradition, genre, function, and the like.[41] Consequently, text can no longer be separated out as something different by species from the oral tradition it records or draws upon; the question becomes not whether but how performance and document speak to one another.

The second shared emphasis, particularly evident among the works by O'Keeffe, Doane, Janko, and Nagy mentioned above, amounts to a corollary of the first. If what we have in the oral-derived document is in some sense an active remembrance of oral tradition, then our interpretive strategies must address that continuation in its fullest rhetorical implications.[42] We are thus led to ask—without primary deferral to a history of composition that can perhaps never be compiled—how a given text continues the tradition of reception. The responsibility for attention to this question does not derive from our knowledge or hypothesis that the work under consideration reaches us as a first-generation transcription of an oral performance, but from the evidence of an oral tradition in its background and some demonstration of the work's continuing dependence upon that oral tradition. Prima facie evidence for such continuing dependence would take the form of rhetorical transformations of the expressive and receptional strategies called metonyms and keys to performance in earlier chapters. Whether we are dealing with living traditions such as the Native American or South Slavic, or with works such as the Old English and Homeric poems that survive only as manuscripts, the question will remain the same: How does the text teach us to read it, how can we be the best possible audience for the singer of tales in performance?

Performance Arena

To begin with *performance arena,* it should be emphasized from the start that a very simple difference must inform everything that can be said about the

40. For some interesting case studies of ways in which oral and literary traditions interacted in the former Yugoslavia, cf. Lord 1986b.

41. Cf. esp. Finnegan 1977, 1988, Street 1984, and Boyarin 1993; also Stock 1990, esp. 5–15, and Foley 1990a, esp. 5–10. For an interesting example of what might be termed *symbolic literacy,* a traditional medium of visual representation that operates without writing, see Carrier and Carrier 1990.

42. Cf. Nagy 1990: 9: "I take it, then, that the questions of meaning in the composition of a song or poem cannot be settled in terms of the composition alone: we must keep in mind what the composition says about its performance or potential performance, and what that says about whoever is the composer, whoever is the performer."

word-power of an oral-derived text: the "place" where the work is experienced by a reader, the event that is re-created, must be summoned solely by textual signals. The phenomenological present conferred by actual performance context—the Rajasthani *bhopo's* episode before his illustrated cloth "map," the folk preacher's retelling of a Biblical tale before his or her congregation, the Serbian *bajalica's* whispered spell in her client's ear[43]—vanishes, and along with it the unique and enriching primal connection between this particular visit to the performance arena and the traditional sense of having been there before. The face-to-face interaction, not only between performer and audience but also among audience members, cannot be played out in a written text, no matter how multi-channeled that document may be.[44] Nothing can wholly replace the personal exploration of an oral traditional performance by a person steeped in the significative geography of the event.

In the case of a work that one cannot automatically assume to be a first-generation transcription of a performance, a similar caveat is necessary. The ideal preparation for faithful reception of such a work is prior immersion in the oral tradition from which it derives, that is, familiarity not only with the descriptive or analytically measurable parameters of a culture but, much more importantly, with its "ways of speaking."[45] Knowing how to use the idiom in which a work presents itself is an accepted (if silently acknowledged) sine qua non for literary studies, so it should come as no surprise that interpretation of a traditional oral form requires as thorough as possible an understanding of its particular, dedicated register. Of course, as composition in writing becomes more and more the rule, and native artists themselves move further and further away from actual performance, the special valence of the register that gains intelligibility precisely from its employment within the performance arena will begin to wane. This diminution of illocutionary force will be a problem first for the involved culture, which may resort to strategies such as "textual communities" to preserve intelligibility, and then, at much greater distance and correspondingly more severely, for the modern reader who attempts to decode what present themselves as decontextualized (in Nagy's term, "destabilized") messages.[46] A textual rhetoric of traditional, performance-derived forms will keep the delicate umbilical of metonym and meaning in place temporarily, but as textuality develops its own

43. On the Rajasthani *bhopo,* see Smith 1991; on folk preaching, Rosenberg 1970, 1986 and Lawless 1988; on Serbian charms, chap. 4 below.

44. Cf. Tedlock's observation (1990: 136): "The sheer process of notation can open our ears to things we never heard before and lead us to revise our picture of the world projected by an oral performance, but once again there arises the question of how much our readers can keep track of all at once." It is worth mentioning in this regard how partial and parochial audio, and even video, tapes prove to be. Although each offers the opportunity to encode additional communicative channels, each also has shortcomings. For example, the directionality of the audio record will make its version of the performance in some ways idiosyncratic, while the video technology may intrude on the event so severely that it deflects or masks many of its performance features.

45. Thus Tedlock's ethnopaleographical program (1987), for instance.

46. Cf. Stock 1983, esp. 90–92, who uses the concept of textual communities to explain how medieval groups fostered internal coherency, that is, how they maintained a continuity of reception.

significative dynamics, that umbilical will wither and eventually lose its function as a conduit of extratextual meaning.

Standing at the far end of the process, at a point far beyond the rhetorical transformation of traditional oral forms, latter-day readers of ancient Greek, Old English, and other oral-derived works must first set realistic goals for entry of the performance arena, which itself may have been rhetorical (but still powerfully determinative) when the extant texts were created. It will of course not be possible to bring to the interpretive encounter anything approaching the ideal—an intimate intracultural knowledge of the prior and informing oral tradition. Nor can one assume, without fear of jeopardizing the viability of the entire enterprise, that the work as it survives represents what was without doubt an oral performance. Whatever is attempted as a methodology, and whatever emerges as a reading, must be assessed against this background.

But let us not focus exclusively on what cannot be recovered. With a realistic calibration, a latter-day reader can indeed hope to make some gains in understanding by entering the performance arena as a partial if inevitably not a full participant in the specialized communicative exchange. With Hymes, I find the idea of a partial but finite gain—particularly one that can be made in no other way—worthy solace for the certain impenetrability of the barriers of both culture and history.[47] Limited access to the arena becomes an option open to the reader of both transcribed performances and works with roots in oral tradition, on the condition that one is willing to concentrate on the dedicated system of signification that bears institutionalized, metonymic meaning, on the keys to performance that survive transformation to text. Even against the inevitable loss that accompanies textualization, we can still sense a work's empowering relationship to the enabling event of performance (real or rhetorical) and the enabling referent of tradition.

In other words, the continuity of reception of a work that stems from oral tradition but which survives only as a text will depend on the reader's ability to recognize the rhetorical signals that are the bequest of performance and tradition, and then to credit these signals with the institutionalized meanings they carry as a dedicated register of verbal communication. Only when the text has been made to yield the kind of augmented discourse that mirrors a traditional oral performance in the highly focused mode of signification we have earlier identified as communicative economy can the message be faithfully received. In addition to the meaning-laden signals, and perhaps less obviously, it will also be the gaps of indeterminacy in such texts that reach out beyond the confines of the document and conventional literary modes of reference to the extratextual event of performance and the referent of tradition. Not only the value-added signals—whether special formulae or other verbal strategies that encode so much more than the sum of their denotative parts—but just as crucially the "blank spots" or logical cruces within a text will require the reader to configure the work of verbal art on the basis of his or her active presence in the performance arena.

47. Cf. esp. Hymes 1981 (1977): 337–40 and 1989b.

That signals and gaps, to be examined in detail immediately below, constitute a topography visible and resolvable only from the vantage point available within the performance arena proves important for texts throughout the spectrum from transcribed performances to "literary" works with roots in oral tradition. At one end of the spectrum, the transcribed performance obviously requires engagement of the tradition's rules for generating meaning in performative context: what is committed to writing or print has its primary allegiance to what remains unwritten, and cannot be successfully addressed as something it is not. In a broadly defined middle area, where the signals and gaps have been transformed into a textual rhetoric and employed by a writer, the reader's responsibility is not dissimilar. Augmenting the discourse will still require, albeit to a lesser extent and with a variant dynamics, activation of the network of signification that derives from oral tradition; performance, even in this altered mode, will still have to be keyed if the work is to be made intelligible.[48] At the far end of the spectrum, as textuality asserts its primacy over the word-power that depends on oral tradition, the metonymic meaning of signals may become muted (or at least the signals may become more limited in range and analytical in focus),[49] and those gaps that both result from and depend on an implied referent may become fewer or nonexistent. As much recent scholarship has shown, however, even those works we consider most highly textual still resonate with traditional oral meaning—if we can learn to identify it.[50]

Register

The fundamental criterion for such an identification, and the entrée to the performance arena, is recognition of and fluency in the traditional, oral-derived, performance-derived *register* in which the work presents itself. As the idiom in which the work was created and through which it must be interpreted, the register contains at once the keys to performance (and to its specialized, highly economical discourse) and the immanence that (re-)vivifies not only the transcribed performance but also the work composed in writing but with roots in oral tradition.

Let us consider more specifically how the signals that constitute the register are transformed into a textual rhetoric, and with what implications for the interpretation of oral-derived texts. Our examination will concentrate on the signals themselves, as defined according to three approaches: the Ethnography of Speaking as practiced by Richard Bauman, the Ethnopoetic perspective as advocated by Dell Hymes, and the Oral-Formulaic Theory as extended to

48. One thinks here of the "translations" of Latin works into the Old English poetic idiom, some closer or more literal than others (cf. the two parts of *Genesis,* for example), but all of them employing the register of Old English poetic diction, an oral-derived traditional register that projects a certain mode of reception. See below the study of "indexed" translation in the Old English *Andreas* in chap. 6.

49. Cf. the rhetorical handbooks so common in the later Middle Ages, esp. the *topoi* discussed authoritatively by E. R. Curtius (1953: 79–105 and 145–66).

50. Cf. esp. Renoir 1988, Doane and Pasternack 1991, Foley 1991: chaps. 5–6; and Amodio 1994.

Immanent Art. Although the focus will be on those features and structures that are understood as meaning-bearing aspects of oral traditional style, we should also note the other side of the representational coin: the gaps of indeterminacy that are, as we have seen, a crucially important part of the ongoing challenge of signification and reception. These gaps open when the surface of the narrative proves itself insufficient to the task of what Iser calls "consistency-building," when the expressive integers of the performance or text must reach beyond the immediacy of the literal level and invoke the specialized, extratextual meaning available only under the double aegis of performance and tradition. Thus, in focusing on signals we are not ignoring gaps; from a Receptionalist point of view, it is the access provided by signals that allows the audience or reader to participate actively in the closing of gaps. In the process of this three-part investigation, it will be possible to glimpse once more how the Ethnography of Speaking, Ethnopoetics, and Immanent Art are addressing parallel, and in many cases identical, concerns.

1. To begin with the Ethnography of Speaking, and with the event of performance, we might inquire how many of Bauman's "keys to performance" persist in texts, and further what form they take and how they condition the message sent by the composer (and tradition) and received by the reader (as audience).[51] First in the order he presents them is the feature of *special codes,* which he instances with the phenomenon of linguistic archaism. Examples of such codes abound in oral and oral-derived discourse alike, and translate readily from voiced event to textual document. Both the Homeric and Old English poems have frequent recourse to archaism, the former so much so that scholars have long disagreed over the absolute historical provenance of the *Iliad* and *Odyssey* that survive. As diachronically based studies have shown,[52] the Homeric epic register consists of a kind of linguistic equilibrium that records the ever-modulating outcome of the competition between archaism and contemporary usage. Over time some battles are won and some are lost, according to the rules of contest in the medium,[53] with the result that the register attains a special character as a way of speaking, constituting a marked species of language that no one used as an idiom for everyday communication (as would be expected because of its dedicated function). Some have thus viewed the diachronic mixture typical of Homeric diction as "artificial," but from the perspective of register we can see that it is no more unreal or deviant than any other speech variety; it is simply different, distinctive, and, as a special code, inherently indexical of certain kinds of meaning.

Dialectal heterogeneity offers another example of "special codes" in the Homeric poems, and has often been studied along with forms apparently char-

51. As noted earlier (chap. 1), Bauman specifically notes that this group of "keys" is a generalized set that he offers as illustration, and certainly not with the assertion that they are in any way universal. With similar caution in regard to tradition- and genre-dependence, and in order to preserve as clear a link as possible with his interpretive program, I use the same set as illustration.

52. Cf. Parry 1932; also Hoekstra 1964, Nagy 1974, 1990, Janko 1982.

53. On traditional rules, see Foley 1990a, esp. chaps. 3–6.

acterized by linguistic anachronism. Like archaism, dialectal irregularity marks the phraseology as a way of speaking and prescribes entry into the performance arena as a precondition for continuing a tradition of reception. The concern that such departures from "standard" speech, departures that I emphasize should not be considered deviant or substandard but rather alternative and empowering, constitute an editorial or critical problem reflects a textual parallax: only if textual strategies for signification are absolutely in the ascendancy— and performance and tradition are forgotten sources of word-power—can these special codes be considered aberrant. Confirmation of this ecumenical view of registers is available in living oral traditions all over the world,[54] and it should come as no surprise that, even under the leveling program of standardization practiced by editors throughout the centuries,[55] the Homeric epic register retains special codes as a key to performance.

Of course, archaisms, like any another characteristic, do not universally mark oral traditional registers.[56] Some traditions may depend at least partially upon word order, for example, to signal the performance arena and a specialized discourse, or on some other linguistic or nonlinguistic feature. Both the Old English and the Homeric Greek poetic registers exhibit an idiosyncratic word order, very different from the expectable prose sequences, and South Slavic epic reveals the same general operational principle behind the formation and variability of phraseology. In both ancient and medieval texts, the deflection from prose word order takes a tradition-dependent and genre-dependent direction, but the larger and more telling point is that each diction demonstrates a markedness in this special coding that carries over into both dictated transcripts and works with roots in oral tradition. To depart from the coding that defines the register is—in either actual oral performance or the second generation of rhetorical transformation—to relinquish the performance arena and by definition to exit the highly economical discourse it promotes. It is also to fracture the necessary illusion created by transaction through the register, and to denature either species of traditional verbal art.

As far as special codes are concerned, then, this broadest of categories in Bauman's list of keys to performance can encompass many different features, depending on the particular linguistic texture of the language that supports the given register. Such features as we have examined will persist in texts as a specialized rhetoric that—for the appropriately prepared reader—will direct response and reception through a series of value-added signals. As we will see in chapters 5 and 6, these signals can invoke both generalized and specific levels of response, from simple establishment of the performance arena (with little or

---

54. Within the South Slavic tradition, for example, one can (and must) readily distinguish among the registers associated with epic, lyric, magical charm, metrical genealogy, and funeral lament. See further the discussion of charms in chap. 4, below.

55. Cf. n. 35.

56. There is naturally great variance in the amount and especially the kind of deflection from the contemporary unmarked "standard," according to tradition- and genre-dependence, with some registers showing more syntactic and/or morphological specialization than others.

no additional value-added meaning) to highly focused metonymic signification. For the experienced reader who can "re-create" the event and harness the implications of the tradition, texts can image the oral traditional strategies as rhetorical functions, mimicking a phenomenology of action and involvement even in the segregated encounter of reader and document. Although the performance cannot be relived or the tradition made as immediate as the event that instances it, an oral-derived, performance-derived text can reflect a way of speaking through special codes.

Figurative language is, of course, a typical feature of virtually all verbal art, oral traditional or not, so it is important to distinguish this second of Bauman's keys to performance from the more widely distributed poetic principle. He observes, for instance, that "the semantic density of figurative language, its foregroundedness, make it especially appropriate as a device for performance, where expressive intensity and special communicative skill are central" (17–18), and goes on to describe three varieties of this trope: figures that are created by the performer, those that are recurrent in fixed-phrase performance (where accuracy is paramount), and ready-made phrases pressed into "employment in novel contexts" (18). Foregroundedness implies markedness, especially in a situation wherein the figures are dynamically constitutive of the idiom. If a register in part depends on figurative language for the establishment of the performance arena, then this feature is acting not as a neutral or optional embellishment but as a defining feature of the linguistic code. By recalling the spectrum of signification typical of such signals—from simple demarcation of the performance arena and opening of the idiomatic channel to highly focused and particular connotative specificity—one sees that figurative language can be much more than an option harmonizing with the general outlines of a poet's artistic program; it can serve as an institutionalized trope that helps to encode directions for a way of speaking.

As for transferral from the experienced event of performance to the rhetorically induced event in the textual libretto, Bauman's three types of figurative language will translate somewhat differently, but with certain similarities as well. Individual creativity in the coining of such tropes must operate against a background of traditional, performance-centered expectation; if the compositional and reception-al rules for the making of figures do not license a given creative act, it becomes contextless, occurs in an affective vacuum, and loses any significative effect beyond that which the work as a text can summon. Old English poetry, particularly *Beowulf*, offers numerous highly successful instances of this kind of individual artistry in traditional context, especially in the formation of compounds. This typically Germanic linguistic phenomenon becomes the occasion for displays of verbal dexterity that situate singular creativity against the informing context of tradition.[57] The latter two varieties of figures, both employing ready-made phrases but differing in their deployment in fixed-phrase or variable performance, have

---

57. For an excellent study of compound diction in *Beowulf*, with full attention to its oral traditional roots and implications, see Niles 1983: 138–51.

direct and primary reference to extratextual meanings; the distinction is between the recurrence of these phrases alongside other ready-made elements on the one hand and their irruption into "unfamiliar" situations on the other. In both cases (and the spectrum that intervenes between these extremes) the transformation to textual rhetoric can continue a tradition of reception, provided that the figurative language in question is perceived against the backdrop of implication that is its larger and most natural context. Given the textual predisposition of the modern reader, we may anticipate that the fixed-phrase performance will run a greater risk of being devalued as unduly repetitive, perhaps as cliché, and that the poet who shows individual creativity in his or her formulation of figures will be the more admired. But we can offset that kind of parochial assimilation to literary principles by attention to the kind and degree of word-power institutionally engaged by this second key to performance.

Parallelism likewise proves a nearly universal poetic strategy, and the distinction between the general phenomenon and the constitutive nature of parallelism in oral traditional registers should be stressed. At the level of a specific, tradition-dependent example, we may cite the feature called "variation" in Old English poetry. Defined by Fred Robinson as "syntactically parallel words or word-groups which share a common referent and which occur within a single clause," and understood as linking two or more items paratactically without prescribing the logical nature of that relationship,[58] this kind of institutionalized apposition marks the Old English poetic register with a recognizable stamp; when it occurs—not as a metrical necessity but as a stylistic constituent—it signals a particular, familiar mode of reception. Once again, then, it is not merely the individual occurrence of the feature but its recurrence as an expressive habit that marks it as a key to performance.

But can parallelism key performance when the items it comprises become textual rhetoric operating upon a reader? At the most superficial level, reduction of Old English variation, for example, to a local phenomenon—the individually realized trope chosen for implementation by a single author—demotes parallelism to the status of any other textual figure by silencing its particularly traditional resonance. If, on the other hand, variation is recognized as a vital stylistic component, nothing less than a defining feature of the register, the way is open to hear a deeper meaning in both its general deployment and its specific usages. As we discovered above, however, the most important question will concern the level of experience brought to each occurrence by the reader: can he or she interpret variation as a strategy that summons the performance arena and helps set the rules for reception of the work (now become a text)? Without that experience—or some simulation of it—the continuity of reception will be broken, and perhaps forever lost; but with such an enabling context the poetic discourse can recover that measure of its original word-power that remains

58. Robinson 1979: 129; he also argues in respect to *Beowulf* (1985: 5–6) that "the logically open, implicit quality of apposition is shared by other stylistic devices in the poem, and in concert these create a reticent, appositive style which is immediately cooperative with the tone and theme of the poem." See chap. 6 below for treatment of instances of variation in the Old English *Andreas.*

encoded and decipherable in the persistence of an oral-derived and performance-derived rhetoric.

Of the remainder of Bauman's keys, let us pass over *special formulae* for the moment, since they will be covered in the comments on register and Oral-Formulaic Theory just below. Likewise, I will not treat either *appeal to tradition* or *disclaimer of performance* at any length. The former, which amounts to an individual's explicitly setting the personal present of the ongoing performance against the standard of the transpersonal present, is in an important sense the (implicit) ritual act in oral traditional performance. All performances—and every aspect of each performance—take a certain measure of their meaning, their word-power, from tradition; every performance is a melding of individual and traditional artistry, with the absence or graphic diminution of either component leading to a profound change in the nature of the communication. Appeal to tradition can thus translate to a textual rhetoric, with the same proviso as before—that there is a body of implication to which one can appeal. And, although rare in ancient and medieval texts,[59] disclaimer of performance assumes roughly the same relationship between individual and tradition, and thus undergoes textual transformation under approximately the same conditions.

The last of the keys to performance, *special paralinguistic features,* calls deserved attention to the primary role of sound in the prescription of a dedicated channel for expression and reception. A highly tradition- and genre-dependent set of characteristics that could be enumerated almost endlessly across different language traditions, this category would include such features as pause, loudness, intonation patterns, duration, rate of delivery, gesture, and audience responses (the last category employing all of the preceding qualities). Nonacoustic recordings of actual performances—that is, oral dictated texts—rarely preserve any of these aspects of performance, which can serve crucial keying functions.[60] Given the textualist bias of our scholarship, with its easy assimilation of all forms of verbal art to the literary-textual model, paralinguistic cues are the very most perishable of keys to performance, in virtually all cases not outlasting their temporal and spatial occurrence as aspects of the event. They therefore almost never translate to a textual rhetoric, which is at any rate inherently ill equipped to image them with any fidelity.[61] For similar reasons, composition in writing will not customarily entail the deployment of these performance cues, nor is it easy to imagine how a tradition of reception of such signals could be established or maintained. Leaving the door open for advances in editing and representation, we must unfortunately conclude that paralinguistic features—alone of Bauman's keys to performance— usually do not and cannot persist in the transformation to textual rhetoric.

---

59. But note the poet's extraordinary interruption of the *Andreas* narrative (lines 1478–91) to comment on the exigencies of telling this apocryphal tale; see further chap. 6 below.

60. One example of a paralinguistic key to performance would be the extremely rapid, sotto voce presentation unique to the Serbian magical charms, on which see further chap. 4 below. Tedlock's Zuni texts (1972a) and others that aim at similar revoicings are of course the exception to the rule in preserving or reflecting some of these keys.

61. On the shortcomings of such libretti, cf. Tedlock's observation quoted in n. 44.

2. Especially since the issue of transformation and representation lies at the heart of Ethnopoetics, let us also consider the prospects for modulation of Dell Hymes's taxonomy of structure from actual performance to transcribed text.[62] It will be recalled that he proposes seven levels of rhetorical segmentation,[63] and that each of the levels has a definite traditional role in constituting the given work. The core of the system is the *verse*, a poetic unit marked regularly, though not always, by an initial particle.[64] Within verses he distinguishes the smaller units of the *line*, indicated many times by predications, that is, verbs, and the *versicle*, a grouping of lines smaller than the verse. This lower end of the scale, the microstructure of the narrative, is complemented by the macrostructure of, in increasing order of size and extent, the *stanza*, a grouping of verses according to the pattern number of the given culture; and the *scene*, *act*, and *part*, dramatic modes of organization in ascending levels. From both the theoretical analysis that supports this grid of features, now attested in more than thirty Native American language traditions, and the demonstration of text-making for a narrative by John Rush Buffalo (Hymes 1987b: 45–52), it seems clear that Hymes considers the seven-part structural scheme a traditional form that encodes a certain kind of signification and prescribes a certain mode of reception.

In the case of acoustically recorded oral narratives, one can envision how Hymes's linguistic and dramatic poetics serves to establish the performance arena. "Interpret what follows in terms of the sevenfold traditional grid," the audience and later the reader are being told; "understand this utterance within its register." But how do those implicit directions translate to a written document, particularly the kind of document in which Hymes has shown much interest—performances transcribed by much earlier investigators before the development of Ethnopoetics and therefore rendered essentially as written, run-on prose?

First, we must recall that Hymes's system does not comprise or depend on acoustic features limited to a single occurrence in a given performance. His rationale for moving from oral recordings to written texts, from one performance to another, and from one language tradition to another is founded on the system's traditional nature—its recurrence as a stylistically constitutive set of features. Under the requirement that truly determinative elements show a co-variation between form and meaning,[65] his seven levels of poetic structure are

62. Note that our task is in this case somewhat simplified, since we are not dealing with works composed in writing, but with actual performances of two kinds—those for which an acoustic record exists and those for which we have only a transcription.

63. In what follows I refer primarily to Hymes 1987b, the latest and most elaborate description of the structural system. Cf. the lengthier discussion of his method in chap. 1 above.

64. It may be worth noting that lines of South Slavic epic are also often marked by initial particles, and further that these particles are not seldom extrametrical (in relation to the ten-syllable *deseterac*) and syntactically unnecessary. On this phenomenon, which is particularly evident in unedited texts and acoustic recordings, cf. Foley 1990a: 89–90.

65. E.g., 1987b: 22. Elsewhere (1981 [1977]: 340) he notes that "to lack tape recordings would be to miss something valuable, the realization in performance to which Tedlock so rightly and creatively calls attention; but it would not be to lose everything. Poetic structure could still be found. The indispensable tool would not be a tape recorder, but a hypothesis."

brought forward and applied to older texts precisely on the basis of their systematic ubiquitousness and demonstrated rhetorical implications. If the signals he describes have a rhetorical function in orally recorded traditional narratives, then transferral to a written medium—in this case a re-editing of earlier texts to reveal their ethnopoetic character and dynamics—seems not only possible but highly desirable. How, then, is the transformation accomplished for the various segments of the performance?

To begin at the simplest level, note that while Hymes's *line* of Native American narrative does not correspond to a typical Indo-European unit marked by syllable- or stress-count, it is nonetheless a traditional unit of expression usually marked by a verb. As such, it can be mapped into a textual format with typographical indication of boundary, and this visual strategy can alert the reader to its structural function. As Hymes points out repeatedly in a variety of writings,[66] failure to "edit in" this—or any other—level of segmentation is to deprive the work of its expressive potential, and thereby to denature reception. Likewise with the *verse,* whose onset is often indicated by an initial particle; once again, the choice rests between a run-on prosified representation that actively obscures the narrative's harmonized layers of structure and a libretto that guides the reader in re-creating the performance arena and in managing the communicative transaction.

As an illustration, consider the following example of line and verse segmentation, drawn from Hymes's scoring of John Rush Buffalo's "Coyote and Eagle's Daughter" (1987b: 36):[67]

A (a) And then Coyote went off from the place, and, galloping,
          "Quick! This camp is on fire!" they say he said.
   (b) When he did, they say, nothing happened.
B (a) Then again he went off, and,
          coming at a run,
          "Hurry! This camp is on fire!" they say he said.
   (b) Then, they say, nothing happened.
              *   *   *
D (a) Then the last time he went off, and,
          coming at a run,
          "Hurry! This camp is on fire!" they say he said.
   (b) Then, they say, many people ran out.

Within the three *stanzas* A, B, and D, which adhere to the Tonkawa pattern number of four (lines per stanza), the verses, marked as are many others by initial "then" or "when," consist of discrete lines. While these lines are in no

66. Most fundamentally, 1975a and 1977; further illustration in 1994.
67. Stanza C (Part I, Act IV), not given here because of space considerations, is nearly identical to the preceding stanza. In what follows I am only too aware that we are dealing with a translation rather than with original-language material, but make bold to do so because the points to be covered are general and theoretical in nature. For more thorough applications of related ideas to works in the original languages, see chaps. 4–6 below.

way amenable to definition by syllable- or stress-count, they are marked by, at minimum, a predication, and they also exhibit the kind of grammatical wholeness or independence widely cited as typical of traditional linear units in ancient Greek and South Slavic narrative.[68] Once this rhetorical structure is made plain by typographically prompting the reader to perceive according to the natural cognitive categories of the communication, one also notices more clearly the formulaic nature of the phraseology—although of course the diction does not exist in symbiosis with a conventional Indo-European prosody.[69] What Hymes has done is to recognize the tradition-dependent nature of this poetry and use the virtues of typographical conventions to promote the reader's faithful reception of this long-silenced performance. While such latter-day readers cannot experience this libretto as an actual performance, they can begin to establish a performance arena by learning to communicate in the register devoted to Tonkawa taletelling.

The other levels of Hymes's system function according to the same basic principles, with versicles, scenes, acts, and parts constituting signals for reception. Because this rhetoric of performance—whether the incremental logic of verses or the dramatic dynamics of the larger units—engenders certain expectations, the listener who would make optimal sense of a given narrative must be able to construe its signals appropriately. For a reader who depends wholly on resurrecting the event from a script, Hymes's visual conventions provide a point of entry into a system of phraseological and narrative organization that would otherwise remain beyond reach. Thus the ethnopoetic libretto makes possible a higher degree of what Iser calls "consistency-building," in that it amplifies the word-power of the work by helping to define its register and to admit the "outsider" to the performance arena.

3. The Oral-Formulaic Theory, particularly as extended to Immanent Art, offers a third perspective on the process and implications of an oral traditional register persisting as a textual rhetoric. In this case we shall be inquiring how the compositional features of formulaic phraseology, thematic structure, and story-pattern translate to deployment in texts, and especially how their significative ability is affected by that translation.

Formulaic phraseology proves not just a typical but a constitutive dimension of many oral traditional registers. With the caveat that any phraseology takes shape from the traditional rules that underlie it, and that therefore no two dictions will answer the same set of definitions,[70] we can observe that many poetic registers in oral traditions will demonstrate some level of phraseological patterning. Depending in part on how the formula is defined and in part on the individual tradition, genre, and work, that level may be quite high, with all or nearly all of the work derivable from a grammar of formulaic patterns; quite low, with a very few phrases ostensibly generated from formulaic systems; or

---

68. E.g., Lord 1960: 54.

69. That is, the phraseology evolves according to its own set of tradition- and genre-dependent rules. Cf. Foley 1990a: chap. 3.

70. Cf. Foley 1990a: chaps. 3–6.

somewhere on the spectrum in between. Whatever the density of obvious "repeated phrases," which at any rate represent the product of composition rather than the process behind it, the larger point is that many registers operate according to traditional rules that foster the creation and maintenance of formulaic phraseology.

The danger inherent in the textualizing of such phraseology can take at least two forms, both stemming ultimately from the same source. For both the transcribed oral performance and the work composed in writing but employing the oral traditional register, the interpretive shortfall lies principally in the privileging of the fossilized product over the ongoing generative process. Once written down and perceived as textual, formulas are only too easily interpreted as the "dead letters" of cliché; instead of being understood as the natural result of rules for discourse, they may be consigned to the status of metrical stopgaps or fillers. In the case of the transcribed oral performance, such fillers are envisioned as stemming from the pressure of rapid and "extemporaneous" composition, while the writing poet, likewise seen as the prisoner rather than the master of a demanding idiom, may seem to resort more than a truly creative artist should to a hackneyed style of expression.

These two versions of a common dilemma highlight the problems inherent in textualizing formulaic phraseology. Focusing on composition at the nearly total expense of reception will foreground the integer at the expense of the mathematics—the mere item at the expense of its connotative, metonymic meaning, and in the presence of a silent text, in many cases stripped of its traditional context, the natural tendency will be for scholars and other readers to assimilate the work to the familiar literary model. This archetypal act of assimilation of course predetermines the mode of reception—fundamentally foreign to the work itself—and precludes a reader's faithful performance of the libretto.

If, on the other hand, the formulaic system of signification is interpreted as indexical of the extratextual tradition, if the phraseology can be understood as opening a channel to a special kind of word-power through a dedicated register, then even a textualized work can be addressed in something approaching faithful terms. As with the Ethnography of Speaking and Ethnopoetics approaches, then, we must deal with the crucially important matters of audience and context, which are in turn central to the move from Oral-Formulaic Theory to Immanent Art. Does the phraseology in the manuscript text have institutionalized reference to something larger and inherently more resonant than its immediate semantic meaning and localized application? Is the reader of the text in question able to project a metonymic reality from the cue provided by the phrase? Is a "way of speaking" vividly keyed by the presence of a given formula, or more broadly by evidence that traditional rules for phraseology are being followed? To what extent does the formulaic aspect of the register establish the performance arena? These are all questions whose answers will speak to the continued efficacy of formulaic phraseology as it modulates from an event-centered, emergent way of speaking to a textual rhetoric that, if successful, recalls and even re-creates an oral traditional and performance-centered word-power. And in the end the answers will all depend on the preparation of the audience and the process of reception—that is, on both the reader's prior familiarity with the immanent meaning of the phraseological integers and that same reader's self-education in metonymic signification through the interpretation of this and other texts.

The situation is much the same with theme and story-pattern, the other two integers or levels of structure discerned by Oral-Formulaic Theory. Themes, or typical scenes, can be taken out of context as in fact too typical, as another sign that the performer or writer is laboring, unable to come up with anything new, fresh, or original. Or, much preferably, a given pattern, for example the Homeric Feast or Old English Sea Voyage,[71] may be proven indexical not only of other occurrences in this particular text, but of a traditional idea that finds expression in many texts and cannot be prisoned solely in this or that situation. In this sense the register will be marked by narrative "words" with considerable "power," scenes or series of actions that signify metonymically and thus mean enormously more than the sum of their semantic parts. The extent to which the reader can grasp the resonance they index will depend upon how well he or she is prepared to (re-)instill the textualized linguistic integers with the kind of values made possible by the enabling event of performance and the enabling referent of tradition. Performance and tradition clearly and unquestionably undergo a radical change in the transformation to textuality, losing the immediacy and presence of the actual event in their modulation to rhetorical representation in a text. As we have already seen, this modulation results in the loss or at least the muting of various features. But if the register functions as an instrument that empowers not simply fluent composition but, much more important for our purposes, *fluent reception,* then the reader can in a real sense perform the work and continue its tradition of reception.

At a third oral-formulaic level, story-patterns can also enable reception by providing a large-scale "map" to complement the finer, inset detail of formulas and themes. If we are prepared to decode the signals that constitute this aspect of the oral-derived, performance-derived register, we may be able to confer a deeply traditional kind of unity on the work being read—not by concentrating on the articulation of parts in this given text, but by relating its succession of events to an untextualized paradigm that we know from the sum of its other instances. Thus, for example, hearing the echoes of other Return Songs will enrich and direct reception of *The Captivity of Djulić Ibrahim* or the *Odyssey,* and familiarity with the "unfaithful mother" song type will gloss the South Slavic *Udovica Jana* (*Widow Jana*) as a work that emerges from a way of speaking, and which is most faithfully interpreted from within the performance arena.[72] Immanent Art prescribes a sensitivity to signals at all levels of structure, under the programmatic commitment to interpret all structural integers as metonymic in mode of signification, and story-pattern will prove no exception.

71. For an analysis of these two themes, cf. Foley 1990a: 265–76 and 336–44, respectively.
72. On Return Songs, cf. Lord 1960: 242–59, Foley 1990a: chap. 10; for the "unfaithful mother" pattern, Foley and Kerewsky-Halpern 1976.

Communicative Economy

Whether from the perspective of Bauman's keys to performance, Hymes's rhetorical structure, or the Parry-Lord levels of patterning as projected by the theory of Immanent Art, then, an oral traditional register is marked in some tradition- and genre-dependent way as an idiom dedicated to the special purpose of communicating through a particular channel. The narrow focus—or dense encoding—of this idiom permits a correspondingly economical conveyance of meaning, as the performer and audience employ a highly resonant species of linguistic, paralinguistic, and nonlinguistic cues to co-create a rich and complex work with relatively few expressive integers. The density of the coding, and in particular the nominal function of its superficial denotation as compared with the multivalent, immanent connotation of the various features or items that make up the register, exacts a certain price: such a register carries out a limited, dedicated function extraordinarily well, with great communicative economy, precisely because it has largely relinquished the much wider range of cultural functions that can be (less economically) managed in less specialized language. A traditional oral register, however it is configured within the expressive reper-toire of a given culture, musters greatly augmented word-power because it has little or no primary responsibility to serve other communicative purposes.

When that register is pressed into service in a textual format, certain aspects of its function naturally change, but there is also a continuity of representation. The Ethnography of Speaking alerts us to the fact that performance can be keyed through many of the same features that characterize an actual event: special codes, figurative language, parallelism, special formulae, and the like can indeed be operative in a textual rhetoric. If these features are to be active, however, there must also exist a reader prepared to receive the signals in something approaching their fully coded significance. Otherwise what was communicative economy becomes tendentious, cliché-ridden indirection, as the performance-derived, traditional implications of the register fall on deaf ears. Whether in relation to a transcribed performance that survives only as a text or in the case of a work composed in writing that employs an oral traditional register, the requirement is the same: a reader who can make the text more than a text by hearing its rhetoric as a signal that establishes the performance arena and opens a channel of highly economical communication.

In considering individual written texts, we will want to inquire how actively the register—now transformed into a textual rhetoric—is operating in a partic-ular textual environment. One might start by gauging the extent to which the performance arena is simulated by the given set of textual cues. How readily do features such as a proem, an address to the reader/audience, or other patently performance-derived signals persist in conveying an empowering sense of how the work is to be received? Perhaps they have, for the composer as well as the reader/audience, become "only rhetorical," projecting the work into a vaguely defined context or simply adding a patina of otherness that is more decorative than determinative. Perhaps these cues have become so thoroughly rhetorical that they cease to create a recurrent, familiar context in which the work must be received to be intelligible.[73] Invoking the performance arena may, on the other hand, be much more than a gesture; it may amount to the rhetorical apotheosis of the work as an emergent event, and thus engage the meaning-bearing potential of performance and tradition, even if at one expressive remove.

As has been emphasized throughout this chapter, most of the interpretive judgments we make about the persistence of traditional oral forms in texts will rest on a realistic evaluation of the audience for whom they were composed. In the case of transcriptions of oral performances, there can be no hesitation in crediting what has become a textual rhetoric with as much resonance as can be discovered. If the only factor that keeps an instance of verbal art from prima facie participation in the ongoing loop of performance and reception is its ostracizing textuality,[74] then the way is clear for the editor and reader to enter the rhetorically projected performance arena as best they can, and to represent and read traditional oral signals at full strength—or at least as close to full strength as the intersemiotic translation to text allows.

Assessing the communicative economy of texts that were possibly or probably composed in writing, though still in the traditional oral register, will of course prove more problematic. In most cases of this sort, a precise, externally verifiable fix on the degree of textuality will not be forthcoming, and it may even be difficult to find a reasonable consensus. One strategy, discussed briefly above, will entail asking not whether literacy simply existed in a given culture at a given time, but more incisively what the verifiable functions of letters might have been at that juncture. Still, even though we press such methods to their limit, there will be situations, especially in the ancient and medieval worlds, that will remain largely in the shadows, with no definitive estimation forthcoming of the particular role of writing in the composition and transmission of a given work.

In such inherently uncertain situations, for which there will be no unambiguous external profile, we may gain a partial but still illuminating perspective by focusing on the internal coherency and expressive dynamics of the register per se. With the certainty of a traditional oral heritage behind the work, we then inquire about the extent to which its register operates through the kind of word-power that is the principal subject of this study. For example, in reading the text, do the signals, many of which may appear with great regularity, seem to bear metonymic significance beyond their usual semantic content? Are the gaps of indeterminacy closed most effectively (even uniquely) by referral to the extratextual body of tradition? Does the unusual density of archaisms, or instances of parallelism, or special formulae encourage a special mode of recep-

73. Cf. Renoir (1988: 171) on such an instance: "the handling of the theme of the hero on the beach in *Sir Gawain and the Green Knight* does not pass muster from the point of view of oral-formulaic rhetoric. As far as I can tell, much of the mechanics of this rhetoric are affectively unproductive within the context of the poem, and the much-acclaimed quality of the narrative is due mostly to the poet's mastery of written rhetoric."

74. Of course, ironically this same textuality is usually the only reason a performance survives beyond the event.

tion? Does the verse structure, sorted by pattern number into regularly configured stanzas, bespeak a dedicated traditional strategy for composition and a
correspondingly dedicated channel of reception? Questions such as these will
not solve the open question of the precise degree to which, or better the exact
ways in which, writing was involved in the making of a text, but they will help
us to understand what is finally much more important: the extent to which a
text still depends rhetorically on the enabling event of performance and the
enabling referent of tradition.

Strategies for Reading: Traditional Rules, Metonymy, and Word-Power

Unlocking the textually kept secret of the extent to which traditional forms
and strategies persist in texts as rhetorically active signals will require a number
of steps, to be illustrated over the course of chapters 5 and 6 for ancient and
medieval poems. First, and at the most basic level, it will be necessary to ascertain
the nature of the traditional rules that underlie the shape and texture of the
register, and this inquiry will work hand in hand with locating the keys to
performance that survive textualization. Under what conditions does phraseology coalesce? What characterizes units of narrative, and what kinds of morphology are observable in the instances at hand? Is parallelism a constitutive
feature of the register that keys performance, or does this duty devolve upon
other stylistic features? In short, the first step will be a kind of calibration for
the individual tradition and genre, to determine as far as possible how it works—
the foundation for how it signifies—in summoning the performance arena and
fostering its own brand of communicative economy.

Once these "philological" judgments are made and the base-level identity of
the register is established, then the next step is to inquire about the special
content of the communication signaled by the text. For a transcription of an
oral performance, the approach is relatively simple and straightforward (but not
necessarily easy of achievement). By comparison with other performances, both
acoustically recorded and transcribed, as well as by comparison of instances
within the textualized performance, one attempts to determine what sort of
special metonymic meaning—if any—a given signal summons.[75]

In South Slavic Moslem epic, for example, any singer's repertoire of "He/she
spoke" phrases is essentially a collection of equivalent elements: parameters such
as idiolect or selection by acoustic patterns may condition deployment at a
superficial level, but none of the functionally associated phrases carries a highly

---

75. In the examples to follow, I choose to adumbrate the strategies employed in later chapters by
reference to the example of patterned phraseology, a familiar constituent of the works to be studied.
As explained in later chapters, however, the whole range of traditional oral features—from the merest
metrical predisposition through the most complex narrative pattern—all assist in creating the
performance arena and constituting the register.

focused metonymic meaning.[76] In marking speech introduction, these phrases inherently announce a certain kind of speech act, but that is the end of their significance. On the other hand, a verbal phrase of precisely the same metrical extent, "He cried out,"[77] when delivered at or near the beginning of a performance, has deep and telling reverberations, signifying the lament of the prisoner-protagonist in the Return Song, a particular brand of shrieking loud and persistent enough to move the captor and his wife to bargain for the prisoner's release and leading eventually to his Ithaka-like arrival, disguised as a beggar, to compete against a gathering of suitors and attempt to reclaim his South Slavic Penelope and his home. These two examples illuminate the extremes of the register's spectrum of rhetorical signification; in fact, most phrases will fall somewhere between these poles. Our task as readers of transcribed performances is to use what evidence we have of other performances to gauge just where the various features fall on that spectrum, and then to coordinate their extratextual resonances in an informed reading of the work as a traditional event.

Informed reading of traditional works probably composed in writing will be inherently more problematic, given both the uncertainty as to the provenance of the text before us and the likely paucity of comparative material on which to base our estimation of a given feature's continuing, that is, rhetorical, word-power. Although we may be able to conduct the "philological" calibration with reasonable confidence, the trajectory from structure or feature to meaning will be much more difficult. In such situations it is necessary to begin by acknowledging that inevitable shortfall: there will be some keys to performance, some ethnopoetic structures, and some oral-formulaic patterns whose resonance will for practical, insurmountable reasons remain unheard. There will indeed be occasions when the information we have is simply insufficient for us to decide just how active a given element is, and our reading of the text will suffer accordingly.

But attention to word-power will bring us part of the way toward a more faithful reading of such hybrid or transitional texts, and that finite gain represents a far better prospect than ignoring the traditional oral nature of the register in which the work was composed, and through which it ideally should be received. We know enough, for example, to say that Homer's "rosy-fingered dawn" line acts as a signal for the introduction of a new episode or activity; what proves important is not just the semantic content—the dawning of a new day—and certainly not just the metricality of the line, but rather the idea of

---

76. Encoding an institutionalized meaning, however general or specific, may involve muting the semantic content of a given element in favor of foregrounding its traditional function. For example, the common phrase "On besjeda," literally translated as "He/she announced, orated," deflects *within the epic register,* along with many other phrases of various literal meanings, to simply "He/she spoke." Within this specialized way of speaking, all such phrases signal the start of a speech, and it is to this broad metonymic function that their semantic individuality is sacrificed.

77. E.g., "I pocmili" ("And he cried out"), "I on cmili" (same translation), or the more obviously determinative "Sužanj cmili" ("The prisoner cried out"). All instances of (historical) present tense are rendered as past, in accordance with general practice.

initiation, of beginning, that is the rhetorical content of the metonymic phrase.[78] In contrast with this rather broad coding, we might consider the special content of the Homeric "looking darkly" phrase (*hypodra idôn*), which James Holoka has shown to "convey anger on the part of a speaker who takes umbrage at what he judges to be rude or inconsiderate words spoken by the addressee" (1983: 4). Although of modest enough metrical extent in comparison to the whole-line "rosy-fingered dawn" formula, "looking darkly" provides a much more exact prolepsis through which prior and subsequent action will have to be evaluated if the work is to be given its full resonance.

As in the case of the exemplary phrases drawn from South Slavic Moslem epic, these two instances describe a wide spectrum, with most phrases falling between their poles, and with some less active than the "rosy-fingered dawn" formula and some frankly beyond the reach of analysis. Still, these instances, and others to be considered in later chapters, illustrate that the metonymic significance of traditional elements can be discerned in the persistence of rhetorical patterns in a text. Instead of moving from one performance to another, asking what is conveyed in different situations, the analytic method will many times involve inspecting just the single text, looking for value-added meaning that rationalizes the various deployments of a feature or structure within this one document. Just as different versions of different Return Songs in Moslem epic will demonstrate a shared appeal to the traditional valence of "He shouted," so the various occurrences of "looking darkly" within the much narrower compass of the Homeric texts will reveal a correlative kind of connotation. What we can determine about oral-derived, performance-derived texts will depend on factors such as the extent and nature of comparative material (if any) and the length and texture of the surviving text itself. Once again, the search can never be complete and final, even under the best of circumstances.[79] But careful triangulation among instances of a given traditional feature—whether a key to performance, an ethnopoetic pattern, or an oral-formulaic structure viewed from the perspective of Immanent Art—will often contribute to making the text a true libretto for the reader's performance.

From this point we move from theory to practice, examining first a living tradition, Serbian magical charms (*bajanje*), and then two examples of works composed in traditional oral registers but making their initial extant appearance as texts—the *Homeric Hymn to Demeter* and the Anglo-Saxon hagiographical narrative *Andreas*. In each case our focus will be trained on the nature and dynamics of word-power, that is, on the role of oral tradition as manifested in the areas of performance arena, register, and communicative economy. Drawing

---

78. Cf. Vivante 1979: 136.

79. Even a living and well-collected tradition will not yield up all of its secrets, particularly not to a person from outside the cultural and expressive community. Moreover, even among the "insiders" to a performance event, different life experiences will make for somewhat different receptions of the event. On the role of the traditional work in unifying—but not absolutely leveling—audience response, see Foley 1991: chap. 2.

on the methodologies of the Ethnography of Speaking, Ethnopoetics, and Oral-Formulaic Theory as extended to Immanent Art, three approaches that by this point should be understood as having overlapping hermeneutical agendas, we will attempt to deepen interpretation by paying particular attention to both the said and the unsaid, the semantically explicit and the metonymically implicit. We will try, in short, to become audiences better attuned to these different ways of speaking.

IV

SPELLBOUND
THE SERBIAN TRADITION
OF MAGICAL CHARMS

U kurjaka čet'ri noge, peti rep,
Od mog odgovora j' bio lek.

Into the wolf's four legs, fifth the tail,
Out of my speaking has come the cure.

Traditional

Izadji, Marija,
Da ti sudi kadija!

Come out, O Mary,
So the qadi can judge you!

Traditional

In this chapter we shall be applying the composite theory of word-power to actual performances of a traditional oral genre in South Slavic.[1] In the past it has been almost exclusively the Moslem epic, familiar to Slavic and comparative scholarship as the benchmark according to which other genres and other traditions have been measured and analyzed in the Parry-Lord methodology,[2] that has provided such illustration. But in the present chapter our focus will fall on a very different singer of tales in performance, and on the very different genre of *bajanje,* or magical charms, from Serbia, an expressive form that contrasts vividly with Moslem epic in performance arena, register, and mode of communicative economy. In this way I hope to take a step toward widening the South Slavic basis of comparison, thus grounding the investigation pluralistically in a living tradition. One may add that whereas the Moslem epic has virtually died out, *bajanje* still functions as an important dimension of rural Serbian daily life.

---

1. As stipulated in the preface, I use the term "South Slavic" as a way of designating the traditions of the former Yugoslavia. Likewise, the adjective "Serbian" will be used to refer to a historically defined ethnic population, and more particularly a set of expressive traditions, within the former Yugoslavia, and is in no way meant as descriptive of current political entities or events.
2. See esp. Parry 1933–35; *SCHS* I: 3–20; Lord 1960; Foley 1988: 32 and 1991: chap. 3.

As recently as 1975 our research team made extensive recordings of charms in and around the village of Orašac, approximately eighty kilometers south of Belgrade, and subsequent fieldwork has established their continuing currency.[3]

Magical charms represent a simple, straightforward test of the efficacy of the approach through word-power. That is, they can be studied as performances experienced in a more or less well known environment, within contexts about which we have some general information and some specific details. In other words, this genre does not present the additional complication of surviving only as a transcript of an oral performance or, at yet a further remove, in a prosified manuscript of uncertain provenance, such as the ancient and medieval works.[4] In terms of the interpretive program developed in the first three chapters, this means that in the case of the charms we are able to (re-)construct the *performance arena* by direct report of the event, that is, by our firsthand experience of it as an emergent reality. Likewise, the *register* employed by the *bajalica* ("conjurer"; lit. "enchanter, speaker") can be analyzed from acoustic records and field reports compiled by participants in the performances, with attention to linguistic, paralinguistic, and nonlinguistic features, and the dedicated idiom can thus be presented as the multi-channeled instrument it is. The result, of course, is that we are in a position to become beneficiaries of the *communicative economy* made possible by entering the performance arena and using the specialized register that is each genre's privileged and dynamic idiom. In short, we are in a position to become a relatively well educated audience, one that understands both the enabling event of performance and the enabling referent of tradition.

Bajanje differs from the much better known South Slavic epic in significant ways, and such differences offer some glimpse of the natural variety of traditional oral forms within a given culture's repertoire. The Moslem epic, having served as the foundation for the Parry-Lord approach and thus as the basic comparand for traditional oral genres in more than one hundred language areas, owes its ascendancy ultimately to its similarity in scope and structure to Homeric epic, the original and always the primary focus of Parry's research on oral tradition. From a vantage point now sixty years past that original research, it seems ironic that this initial concept of oral tradition effectively took shape from an ancient exemplar known only in manuscript form and constituting only one among myriad forms of oral and oral-derived traditional art.[5]

---

3. Cf. esp. Kerewsky-Halpern and Foley 1978a, 1978b; Foley 1982; Kerewsky-Halpern 1985, 1986.

4. As for the South Slavic epics collected by Parry and Lord, in some cases we have only the dictated texts written out by their native assistant Nikola Vujnović, himself a *guslar,* who heard and recorded these performances through a regional (dialectal) and individual (idiolectal) filter; on the various levels of traditional idiom, cf. further Foley 1990a, esp. chaps. 5, 8. Even in these cases, however, additional elements of context are provided by the rest of a singer's recorded repertoire (typically part of it acoustically encoded) and the recorded conversations that Parry and Lord regularly carried on with informants. On the more general problem of the fundamental differences among media in which performances are encountered, and the principle of "text-dependence," see Foley 1990a: chap. 2.

5. Cf., e.g., Opland (1975, 1980) on the South African praise-poetry model, which he specifically contrasts to the example of South Slavic epic, and Finnegan (esp. 1977, 1988) on international diversity among oral traditions.

Precisely because the history of studies in this area—at least those within the province of Oral-Formulaic Theory—has been so exclusively (if tacitly) determined by the epic generally, and by the Moslem subgenre of epic in particular, I have elsewhere sought to query other narrative genres from the former Yugoslavia to fill out the picture.[6] In an ongoing effort to widen and deepen our experience of South Slavic genres, and of oral traditions worldwide, I concentrate here on a poetic form that is, as we shall see, nonnarrative and neither sung nor accompanied by an instrument; what is more, as in so many traditional oral forms, the familiar concepts of formula, theme, and story-pattern will prove largely impertinent. Suffice it to say at this point that the expressive integers of the *bajanje* register simply do not square with those of the Moslem epic register. Nor are the facts or assumptions of performance itself simply superimposable upon the familiar matrix of the South Slavic *guslar* and his audience. Nonetheless, we will learn that the heuristic concepts of performance arena, register, and communicative economy will translate easily and productively to the genre of magical charms, in the process illuminating the transaction that occurs during the event of performance and under the aegis of tradition.

Before we turn to a reconstitution of the experience of *bajanje* from these perspectives, it will be well to reiterate a few premises of the approach through word-power. It will be recalled that this composite theory stresses the *un*textual nature of traditional oral art, and in so doing must confront both its structural and its significative dynamics. "Word" in this context thus requires a double definition, as an expressive integer that obeys traditional morphological rules, to be sure, but also as a metonymic key that activates performance and brings into play a network of traditional meaning. In place of the compositional imperative so often cited as the root cause of a register's particular shape and patterning, then, word-power prescribes what is ultimately an *artistic imperative.* Since the "words" that constitute the register amount to the only available way of speaking that accomplishes the particular expressive goal, and since they are so densely coded with information and resonance, the "obligation" to use them lies not in their metricality or the relief they promise a narrator under the pressure of rapid composition, but rather in the unique opportunity they afford the performer for effective communication and artistic creation.

It will thus be not only justifiable but necessary to treat the morphology of the register entailed in the *bajanje* genre, to gain a philological perspective on the structural identity of the idiom. But it will be unjustifiable to stop at that point and to end our inquiry by, in effect, pronouncing the charm to be adequately configured, that is, metrically satisfactory and tectonically sound. Using the common thread informing Immanent Art and the Ethnography of Speaking, we will be most fundamentally interested in what the integers project once they are understood as nodes in the resonant network of a performance tradition. The necessary first step of philology starts us down the path toward more than

---

6. E.g., the discussion of the "more textual" Christian epic in Foley 1991: chap. 4. Cf. Coote 1977 on "women's" (or lyric) songs.

literality and constrained signification; all (textual) appearances to the contrary, it leads eventually to what Pelt Kid's grandmother really means, and to what Tale of Orašac really offers his comrades' cause.

Bajanje: Curative Word-Power

Serbian folk taxonomy distinguishes between *vračanje*, the kind of harmful witchery commonly referred to in other cultures as "black magic," and *bajanje*, the set of healing charms whose function is to restore a person's or animal's health by dispelling the cause or agent of the sickness.[7] This latter variety of "white magic" is practiced widely throughout villages in the area of Šumadija in central Serbia, conventionally and virtually exclusively by postmenopausal women. Such healing spells are often learned before a girl reaches puberty, one customary paradigm involving a transmission from a "granny" (*baba*) to her young granddaughter. In this scenario the girl will then keep what is recognized as a significant part of her dowry locked away in her mind during her childbearing years, performing spells only after the period of what Mary Douglas has called "danger" has passed.[8] An adult woman can also learn charms from her mother, in that case usually just before marriage, or, more rarely, from her new mother-in-law after she joins the husband's household. Whatever the source and timing of the acquisition, however, she cannot normally use the inheritance until she too becomes a *baba*.

For reasons endemic in the social structure of this region, whose core is the multigenerational extended family or *zadruga* that is both patriarchal and patrilocal,[9] the overall transmission pattern for this genre differs radically from that of the more familiar epic. Whereas epic songs, the almost exclusive province of males,[10] tend to follow family lines or to move from one place to another through performance at larger gatherings, *bajanje* can change locales with every generation, as the outmarrying bride brings her mother's or grandmother's inheri-

---

7. Lexicons differ on the denotative meaning of the verb *vračati*, ranging from the negative sense given above through such neutral phrases as "to practice sorcery" and on to quite positive glosses, such as "to heal." The taxonomy presented here is that of the Serbian area in which our research team worked, and reflects the categorical distinction informants made between these two species of verbal magic. One measure of the binary nature of that distinction is the fact that we were forbidden direct access to *vračanje*, whereas no such absolute taboos applied to *bajanje* (see below on qualifying as an audience for *bajanje*). For an anecdotal account of an instance of *vračanje*, cf. further Kerewsky-Halpern 1986: 49–50.

8. Douglas 1966. The convention of avoiding performance during the fertile years "thus places [the woman] within the ancient and widespread belief system in which females of childbearing age are defined as a special class, in possession of dual powers—the one sacred and related to the cyclical properties so similar to the mysteries of nature and the other polluting and negative. Both aspects are potentially dangerous, a fact articulated even by contemporary villagers" (Kerewsky-Halpern and Foley 1978a: 906). Supporting this segregation is the culture's view of the female as primarily part of a procreative unit, rather than as the more clearly defined individual she becomes with the onset of menopause.

9. On the *zadruga*, see Halpern and Kerewsky-Halpern 1972: 16–45.

10. But see Murko 1951: 189–205 for evidence of female epic singers encountered during his travels in the former Yugoslavia in 1930–32 and earlier.

tance—itself usually the bequest of another village and family—into a new context. From a diachronic point of view, the charm is much more mobile than the epic (or any of the other men's genres)[11] over time, and collection within even a single village will perforce produce a correspondingly greater variety of spells than of epics.

Perhaps unexpectedly, *bajanje* exists and seems to flourish entirely outside formal religious and political constraints. But although this form of folk curing relies on non-Christian (in many cases presumably pre-Christian) beliefs and dynamics, it figures forth a pattern observable throughout peasant culture in this area, a pattern whereby secular individuals appropriate certain religious activities to themselves, within a nominally Serbian Orthodox context. For example, the male head of the household conducts the most important observance on the recurring ritual calendar, the *slava* or feast-day of the lineage's patron saint,[12] while women are in charge of nonregularized forms of spiritual and ritual intervention, their responsibility being "to deal with magic and deviltry, to banish diseases caused by mysterious chthonic powers, to counteract the evil eye, to divine, to bewitch" (Kerewsky-Halpern and Foley 1978a: 905). In the terms we have been developing in this study, the register associated with the performance of *bajanje* does not intersect in any major way with formal, regularized religious observance.[13]

Likewise, official political pronouncements outlawing the practice of folk medicine have had no discernible effect on its conduct in the village. Our experience of the Šumadijan area has been that mandates from the state are honored almost wholly in the breach: landholding continues to operate according to an ancient system of inheritance within the *zadruga,* magical charms remain an irreplaceable item in the village medicinal kit,[14] and the two oxen that in some shared fields pulled the plow were—even before the recent demise of the Marxist-Leninist ideology—called "Capitalism" (the stronger, more heavily muscled one) and "Socialism" (the weaker, leaner one). Once again, we have to do here with traditional practices that because of their focused function and dedicated register have limited intersection with even the most pressing of contemporary issues.[15]

Prior collections of *bajanje* have been extremely limited, in fact fragmentary.

11. See "*Bajanje* within the Village Expressive Repertoire," below.

12. On the *slava,* see Halpern and Kerewsky-Halpern 1972: 110–14.

13. This does not mean that Christian figures, processes, and general symbolism cannot enter the charm tradition; as we shall see below, they certainly do. But such symbolism always enters subject to the preexisting and determinative rules of the genre—rules both compositional and significative.

14. Cf. Kerewsky-Halpern and Foley 1978a: 905: "The regional market town now provides most peasant needs, including the services of doctors and pharmacists. 'But,' says one man, 'for some things, what do doctors know? Injections, injections, and nothing! For some things, *treba da se baje* ("you have to cure with charms").'"

15. One might contrast other forms, such as the "partisan songs" that developed from epic during the Serbian resistance in World War II and proved flexible enough to accommodate pressing social and political concerns. A salient example for U.S. citizens in this regard is the heroic song entitled *Smrt u Dallasu* (*Death in Dallas*), chronicling the assassination of John F. Kennedy. Cf. Elizabeth Gunner's (1986) documentation of the use of the indigenous South African (Xhosa, Zulu) genre of "praise poetry" for political protest; also her more wide-ranging study of "genre boundary jumping" in South African popular song (1991).

Scholars have until recently viewed the charms either as a minor aspect of the general ethnographic background, and so have not treated them as verbal art, or as an interesting but primitive form of medicine, and thus a curiosity for practitioners of more modern, typically Western strategies for healing. In neither case has *bajanje* been studied for its own sake or on its own terms, and commentators have usually felt justified in presenting only brief snatches of charms—a few lines here or there—to reinforce a general observation about cultural activity.[16] On the other hand, the excellent and unique anthology of spells published in 1982 by the Serbian scholar Ljubinko Radenković, while containing some 630 poems with apparatus and commentary, suffers from another kind of shortcoming. In drawing his exemplars much more often from printed sources of uncertain ultimate provenance than from archives of material collected during fieldwork, and in presenting them in isolation outside their ethnopoetic context, Radenković has editorially transmuted the tradition of *bajanje* into an inventory of texts. Except by hearing the diminished resonance induced by the group of variants he includes, it is difficult to sense the word-power of these textualized avatars of verbal magic.[17]

Bajanje within the Village Expressive Repertoire

What informs the present study of *bajanje* as a form of word-power is the fieldwork undertaken by anthropologist Barbara Kerewsky-Halpern and me in and around the village of Orašac in central Serbia.[18] Our research team was extremely fortunate in being able to build on the Halperns' two decades of firsthand experience in this area, a period during which they conducted detailed ethnographic and demographic examinations of Serbian peasant culture.[19] In joining forces for the exploration of the repertoire of traditional oral expression shared by the people of this region, we hoped to accomplish two goals. First, from the perspective of studies in oral tradition, since the "Yugoslav analogy" developed by Parry and Lord rested entirely on the Moslem subgenre of epic, an important but by definition only a single and therefore partial basis for comparison, we hoped to pluralize the South Slavic "standard" for oral tradition(s) by sampling whatever nonepic genres presented themselves. Second, from the anthropological side, the Halperns found that their prior work, data-oriented as it was, regularly privileged the "content" of Serbian culture over its transmitting "form,"[20] not having sufficiently taken into account the traditional oral quality of the speech acts that they were committed to observing and explaining.

16. For a sample of this kind of scholarship, see, e.g., Kemp 1935, Knežević and Jovanović 1958, Pavlović 1921, A. Petrović 1939, and P. Petrović 1948.

17. Were there no possibility of consulting actual performances of *bajanje,* as there is no opportunity to reach beyond the textual records of ancient and medieval traditions, Radenković's approach would of course be fully justified as the only possible route. But, as mentioned above, *bajanje* remains a functional way of speaking in the village context, and can be studied directly.

18. For an early summary, see Foley 1982, to which should be added Kerewsky-Halpern 1985, 1986; comparison with Old English charms is the subject of Foley 1980a. Our joint fieldwork was funded in part by the National Endowment for the Humanities.

19. See esp. Halpern 1967 and Halpern and Kerewsky-Halpern 1972.

It was thus a shared concern with the determinative factor of social context that constituted the bridge between these two goals—to pluralize the model and in effect to consider the performance arena and register associated with the various speech acts. Only if the communication were understood as embedded in its situational matrix, we agreed, could it be understood as part of the repertoire of ways of speaking; only if one considered fully the expectations associated with the medium could the message be faithfully received.

Our joint research uncovered several traditional oral genres, some of them unreported or not well known, but very little in the way of extended narrative poetry, which in this region would be the shorter, Christian variety of epic.[21] The Halperns had recorded a version of the *Udovica Jana* (*Widow Jana*) narrative some years earlier, but by 1975 there were few older men left who claimed or were reputed to be able to sing to the *gusle*, and fewer still who were actually willing to do so.[22] One man who did perform for us, for instance, proudly announced that he had learned a particular song from a *pjesmarica* ("songbook"). When we asked to see the published source, he produced a well-worn pamphlet entitled *Borba Jugoslavenskih Partizana* (*The Battle of the Yugoslav Partisans*) that he had laboriously pored over and crudely marked, indicating deletions and the like. Nonetheless, comparison of his acoustically recorded performance to the text revealed that the integrity of the register had superseded his avowed fidelity to the printed source: the actual version he sang followed the songbook only occasionally and loosely.[23]

In compensation, as it were, a number of nonepic genres were still flourishing, even as incipient literacy was becoming established in the village.[24] But, as we have seen in chapter 3, reliance on traditional oral expression is a function not

20. Cf. Bakker 1993, who emphasizes the special inappropriateness of the Western dichotomy of form and content for works of verbal art in oral tradition.

21. See n. 6 above.

22. During a visit to one household, in which we had been told there was an older man who could still sing the epic songs, we asked the seventy-year-old patriarch himself whether he was willing to perform. He demurred, while his son, approximately twenty-five years younger and much more "modern" in his preferences, swaggered forth to show us how it was done. He played a few lines, apparently from rote memory, and then rather sheepishly relinquished the *gusle*, unable to go any further. At that point his father took over and performed a Christian song from start to finish. While this episode was unique in its particulars, we encountered many instances of older men who could perform the epic songs but who in effect had lost their audiences. In this region, where the Christian tradition prevailed, it was the family setting, or more rarely events such as weddings, that once provided such an audience; with the younger family members' loss of interest, the creation of what I have called the "performance arena" became less and less possible. Not merely the onset of literacy, then, but much more tellingly the impossibility of situating the act in its enabling context, has proved the principal cause of the epic tradition's demise in this area.

23. This interstitial case deserves more detailed attention than can be devoted here, but we may remark in general that the intercession of a text—the songbook—has in this instance not deflected the continuity of the performance tradition in any determinative fashion. Cf. Lord 1986b, which studies three specific cases of the encounter between oral tradition and the world of literacy and print in the former Yugoslavia.

24. In the most general terms, people aged forty-five to fifty and over in this particular region had at most four grades of schooling; some of them were thus marginally literate, while many were unable to read or write. Below age forty the number of years in school increased, and many more people were functionally literate.

of the mere existence or availability of literacy, but of the specific, socially defined uses to which it is put. Many people could read and write well enough to communicate with their children working as *Gastarbeiter* in Switzerland or Germany, but they would never consider employing that communicative technology for the many forms of expression that remained, in effect, traditional oral registers. To turn to the imported and irrelevant technology for such needs would be to destroy the sociolinguistically constituted performance arena, and thus to disable the special kind of communicative economy it fosters.

Among the genres we encountered was the *metrical genealogy,* a digest of a given lineage's family tree "kept" and performed by older men in the ten-syllable line of the epic.[25] This multigenerational history customarily involved in excess of ten generations and a total of more than 100 individuals, and essentially documented the entire lineage from its founding namesake ("Stojan" for the Stojanović clan, e.g.) to the present day of the speaker. Another type, or collection of types, was what the nineteenth-century ethnographer Vuk Karadžić called the *women's* or *lyric song,* in order to distinguish it from the (men's) epic narrative.[26] Like the other women's forms, the various species of lyric were composed in symmetrical octosyllables (4–4); mostly love songs, they were not seldom sung in unison or associated with particular events, such as weddings. Women also bore the responsibility for promoting familial and community healing following the death of a loved one. These *funeral laments* represented another form of traditional word-power, with the closest female relative returning to the graveyard at least monthly to recompose her mourning chant according to the rules of this particular genre.[27]

In addition to these genres, we also found evidence of traditional oral forms that could be labeled *folktale* (prose narrative with occasionally interspersed poetic lines, told by men), *recipe* (a women's speech act, apparently only sparsely distributed), and not least what we chose to call *poetic speech.* This last category designates the tendency for certain informants, chiefly older men, to shift register from the unmarked conversational standard to the poetic (epic) idiom.[28] In what amounted in Hymes's terms to a "breakthrough into performance," they would summon this other register for a very brief or a somewhat longer utterance, ranging from a single phrase to a quasi-historical account that required a few minutes in the telling, and then would shift back to the unmarked standard. Perhaps the best examples of this expressive trait came from Milutin Matijašević, a farmer and epic singer from the nearby village of Velika Ivanča, who not only enumerated his World War I battalion in decasyllables, but offered the ensuing observation on having his photograph taken for the first time:

25. For a full discussion of the metrical genealogy, called *istorija* ("history") by native informants, see Kerewsky-Halpern 1981a.

26. See esp. Lord and Bartók 1951 and Coote 1977, 1992.

27. The laments are called *tužbalice* by native informants; see further Kerewsky-Halpern 1981b. Cf. the women's subgenre of lament in the ancient Greek *Iliad* (Foley 1991: 168–74).

28. One can glimpse the same occasional modulation in the Parry-Lord conversations with epic singers; see the account of Halil Bajgorić's telling of his own "personal story" (Foley 1990a: 45).

Ja od Boga imam dobrog dara,
Evo mene mojega slikara;
Kogod 'oće, ko me lepo čuje,
On mene lepo nek' slikuje.

Yes, from God I have a fine gift,
Here comes my photographer;
Whoever wishes, whoever hears me well,
Let him take my picture well.

Milutin was in fact using the resources of the epic register to compose this little quatrain; we can track counterparts to its phraseology in the epic songs he sang, and all of the involved lines follow traditional rules.[29] But, more important, he made the choice of the performance idiom to frame his reaction to the picture-taking, and was fluent enough in this dedicated register to modify it to serve a unique purpose, doubtless a purpose for which he had never employed it before.[30] Why did Milutin shift communicative channels at this point during our visit with him? It would be dangerous to pronounce an answer with certainty and without qualification, but we may observe that expressing himself through this augmented code places the event within the performance arena of epic, divorced from the mundane activities of daily life, in short in a context in which *guslari* are honored members of the community (as they seldom are anymore) and in which heroic achievement and permanence of reputation are the rule. This seems an entirely appropriate arena for confronting and discussing this unquestionably unique—but now also traditionally situated—act of photography.

Before turning to the performance arena associated with the healing charms, it may be well to say a few words about the field methods we employed, particularly because this dimension of the investigation speaks directly to how "breakthroughs into performance" are to be understood. Because the fieldwork was a joint venture undertaken by an anthropologist with extensive training in linguistics and a "literary folklorist" trained in comparative oral traditions, it reflected an array of concerns. The anthropologist, Barbara Kerewsky-Halpern, brought to the project a well-honed sensitivity to social context, the more so since she was working in an area and with a group of informants she had known for more than twenty years. Not only did we strive to record and interpret performance events in their originative contexts, but because of the Halperns' prior experience in this area we were able to gain admission to certain circles and events, such as the performance of *bajanje,* which otherwise would have been denied to us as outsiders. Complementing this ease of entry was the

29. On traditional rules for South Slavic decasyllabic phraseology, see Foley 1990a: chap. 5. In brief, these lines follow the principles of right justification and word-type localization that underlie the formation and maintenance of traditional diction as a whole. The relatively unusual rhymed couplet structure of Milutin's four lines is a measure of his virtuosity as well as another manifestation of right justification.

30. Or so we suspected during the performance and initial interview; Milutin confirmed our suspicion in later conversation.

diachronic, evolutionary perspective that extended experience in a single region can bring: over more than two decades the Halperns had witnessed processual changes in all aspects of village life (and in themselves as well),[31] and the local repertoire of oral traditions was no exception.

Paired with the anthropologist's concern for understanding verbal art as socially situated was the literary folklorist's commitment to participant observation and subsequent analysis on a number of levels. Investigations by Parry and Lord and by numerous others had convinced me of the importance of observing from within, with as little deflection as possible, that is, of minimizing the "uncertainty principle" Tedlock describes in another of its manifestations.[32] One of the ways to approach this goal was to pluralize the experience: for this reason we visited each informant time and again, holding the controllable variables constant as well as we could and reexperiencing the reenacted event as many times as was practicable. Subsequent analysis could then address not one but a multitude of witnesses, in effect restoring multiformity to the performance event instead of insisting on what amounted to the single, privileged, textual transcription of a once-living reality.[33] Such analysis could also proceed on paralinguistic and nonlinguistic levels, as we shall see below, rather than being limited strictly to whatever phraseological tracks Proteus had left behind him.

By applying this multidisciplinary program for fieldwork to what we expected to be a full repertoire of traditional oral forms, and by confronting the experience (and later analysis) on its own tradition-dependent and genre-dependent terms, we hoped to better understand the expressive strategies employed by Serbian villagers in the course of daily life as well as on special occasions. And by paying full attention to what we as observers brought to the experience and perception of the events we attended, we hoped to calibrate our re-creation according to the tenets of what has been called "reciprocal ethnography."[34] What we were after, it is fair to say in summary, was a realistic perspective on word-power.

The Performance Arena of Charms

As we began during exploration of other genres to hear more and more about the existence and efficacy of *bajanje* or magical charms, the possibility of recording and learning about this largely unstudied speech act presented itself. There were of course many barriers to successfully doing so, some real and, as it turned out, some imagined.

Before actually starting to seek informants who were reputed to be *bajalice*

31. See, e.g., Halpern and Kerewsky-Halpern 1972: 1–3.
32. 1990: 139f. The emphasis here is on "minimizing"; the nature of such uncertainty is that it can never be entirely eliminated from a physical or linguistic observation.
33. Cf. the editorial strategy of employing a computerized text-processor to avoid privileging any single version of a work of verbal art (e.g., Foley 1984).
34. On "reflexive ethnography," see esp. Ruby 1982 and Clifford and Marcus 1986.

("conjurers"), we envisioned what proved a rather romanticized figure and process: an older and extremely mysterious woman, not unlike a fairytale hag or crone, who plied her liminal trade strictly behind closed doors, employing all manner of ritual objects and in general operating well away from polite village society and its central concerns. We anticipated all aspects of the conjuring procedure to be marginal, with the patient daring the threateningly eccentric encounter only for the chance of being cured. We assumed that the entire charm tradition occupied only a dark and forbidding corner of the cultural repertoire, and that people's initial reticence to talk much about it stemmed primarily from their uncertain relationship to an unsettling custom within their society.

It is now instructive to counter this preconception with the actual experience, and to remark explicitly that the "Balkan crone" image had reality only as an external dimension of a facsimile experience—our own personal performance arena.[35] For we were soon surprised to learn that *bajanje* is regularly performed with third parties present, in the midst of doing other things such as household chores, and even in public. The women who know how to use the charms are perfectly pleasant, grandmotherly people who not seldom intone the spells with grandchildren sitting nearby or in their laps, and with ritual objects only rarely employed as part of the conjuring process. Everybody in the village knows about *bajanje,* and most adults have frequently sought out specialists to cure one or another malady, from skin disease to impotence to a dry cow. *Bajalice* are paid, just as one would pay for any service in the village—that is, usually in kind—and there is no more shame or uncertainty involved with securing this kind of aid than there would be with engaging any available and culturally approved service. In its external appearance, the performance arena associated with *bajanje* erects few barriers to those who wish to enter.

This does not mean, however, that entry is automatic or necessarily even easy to gain. Beyond the quotidian fact of reimbursement for services rendered looms the question of admissibility of outsiders. Barbara Kerewsky-Halpern was straightforwardly told that she was eligible to hear and record these charms because her position as mother of two daughters of marriageable age had made her what amounted to an honorary *baba* ("granny"), a person who according to the scheme of fertility and charm transmission—not to mention her long residence and synthetic kinship connections in the village—now qualified as an approved recipient of these valuable gifts. Informants were discriminating, it is

---

35. This false expectation resembles the instance described earlier (chap. 1, n. 59) wherein students conditioned to "dramatic" oral presentations found the repetitive, "undramatic" melodic line of the *guslar*'s performance extremely puzzling in its apparent lack of expressiveness (on this little-studied area, see Herzog 1951, *SCHS* I: 435–67, and Bynum 1979). A similar situation arose some years ago when at a conference in Boston the late Albert Lord was confronted with what seemed at first blush a reasonable question from a member of the audience attending his paper. "Professor Lord," the well-meaning fellow asked, "does the singer gesture meaningfully with his hands as he delivers the epic?" "No," Albert replied carefully, "he's playing the *gusle,* you know." Both the students in the first example and the audience member at the conference had constructed their own performance arenas, based on what they knew of verbal art in their own and other cultures, and in the process had simply erased the possibility of other channels for expressiveness.

now apparent, between the use of healing charms in practice, in which case no bestowal occurs, and their transmission to another person, in this instance via the tape recorder. Only because Barbara qualified on socially approved grounds were we permitted to receive *bajanje*.[36]

Apart from the external features of the ceremony, which will be further addressed as part of the discussion of register below, it should be noted that to enlist a *bajalica*'s aid very clearly meant to enter the performance arena. In that recurrent and highly charged setting, and only there, was the conjurer understood to be able to intervene with the imbalance of natural forces that had produced the anomaly in her patient, and to restore the cosmic status quo and thereby relieve the client of his or her symptoms. The process seemed to work in much the same way when the afflicted party was an animal demonstrating some physical malady.[37] For our purposes, and specifically from the point of view of word-power, entry into the performance arena of *bajanje* entails the suspension of everyday discourse in favor of what Bauman has called "situated behavior" and "a transformation of the basic . . . referential uses of language" (1977: 9). It is also the locus where, in terms of Immanent Art, the nominal features of this situated behavior give way to their metonymically implied meanings, in sum their traditional referentiality, and finally where, in terms of Ethnopoetics, the *bajalica* and her patient utilize a marked and differentiated way of speaking to reach a well-defined and socially approved goal. Let us now examine the medium through which they accomplish this specialized communication.

The Charm Register

Each register, each way of speaking, we have argued in earlier chapters, enables a narrowly focused and greatly amplified communicative exchange precisely by virtue of its limited scope. Because of the constraints that the performance tradition has placed on this dedicated medium, constraints that from the perspective of relatively unmarked and unspecialized discourse might seem inhibiting and counterproductive, such a register can support a unique level of expressive economy. A few words, a melodic phrase, a sequence of gestures can summon enormous meaning, as word-power effectively takes advantage of the medium's limitations to convey information and experience in a densely packed code.

One would look far and wide for a register more dedicated, and correspondingly

---

36. Note that our claim to be interested in the charms *kao poezija* ("as poetry") effectively fell on deaf ears. These spells had value for their bearers only as curative rituals passed down in the female line and brought to marriage as a dowry. The synthetic kinship (cf. Foley 1992) that the Halperns enjoyed with people in Orašac, a history of relations that prominently included godparenthood (*kumstvo*), an extremely important institution in Serbian culture, acted as a background for the intercultural transaction. My presence as a younger male was presumably overlooked because of the combination of gender impertinence and licensing by association with the new *baba*.

37. See the discussion of "Against Snakebite" below.

more superficially terse yet metonymically rich, than that associated with *bajanje*. In comparison to the broad expanse of the epic, or even the more modest range of the lyric song, the words and actions that constitute the Serbian charm are remarkably few.[38] In turn, this extremely focused and dedicated mode can prove difficult to decipher, even when the performance context has been observed and in some fashion preserved. Because each expressive integer naturally implies so much, and thus because nominal, denotative meanings prove so effervescent in and of themselves, the problem of entering the performance arena—and specifically of construing the register—can prove extremely challenging.

In attempting an incipient fluency in this way of speaking, then, it seems especially important to cast our interpretive net as widely as possible, seeking as many different kinds of performance features as we can and then evaluating their specialized valences. To illustrate, let us start not with a string of (sounded and heard) words reduced to the silence of a textual format, but with what Tedlock has shown the ritual gesture of text-making to leave behind and Bauman has established as one of his keys to performance—namely, paralinguistic features.

Unlike the epic, in which lines composed in a much different language variety are intoned in a comparatively slow, heavily stylized manner that often includes a melodic line and instrumental accompaniment,[39] *bajanje* is spoken very softly, sotto voce, and extraordinarily rapidly without vocal or instrumental melody. Typically the conjurer leans over and whispers the charm into the patient's ear; in this scenario the spell is not audible to anyone other than the two of them. Also very much a part of the articulatory profile in the longer charms is a strong tendency to pause briefly between what are, as we shall see below, constituent sense units of the charm; these pauses are predictable and traditional aspects of performance.[40] Rarely the *bajalica* might introduce a ritual object, such as a knife (for cutting out the disease), a piece of silver (symbolizing the hoped-for state of purity), or a burning ember on a coal scuttle (for burning out the infection), but these items would best be considered optional material features of the register. The communicative emphasis is first and foremost on the sounded and heard *words*—their actual utterance—as the source of the charm's magical power,[41] which depends as much on the paralinguistic features of whispering, extremely rapid articulation, and regular (if momentary) pauses as on any other aspect of the performance event.

Within this articulative mode, a number of linguistic features reenforce the

38. Cf. the limited but richly associative repertoire of expressive integers used in traditional pictorial media, as discussed in Foley 1991: 48–53.

39. See n. 35. The point here is that the two registers are dramatically different in their linguistic, paralinguistic, and nonlinguistic features. Nonetheless, the basic dynamics of signification—entry of a performance arena and projection of meaning according to a traditional contract—are largely the same.

40. Cf. Tedlock (e.g., 1972a, 1977) on pauses; note that the pauses in the performance of *bajanje* constitute an institutionalized, traditional feature, not a momentary, variable aspect of the communication (cf. chap. 1 above).

41. The Indo-European force of the root *2bha-*, which underlies Serbo-Croatian *bajati* ("to charm, enchant"), is, according to Pokorny (1959/1969, I: 428), *sprechen*.

marked quality of the *bajanje* register as a medium with a single, well-defined social function and therefore with a unique kind of word-power. Starting with the more expectable, we may note that charms utilize the "women's prosody" in a Serbian village, that is, the symmetrical octosyllable (4–4) as opposed to the asymmetrical decasyllable (4–6) typical of the men's genres.[42] Along with this level of regularity, and best understood as in symbiosis with it, is a patterned phraseology, a recurrent diction. To call this patterning formulaic, however, could well be more misleading than helpful. To put the matter most straightforwardly, the charm phraseology operates according to a different set of traditional rules from that of the epic.[43] This is not to say that it is more or less stable or variable, but simply to point out that it is different in shape and dynamics, as would be predicted by the comparative criterion of genre-dependence. What is more, this diction is in fact different enough from that of the decasyllabic epic, long the sole model of traditional phraseology in South Slavic and by comparative extension much more widely, that it proves more accurate to avoid the assumptions associated with the label "formulaic" and to examine what patterning actually exists in this genre, as will be done below.

In addition to the octosyllabic prosody and the diction with which it is in symbiosis, we may denominate the feature of *frames* as a defining aspect of the charm register. These strophe-like units, from two to twelve lines in our collected samples,[44] act not unlike themes or typical scenes in narrative genres: that is, they are integral clusters with semi-independent lives of their own, units that are structured at least by idea-pattern and often by acoustic or phraseological networks as well. They differ from such typical scenes in the same way that charm differs from epic—*bajanje* foregrounds lyric, fleeting, intense moments, in place of the more expansive, detailed, broadly representational style associated with narrative forms. Thus a frame can, for example, simply list the color-coded attributes of the otherworldly helper whom the conjurer summons to assist in the curative process invoked by the "Nine Winds" spell:[45]

> Otud ide crveni konj,
> crveni čovek, crvena usta,
> crvene ruke, crvene noge,
> crvena griva, crvene kopite.

---

42. For a comparative view of the octosyllable, decasyllable, and related meters, see Jakobson 1952; for a recent analysis of the epic decasyllable with special reference to formulaic phraseology, see Foley 1990a: 85–106. As will be discussed below, Serbian *bajanje* represents a symbiosis of the octosyllabic women's meter and the particular array of linguistic strategies that help to make up the phraseological dimension of the register; because these strategies frequently enough override the eight-syllable constraint (as a consequence of the substitution system for curing various related diseases, for example, and also of the unaccompanied, extremely rapid, solo performance), "the meter" of the charms is a less dependable abstraction than "the meter" of the epic.

43. See n. 74 below.

44. This merely designates what our fieldwork uncovered as an empirical measurement; there seems to be no inherent reason why they could not be somewhat longer. See below for further discussion.

45. This frame, which we have named *horse and rider*, opens both versions of the charm examined below ("A Performance in Context"); for more on the conjurer and the event, see that section.

> Out of there comes the red horse,
> red man, red mouth,
> red arms, red legs,
> red mane, red hooves.

Or a more generic frame, useful both in other charms and at various junctures within a single given charm, can describe a therapeutic arrival, with the actual arriving agent left unspecified:

> Kako dodje, tako stiže;
> Ovu boljku odmah diže.
>
> As he comes, so he approaches;
> He lifts out the disease immediately.

More examples of frames will be given below when two entire charm performances are scored for reperformance, but suffice it to say at this point that this keying feature acts as a kind of nonnarrative theme, a lyric cluster with a traditional structure and, as we shall see, a traditional referent.

Other characteristics of the *bajanje* register include the frequent occurrence of archaisms. A short passage from another healing spell recorded in Orašac will illustrate some of the involved phraseology. Speaking of the "other world" that is the natural locus of disease and the place to which she seeks to return the intrusive malaise, the conjurer begins as follows:

> Otud ide aloviti,
> Aloviti, viloviti,
> Orloviti, šaroviti, . . .
>
> Out of there comes *aloviti*, etc.

I have left the sequence of rhyming items untranslated for two reasons. First, one looks in vain for dictionary definitions of these words that as a group make even minimal sense in this context: *(v)alovit* may denote "wavy" or "hot-tempered, powerful," *vilovit* "lively" or "magical," *orlovit* "eaglelike" and thus "heroic," while *šarovit* is quite clearly "striped" or "multicolored."[46] Applied to the nine incursive wind-borne diseases, these archaic terms—long vanished from "standard" village speech (if indeed ever present in that larger, relatively unmarked register) and apparently never a part of the "standard" urban or literary languages—seem to name various attributes of infections that are also literally

---

46. Glosses from Benson 1984, Stevanović et al. 1967 (my English translations here and below). On *aloviti*, cf. *SAN*, which defines the adjective as "(in folk belief) having the supernatural characteristics of a dragon"; on *viloviti* cf. Karadžić 1852, which renders it as *lymphaticus* ("mad, frantic"), and *SAN*, which gives an etymological reading: "having supernatural features or traits that may be attributed to vilas [semi-divine nymphs] or various other supernatural beings." It is tempting to see *aloviti* and *viloviti* as offering a glimpse of a mythos associated with the "other world," the place where, as we learn in other charms from the Šumadijan region, "the rooster doesn't crow, the sheep don't bleat," and various other natural phenomena are suspended (while their *un*natural opposites reign supreme); on this point see the discussion of the "Nine Winds" below.

"winds" (*vetrovi*), but there is hardly enough information in their collective lexical yield to allow construal of the folk epidemiology that presumably lies behind and comprehends them.

The second reason that I have left these puzzling adjectives untranslated is that none of the informants understood their underlying lexical matrix either. In fact, when questioned about the meaning of various of the words, they all professed complete ignorance of the meaning of *aloviti* and *viloviti;* they were able to relate *orloviti* to its etymon *orao* ("eagle") and *šaroviti* to the common word *šaren* ("variegated," "striped"),[47] but no overall picture of what was happening was available to any of them. Nonetheless, they used the sequence of *-oviti* terms quite regularly, with expectable variation from one performance to the next, and appeared to feel that the series of syllables they encoded was a crucially important part of the curative ritual. Whatever their designation outside the moment of performance, these archaisms served an important keying function within the *bajanje* register.

Alongside terms whose nominal meaning had over the passage of time become indistinct existed "new" words, ostensibly fashioned exclusively for this way of speaking.[48] Examples of such words, which appear in the libretto given below, include the names for three of the otherworldly helpers the *bajalica* calls to her aid: Ugimir, Stanimir, and Persa. Ugimir is instructed to "kill" (*ugini*) the disease and Stanimir to "halt" (*stani*) it; the result of their heroic accomplishments will be the patient's *mir* ("peace, calm"). The third agent, Persa, whose differently configured name represents an accommodation to the problem posed by a four-syllable combination of "stop" (*prestani*) plus *mir,* serves the same acoustically iconic function as his fellows, first halting the disease's progress and then (by implication) restoring the patient's peace. Unlike the archaisms, which probably had some lexical content outside the charm register at an earlier time, these neologisms seem to be creations of the genre, direct and dedicated manifestations of its word-power.

Both types of expressive integers, however, and even the lexically opaque "words" that constitute so-called "gibberish" charms in Serbian and Old English,[49] are but a special case of metonymy, the root dynamic of signification in this and other traditional oral genres. As such integers stray further and further from the standard, unmarked register, they reveal without lexical distraction the truly arbitrary relationship of sign to its signification, and at the same time embody a semantically unencumbered species of coding in which the concrete

---

47. The nominal nature of *šarovit* as an epithet is again illustrated in the very common formula *knjiga šarovita,* which appears frequently in both Moslem and Christian South Slavic epic (cf. Foley 1990a: 180–81). This phrase literally means "variegated paper, letter," but it metonymically signifies the kind of epistle sent by one important personage to another in order to convey a message of some significance (summons to war, invitation to a wedding, intelligence about the enemy, and so on).

48. It is well to note that archaic and "new" words in this register may not be distinguishable in all cases, and that beyond mere typology or etymology the important point is that both summon meaning in the same way—not via the conventional lexicon but by register-specific metonymy.

49. On "gibberish" or "nonsense" charms in these two traditions, see Foley 1980a: 81–82 and below, n. 76.

integer (now "nonsense" or "gibberish") can stand for a complex and richly nuanced traditional idea under the aegis of the performance event. With these specialized dimensions of word-power in mind, let us now bring what we have discovered about performance arena and register into the context of an actual performance.

A Performance in Context

After becoming aware of the prevalence of *bajanje* in the village of Orašac and in the general region of Šumadija, we began to query informants about who were the best, most frequently consulted *bajalice* and to visit those women who were thus recommended. Just as with any other genre in the traditional oral repertoire, there were some who enjoyed fine reputations for the variety and efficacy of their cures and some who were more limited in their practice of the healing arts. We also found that many of the conjurers included massage and other nonverbal therapies (e.g., remedies for post-childbirth discomfort) in the category we translated somewhat narrowly as "charms," but we had decided to focus on the verbal arts and so concentrated virtually exclusively on their spoken crafts.[50]

The most accomplished and respected practitioner of healing arts in the area was Desanka Matijašević, a woman of about fifty-five who had married into the most affluent extended family (*zadruga*) in Orašac.[51] Desanka was particularly well recognized in this region as a specialist in dealing with diseases called the "nine winds." Villagers perceive these illnesses as both borne on and caused by the powers of the wind (*vetar*), which can blow them from their right and proper place in the "other world" to a destabilizing and threatening presence in the world we know. Although some of the terms used in the classification of winds are, as we have seen above, obsolete in the standard discourse register, certain of the indexing labels can be translated to the contemporary vocabulary: for example, after consultation with physicians we were able to determine that villagers call erysipelas the "red wind," eczema the "white wind," jaundice the "yellow wind," and anthrax the "black wind."

When we stopped by the family household for the first time, Desanka was pasturing pigs. Following traditions of Serbian peasant hospitality, she ushered us inside the whitewashed mud-brick house and offered ritual servings of *slatko* (sweet preserves), mineral water, homemade brandy, and Turkish coffee.[52] Even-

---

50. This was but one area where the "fit" between, in Dan Ben-Amos's terms (1969), "ethnic" and "analytic" perspectives was less than exact. Emphasis on the outsider's notion of a coherent body of material must be made on the grounds of analytical convenience, and in the present case this emphasis made possible direct comparison with other genres in the traditional oral repertoire as well as with other charm traditions, such as the Old English, which is known only via manuscript preservation (cf. Foley 1980a, 1981).

51. Pseudonyms are employed throughout this account of *bajanje* in the Orašac area.

52. This custom has been preserved in the urban environment among many older people, even those whose families have been out of the village for generations. There is evidence, however, that it is rapidly dying out among urbanites fifty years of age and under.

tually, reassured by the presence of her husband, who had come in during a midday break from working in an adjacent hayfield, she raced through—or so we thought at the time—a recitation of the charm to dispel the "red wind" (*crveni vetar*). When she hesitated at one point in this first performance, apparently because of the unusual nature of the audience and its interests, her seven-year-old grandson Marko prompted her.[53] The resultant uneven pace provided a logical reason to ask Desanka to repeat the *basma*. A third version was elicited by asking for clarification of a certain passage; in order to retrieve that small section, she had to go back and start from the beginning.[54] This third version (A3) is the first of the two presented below.

After making a preliminary analysis of these three performances, and having interviewed other *bajalice,* we returned to Desanka eight days later, explaining that some of the archaic language was unfamiliar to us. During the discussion that ensued, we came to understand better the folk interpretations of the role of the conjurer as mediator, attitudes toward psychic healing, notions of many different wind-borne diseases, and the dynamics of transmission and performance. This session also produced five additional versions of the "Nine Winds," the first of which (B1) serves as the second example below. In the course of this latter visit, Desanka's daughter-in-law, Nada, was present most of the time. Toward the end of the interview she suggested fetching her mother-in-law's "equipment" (*pribor*), so that they could enact what the younger woman saw as a "real" cure, with Nada assuming the role of the afflicted person and kneeling before the conjurer. The result was an irregular version of the charm, a situation recognized by Desanka herself, preoccupied as she was with the uncharacteristic demonstration of the rarely used conjuring tools and conscious of enunciating at the same time for the tape recorder.[55] In a memorable observation, she explained that she was not accustomed to thinking of the words: "Što, ovaj, upamtim, ja upamtim; / Što ne upamtim, ja sasnim noći" ("Well, what I remember, I remember; / What I don't remember I dream at night").

Here, then, are libretti for her two performances, lineated according to rhythmic and syntactic structures. Multilinear frame units, paralinguistically marked

---

53. This small vignette fairly illustrates the disparity between our expected performance arena and what actually occurred. As a boy, Marko was decidedly not the proper recipient of *bajanje*, but he had apparently picked up some part of the charm simply by being present when his grandmother healed her clients. In many ways *bajanje* is a surprisingly public performance, and, as discussed below, its efficacy—its word-power—depends on the recognized status of the speaker, the invocation of a circumscribed performance arena, and fluency in the dedicated register.

54. Cf. the practice of epic *guslari,* who may stop their performance at any point for rest (Lord 1936), but customarily backtrack to the last traditional boundary upon resumption (Foley 1990a: 284–88).

55. It will be remembered that the *bajalica* customarily whispers the charm into the patient's ear. This need to speak somewhat more loudly and openly seemed the major articulatory discrepancy between Desanka's performances for the tape recorder and her customary practice; her speed of articulation was apparently about the same as usual.

in performance by intervals of from one-half to one second, are indicated by vertical (line) spaces and assigned letters to distinguish them.[56]

[Spoken sotto voce and very rapidly]

	Version A3 (7/31/75)	*Version B1* (8/7/75)
a	1. Otud ide crveni konj,	1. Otud ide crveni konj,
	2. Crveni čovek, crvena usta,	2. Crveni čovek, crvena usta,
	3. Crvene ruke, crvene noge,	3. Crvene ruke, crvene noge,
	4. Crvena griva, crvene kopite.	4. Crvena griva, crvene kopite.
b	5. Kako dodje, tako stiže,	5. Kako dodje, tako stiže,
	6. Ovu boljku odmah diže;	6. Ovu boljku odmah diže;
c	7. I odnose i prenose,	7. I odnose i prenose,
	8. Preko mora bez odmora—	8. Preko mora bez odmora—
d	9. Gde mačka ne mauće,	9. Gde mačka ne mauće,
	10. Gde svinjče ne guriće,	10. Gde svinjče ne guriće,
	11. Gde ovce ne bleje,	11. Gde ovce ne bleje,
	12. Gde koze ne vreće,	12. Gde koze ne vreće,
		13. Gde konj ne vrišti,
		14. Gde pile ne pišti,
		15. Gde pevac ne peva,
		16. Gde kokoška ne kakoće,
		17. Gde konj . . . pop ne dolazi,[57]
e	13. Gde pop ne dolazi,	18. Gde krst ne donosi,
	14. Gde krst ne donosi,	19. Da se kolač ne lomi,
	15. Da se kolač ne lomi,	20. Da se sveće ne pali.
	16. Da se sveće ne pali.	
f	17. Beži boljku u polje,	
	18. Beži boljku u more,	

56. For a digest of frame occurrence in our recordings of this charm, see Kerewsky-Halpern and Foley 1978a: 918–19. Interestingly, although lines and even whole frames from the following performances can be found in the anthology of *bajanje* published by Radenković (1982), no real parallels to the spell as a whole are included among the forty-one texts given under the headings of "Od crvenog vetra" ("For the Red Wind," nos. 89–109) or "Od vetra" ("For the Winds," nos. 110–29). Such loose resemblances mirror a similar set of "dialectal" relationships among epic performances from different regions (cf. Foley 1990a: chaps. 5 and 8). The idiolectal level of traditional variation is harder to generalize about, since as noted above, the charms involve complex intergenerational transmission from in-marrying grandmothers and mothers to out-marrying young girls and brides, a pattern that contrasts sharply with the lineage-centered and largely local transmission pattern of epic.

57. Desanka "misspoke" by initially saying *konj* ("horse"), and then "correcting" immediately to *pop* ("priest"). I have put quotation marks around "misspoke" and "correcting" to indicate that these pejorative terms are descriptive only of the surface of the charm performance, and that the "slip" actually helps us glimpse its underlying expressive logic. Note first that it is the horse that begins line 13, within a very similar traditional frame (*d*) and employing the same phraseological pattern, so that there is certainly sufficient precedent for its occurrence here. More important, however, line 13 begins the second four-line unit within the *animal* catalog—part II as it were; to the considerable extent that the "pattern number" for frames is four, it is inherently logical that Desanka should have turned to either line 9 or line 13 as an unintentional substitution for the beginning of the next four-line increment (part III). This evidence of quanta within the performance of charms is similar in compositional logic and function to epic singers' returning to traditional boundaries to restart a song, as well as to their large-scale "errors" in story-pattern being driven by "improper" recourse to alternate traditional units (on these two points, see n. 54 and Foley 1990a: chap. 10, respectively).

	19. Beži boljku pod kamen;	
	20. Tu ti mesta nema!	
g	21. Otud ide crvena krava,	21. Otud ide crvena krava,
	22. Crveno telo otelila,	22. Crveno tele otelila,
	23. Crveno mleko podojila.	23. Crveno mleko podojila.
h	24. Otud ide crvena kvočka,	24. Otud ide crvena kvočka,[58]
	25. Vode devet crvenih pilića,	
	26. Padoše na crveni bunjak,	25. Padoše na crveni bunjak,
	27. Pokupiše crveni crvići.	26. Pokupiše crveni crvići.
c	28. I odneše preko mora,	27. I odneše / preko mora / bez
	29. Preko mora bez odmora.	odmora.[59]
k		28. Deset, devet, osam, sedam,
		29. Šest, pet, čet'ri, tri, dva, jedan.
f	30. Idi . . . beži vetra u polje,[60]	
	31. Beži vetra u more,	
	32. Beži vetra;	
	33. Tu ti mesta nema!	
i	—(Ime) ostaje[61]	
	34. Lako kao pero,	
	35. Čisti kao srebro,	
	36. Blaži kao materno mleko.	
j	37. Otud ide Ugimir,	30. Otud ide Ugimir,
	38. Ugini boljku, ugini!	31. Ugini boljku, ugini!

58. By comparison with version A3, the next line of B1 seems simply to be missing, but in fact the *hen* frame (*h*) occurs twice in this form (and three times in its "fuller" form) over the eight recorded versions. More pertinent, we should also recall that there are both explicit and implicit aspects of an utterance made in performance, and that the transcribed text cannot by definition provide a fair measure of any single version's "completeness." For further discussion and examples of this phenomenon in the Moslem and Christian epics, see Foley 1991: 75–83, 111–15. Both the "instability" of the *hen* capsule and the strength of the pattern number of four (see n. 66 below) suggest the possibility that we are also "missing" a line in the *cow* capsule (*g*).

59. Line 27 of version B1 is actually a triplet of three half-lines, telescoped by the *bajalica;* cf. the terracing of *preko mora* in the corresponding lines (28–29) of version A3. Such foreshortening is a common enough compositional feature, especially in symmetrical meters such as the octosyllable (4/4), in which any one half-line is prosodically equivalent to any other. Telescoping does occur, but much more rarely, in the asymmetrical (4/6) epic decasyllable, as we observed with a singer in nearby Velika Ivanča, who in the heat of performance would characteristically omit the instrumental break between lines and fuse one decasyllable directly to the next. On the possibility that "extra half-lines" in Anglo-Saxon poetry may result from a similar process involving the (symmetrical) alliterative line, see Foley 1980b.

60. Another slip of the tongue, with Desanka substituting the verb "go" (*idi*) for the expected "banish" (*beži;* both imperative forms) and then immediately correcting. The slip may have been induced by the upcoming uses of the same verb (*ide*, present indicative) in the *peace* capsule starting at A3.line 37.

61. Here, in a frame that occurs in only four of her eight recorded performances, the conjurer names the afflicted party—"Let X remain"—and projects the cure's result in terms of common cultural symbols of purity. Because Desanka broke rhythm (and performance) in speaking "(Ime) ostaje," and because that phrase thus functions somewhat differently from those contiguous to it, I have chosen not to number it as a line of poetry.

39. Otud ide Stanimir,
40. Stani boljku, stani!
41. Otud ide Persa,
42. Prestani boljku, prestani!

32. Otud ide Stanimir,
33. Stani boljku, stani!
34. Otud ide Persa,
35. Prestani boljku, prestani!

k 43. Deset, devet, osam, sedam,
44. Šest, pet, čet'ri, tri, dva, jedan.

l 45. U kurjaka čet'ri noge, peti rep,
46. Od mog odgovora j' bio lek.

36. U kurjaka čet'ri noge, peti rep,
37. Od mog odgovora j' bio lek.

Translation

a 1. Out of there comes the red horse,
2. The red man, the red mouth,
3. The red arms, the red legs,
4. The red mane, the red hooves.

1. Out of there comes the red horse,
2. The red man, the red mouth,
3. The red arms, the red legs,
4. The red mane, the red hooves.

b 5. As he comes, so he approaches,
6. He lifts out the disease
   immediately;

5. As he comes, so he approaches,
6. He lifts out the disease
   immediately;

c 7. He carries it off and carries it
   away,
8. Across the sea without delay—

7. He carries it off and carries it
   away,
8. Across the sea without delay—

d 9. Where the cat doesn't meow,
10. Where the pig doesn't grunt,
11. Where the sheep don't bleat,
12. Where the goats don't low,

9. Where the cat doesn't meow,
10. Where the pig doesn't grunt,
11. Where the sheep don't bleat,
12. Where the goats don't low,
13. Where the horse doesn't neigh,
14. Where the chick doesn't peep,
15. Where the rooster doesn't crow,
16. Where the hen doesn't cackle,

e 13. Where the priest doesn't come,

14. Where the cross isn't borne,
15. So that ritual bread isn't broken,
16. So that candles aren't lit.

17. Where the horse . . . priest
   doesn't come,
18. Where the cross isn't borne,
19. So that ritual bread isn't broken,
20. So that candles aren't lit.

f 17. Banish the disease into the field,
18. Banish the disease into the sea,
19. Banish the disease under a stone;
20. You have no place here!

g 21. Out of there comes the red cow,
22. She gave birth to a red calf,
23. She nursed it with red milk.

21. Out of there comes the red cow,
22. She gave birth to a red calf,
23. She nursed it with red milk.

h 24. Out of there comes the red hen,
25. She leads nine red chicks,
26. She fell upon a red dung-heap,
27. She gathered up red worms.

24. Out of there comes the red hen,

25. She fell upon a red dung-heap,
26. She gathered up red worms.

c   28. And she carried it off across the   27. And she carried it off / across
           sea,   the sea / without delay.
       29. Across the sea without delay.

k   28. Ten, nine, eight, seven,
                                                               29. Six, five, four, three, two, one.

f   30. Go . . . banish the illness into
           the field,
       31. Banish the illness into the sea,
       32. Banish the illness;
       33. You have no place here!

i   —Let (Name) remain
       34. Light as a feather,
       35. Pure as silver,
       36. Mild as mother's milk.

j   37. Out of there comes Ugimir,   30. Out of there comes Ugimir,
       38. Kill the disease, kill it!   31. Kill the disease, kill it!
       39. Out of there comes Stanimir,   32. Out of there comes Stanimir,
       40. Halt the disease, halt it!   33. Halt the disease, halt it!
       41. Out of there comes Persa,   34. Out of there comes Persa,
       42. Stop the disease, stop it!   35. Stop the disease, stop it!

k   43. Ten, nine, eight, seven,
       44. Six, five, four, three, two, one.

l   45. Into the wolf's four legs, fifth the   36. Into the wolf's four legs, fifth the
           tail,   tail,
       46. Out of my speaking has come   37. Out of my speaking has come
           the cure.   the cure.

Performance Notes

One way to gloss these two performances—or at least to adumbrate what they signal through the register dedicated to *bajanje*—is to place their differences against the background of their similarities and thus to highlight what features, whether linguistic, paralinguistic, or nonlinguistic, appear most crucial to their word-power. As noted above, the charm tradition mandates certain paralinguistic features as constitutive of the way of speaking: whispering, extremely rapid articulation, regular pauses, and (less regularly) delivery of the utterance directly into the ear of the afflicted party. The "tools" displayed by Desanka's daughter-in-law, partly out of filial respect and partly out of an obvious wish to help the outsiders understand the special nature of the event, turn out to be quite optional; in actual practice, the *bajalice* of this region seem seldom if ever to employ them. Likewise, the patient assumes no particular posture relative to the conjurer, and may even be standing in a relatively crowded room while other conversations are going on.[62] What is absolutely requisite is that the charm be performed by a "licensed" practitioner, a post-menopausal "granny" known for her particular abilities and rewarded financially or in kind for her services.

Within this performance arena, which the *bajalica* and her patient create based on cultural negotiations embedded in tradition and instanced in the event, the utterance as delivered through the register is believed to have great impact on the wished-for realignment of the two worlds—the natural universe that we all know and the unnatural "other place" from which the disease has emanated and to which it must be returned. Both performances by Desanka begin with the *horse and rider* frame (*a*) described above, with this heroic figure being summoned from the other world to cross the border and assist the conjurer in the process of curing. Like other agents of change in the charm, his color—here red—identifies the particular skin disease and "wind" he is asked to help dispatch. This is the standard opening for this kind of verbal magic, and part of its force derives from its recurrent initial position. Lines 5–6 of the two versions, the *as/so* unit (*b*), constitute what might at first sight seem a much more mobile frame, being both less specific and half the size of *horse and rider,* but other performances show that that part of its illocutionary function derives from consistently occupying second position in the sequence, and in thus rounding off the summons of the initial agent.[63] The phraseological patterning of lines 7–8 (*carry, c*) varies, with internal repetition of morphs and in-line rhyme forming the phonological backbone of this ubiquitous frame,[64] whose content gives us a clearer idea of the cosmic geography by referring to a "sea" interposed between the two worlds.

With the series of "where" (*gde*) lines that make up the *animal* catalog (*d*), we encounter the first disparity between Desanka's two performances, although it is not so much a wholesale deviation as a difference in explicitness. The entire "Where X doesn't Y" sequence, with X being a domesticated animal and Y its predictable barnyard sound, provides the first real example of a Parry-Lord formulaic system, a phraseological pattern with two semantically linked substitutable slots. More important for understanding how word-power works in this genre, however, the series metonymically designates the otherness of the world from which disease has arisen, remarking in memorable fashion its diametrical and unnatural reversal of baseline, customary phenomena taken for granted in a Serbian village environment.[65] But whether the conjurer explicitly details the curious silence of all eight animals or leaves four of them implied by the event of performance and the referent of tradition is finally not the ultimate measure

---

62. One should not absolutely discount the possibility that the charm tradition in Nada's home region made more emphatic or even regular use of such ritual objects. The same should be observed about the kneeling posture she demonstrated. What we may be facing here is a dialectal difference manifesting itself in nonlinguistic aspects of the performance genre.

63. *As/so* occurs in no other position in any of the recorded versions.

64. Cf. A3.28–29, B1.27. The other six versions reveal that the *carry* frame can occur at different spots throughout the performance; three of these contain two instances each.

65. Cf. the same strategy operative in the proem (*pripjev*) to epic songs, where a series of comparisons underline how unnatural it is for a singer not to perform his song (see Foley 1991: 68–75).

of the charm's "completeness" or efficacy. It is rather a question of whether the irruption of magic created by verbal negotiation within the performance register is sufficient to the task of the cure. Desanka's quantum-based alternation between four and eight animals—never any other number—over the series of performances we recorded leaves little doubt that the force of the spell or *basma* is indexed metonymically, rather than literally (or textually) linked to a "complete" representation.[66]

Whatever the multiform of the *animal* frame, it leads regularly to the *liturgical* frame (*e*), to which it seems to be conjoined idiomatically.[67] Here the charm embodies and intensifies otherness by describing a world so religiously heterodox that a priest dares not visit, and therefore the central symbol of Orthodox Christianity, the cross, cannot be borne. Added to this reversal is the confutation of the *slava* ritual, the feast-day of a clan's patron saint, through denial of its central rituals: breaking the ceremonial loaf (*kolač;* the panspermia) and lighting the holy candles. Interestingly, then, the strangeness of the world that is the locus of the intrusive disease is portrayed negatively through two intrinsically dissimilar metonymic series that are nonetheless united by a single referential strategy: the organic functioning of the natural world and the religious functioning of the ritual event share the role of master calibrator in picturing the "otherness" that characterizes the origin of (and proper environment for) windborne illness. Word-power depends on the unquestioned centrality of these expectable and "normal" phenomena, and on the equally clear implications of their suspension.

The next four lines of version A3 constitute another frame, *banishment* (*f*), but this time a highly variable one that appears in only five of the eight performances we recorded, and then in different positions within the charm and in different forms.[68] It also occurs later in version A3, but not at all in B1. Not unlike certain narrative themes in the epic, then, it seems to have more of a life of its own than many other frames. The first three lines can be interpreted as three manifestations of the same formulaic system, but the closing expostulation, "Tu ti mesta nema!" ("You have no place here!"), proves the most stable of the frame's constituents even though it bears no phraseological relationship to its fellows.

More important than the *banishment* frame's flexibility and range of occurrence per se, however, is the fact that in version A3 it leads to and contrasts markedly with two other frames, each of them quite stable and highly focused

66. This variation implies what Hymes would call a "pattern number" (see chap. 1, n. 51 above), that is, a numerical structure or performance key that helps to characterize the register; in the case of frame structure in charms, that number seems to be four. This is not to say that all frames must be composed of four (or a multiple of four) lines; indeed, we have examples in the "Nine Winds" of other configurations, with two taking an especially prominent role. But it is to notice that four lines of roughly octosyllabic verse do form a relatively consistent vehicle for expression.

67. Primarily because there is no pause between these two catalogues in Desanka's performances, and also because they employ the same phraseological pattern and exhibit no significant break in sense, I have left no vertical space between them in the libretto.

68. Twice, in versions B4 and B5, the last two lines of this frame are "omitted"; the remaining variations are minor.

in both morphology and metonymic signification.[69] These two units, *cow* (*g*) and *hen* (*h*), both of which involve a domesticated and food-producing female animal mothering her young, are color-coded so that their expressive and curative force can be enlisted by the *bajalica* as part of the overall healing operation. In this way the mother cow and mother hen serve as confederates of the horse and rider, and also of the three named agents (Ugimir, Stanimir, and Persa) described above. Typical of the charm as a whole, and of other traditional oral genres as well, the *banishment, cow,* and *hen* frames demonstrate a morphological and significative spectrum: fluency in the register demands the ability to manipulate capsules of widely variant form and immanent meaning.

This observation on fluency presents an opportunity for an interim summary of frame and line features before continuing with a description of the rest of the charm register. At the most basic level, the octosyllabic line must be understood as an analytic approximation of one aspect of the symbiosis of prosody and phraseology. To take the simplest example of extremes allowed by this equilibrium, dispelling the red (*crveni*) wind involves a three-syllable substitution, while the cognate cure for jaundice (*žuti*) and most other skin diseases calls for a two-syllable increment. In the first frame, the *horse and rider,* the red wind spell thus mandates what some would label a hypermetrical or even unmetrical series of lines: "crveni konj," "crveni čovek," and so on are five-syllable hemistichs; line 1 thus measures nine, lines 2–3 ten each, and the fourth line eleven syllables. But such a characterization by supposed "norm" and departures from that norm, proceeding as it does from a bias that privileges the syllabic regularity associated with other genres and other media, misrepresents *bajanje*. Where sound is truly the primary engine of word-power, the sonorous recurrence of the color name must override the textual niceties of exact syllabicity. Even the Moslem epic, usually an accompanied genre that employs vocal and instrumental melodies as regulators of phraseology, allows for some syllabic variation;[70] charms, performed without melody or instrument and preternaturally quickly, are that much more likely to subordinate "our" measure of regularized meter to the inherent dynamics of the register.

At the next level of complexity, that same dynamics—at its core an art of sound-patterning—takes a number of forms in keying performance. One of them consists of echoing a touchstone morph,[71] such as the color word "red" in the *horse and rider* frame, throughout the frame or entire charm, and thereby indexing the cure by implied reference to the folk-epidemiological background.

69. On the "marker" role of frames such as *banishment,* cf. the function of *boundary lines* in epic, highly generic decasyllables such as "But you should have seen X" ("Pa da vidiš X"), whose metonymic force is more to provide limits and transitions than to contribute specifically to the ongoing narrative; see further Foley 1990a: 286–87, 295–96.

70. Cf. Foley 1990a: 85–94.

71. I here specifically avoid describing the process as one of "repetition," since the features of *horse and rider,* like other traditional oral integers, are more accurately understood as accruing traditional meaning by recurrence in performance. It is their indexing of traditional referentiality—rather than their linear "repetition"—that enables communicative economy. See further Foley 1991: 56–58 on repetition versus re-creation.

Another linguistic feature of the *basma* phraseology is the "Out of there comes" ("Otud ide") beginning to a number of lines and frames, a phrase not unlike "Once upon a time" in its keying function. In addition to its traditional reference to the other world, this rhetorical byte in the performance register signals incipience: each recurrence both begins anew and anaphorically relates what follows it to foregoing (and subsequent) capsules begun with the same verbal cue. In this way, the three named agents we are about to meet in the latter part of the charm—Ugimir, Stanimir, and Persa—are projected as confederates of the *bajalica,* as are the other helpers summoned to assist in banishing the disease and healing the patient.

Other features of the *bajanje* register include rhyme (both end-line and in-line), parataxis and parallelism, syntactic patterning, and various semantic patterns. Rhyme, already pointed out above, can occur as a result of either morphological (*stiže/diže,* "approaches"/"lifts out," 5–6) or homophonic (*mora/odmora,* "sea"/"delay," 8) pairings; in this respect word-power arises from the harmony of sound, largely independent of any semantic correlation between the words involved.[72] Parataxis manifests itself everywhere, from the generalities of line and half-line structure through the incremental nature of the *animal* catalog and on to the relationship among frames. Syntactic patterning of different kinds, some as formulaic as the animals and their sounds and some as unformulaic as the co-occurrence of near-synonyms in the same phrase (e.g., *odnose* and *prenose,* "carries it off" and "carries it away," 7), proliferates throughout the charm, lending a recursive character to the utterance and imaging a phenomenological control in the texture of the articulation. Semantic patterns also help bind together the *basma*'s active parts, causing frames to cohere (*horse and rider, cow,* or *chicken*), for example, or contributing to the integrity of a formulaic series (the *animal* catalog). The thrust of all these features is to convey via a dedicated way of speaking the word-power necessary to a successful cure. By negotiating within this specifically focused register, an idiomatic network of highly structured utterance that is directly and unambiguously constitutive of the desired cure, the *bajalica* has access to enormous word-power.

Beyond prosody and the various aspects of phraseology lies the performance unit of frame. Many of these capsules measure four (approximately) octosyllabic lines in length, or double that number,[73] but a few are either two or six lines long. More important than attempting to establish an absolute "standard" length, however, which on reflection must prove a textual preoccupation, is recognizing that frames have an internal logic, partly acoustic and linguistic and partly idea-based, that determines their wholeness and integrity. The *horse and rider,* for example, consists of a catalog of visual details, all calibrated for the particular illness, with the whole image being expressed through synecdoche of key parts. The *cow* and *chicken* strophes, treated in detail below, cohere primarily

---

72. Cf. the discussion below of the immanent force of the so-called "nonsense" or "gibberish" charms.

73. See n. 66 above.

through the nurturing paradigm they present in a miniature narrative, although many of the phonological and phraseological strategies discussed above also apply to their dynamics. The *reversed numbers* capsule (*k*), designed to reduce the disease to mathematical nothingness, has its own inevitable logic; for obvious reasons, it does not share other units' capacity for change within limits.

And just as frames vary in their modes of internal cohesion and stability over a series of performances, so they also vary one from the next in their localization within the charm and their attachment, if any, to other frames. The horse and rider always begin the "Nine Winds," and the animals and liturgical capsules always occur in succession, while many other frames—*as/so* (*b*), *carry* (*c*), *banishment* (*f*), and *reversed numbers* (*k*)—can occupy a number of different positions. This diversity in traditional linkages reflects idiosyncrasies within the *bajanje* register, and mirrors as well the diversity among phraseological and thematic patterns in Moslem epic, where all elements are decidedly neither created equal nor deployed with equivalent compositional latitude or metonymic meaning. As has been suggested for the epic, traditional rules for the composition of register underlie the products we glimpse in performances, and it is this set of compositional rules that both focuses and promotes variety in the expressive integers.[74] Under the aegis of such a process, a register becomes differentiated and stabilized as a situational variety of language, dedicated to fostering highly economical, even privileged communication within a given genre; within this necessarily flexible definition, the larger unit of the frame, as well as an array of microstructural features, exhibits the rule-governed free play of morphological variation.

In fact, the very next frame (*naming, i*) in version A3 encourages us to look beyond a static textual model for the morphology of elements and to ponder the multiformity that, without paradox, is at the heart of traditional oral expression and its singular word-power. Although we might imagine that the four-line sequence in which the patient is denominated by name would be among the most indispensable parts of the utterance, crucial to its therapeutic success, *naming* actually occurs in only four of the eight versions recorded in Orašac. Once again the event of performance and the referent of tradition "fill in" the perceived gap: with the utterance passing from conjurer to patient as a physical stream of sound in real time, and with both having entered the performance arena and subscribed to belief in the act of healing through this specialized register, identification of the individual by given name is not as pressing an issue as it would be under other, less ritualized circumstances. Likewise, the invocation

74. A thoroughgoing philological explanation of the traditional rules underlying the charm register is beyond the scope of the present exposition. Nonetheless, consider a few of the rule-governed processes that have been touched upon during this discussion: a symbiosis of prosody and phraseology (but with the symmetrical octosyllable rather than the asymmetrical epic decasyllable, and with more "departures" from metrical strictness than in the epic), various phonological patterns (again comparable to acoustic networks in epic, but in a greater variety), and the repertoire of frames (similar to themes or typical scenes in epic, but much shorter and nonnarrative to serve the dynamics of this genre). Cf. the discussion of traditional rules in ancient Greek, South Slavic, and Old English epic in Foley 1990a, esp. chaps. 3–9.

that this individual become—as a result of the charm—unburdened ("light as a feather"), unblemished ("pure as silver"), and innocent ("mild as mother's milk") appears not to be a sine qua non in the *bajalica*'s curing process.

The perspective offered by the *naming* capsule foregrounds a version of the more general question with which we began this section of the inquiry: What is absolutely requisite to a successful, that is, effective, performance of such a magical charm? We have seen that frames behave differently, some of them recurring with great regularity at particular spots in each version and others seemingly less important in the overall scheme of things, at least as evidenced by their inconsistent appearance or their relative ubiquitousness. As a first principle, it is well to remember that the textual notion of "completeness" is categorically impertinent to traditional oral genres, since the pars pro toto dynamic of metonymy is the primary source of meaning, and *bajanje* is certainly no exception to this scenario. Then too, the final judgment on adequacy of the utterance must be left to an audience trained to receive the charm according to the principles brought into play by performance arena and register, and non-members of the culture are of course disadvantaged in their ability to render such a verdict. What we can say, on the basis of the Receptionalist approach detailed earlier in this volume, is that, assuming that the eight recorded versions of the "Nine Winds" reflect in their morphology some idea of the comparative importance of individual frames, those units that recur with absolute regularity can be considered more crucial to fluent, and therefore efficacious, communication than those that occur only irregularly or in different configurations.[75] This does not mean that the less frequent frames are devoid of signification, acting solely as fillers; such an all-or-nothing model would amount to a reductive binary concept of immanent implication, based ultimately on a textual apprehension. Frames must rather be understood as occupying a whole spectrum of morphological and meaning-bearing possibilities, with generic, multi-purpose, moveable units playing their significative roles alongside the more particular, single-purpose, single-location capsules in the register.

An example of the latter variety of frame presents itself as the next unit in the "Nine Winds" charm, with the summoning of the three agents Ugimir, Stanimir, and Persa (*peace, j*). As explained above, these three constructed figures lexically embody the double action of removal ("kill," "halt," "stop") and restoration ("peace") that the conjurer is undertaking, and in so doing they act as co-participants in the healing act. From this point Desanka moved quickly to closure, in one case (A3) interposing the generic capsule of *reversed numbers*, and in the other proceeding directly to the final, two-line frame.

---

75. On one level, this is simply an empirical judgment made on the basis of multiple versions and assuming that certain frames are in fact more crucial to the communicative economy, or cure, than others. The argument from word-power would proceed similarly: any given performance-event must deploy enough of the register to engage the traditional force enabled by this way of speaking. The final judge of "sufficiency" would of course be the traditional audience (here the client) who serves as the communicative partner in the exchange.

Communicative Economy

If the conjurer and patient have entered the performance arena, accepting its institutionally implied agenda for the performative and traditional constitution of the curing ritual, the result must be a cure. Thus the last two lines of the charm (*wolf, l*; in all eight versions):

> U kurjaka čet'ri noge, peti rep,
> Od mog *odgovora* j' bio lek.
>
> Into the wolf's four legs, fifth the tail,
> Out of my *speaking* has come the cure.

I translate *odgovor* as "speaking" to emphasize two fundamental dimensions of the performed charm: its palpable "spokenness" and its identity as what Hymes has called a "way of speaking." Although dictionaries customarily render the unmarked noun as "response," the context in which *odgovor* occurs here keys other shades of meaning: both the sounded physical reality of the experienced event and the dedicated, highly focused nature of an expressive act aimed at a single, well-defined goal. Another way to say the same thing would be to observe that *odgovor* could equally well be translated as "word-power"; from the conjurer's word-power, enabled by the event of performance and the referent of tradition, "has come the cure."

Having sketched the *bajanje* register in its linguistic, paralinguistic, and non-linguistic dimensions, we are now in a position to observe that it is this set of performance keys, of metonymic signals, that engenders the communicative economy otherwise understood as the cure. In other words, although responsibly we must preface each annotation on word-power with a stipulation that as mere analysts we can never wholly recover the insider's perspective on a work of verbal art, some of the metonymic referentiality naturally associated with a given register can be reprojected by a careful consideration of the internal logic of the speech act. By bringing into play as much of the context as possible—multiform versions, physical setting, paralinguistic gestures, and so on—we can understand at least some of what the *bajalica* is attempting to accomplish, both as a speaker and as an intercessor.

Discovery of the link between the charm as a sounded reality and its contextual meaning thus rests in a recognition and reemphasis of a long-honored property of language in general: the arbitrary nature of the relationship between sign and meaning, a relationship here intensely magnified in the pars pro toto metonymic relation between performance signal and its dedicated signification. One of the most telling examples of this rule as it applies to the keyed implications of traditional oral registers may be found within the same genre of magical charms, namely, in the so-called "nonsense" or "gibberish" charm, mentioned briefly above, that surfaces in many different traditions.[76] In such semantically opaque forms of verbal magic, often the only trace of standard language is an acoustic pattern based on the natural linguistic features of the language in question: an alliteration or rhyme or pattern of accents, for example. And yet the "nonsense" syllables have sufficient word-power that they cannot be greatly modified from one performance to the next without destroying the charm's communicative integrity and proscribing the cure.[77] Quite clearly the link between expressive integer and word-power is strong and focused, even if (and in an important way because) the integer itself makes little or no sense outside the arena and register of magical spells. Such a situation illustrates just how nominal the bare semantics of metonymic cues can be—a string of supposedly meaningless syllables becomes the sole pathway to the desired goal of healing, with "gibberish" assuming an expressive responsibility that no amount of verbal dexterity within the standard, unmarked register can match.

Coda: The Snake and the Virgin

In order to widen our experience of word-power and *bajanje* beyond the (already quite extensive) morphology of the "Nine Winds," and to provide a closing emphasis on the core concepts of performance arena, register, and communicative economy, let us turn to some quite unusual performances of a charm that seems to be relatively sparsely distributed, at least in the region of Orašac.[78]

This spell, which we will entitle "Against Snakebite," was contributed via oral performance principally by a man, Vojislav Stojanović, the sole possessor of the remedy in Orašac and over the entire geographical area, and later by his sister Radojka, who was visiting the village from Belgrade, having permanently left her birthplace some years before. Although the rules of the genre forbid male reception and practice of *bajanje*, Vojislav was known to have the spell at his disposal and was apparently quite frequently called upon by his neighbors to

---

76. Consider the following example from Old English (Grendon 1909: 194–97):
    Ecce dolgula medit dudum,
    bethegunda brethegunda,
    elecunda elevachia,
    mottem mee renum,
    ortha fuetha.
Largely unintelligible except for a few familiar Latin and Old English words or word-parts, these five lines are labeled "gibberish" by the two major editors, Grendon (1909) and Cockayne (1965). And yet the sequence exhibits rhyme, alliteration, traces of a nonsyllabic meter, and indications of classic Anglo-Saxon half-line and whole-line structure. Whatever the origin of these curious sounds, they are ordered by responsional and echoic functions typical of the charm register, and they can plausibly be understood as serving a (now-lost) magical function through that register's invocation of the performance arena.
    77. Cf. the examples of metonymic referentiality cited in chap. 1 above; also in Foley 1991: chap. 1 and passim.
    78. As with the "Nine Winds," most lines in "Against Snakebite" as recorded in the Šumadijan area can be found in one or another of Radenković's charm texts (1982: cf. nos. 1–45), but there is no overall parallel. Again we may be dealing with "dialectal" variation in traditional form.

use it to cure their sick animals. Likewise, although Radojka still remembered the charm, she had become a confirmed city-dweller and, far from being in a position to use the spell, regarded such practices with the self-defining and self-reenforcing suspicion of an urbanite. Because Vojislav knew we were interested in charms and had been a dependable informant for the Halperns' anthropological investigations for two decades, he suggested performing the *basma* for us, but at first resisted the presence of the tape recorder. Only after assurances that his valuable property would not be transferred to anyone else in the community did he agree to an acoustic record of the event. Thus it was that we received four versions of "Against Snakebite" from him, with the added instructions that plum brandy be applied to the actual bite and the ritual be repeated three times—"today, tomorrow, and the day after tomorrow." Here is the first of Vojislav's four versions alongside Radojka's (very similar) single performance; since neither informant paused during utterance of the charm, the vertical spaces signal what I take as the frame structure of this charm:[79]

Vojislav, version #1	*Radojka, unique version*
Nije zmija kravu ujela;	Dobro jutro, zlo jutro,
Dobra druga drugu poljubila.	Koliko te o zla!
Dobro jutro, zlo ti jutro,	Dobro jutro bilo,
Toliko te do ujutru bilo!	Toliko te do ujutru bilo!
Zemlja zemlju jela,	
Zemlja zemlju ručala,	Zemlja zemlju ručala,
Zemlja zemlju večerala;	Zemlja zemlju večerala;
Nij' od zemlje večera,	Nij' od zemlje večera,
Nij' od trnja postelja.	Nij' od trnja postelja.
Ajd' izlazi, Marija,	Izadji, Marija,
Da ti sudji kadija.	Da ti sudi kadija.
Nije radi zle žene,	Nije zbog zle žene,
Nego pored oca i dece.	Ni već zbog oca i dece.
	Nije zmija (po imenu) ujela;
	Dobra sestra sestru poljubila.

* * *	*
A snake did not bite the cow;	Good morning, evil morning,
One good friend kissed another.	How much evil you brought![80]
Good morning, your evil morning,	It was a good morning,
[But] you brought so much evil in the morning!	[But] you brought so much evil in the morning!
Earth ate earth,	
Earth ate earth at midday,	Earth ate earth at midday,

79. The four versions recited by Vojislav are virtually identical, the only differences being his variation between *radi* and *pored* in lines 12–13 (both mean "on account of" in the local dialect; Radojka uses *zbog,* "because," a more general word unmarked for this area or register), and occasional alternate endings or pronunciations.

80. Literally (here and below), "How much to you about evil!"

Earth ate earth in the evening;   Earth ate earth in the evening;
The evening meal is not from earth,   The evening meal is not from earth,
The bed is not made of thorns.   The bed is not made of thorns.

Get out, O Mary,   Come out, O Mary,
So the qadi can judge you![81]   So the qadi can judge you!
It is not because of an evil woman,   It is not because of an evil woman,
Nor because of the father or   Nor yet because of the father or
    children.   children.

A snake did not bite (for the name);
One good sister kissed another.

The circumstances under which the two unlikely bearers (one active, one passive) received the *basma,* and which continued to license Vojislav's performance of it, are unusual and instructive. Because their aunt, the original possessor of this potential gift for a granddaughter's dowry, lay on her deathbed and Vojislav and Radojka happened to be the only people present at the moment she passed away, the old woman had no choice but to transmit the charm to them; the only alternative, unacceptable to the village society as a functioning unit, was to let the tradition of this important healing remedy die with her. The more remarkable transmission was of course to the nephew: in taking him into her confidence in such an unprecedented way, she effectively designated Vojislav a conditional *bajalica,* a ritualistic position and relationship itself unparalleled but in effect and function not unlike the kind of synthetic kinship practiced in village institutions such as *kumstvo* ("godparenthood") or *pobratimstvo/posestrimstvo* ("bloodbrotherhood/bloodsisterhood"), in that powers and responsibilities beyond conventional or quotidian definition are specially stipulated.[82] For this one purpose only, Vojislav was allowed to transcend the limits of gender construction and village identity, appointed and acting in his aunt's stead as an honorary conjurer. At the same time, Radojka's marrying out of the village and into the sophisticated, Western environment of Belgrade, where conventional modern medicine is of course the rule, left her male cousin the only practitioner able to treat this particular malady.

In the terms we have been developing in this chapter and earlier, Vojislav was thus able—again for this one purpose only—to enter the performance arena wherein "Against Snakebite" was practiced and could effect change. What is more, he apparently did so with some frequency, being hired once every few weeks to treat lactating animals that had gone dry because of the imputed snakebite. On these grounds his disinclination to have the charm acoustically recorded offers some insight into its dynamics and the nature of the performance arena. Not only did Vojislav, like other *bajalice,* guard his inheritance zealously; he also regarded its sounded reality—not its *text*—as being too powerful to be

---

81. From Turkish *kadi* ("judge"), ultimately Arabic *qadi,* this word stems from the Ottoman era and is here applied, as we shall see, in a very different, Christian context.
82. On these modes of synthetic kinship as manifested in verbal art and in daily village life, see Foley 1992.

in the possession of others, for whatever reason. I do not know in what exact proportion professional jealousy and the danger of the utterance's word-power mixed in his reluctance to speak the charm for the tape recorder, but his conversation made it evident that both concerns were active. He was, as noted above, the sole possessor of this important village remedy, and he knew how powerful his words could be. In wanting to prescribe the conditions under which we were permitted to collect this *basma*, Vojislav was insisting on the retention of sole authority over who entered the performance arena to enact "Against Snakebite."

As for the register employed once one gains entry, this charm, although considerably shorter and simpler than the "Nine Winds," still manifests many of the same expressive features. The basic poetic line reflects a symbiosis between phraseological patterns and the women's octosyllabic meter: although the actual syllabic count of individual lines varies widely, with euphonic and syntactic desiderata overriding absolute fidelity to a metrical constraint, still the line approximates a symmetrical octosyllable in overall structure. It also seems only prudent to acknowledge the possibility that some (but certainly not all) of the divergence from octosyllabic rhythm may derive from the informant's relative unfamiliarity with the register of this genre. In other words, because this charm represented what was for him a unique speech act, divorced in his particular expressive repertoire from the rest of the *bajanje* tradition, Vojislav may have been somewhat less fluent in managing the way of speaking than the usual *bajalica*. If so, this caveat would also apply to other linguistic features of the performance. Given the fact of intrasocietal knowledge of speech acts, however, as evidenced for example in Desanka Matijašević's grandson's prompting her when she hesitated during performance of the "Nine Winds," I would caution against overestimating Vojislav's unfamiliarity with the register.

We are able to comment on paralinguistic features only generally and sparsely, since this charm, unlike the "Nine Winds," is so short that such characteristics are not graphically foregrounded.[83] Vojislav spoke the snakebite charm with the same whisper and rapidity typical of other conjurers' performances, and observed beforehand that he delivered it straight into the ear of the afflicted animal, again mirroring the paralinguistic and nonlinguistic features of the "Nine Winds" performances and affirming the sense of power in the physical sounding of the spell. As far as I know, he never employed implements of any sort—which even in Desanka's case (and in others') seemed optional and relatively unimportant—nor was there the kind of secret ceremonial rite entailed that we had impertinently projected as the probable performance arena before learning how the spells were really performed. As with the "Nine Winds," the register exhibits the linguistic features of repetition (line 3), syntactic patterning (5–7), and acoustic effects (5–7; 9–10), although no clear neologisms occur and the only

---

83. What follows is at points confirmed by reference to Radojka's version, but the singularity of her charm (a unique performance by an individual long removed from the village and now openly suspicious of *bajanje* in general) must limit its usefulness to simple confirmation.

possible archaism is *kadija* (qadi, "judge"). In short, the repertoire of performance keys is narrower than that in the other charm, again at least partly because the spell itself is markedly briefer in overall extent and less complex in its make-up, but enough of the same features are manifest to demonstrate that "Against Snakebite" employs the same register.

Another hallmark of the charm register, organization by frames, also characterizes "Against Snakebite," although let me repeat that the paralinguistic cue of pause between frames did not constitute a dimension of performance in this second charm.[84] The strophic units, composed of from two to five lines,[85] embody separable but complementary acts or perspectives. The opening frame in Vojislav's version tackles two discrete but finally interrelated issues: after denying the feared (and of course tacitly admitted) reality that it was a snake that bit the cow, he redefines the act in question as the benign image of a good (female) friend kissing another good (female) friend. This is the same frame that serves as coda to Radojka's unique performance, and, as we shall see below, it constitutes an utterance heavy with implication. The next two lines establish the modulation from good to evil, from health to illness, that provides the incipient condition and overall reason for the performance: the imbalance that the *bajalica*—here Vojislav and Radojka—will seek to correct. Lines 5–9, like the *animal* capsule in the "Nine Winds," deepen the description by invoking the unnatural, the counterexpectation that the charm must combat. After this "citation" of the irruption of the profane into the present, the conjurer summons the offending party, the snake, (re)naming it "Mary" and asking that it be judged, presumably as to its residual danger. While this sequence of frames has no direct parallel with the units that make up the "Nine Winds," the mode of organization—short, internally logical idea-clusters—is quite similar, once again arguing that the two functionally quite diverse charms employ the same traditional performance register.

If Vojislav is licensed to admit his patients into the performance arena, where the event empowers his words, and if further he can speak in the dedicated register that institutionally engages the referent of tradition, then we would be led to expect a high degree of communicative economy. We would be led to anticipate a cure accomplished by the word-power at his command, and, if village opinion is any guide, we would not be disappointed: dry animals treated

84. I take the absence of pause not as a sign of a different genre or register—the similarities between the "Nine Winds" and "Against Snakebite" are simply too numerous and thoroughgoing to support such a hypothesis—but as an indication that the latter charm does not present a sufficiently extensive or elaborate vehicle for the paralinguistic index of interframe pause to emerge. Since that particular register-specific feature seems to characterize all of the longer, more internally heterogeneous charm performances we recorded from various *bajalice,* it seems safe to confirm this theory on empirical grounds.

85. Vojislav's "Earth ate earth" capsule has five lines in all versions (four in Radojka's performance), but might well be understood as two units of three and two lines, respectively; it is difficult to make such a determination (or rather to support either interpretation) without the paralinguistic cues that define frame division in the "Nine Winds." I have chosen to indicate a single five-line frame here because of the lexical echo in the seventh and eighth lines between the phrases *zemlju večerala* and *zemlje večera.*

with this medicine do begin to lactate again, and the ill effects of the snakebite are magically dispelled. But just what does the malady consist of and what is the dynamic process behind the cure?

On these points the charm itself is so telegraphic that only further discussion with Vojislav and others enlightened us,[86] and there may well be a lesson entailed in our struggle to understand. Depending on genre and, as in this case, on individual items within genres, a given performance may appear more or less opaque to the outsider (outsiders being defined here as first the most peripheral personalities, that is, the fieldworkers from without the culture, and secondarily those people within the culture whose knowledge of the given traditional genre is limited). As a rule of thumb, the more densely coded and functionally focused a speech act, the more "additional" information is required to receive it in something approaching its cultural context. For members of the society, and especially for those skilled in performance of the particular genre, that enabling context is never "additional" but always implied, always immanent. Whether it constitutes a part of the utterance amounts, in other words, to a phenomenological question: for outsiders no, for insiders yes. "Against Snakebite" proved one of those items—in an already highly focused genre— that largely resisted the outsiders' analytical approach and seemed obviously to require a cultural context to which we were not automatically privy. In our questioning of Vojislav and others, we thus set about discovering the traditional referent of this terse but uniquely effective utterance, attempting to establish its immanent meaning.

The initial step was a full appreciation of the malady being addressed: we learned that a dry cow or other lactating animal is extremely threatening in the village, since most households have only a small number of milk-producing animals and depend upon them for basic needs (milk, cheese, derivative foods). When the cow stops producing, a significant obstacle presents itself, since there may be no alternative source for what she provides. Villagers explained the phenomenon as the surprisingly common occurrence of a snake (*zmija*) that has found its way from the creek (*potok*)[87] to the livestock shed and bitten the milk-producing animal on the udder. In explaining the scenario to us, they often referred or pointed to an inflamed udder, sometimes to an udder that to our eyes looked normal enough, claiming that the toothmarks were visible. The problem was thus understood to arise from recurrent, inevitable causes, and the *bajanje* was, as with the "Nine Winds," perceived as restoring the cosmic status quo.[88]

Extensive background research eventually established that the spell was thought

86. To a lesser degree, the variants in Radenković 1982, especially nos. 1–9 and 18, have also been helpful.

87. In many ways the *potok* is understood as a liminal area in the village, a boundary region that can either promote or threaten health. On the positive side, it is apparently associated with fertility (particularly female fertility); but it is also linked with disease and death.

88. In this way the problem and its cure were seen as quite different from the pernicious black magic (*vračanje*) used by one person, for example, to intentionally dry up a neighbor's animal. See n. 7 above.

to counteract the snakebite by transforming the enemy agent, the snake, into a "good friend or sister" and, perhaps less explicitly, by calling for a "judgment"—presumably positive and exculpating—on the snake–become–Virgin Mary. Both appeals have a certain elemental significance with respect to the culture and the charm tradition. Transformation into one's (female) friend or sister invokes the cultural construct of the nourishing and unthreatening female, a figure who would only promote and share the animal's natural function. Throughout the cultural repertoire and the repertoire of local verbal art, the female agemate or sister is she who succors the younger siblings, helps manage the household, prepares the hero, warns her father of treachery, and so on.[89] One simply could not involve a more sympathetic, positive figure—not, that is, unless one invoked the Virgin Mary. Here we glimpse syncresis at its most suggestive, as the kinship image meshes with the Christian religious figure to complete the "defanging" of the *zmija*. Not only is the snake made a friend or member of the family, in either case a most supportive and nonthreatening confidante, but it is eventually transfigured into the virgin mother of God, the religious symbol par excellence of selfless concern for all that is natural and good.[90]

It may now be apparent why "Against Snakebite" proved such a challenge to decipher. Granted that the performance arena and register created the site and medium for the curative transaction, the specific referents of the various figures and actions remained obscured by the lack of context. To put it another way, so much remained implicit that the nominal surface of the charm—all that was visible at first—appeared more a hodgepodge of mysterious innuendoes than a coherent healing utterance. But with the immanent mythos brought within the outsider's reach, and effectively restored as a part of the charm, the word-power that is the cure becomes plain enough. The conjurer seeks to exit the present "evil morning" of the animal's dryness and return to the "good morning" of natural function and cosmic balance. As things stand now, *ručak* (the midday meal) and *večera* (the evening meal) and all that they represent are under threat; expectable processes are so fundamentally disturbed that "earth eats earth" (5–7)[91] and food is not forthcoming from the land (8), no more than one can make a bed from thorns (9). Instead of removing the "red disease" with the cooperation of the horse and rider, mother animals, or three named agents of the "Nine Winds," the *bajalica* herself transmutes the offending snake to a friend or sister and then to the Virgin Mary, thus casting out evil by rendering the *zmija* not only nonthreatening but unambiguously benign. Once these forces are

---

89. This figure is ubiquitous in both Moslem and Christian epic; one example is the sister in the very common "unfaithful mother" (*neverna majka*) tale, a young girl who helps her brothers avert the mother's (and mother's lover's) plans to murder them (see, e.g., the Christian song *The Widow Jana*, as discussed in Foley and Kerewsky-Halpern 1976). On the nourishing female figure in South Slavic Moslem epic, cf. Foley 1991: 91–94.

90. Cf. the summoning of Mary in Radenković 1982: nos. 2 and 9, wherein a snake has disturbed the cosmic order.

91. Cf. Radenković 1982: nos. 2, 3, etc.; this dysfunction is also expressed as earth *kissing* earth (nos. 1, 4, 6, etc.).

summoned and engaged, the curative process engendered by this brief but densely echoic spell is complete.

In summary, we have seen in this chapter what it means to enter the performance arena, to speak and to hear within a special, dedicated register, and to experience the communicative economy of word-power in a traditional oral genre. The object of our attention, the genre of Serbian magical charms or *bajanje,* has been shown to operate according to its own traditional rules, some of them familiar from earlier scholarship on South Slavic epic and some of them quite idiosyncratic. The two example spells, "Nine Winds" and "Against Snake-bite," have illustrated the linguistic, paralinguistic, and nonlinguistic aspects of the speech act, and have shown—through version-to-version morphology and restoration of context—how the event of performance and the referent of tradition enable the situated utterance, how they provide it with a word-power far beyond its nominal, superficial semantics. In respect to this healing art, which serves a crucial, well-recognized social function and depends fundamentally on word-power for its expressive force, we can now more fully understand and credit Desanka's (and the tradition's) pronouncement that "out of my *speaking* has come the cure."

Over the course of the next two chapters we shall turn our attention to the *Homeric Hymn to Demeter* and the Anglo-Saxon verse hagiography *Andreas,* seeking to understand what happens to that speaking when its vehicle becomes a text.

V

CONTINUITIES OF RECEPTION
THE HOMERIC HYMN TO DEMETER

κρατὺς Ἀργειφόντης

mighty [infant] slayer of Argos

Traditional

Zeus spoke and Iris did not disobey his behests.
Speedily she rushed down from the peaks of Olympos
and came to Rharion, life-giving udder of the earth
in the past, and then no longer life-giving but lying idle
without a leaf. It was now hiding the white barley
according to the plan of fair-ankled Demeter, but later
the fields would be plumed with long ears of grain,
as the spring waxed, and the rich furrows on the ground
would teem with ears to be bound into sheaves by withies.

Hymn to Demeter, lines 448–56

From Performance to Text

In the foregoing chapter we examined how the theory of word-power opens up
the traditional oral genre of Serbian charms, or *bajanje,* by emphasizing the
enabling event of performance and the enabling referent of tradition. Through
her speech act, the conjurer situates her patient and herself in a well-defined
performance arena, where the special words and actions that constitute the
charm register are specially efficacious. That is, she harnesses the singular communicative economy of the charm genre—as terse and yet as reverberative an
idiom as one is likely to encounter—in order to initiate a highly focused discourse, in order to banish the disease and bring about the cure.

As we move from the actual, textually unmediated experience of performed
charms to the ancient Greek texts that are the subject of this chapter, we must
contend not only with a shift in genre but, more fundamentally, with a radical
shift in medium. No longer will the relative luxury of acoustic records and
participant observation of performance be available as guides to understanding
the dynamics of an unambiguously traditional oral art; rather, we must now

deal with silent, disembodied textual artifacts that may have involved the use of writing in the very composition of the work as well as in its transmission. Clearly, this is a different kind of singer of tales in performance. As discussed in chapter 3, this latter change adumbrates important, far-reaching modulations, but not so simple or absolute a quantum difference as the Great Divide theorists have often assumed.

In considering the dynamics of such oral-derived traditional texts, we argued that the most productive avenue of inquiry was not to attempt to gauge the "orality" of the surviving works (whatever that might mean), but rather to try to judge the extent to which traditional oral integers persist as textual rhetoric. To put the same matter in another way, the core interpretive question addresses not solely the extant text itself, as an object simply to be analyzed stratigraphically for its "layers" of signification, but *the degree to which the text promotes— and its readership continues—a tradition of reception.* This approach takes account of the basic communicative act of traditional oral art: negotiation of meaning between a performer and an audience under the aegis of word-power, that is, with institutionalized and empowering reference to a now-rhetorical performance act and immanent tradition. To the extent that an audience is able to co-create the work by enriching its textual integers and bridging its gaps of indeterminacy according to the rules of the idiom, that audience can recover its traditional, performance-centered resonance. And since such works, which emerge from oral tradition and yet involve textuality in various ways, clearly lay claim to a double heritage, it seems indefensible to eliminate either dimension from our own reading strategy, our role in the making of the work of art. A composite or syncretic poetics can be stripped of its natural bivalence only at the heavy price of reductionism.[1]

Traditional texts, we discovered, can preserve certain of the significative strategies familiar from traditional oral performances, while they necessarily must discard others. The *performance arena,* that privileged locus where the business of specialized communication is uniquely enfranchised, becomes purely rhetorical. In simplest terms there no longer exists an actual, tangible "place" devoted to this function, no locus defined temporally and spatially, but then such tangible locations were never more than sequel concretizations of the performance arena, nominal instances of an intangible "place" or "moment" that harbored much wider and deeper implications. Thus transition from a series of nominal instances to a rhetorical function independent of concretizations does not represent as severe a shift as might first be imagined. In both cases the experience of performance, real or projected, energizes the relationship between performer, now rhetoricized as well, and the audience/reader. In both cases

---

1. The present discussion will of course concentrate on the traditional oral aspects of such verbal art, those aspects that have been downplayed or ignored in most other treatments of the works to be examined in this and the next chapter. But this emphasis should not obscure the fact that textual strategies can and do coexist within a traditional oral poetics. It would in fact be more accurate, as we shall see, to speak of a poetics that comprises tropes and strategies associated with both the immanence of oral tradition and the textuality of manuscript traditions.

entering the arena means designating a preselected and dedicated channel for communication, with all of the limitations and advantages that channel entails.

Rhetorical preservation of the performance arena as a determinative (because indexical) force represents another reason to envision traditional oral and oral-derived works as a spectrum rather than as two separate or separable types. Of course, the fundamental unity of works across such a spectrum does not relieve us of the responsibility to make our best efforts at individual calibration of texts: the principles of tradition-, genre-, and text-dependence must always precede and complicate—even problematize—our interpretive approach to any of these works.[2] But amid the differences mandated by a responsible reading program, it is well to remember that such oral-derived texts rhetorically continue the tradition of reception by maintaining the imperative to return to the "place" where traditional oral discourse operates most economically.

Likewise, we learned in chapter 3 that the *register* or idiom uniquely licensed to support the dedicated discourse of the arena can in part survive textualization, and this discovery led to the further observation that a reader's own fluency in the register was therefore crucial to an understanding of the work on its own terms. In terms of the Ethnography of Speaking, paralinguistic features in most cases perish, and efforts to reinstill them in a libretto have met with mixed success. But the performance keys known as special codes, figurative language, parallelism, special formulae, appeal to tradition, and disclaimer of tradition can and do survive the semiotic translation to text, albeit in altered form and according to the variant dictates of different traditions, genres, performers, and so forth. That is, they survive as long as they are functional, as long as the tradition of reception remains more or less intact.

The same proved true from the perspective of the Oral-Formulaic Theory, whose integers of formula, theme, and story-pattern prove less important in and of themselves than does the systemic mathematics they make possible.[3] As long as the phraseology, for example, retains its more-than-textual significative powers, it will maintain its word-power as a register of discourse, a way of speaking and meaning, whether it is deployed and perceived as a string of heard syllables or as a textual coding that summons those syllables. In both cases the role of the idiom is to make institutionalized reference—either directly or rhetorically—to performance and tradition, and thereby to engage fields of meaning that are otherwise beyond the reach of any performer or audience (including either authors or readers as well). Likewise with the theme and story-pattern: textualization does not wholly dampen their endemic reverberations, not as long as the reader/audience remains fluent in the register. Interrupt that fluency, however, and even the most densely encoded traditional signals—whether emergent in performance or latent in texts—will fall on deaf ears.

2. On these concepts cf. Foley 1990a: 5–19.

3. As has been discussed elsewhere (esp. Foley 1990a: chaps. 4–10), these "products" are merely the most visible evidence of more radical and more important processes. For examples of the metonymic meaning of various levels of oral-formulaic units or patterns, see Foley 1991, esp. chaps. 3–6.

Such an interruption was precisely the reason that Ethnopoetics was originally formulated. Whether through Tedlock's augmented scripts for performance and program for ethnopaleography or Hymes's redramatization by line, verse, versicle, stanza, scene, act, and part, this approach seeks not simply to fashion a suitable or faithful textual object but, in the process and much more importantly, to make it possible for the reader/audience to continue the tradition of reception. All differences in their individual programs aside, Tedlock and Hymes are both attempting to reconstrue the register in which Native American oral traditions were and are performed and apprehended. In helping us to move away from culturally and cognitively narcissistic assimilation to prosified literary texts, they point toward an appreciation of traditional oral art on its own terms, as informed by performance and tradition.

If oral-derived traditional texts can preserve both access to the performance arena and a rhetorical reflex of the dedicated discourse register, then they can, subject to the reader/audience's preparation, promote at least a measure of *communicative economy*. In terms of the Ethnography of Speaking, this means that performance will be keyed and the connection vitalized between the words of the text and the power they can be made to wield under the contract of the performance tradition. From the perspective of Oral-Formulaic Theory, the units of discourse will persist because they still convey a wealth of extralexical and extratextual reference, only now with their metonymic, immanent associations made rhetorically present. Ethnopoetics ensures such singular economy by removing works from conventional textual straitjackets that only hinder their natural dynamics and by fitting them to a textual format that helps to release that dynamics. It cannot be denied that traditional texts purchase communicative economy only at the expense of one semiotic remove, and we will do well to remember that a syncretic or composite poetics will customarily be the most productive solution for texts of uncertain provenance.[4] But neither can we claim a responsible "reperformance" of such works without taking into account the substantive extent to which these same texts maintain a strong and nourishing link to oral tradition through a continuity of reception.

Methodology

Establishing a continuity of reception for oral-derived traditional texts requires a methodology sensitive to the features that survive semiotic translation from event to text, and one at the same time able to locate and describe tradi-

---

4. As discussed in chap. 3, there are of course real differences between transcriptions of actual traditional oral performances on the one hand and, on the other, texts (such as ancient and medieval vernacular poetry) whose precise relationship to a prior or ongoing oral tradition cannot be ascertained. In these latter situations, examples of which we will be confronting in the present chapter, I strongly advocate admitting uncertainty and adhering to a syncretic poetics, a position that nonetheless provides for the simultaneous consideration of traditional oral forms as full partners in the expressive format. Cf. also Fine 1984 and Foley in press.

tional integers and meanings without recourse to the plethora of evidence and unambiguously oral performances typical of many living traditions. As noted above, there are certain aspects of performance registers that transfer quite readily to texts, with inevitable shifts in nature and deployment, and there are some that do not. Potentially more problematic, however, is the question of the metonymic meaning such transferred integers project. Granting a fluency on the part of the contemporary reader/audience accustomed to dealing with such a text, how does the latter-day scholar aspire to anything approaching a similar fluency? If all we have left is the text, isolated from its ambient tradition, how do we enter the performance arena, learn the particular register, and participate in the act of economical communication?

One must start, I believe, by admitting that outsiders to a performance tradition can seldom if ever achieve a mother-tongue fluency in a register outside their own cultural repertoire, even if the tradition is ongoing and readily available for study. There will always be an endemic shortfall for the "analytic" or "etic" interloper, a comparative lack of the kind of firsthand knowledge gained only through active, iterative experience of the tradition. Hopefully, the external perspective available to the outsider will in part compensate for that shortfall: he or she may be able to offer new insights by intentionally stepping outside the performance arena, by citing comparative material from other traditions, and so on. But we should be under no illusion that we can recover the insider's perspective, and the necessary alterity of an oral tradition outside one's experience only deepens when the sole contact with the work(s) involved is mediated through the distancing function of texts.

That endemic limitation notwithstanding, we can conduct a self-tutorial of modest proportions leading to a fuller grasp of the performance register in which the work is presented. The fundamental move in this inquiry is a deceptively simple one: to ascertain whether traditional integers, in whatever multiformity they occur in a text or texts, project associative meanings beyond the lexical, syntagmatic surface of the narrative or lyric form. In other words, we first define and locate what can be classed as traditional, performance-derived integers or keys, and then ask whether the patterns or features so defined can be shown to bear a value-added signification, what has been termed a metonymic or immanent meaning, in addition to the signification accorded them by membership in the textual cadre of expressive components. Do any of the integers stand pars pro toto for a larger, extratextual reality? Can we establish that an element of phraseology or narrative patterning institutionally implies more than the sum of its parts? Does the advent of a figure, a phrase, or an action constitute a traditional prolepsis, and therefore a "map" for construal of what is to follow? These are the sorts of questions that a self-tutorial in register will comprise.

In this and the next chapter, we will be dealing not with transcriptions of oral performances but with texts whose precise provenance remains unclear, despite their evident roots in oral tradition. Besides specifying this oral-derived character, our methodology must therefore operate on a sharply limited textual sample. Few of the Homeric Hymns, even though they may be dedicated to the same god or goddess, show much sustained resemblance beyond their opening and closing formulas. Likewise, the Anglo-Saxon poem to be examined in chapter 6 is clearly an individual, separate text, with no alternate versions. The next methodological concern therefore centers around the problem of comparanda: the extent to which comparative material necessary to the establishment of metonymic meaning really exists for the texts under consideration.

Once again, we start by not just admitting but indeed stipulating the shortfall; some traditional signals will go unreceived and some gaps of indeterminacy will remain unbridged simply because we lack the background for a fully successful self-tutorial. But, especially in a contemporary critical climate that values the continuing conversation and the ongoing discussion over the illusion of a final solution, the partial nature of the interpretive journey should not deter us from setting out. Any gain in understanding the dynamics of a work can only bring us another step forward, fueling a developing awareness that will, naturally, require more and more interpretation.[5] And the inquiry proposed here is sufficiently radical—in calling for attention to a largely neglected aspect of the very communicative medium of the works involved—that there can be no question either of regretting the partiality of these early, illustrative results or of being disappointed with the magnitude of the nonetheless finite yield.

But, this much stipulated, exactly how do we proceed with even a partial projection from traditional *textual* integer to metonymic, immanent meaning? How, in short, do we go about restoring word-power? Moving from least to most restrictive scenarios, let us begin by considering the kind of situation in which some variant texts that can serve as comparanda do exist. In such cases one can gather instances of surviving traditional integers or performance keys, such as formulaic expressions or other signals, and analyze their deployment across different texts, versions, and instances. Do these variously contexted witnesses of a given traditional form seem to bear any special, associative signification that cannot be predicted according to customary lexical and textual criteria? It may be, as with certain features in traditional oral performances, that the form in question really has no such value-added meaning; speech introductions are usually not echoic in this sense, for example, serving only the basic function of marking the start of a character's assertion, narration, or response without any particular metonymic valence. Some of the now-rhetoricized forms will, however, bear heavier connotation, adding an immanent meaning that cannot be discovered as long as one treats the traditional register as an unmarked idiom. Comparison among existing witnesses from whatever sample of texts is available—under the discriminations informed by the principles of tradition-, genre-, and text-dependence, of course—will begin to make plain what this added valence brings to the various appearances of its nominal signal, enriching the textual presentation with a traditional, performance-derived reverberation.

---

5. Walter Ong describes the necessarily ongoing nature of interpretation as follows (1986: 147): "All utterance both reveals and conceals. The quest for utterance that reveals all and never needs interpretation is a quest for a will-o'-the-wisp."

The approach is basically the same for texts that unfortunately lack a plurality of versions. In these cases the only recourse will lie in triangulating among instances not from different versions but from different passages in the same work or, with appropriate calibration,[6] different works. This is not as limited or as speculative a procedure as might be imagined, especially for a longer text such as the *Iliad* or *Odyssey,* or for a reasonably well populated and coherent genre of shorter works such as the Homeric Hymns, which, as we shall see below, share many aspects of register with the much more thoroughly studied epics. This congruency enlarges the possible scope for analysis in another direction. The Anglo-Saxon *Andreas,* to be treated in the next chapter, presents a different but ultimately related species of challenge. No alternate versions of this particular poem survive, or are likely ever to have existed, and the genre we name "hagiography" in Old English is much more heterogeneous than that of the ancient Greek epic or Hymn.[7] Compensatorily, however, Anglo-Saxon poetry does not appear to be brachiated by genre as dramatically as some other oral-derived poetries, and as a result traditional elements such as formulaic phraseology and narrative patterning tend to be shared broadly among otherwise quite disparate poetic types.[8] While genre-dependence must continue to guide our investigations, this idiosyncrasy of Old English verse substantially widens the sample of traditional texts that can serve, again with appropriate calibration, as comparanda.

Triangulation among multiple instances of traditional forms, then, will constitute the fundamental methodology of our analysis of oral-derived traditional texts. By asking what these witnesses share—as their joint contribution to a series of mutually distinct narrative or lyric situations—we will be inquiring what they encode in addition to what their lexical and syntagmatic functions make available to the reader/audience. We will in short be reaching beyond the immediate context of each occurrence to the larger context of a (now rhetorical) performance tradition, beyond textual to extratextual, immanent meaning.

In order to illustrate the important contribution that traditional oral forms can make to a work of verbal art, we will be considering poems from the ancient Greek and Anglo-Saxon canons over this and the next chapter. In lieu of the *Iliad* and *Odyssey,* obviously the locus classicus for studies of ancient Greek *epos,*[9] we will be consulting the Homeric Hymns, a relatively neglected corpus

---

6. An example of such calibration will be given below in the discussion of *epos*-wide patterns in the *Homeric Hymn to Demeter.*

7. Compare the hagiographies *Juliana* and *Elene,* which differ from *Andreas* (and from each other) in dimensions such as the emphasis placed on heroic behavior and spiritual strife, and in "fidelity" to their probable sources. On the matter of correspondence between source and Old English "translation," see chap. 6.

8. Cf. the case of South Slavic oral traditions, which include two epic meters—the decasyllable (see esp. Foley 1990a: 85–106) and the *bugarštica* (see espec. Miletich 1990; Stolz 1969)—and an octosyllabic line that underlies the *ženske pjesme* ("women's songs") and many other genres customarily performed by women (see further the study of charms in chap. 4 above).

9. But cf. esp. G. Edwards 1971, Nagy 1990, Janko 1982, and Peabody 1975, all major studies of composition and the *epos* that involve the Hesiodic corpus or the Hymns or both. For a magisterial overview of scholarship on Homer and oral tradition, see M. Edwards 1986, 1988, 1992.

that many scholars from the ancients onward have understood as prolegomena *(prooimia)* to the performance of epic poetry *(oimê)* in early Greece. From the Old English texts I choose the verse hagiography *Andreas,* so close to *Beowulf* in phraseology while so far removed in subject and apparent purpose.

Before beginning with the Hymns, let me restate that the selection of instances below is presented only as a series of examples of how traditional integers can and do persist as a mathematics of rhetorical forms in an oral-derived traditional text. As such, it is intended merely to sample, and hardly to exhaust, the resonance of oral tradition in a few passages from the vast digest of ancient and medieval vernacular poetry. In this sense, the examples are best taken as an invitation to further study, as an exordium to more extensive and intensive analyses. For the moment, in other words, I am concentrating on explication of the *principle* of word-power and its relationship to performance and tradition; if this approach is to fulfill its potential for deeper appreciation of the art of traditional oral poetry, then practical, sustained applications to entire individual works will eventually be appropriate and indeed necessary.

Word-Power in the Homeric Hymns

Selecting the Channel

Specific illustrations from the Homeric Hymns will follow, but in accordance with what has been developed over the first three chapters about the singer of tales in performance, it is well to make at least brief mention of the "gross anatomy" of the poetic register before moving on to examples of its finer, more articulate expressive function. Because the actual performance parameters of this ancient art are largely irrecoverable from the extant texts, we are chiefly dependent on those aspects of register that can be isolated as textual survivals. As explained above, we can to an extent glimpse the compositional lineaments of formulaic phraseology, thematic structures, and story-pattern, as well as the performance-based features of special codes, figurative language, parallelism, special formulae, appeal to tradition, and disclaimer of performance (though not paralinguistic features).

What must be emphasized for the oral-derived traditional texts is that the mere presence of these survivals—the persistence of traditional forms as textual rhetoric—projects the performance arena and enables communicative economy for the reader/audience who can continue the tradition of reception.[10] In other words, it is not only the specific metonymic valences of this or that integer that constitute word-power, but also the mere base-level invocation of the idiom. By

---

10. It should be stressed that these survivals must persist as the basic expressive idiom of the work of verbal art, not as inessential elaborations on a primarily textual form that depends chiefly on a different register; cf. Renoir 1988: 169–74 on the Middle English romance *Sir Gawain and the Green Knight.* In what follows I draw the Greek quotations from Allen, Halliday, and Sikes 1980; the English translations are quoted from Athanassakis 1976.

the very act of composing (and prescribing reception) in the particular register of Homeric phraseology and narrative pattern, Homer and his counterparts have selected the channel through which the communication will occur. Whatever particular tropes—the Feast scene, the "intimate word" (*pykinon epos*),[11] or myriad other integers—are then deployed as signals with which a focused response is institutionally associated, each depends for its singular word-power upon the basic keying function of the register as an idiomatic whole.[12]

Genre and the *Epos* Tradition

The Homeric Hymns present a fascinating variety of thirty-three shorter and longer praise poems celebrating the ancient Greek pantheon of gods. Composed in the hexameter phraseology shared by the *Iliad, Odyssey,* and Hesiodic works, the Hymns have historically resisted critics' best attempts at a tidy generic taxonomy. Thucydides and Pindar were the first to call them *prooimia,* that is, "proems, preludes" to a subsequent main event—a longer (presumably narrative) poem (*oimê*)—and most ancient sources concur with this opinion.[13] No less revolutionary and influential a Homeric scholar than Friedrich Wolf lent his considerable weight to a version of the same position, observing that "Pindar and Plutarch report clearly enough that the hymns were composed by rhapsodes, by which they furnished preludes to the formal recitation of the poems of Homer and of others."[14] In the standard edition of the Hymns, Allen, Halliday, and Sikes suggest that this blanket statement needs qualification, and propose to reserve the concept of *prooimion* "to apply only to certain of the minor hymns."[15]

Designating function as the defining criterion for genre is made more difficult by the endemic heterogeneity of the Hymns. Although most are brief, lyrical

11. See Foley 1991: 174–89 and 154–56, respectively.

12. Scholars have searched to establish what we might call the general philology of the register, as distinguished from individual phrases and patterns within that register, in various ways, beginning of course with the work of Milman Parry (see M. Edwards 1986, 1988, 1992). What each of these studies offers is a view of the register-specific parameters for setting and entering the performance arena, a perspective on the variety of language to be employed. Whether we look at that language in terms of its traditional rules or in the exacting mathematical analysis done by William Sale (e.g., 1993), or for that matter via some other methodology, the essential point is that the register so constituted preselects and reinforces a range of responses; in addition to the specific keys we shall investigate below, the register as a significative system summons the immanent backdrop against which they will be played out.

13. See Allen, Halliday, and Sikes 1980: lxiv-lxxxi on "The Homeric Hymns in Antiquity" for the pertinent citations from the fifth century B.C. onward. This discussion will assume that the *Hymn to Apollo,* its Delian and Pythian sections notwithstanding, constitutes a single work; cf. Nagy (1979: 6–7), for whom "the integrity of the poem results from the fusion of two traditions about Apollo, the Delian and the Pythian, but the artistic fusion of two distinct traditions implies a corresponding social fusion of two distinct audiences."

14. Wolf 1985: 112. On the importance of his *Prolegomena ad Homerum* for the development of studies in oral tradition, see Foley 1988: 4.

15. 1980: xcv, adding that "there is nothing incongruous in supposing Homerid rhapsodes at one time prefacing their recital of portions of Homer with invocatory verses of their own, and at another reciting, at *agônes* [ritual games, contests] and festivals, longer independent compositions in honour of the God of the place."

celebrations consisting primarily of formulaic addresses and closures,[16] four of them—namely, the Hymns to Demeter, Apollo, Hermes, and Aphrodite (nos. II, III, IV, and V)—are much more extensive poems, on the order of 300–600 lines each, and are characterized mainly by long narrative middle sections detailing the god's or goddess's birth and/or later mythic history. While it may be possible to understand a modest-sized hymn of, say, five to fifty hexameters as a prelude to a more substantial recitation or performance, the four major Hymns seem unlikely to have performed that function, and the most recent scholarship has moved toward treating them as free-standing works in their own right.[17]

This considerable subgeneric span, from brief lyric through well-developed mythic history, has a historical dimension as well. Although dating of the Hymns remains for most scholars an approximate science, the more so since the works involved are traditional and (at least) oral-derived,[18] the conventional wisdom holds that most of them must have been "post-Homeric," that is, somewhat later than Homer, with conjecture locating their emergence from the eighth through the fifth century B.C., a few possibly later.[19] Equally unsure is the matter of possible authorship: Pausanias speaks of Olen, Pamphos, Musaeus, Orpheus, and Homer as composers of hymns, but these attributions are as problematic as the overarching Homeric Question,[20] and therefore as subject to hypothesis, proposal, and counterproposal.

Especially for our stated purpose—an understanding of the word-power associated with the *Homeric Hymn to Demeter*—the textual dimensions of authorship and date are far less important than the basic unity of most of the Hymns as a group and their general homology in register with the Homeric epics.

16. These shorter Hymns include poems addressed to Aphrodite, Apollo, Ares, Artemis, Asklepios, Athena, Demeter, Dionysos, the Dioskouroi, Gaia, Helios, Hephaistos, Hera, Herakles, Hermes, Hestia, the Mother of the gods, the Muses and Apollo, Pan, Poseidon, Selene, and Zeus. The relationship between the two Hermes hymns, the longer (no. 4, 580 ll.) and the shorter (no. 18, 12 ll.), is problematic. Lines 1–9 of no. 4 are nearly identical to the first nine lines of no. 18, and 4.579–80 resemble 18.10–12 to a degree. Whether these are textually related witnesses (the shorter an abstract or excerpt of the longer), multiforms of the same Hymn, or evidence for the modulation of the simple *prooimion* to a full-blown, free-standing poem must remain conjectural.

17. Cf. esp. Clay (1989), who argues that "the [major] hymns provide a necessary complement to the Panhellenic epic and theogonic poetry of Homer and Hesiod" (16). See further n. 16 above.

18. Basing his remarks on statistical tests for innovation in the diction, Janko (1982: 188) observes: "If we accept, as I believe we should, that writing played no part in the *composition* (as opposed to the recording) of the Homeric and Hesiodic poems, then it is at least clear that the two *Hymns to Apollo* do not differ from them, while . . . the Hymns *to Aphrodite*, *to Demeter*, and *to Hermes* (along with the *Shield of Heracles*) are increasingly suspect of being influenced by the use of writing in their composition." His primary evidence for this perspective on *Demeter* is the nature of its enjambment (41; cf. also 183). The argument made in the present volume—that there exists an expressive and receptional logic for the persistence of the traditional oral register in texts—would tend to mitigate the segregative force of such findings. See further Janko 1990 and 1992: 37–38.

19. For our purposes with the *Hymn to Demeter,* Clay's generalization that the four major hymns date "from about the eighth to the sixth centuries B.C." (1989: 5) is a sufficient approximation. See further n. 18 above.

20. See Allen, Halliday, and Sikes 1980: lxxxiii-lxxxviii for what is known about these and other poets as possible hymnists; note that Hesiod is included by some commentators (on this attribution cf. Minton 1970 on the possible hymn-proem of his *Theogony*). On the Homeric Question in general, see esp. Nagy 1992.

Although genre-dependence means that the Hymns must show some variation from the epics, particularly at those levels most governed by genre, the compositional and expressive idiom employed across all forms of Homeric *epos* is in some ways remarkably consistent. At the level of phraseology, the formulaic constitution of the Hymns does not diverge graphically from that of the epics: after studying the repertoires, Janko (1982: 26) concludes that "if there were schools of poets they cannot be distinguished by more than a few regional formulae: the unity of the tradition is impressive."[21] While it is dangerous to base too much on a selection of texts we cannot assign by individual poet or region, as we can the often quite heterogeneous groups of performances recorded from modern oral traditions,[22] the factor of Panhellenism may also be enlisted as a focusing dynamic that may well have shaped surviving witnesses of *epos* into a unified, streamlined tradition.[23] When one adds the rationalizing argument that the most fundamental measure of a traditional, performance-derived register is not the phraseological objects themselves but rather the traditional rules that govern their generation,[24] then the Hymns take their place ever more securely as full members of the family of Homerica.

If the phraseology and its traditional rules plainly suggest a unity of *epos,* the case cannot be so clear for levels of traditional organization beyond the microstructural. For immediately after leaving the relatively unconstrained level of the hexameter diction, we must confront the challenge of a narrative structure that depends in part on the demands of the Hymn genre. The scenic repertoire of even the major Hymns—there will be little beyond (chiefly formulaic) patterns of opening and closing in the shorter poems—must differ in certain respects from that of the immensely larger epic; even a first approximation would assume a markedly more limited repertoire of forms for the Hymns as well as a natural generic divergence in texture and scope between instances of a motif or theme shared across genres.[25] Epic story-patterns such as Return, if indeed they exist, must modulate similarly, in accordance with the presentational possibilities of the nonepic genre. And this is to say nothing of the extremely restricted textual sample—four major Hymns and two epics, all in singular versions—with which

21. Cf. Hoekstra 1969, esp. 57 on *Demeter.* It should be noted that his focus on divergences arises against the background of a strictly evolutionary hypothesis and from a commitment to emphasizing relatively minor differences over broad and general similarities. See further the discussion of idiolect and dialect below. On features shared among the *Hymn to Hermes,* the *Theogony,* two Hesiodic fragments, and the *Iliad,* see Harrell 1991: 309f.

22. On idiolect and dialect in the South Slavic epic register, cf. Foley 1990a: chaps. 5, 8.

23. Clay (1989: 270) summarizes: "Alongside the Panhellenic genres of heroic epic and theogonic poetry, we can now add the major Homeric Hymns as a distinct and complementary genre, an equal partner, as it were, in the great Panhellenic enterprise that molded a unified and systematic conception of the ordered cosmos for the Greeks."

24. Cf. Foley 1990a: chaps. 3–4 on phraseology and traditional rules in ancient Greek *epos;* comparative analyses are available for South Slavic (chap. 5) and Anglo-Saxon (chap. 6).

25. Sowa (1984: 2) argues that "the presence in the *Hymns* of these themes [of the Marriage of the Fertility Goddess, the Journey, and the Hero's Birth], found also in Homer and Hesiod, adds to the evidence that the *Hymns,* too, belong to the oral tradition of composition." Note that she is employing the term "theme" to "mean more or less what Lord means by 'complexes of themes'" (9), that is, "story-patterns."

we must work. Under such conditions, whatever we may find of homologous scenic or thematic material linking the epics and the Hymns will deserve special attention.

To provide a theoretical underpinning for the general interrelationship of the Homerica in terms of register, we may draw on a principle of generic brachiation first elaborated elsewhere.[26] Within a poetic tradition, genres that diverge prosodically must show fewer correspondences between their traditional phraseologies than those that do not. A phraseology exists in symbiosis with the metrical dynamics of the tradition; divergence in meter thus means divergence in diction. Because the Homeric epics and Hymns employ the same hexameter medium, we may expect, within limits, a unified phraseology, with many elements—products of a process that proceeds under the aegis of traditional rules—shared between epic and Hymn. This is also the case, for example, with the Anglo-Saxon poetic genres, all of which employ the stress-based, alliterative line: epic, elegy, hagiography, riddle, maxim, and so on can share phraseology across generic boundaries, subject of course to need and convention. It is, on the other hand, decidedly not the case with South Slavic traditions, wherein diction in symbiosis with a decasyllabic prosody, for example, has little in common with diction supported by an octosyllabic meter.[27] Brachiation by prosody would not be a determining factor per se in the relationship among genres at the narrative level, where the influence of poetic type would loom larger and exert its influence unmitigated by a shared symbiosis of phraseology and meter.

As an avenue toward considering a few traditional, metonymic features of the *epos* register, let us draw some rough formal outlines for the Hymn genre, specifically without prescribing any accompanying social function. I suggest this approach for three principal reasons. First, and most pragmatically, a formal, structural approach will not disenfranchise one or another group of the Hymns on the basis of their unacceptability as *prooimia,* as free-standing works, or as other types of poetry. Second, for oral-derived traditional works, which come to us as decontextualized texts, the relationship between performance and genre will be crucially important in its broad implications while finally unrecoverable in precise terms. In this regard Nagy's view of performance and *epos* is quite compatible with the perspective on such issues developed earlier in this volume:[28]

> If indeed performance "takes on meaning only by referring to the instance of its utterance" [quoting Johnson 1980: 56], then this instance, this occasion, must be the basis for the intent of the utterance, for its rhetoric. If, further, the occasion should ever be lost or removed, then the intent of the utterance is destabilized. We may say that the very notion of genre serves as compensation for the lost occasion.

26. Cf. Foley 1991: 192.
27. We may contrast decasyllabic genres customarily performed by males (e.g., epic, genealogy) with octosyllabic genres customarily performed by females (e.g., charms, lyric songs). See further "*Bajanje* within the Village Expressive Repertoire," chap. 4 above.
28. Nagy 1990: 9; cf. the core concerns of chap. 3 above.

In the terms used in chapter 3, performance context is transformed into a textual rhetoric, which continues to foster a tradition of reception. In such circumstances it seems wisest not to insist on projecting precise functions from texts, lest such insistence exclude certain of the Hymns from consideration, but rather to accept a range of performance possibilities in order to concentrate on their word-power. We circumscribe the performance arena generously, in other words, to avoid fragmenting it and diluting its force.

Third, given the heterogeneity of the Hymns, and in particular their variance across a spectrum from simple praise songs to fully developed mythic histories, we would do well to admit the possibility of a diachronically and synchronically emergent genre, one that subsumes in its repertoire a number of related realizations without declaring any one type primary and the others derivative. Especially because we are involved with an oral-derived type of poetic enterprise, which has continued a tradition of expression and reception into a body of texts, fragmentation for the sake of a simplex typology (defined according to function or any other criterion) seems counterproductive. In what follows, then, I combine the structural analyses of a number of investigators to furnish a first approximation of the Hymn genre; with that modest overview in hand, we will then proceed to examine the implications of performance arena, register, and communicative economy in the *Hymn to Demeter* and, to a lesser extent, in other Hymns.

Genre Models for the Hymns

The system of description proposed by Richard Janko (1981) has the advantage of accommodating the entire spectrum of works involved by admitting to the larger genre both the shorter, simpler type and the longer, more developed sort of poem. Positing as do most commentators a three-part structure, Janko divides all of the Hymns into an introduction, a middle section consisting of "attributes" or mythic material or both, and a conclusion consisting of up to three elements—salutation, prayer(s), and poet's task (a reference to subsequent performance activities, usually the "next" song). The key part of this model lies in the classification of material constituting the body of the given Hymn as either a present-tense account of the god's "appearance, possessions, haunts, and spheres of activity" (Attributes; 11) or as "events that happened in the past, i.e. simply as narrative in the past tense" (Myth; 11). This double definition of the crucial middle section allows not only for disparate contents—the praise poetry of momentary panegyric versus the sustained narrative of a poem such as *Demeter*—but also for the troublesome because substantial variance in length and complexity.[29]

Based on a sample much larger than the Homeric Hymns alone, William Race's taxonomy (1982) also prescribes a tripartite structure, this time of an *archê,* in which the speaker addresses or introduces the god or hesitates over the

---

29. He also prescribes a single device for meshing the two, usually distinct middle sections (12): "The Attributive Hymn may be extended only by the addition of a Priamel leading into a Myth." The resultant pattern he then labels a Composite.

task; followed by the establishment of what he designates as *charis* ("favor, grace");[30] and culminating in a request or petition. As must any such systemic model, Race's categorization of the genre provides for flexibility in the middle section of the hymn, only in this instance by concentrating not on the nature of its contents but rather on the unifying, generic imperative that establishes a particular relationship between hymnist and deity (10):

> The rhetorical τέλος of a hymn, then, is to secure the god's pleasure by a "pleasing" choice of names and titles (especially prominent in the Orphic hymns) and by the "proper" narration of his powers and exploits (especially prominent in the longer Homeric hymns, Callimachus' hymns, and the prose hymns of Aristides and Menander).

Where Janko defines the middle section of the Hymn in terms of its style of presentation, then, Race characterizes its flexibility as derivative of a rhetorical strategy—to cultivate *charis* with the god addressed.[31]

These two accounts of formal structure in the Homeric Hymns harmonize to the extent that they can provide a collective, generic background for study of poetic features less immediately available through individual textual analysis. Moreover, neither perspective eliminates the possibility of viewing the extant body of Hymns as a kind of "anthology"; in this respect we may extend Clay's characterization of the major Hymns as "recount[ing] a critical chapter in the mythological history of the Olympians" (1989: 11) to include all or most of the thirty-three poems that survive, with the proviso that not all chapters of the anthology need be major, or even what Janko calls Mythic, Hymns. One thinks, for example, of the mélange of chapters in Vuk Karadžić's anthology of Marko Kraljević tales from the South Slavic tradition—some of them terse and pithy scenes, others longer and/or composite dramas—but all of them contextualized by a tradition of reception whose central dynamic is word-power.[32] Of course, such a conception of parts implying a (more than textual) whole means that the anthology can be only as successful as its audience is fluent in the dedicated register, and as its necessarily partial contents are evocative of implied contexts. To the elucidation of the Hymn anthology, and especially the *Hymn to Demeter* as one such chapter, we now turn.

---

30. Race chooses the idea of *charis* because "no other word epitomizes so well the relationship which the hymnist tries to establish with the god—one of reciprocal pleasure and good will" (8). Cf. Miller (1986), who likewise divides the Homeric Hymns into three sections (exordium, mid-section, and salute) and observes that "the rhapsodic hymn seeks primarily to *please* the god (and its human audience) through 'objective' (that is, essentially disinterested) praise" (2–3). Minton also accepts a "threefold pattern" as a "traditional guideline" (1970: 375), grouping the Hymns with a Hesiodic tradition distinct from the Homeric (on this last point cf. de Hoz 1964 and Notopoulos 1962).

31. Race also notes (11) that "often prayers for the success of the song are coupled with requests for the wellbeing of the community. In the Homeric Hymn to Demeter (490–94) the poet hopes that his song will succeed in eliciting the bounty of Demeter and Persephone. . . ." We will address below the issue of the homology of this generic pattern of petition with the shape of the particular Hymn and the Return story in general.

32. Cf. Foley 1991: 103–106.

The Dedicated Register

In what follows we will be concerned with understanding the traditional register in terms of three levels. The first of these is phraseology, that is, what Parry-Lord theory calls "formulaic structure" and Performance Theory "special formulae" (although Bauman's "special codes" are also involved here, as is "figurative language").[33] The second step of the examination will focus on a brief survey of the metonymic features of the Hymn genre and some of the modest-sized narrative moments and actions, integers that are shared with the larger Homeric *epos* and on the basis of which the reader/audience can foster continuity of reception. The third and final characteristic of the Hymn register to be considered is the clear evidence of a Return pattern that harmonizes the story of Demeter, the institution of the Eleusinian mysteries, the eternal return promised in the annual cycle, and the act of praise that the *Hymn to Demeter* (re-)presents.

Phraseology: Mighty [Infant] Slayer of Argos

In her brisk and generally helpful foreword to her translation of the Homeric Hymns (1973), Thelma Sargent offers the following observation on what she regards as misapplied epithets in the *Hymns to Hermes* and *to Demeter* (xi):

> While in some contexts *periphrôn* and *daïphrôn* may describe Persephone very well, they do not describe the young and innocent victim in the hymn to Demeter, and *kratus Argeïphontês*—accounting for nearly three of the six feet—is hardly appropriate to the newborn Hermes. Because these incongruities occur usually at the end of a line, I think they can be explained as desperate expedients under stress, and tolerantly overlooked.

The stress of which Sargent speaks is of course the exigency of composition during performance, since she follows a utilitarian brand of Parry-Lord theory.[34] Her comments center on the apparent inappropriateness of these phrases to the particular situations in which they appear, and assume an absolute textual singularity that would be foreign to the dynamic of word-power we have been studying in oral-derived traditional works.

Nonetheless, and granting her the compositional usefulness of the formulaic diction as a metrical register, we need not translate phraseological systematiza-

---

33. In other words, the following analysis considers traditional features and their word-power from the composite perspective advocated throughout this volume, with the explicit credo that, even at one remove in the rhetoric of oral-derived texts, performance remains the enabling event and tradition the enabling referent.

34. Just above she observes (xi): "There is hardly a noun, common or proper, that is not modified, and the modifiers are sometimes incongruous, irrelevant, even contradictory in context. These adjectives are stock descriptions, and the poet, composing aloud as he went along and needing, say, two and a half feet to fill out his line, must have just thrown in the first of an assortment of associated words of varying length that came to mind."

tion to artistic blemish. Let us begin with Hermes, *kratus Argeïphontês*, the "mighty slayer of Argos."[35] The prodigious feats of cattle-stealing and lyre-playing that Hermes manages during his first day alive might seem to offer one avenue for explaining away the attribution of a remarkable deed to a mere babe; if within the hyperbole that is his praise song he can accomplish such deeds within hours of birth, then perhaps nothing is impossible. But the Hymn itself removes this avenue of interpretation, making no explicit narrative mention whatsoever of Hermes' (later) conquest of Argos.[36] It is as if an episode from his future exploits were retrojected into the infancy of this newborn son of Zeus and Maia, and it is precisely this anachronism in the "biography" that cannot be dispatched by a general understanding of Hermes as divine prodigy. He may be *kratus* ("mighty") from birth, but, unless his mythic biography is resequenced, he cannot yet be *Argeïphontês* ("slayer of Argos").

Just how does the poet employ the undeniably formulaic phrase *kratus Argeïphontês*, and how else is the god Hermes named? As it turns out, there are altogether nine occurrences of the phrase in the Homerica: five in the Hymns, and two each in the *Iliad* and *Odyssey*. Interestingly, the instances in the Hymns share no special contexts, nor is the application uniformly or monolithically "appropriate" in a textual sense. At *Demeter* 346, Hermes, sent on an errand from Zeus, approaches Hades to make the case for releasing Persephone. Later in the same poem, at 377, he grasps the whip to drive his deathless horses and golden chariot. Within the *Hymn to Hermes* the celebrated god is named in this way twice: at 294, the infant's double gastric "explosion," delivered while in Apollo's arms, constitutes an omen of remarkable things to come, while at 414 he first seeks to hide from Apollo and then charms the god with his singing and lyre-playing. Finally, in the *Hymn to Aphrodite* (129), the goddess invokes the "mighty slayer of Argos" as the culprit who, according to her lying tale spun to disclaim divinity, stole her away from her father's home in Phrygia and brought her to this place to be Anchises' wife. Some of these usages may be more acceptable than others as decontextualized, situation-specific attributions, but, as we have learned in earlier chapters, traditional phraseology has little allegiance to such a textually significative dynamics.

35. On the uncertain etymological meaning of the epithet, cf. Heubeck, West, and Hainsworth 1988: 79, n. to line 38: "Ancient scholars offer various wild guesses about its meaning; the usual interpretation was 'slayer of Argus', recalling Hermes' role in the story of Io, an obviously ancient tale, even though the first surviving references to it come from the pseudo-Hesiodic *Catalogue of Women* and *Aegimus* (Hes. frr. 122ff., 294ff.). It seems fair to infer that the poet and his audience understood *argeiphontês* thus; certainly the second element was already interpreted as 'killer' when the *Iliad* was composed, since it must have provided the model for *andreiphontês* (*Il.* ii 651 etc., cf. *Poluphontês Il.* iv 395)"; cf. Kirk 1985: 127, n. to line 103. Heubeck et al. go on to give alternate suggested derivations for the formula ("dog-killer," "shining in splendor," "killer *at* Argos") and to observe that while "slayer of Argus" was perhaps not the "original" (etymological) meaning, such uncertainty is irrelevant to the present discussion on a number of scores; we may agree with this position, first because we are not concerned with what the audience of the *epos* did not themselves understand, and second because the lexical meaning of the epithet as an isolate is nominal and thus not germane to its traditional, performance-derived role as part of a signifying unit.

36. For a digest of Hermes' mythological identity, see Morford and Lenardon 1991: 221–40.

We can discover more about the particular force of *kratus Argeïphontês* on its own terms by consulting the Homeric poets' repertoire of related phrases. Over all of the Hymns and both epics, the epithet *Argeïphontês* appears a total of forty-two times, all but one localized at the end of the hexameter line and all but four preceded by a complementary adjective. The distribution of the thirty-eight noun-epithet formulas is as follows:[37]

Phrase	Iliad	Odyssey	Hymns
κρατὺς Ἀργειφόντης	2	2	5
διάκτορος Ἀργειφόντης (incl. oblique cases)	8	7	1
ἐΰσκοπος Ἀργειφόντης (incl. oblique cases)	2	2	2
χρυσόρραπις Ἀργειφόντης (incl. oblique cases)	0	1	3
Κυλλήνιος Ἀργειφόντης	0	0	2
κύδιμος Ἀργειφόντης	0	0	1
	12	12	14

These phrases demonstrate some dimensions of Parryan thrift in their deployment, with traditional integers of all four primary line-ending lengths favored by the hexameter from midline onward:

simplex Ἀργειφόντης	C2 - end (adonean)
διάκτορος Ἀργειφόντης ἐΰσκοπος Ἀργειφόντης	B2 - end (hemistich)
χρυσόρραπις Ἀργειφόντης Κυλλήνιος Ἀργειφόντης	B1 - end (hemistich)
κρατὺς Ἀργειφόντης	C1 - end (colon)

At the same time it should be observed that to an extent these formulas taken together lack thrift, since they offer more than one way to name a given figure in the same metrical fashion, but that they are further sorted by genre.[38]

This system of phraseology amounts collectively to an idiomatic way of naming Hermes that may be understood as "useful," as long as we restrict the

37. Of the four nonepithetic occurrences, two are nominative and line-final (*Il.* 24.182, *Od.* 10.302), one is accusative and line-final (*Il.* 24.153), and the last is vocative and between the A1 and B1 caesurae (*Argeïphonta*, a different metrical word-type; *Hymn to Hestia* [29].7).
38. Cf. Janko 1982: 21. The violation of thrift is not as severe as it might appear, however, since, for example, the epics use only *diaktoros Argeïphontês* (nom.), while *eüskopos Argeïphontês* (the "alternate" nom. formula from the B2 caesura to line-end) occurs solely in the Hymns. But cf. the discussion of *Hermês* phrases below.

application of utility to the coordinated group of integers themselves and not extend it without further examination to the fields of reference governed by any or all of Hermes' Argos-slaying names. To preview where we are headed, we may say that any of these integers has license to summon metonymically the entire, composite character of the god Hermes—not just as he who dispatches the many-eyed guardian of Io, but as prodigy, messenger, and prominent member of the Olympian coterie. The "tell-tale detail" acts as a nominal site for the catalysis of word-power, for establishment of the performance arena and engagement of the extrasituational, traditional whole that is Hermes. In this way communicative economy derives from the focus provided by a limited number of onomastic possibilities.[39]

Let us then widen the perspective and ask how the *Argeïphontês* diction works in the larger context of all of Hermes' names. In order to abbreviate and simplify the presentation of this comparative material, I will resort to a series of compositional rules that illustrate both the options available in the diction and the apparently singular behavior of the Hymns poet(s).[40] We begin with the smallest increment of the hexameter verse, the last two metra or adonean clausula:

Rule (1): To name Hermes from the C2 caesura (or bucolic diaeresis) to line-end (_ u u _ _) in the Hymns, employ the phrase *kudimos Hermês* ("honored Hermes," nom.; *kudimon Hermên,* acc.). This formula is used a total of nine times in the Hymns and not at all in the epics; of the only other possibilities for this part of the line in the Hymns, *Maiados huios* ("Maia's son") seldom stands alone and does occur in the *Odyssey,* while *aglaos Hermês* ("shining Hermes") occurs once in a curious line.[41] Clearly, the poet of the *Hymn to Hermes* has a decided, virtually exclusive "preference" for *kudimos Hermês* under these particular metrical conditions, a phrase absolutely unknown to the *Iliad* or *Odyssey.*[42]

---

39. Cf. Foley 1991, esp. 52–53. To draw the argument to one logical extreme, a "surplus" of ways to name a character would dilute the system of signification by weakening the bridge between nominal integer and traditional, performance-derived meaning. Although most characters can be summoned in more than one phraseological way, there would come a point at which an increasing repertoire of noun-epithet formulas would become too large and unsystematized to economically promote the institutionalized, pars pro toto relationship that word-power engenders. This kind of dysfunction, like an audience's lack of fluency, would seem a precondition to the deployment of textual strategies for encoding and transmission.

40. Let me stipulate that, for the sake of convenience, these rules are framed solely from a synchronic perspective, and thus have built-in limitations; for the complementary perspective from diachrony, see esp. Nagy 1974, 1979, 1990, and Foley 1990a: chaps. 3–4.

41. Only two of thirteen instances of *Maiados huios/-oi/-el-on* over the Hymns and the *Odyssey* appear as the simplex phrase; the most common context is *Dios kai Maiados hui-* ("son of Zeus and Maia," 7 times). As illustrated with the famous "winged words" phrase and associated diction (Foley 1990a: 129–37), the simplex *Maiados hui-* should not be understood as the "core" upon which the longer pattern is erected, but as a separate, individual response to traditional rules. The single simplex instance of *aglaos Hermês* (*Hymn to Hermes* [4].395) may be more a reaction to the consistent word-type placement of the verb *epepeitheto* ("[he] obeyed"; 10 of 14 in this position, favored for the word-type u u _ u u [63.2% for the word-type]), which immediately precedes this unusual clausula, than to any hypothetical formulaic alternative. Word-type percentages are derived from O'Neill 1942, with corrections for natural quantity in the final anceps.

42. Underlining the Hymn-specific usage of *kudimos Hermês* is the unique and unwieldy construction used at *Hymn to Hermes* [4].84, *kudimos Argeïphontês,* which this innovative poet employs to eke out a hemistich after the relative pronoun *ta* ("these things").

Rule (2): With three exceptions, Hermes is never named—with *any* phrase—in this same portion of the hexameter in either the *Iliad* or the *Odyssey*. That is, the two epics, as opposed to the Hymns, share the phraseological policy of employing only longer noun-epithet formulas for Hermes; while we find a total of twenty-four occurrences of longer names in the *epos* as a whole, there are only three instances of an adonean phrase in the epics, and all of them are eccentric accommodations of other traditional patterns.[43]

Rule (3): To name Hermes from the C1 caesura to line-end (u u _ u u _ _), employ the phrase *kratus Argeïphontês*. This name, our focus for this part of the chapter, is evenly distributed throughout the *epos:* five in the Hymns and four in the epics. There are rare exceptions to this rule, all explicable as apparently either ad hoc lines or analogical formations and none involving an alternate system of diction.[44]

Exploration of the larger phraseological context of "mighty slayer of Argos" could be extended to treat the names that occupy other sections of the line, but perhaps enough has been brought to light to make the major and general point: there are finite limitations on the ways in which Hermes can be summoned, and the poets of the *epos*, somewhat idiosyncratically in the Hymns as distinct from the epics, operate within these limitations. But as we have seen earlier, "constraints" are more productively understood as mechanisms that focus and empower rather than exclude and dilute.

In regard to differences between the Hymns and the epics, we should keep in mind the essential unity of the *epos* register, demonstrated by a number of investigators as noted earlier. This empirically established characteristic is reenforced from a theoretical vantage point by what was observed above about the

---

43. Besides being only twenty-nine lines apart, *Il.* 24.153 and 182 share a whole-line formulaic pattern: *toios/-n gar t/hoi pompos/-n _ _ _ Argeïphontês/-n.* In the first case, Zeus is issuing instructions for Iris to carry to Priam, saying "such an escort shall I send to guide him, Argeiphontes"; in the second instance Iris is delivering the instructions, telling Priam "such an escort shall go with you to guide you, Argeiphontes." Unusually, it is the opening section of the hexameter that demonstrates the formulaic phraseology, and the latter hemistich seems a response to that fixity made under traditional rules (note that u _ u u, the metrical word-type of the interstitial material, *ham' hepsetai* and *opassomen,* is localized 95.6% at this position). We should also note that Zeus's original directions and Iris's speech to Priam are nearly identical throughout (cf. esp. 147–58 and 176–87). The Odyssean exception to the second naming rule (10.302) likewise seems a traditional, rule-governed response to a line-initial formula; in this case the construction seems (on available evidence) to be ad hoc, since no relevant patterns with either *pore* or *pharmakon* exist.

44. On the oddity of *Il.* 20.72, which involves the unique phrase *eriounios Hermês* ("helper Hermes," as distinct from the metrically inequivalent *Hermês/-n eriounios/-n*), the rare word *sôkos* ("the mighty"?) perhaps to be taken as part of the epithetic phrase, and metrical license (compensatory lengthening of *-kos-* before a vowel), see M. Edwards 1991: 297, n. to 72. The inexplicit *Dios aglaos huios* ("Zeus's shining son," *Hermes* 432; also applied to Minos, judge in the land of the dead, at *Od.* 11.568) and *Dios alkimos huios* ("Zeus's courageous son," *Hermes* 101) well illustrate the nominal nature of components of a traditional "word": the issue is not whether shining or courageous is more appropriate to a given context, but the fact that each successfully constitutes a metrically acceptable key to performance and thus metonymically summons the named god in all of his traditional complexity. *Kullênios* ("Kyllenian," designating a mountain in Arcadia) and *chrusorrapis* ("with golden wand") combine once each with *Hermês*, and only in the Hymns, to fill this part of the line. The former can be viewed as a cultic, Hymn-specific development, and the latter as an analogical formation from the longer phrase *chrusorrapis/-n Argeïphontês/-n,* which is a hemistich formula that occurs a total of four times in the *epos.*

lack of metrical brachiation in ancient Greek *epos*. Because both Hymn and epic phraseologies stand in a symbiotic relationship to the same hexameter prosody, and therefore follow the same traditional rules, they are unlikely to have developed into wholly separate linguistic idioms. Were this not the case—if, for example, the Hymns employed a pentameter diction with, presumably, a very different intralinear dynamics—then this hypothetical register would have little in common with the Homeric language of the *Iliad* and *Odyssey*.

But dynamic processes governed by generative traditional rules yield similar, not necessarily always identical, collections of "products," and even an instrument as finely calibrated as the Homeric hexameter leaves room for variation and substitution, both diachronically and synchronically. Indeed, the continued existence of a traditional register—at the phraseological or any other level—is directly dependent on its built-in capacity for change, for self-renewal. Even if that capacity must sometimes translate to "errors" when viewed only in the most immediate context of an extant and fossilized text,[45] it is essential to the maintenance of process, or "ongoingness," in a tradition. Hoekstra, Janko, Nagy, and others have convincingly established the evolutionary aspect of the diction, the ways in which the living organism perpetuates itself in effect by replacing itself over time. As a complement to that fruitful diachronic perspective, I propose considering some of the differences between Hymn and epic registers—minor perturbations within an overall unity—from a synchronic point of view as well. For the Hymn-specific usages exemplified above constitute a pattern of variation extremely similar to the synchronically defined levels of idiolect and dialect that can be studied in living oral traditions. Let us consider, in other words, the evidence for idiosyncratic specification of the shared poetic register not solely as a historical or genre-specific development but, in part, as the result of different regions' or even individuals' deployment of traditional rules.[46]

Within the unified decasyllabic register of South Slavic epic, for example, we find numerous instances of variation among the formulaic repertoires of individuals. One idiolectal discrepancy involves the way in which singers begin a Return Song, specifically how they serve notice that the prisoner-hero is raising the required ruckus in prison. In the geographical region known as Stolac in central Hercegovina, a relatively homogeneous dialect area in which a great deal of the total formulaic repertoire is common to singers whose works I have examined, Mujo Kukuruzović and Halil Bajgorić diverge on this point.[47] In such

45. Such momentary "lapses" can occur all the way from the microstructural level (as with hypermetric and hypometric lines; cf. Foley 1990a: 89–95 on South Slavic and Parry 1928b for ancient Greek) to the macrostructural level (as with story-pattern shifts; cf. Foley 1990a: chap. 10). It should be stressed that understanding these moments of apparent infelicity as the poet's "nodding" amounts to removing the works in question from their traditional contexts, which provide both structural and significative support for what may seem mistakes or inappropriate usages when viewed out of context.

46. One must also respect the possibility that such divergences stem, at least in part, from genre-dependence; however, the lack of metrical brachiation in the *epos*, discussed above, would seem to make differentiation by idiolect and dialect a more likely explanation.

47. The basis for these remarks is a computerized concordance of five epic songs from the Stolac region in central Hercegovina, a total of some 7,287 decasyllabic lines; on the nature of the sample, see further Foley 1990a: 50–51. For biographies and other details about the singers involved, see ibid.: 42–50.

a situation Kukuruzović turned without fail to one of two expressions—"He cried out [for a period of time]" or "How he cried out, it was his misfortune"— while his counterpart Bajgorić always employed the phrase "[name] cried out in prison."[48] Notice that these phrases share a number of features without being identical, and we may add that all three obey traditional rules.[49] Other points of comparison lie in their variant lengths[50] and in their flexibility in accommodating different periods of time or different agent names. In short, these three formulas exhibit an idiolectal variation in the South Slavic epic register, representing the particular solutions that these two poets have established as personal compositional "words" in their repertoires of traditional diction.

Idiolectal divergence can also be glimpsed in the "period of time" phrases each *guslar* employs. When he wants to indicate the length of the prisoner's intolerable shouting, so loud and cacophonous that it keeps the captor's infant from sleeping and nursing and thus threatens the very continuation of his lineage, each poet once again resorts to different but related phrases. Only Kukuruzović will say either "a little week of days" ("nedjelica dana") or, much more often, "three white days" ("tri bijela dana"), and only Bajgorić will claim that the noise had lasted "two white days" ("dva bijela dana"). These expressions are obviously related, and lexically they mean about the same thing, but the point is that the two singers handle the symbiosis of prosody and phraseology individually; what is more, that individuality is absolutely consistent. In this case, however, the two idiolects also exhibit a point of contact with yet another phrase used for the same purpose, a phrase that actually appears in both singers' performed repertoires: "for a week of days" ("za nedelju dana"). This and many other phrases shared between and among the singers of the Stolac region constitute evidence of a regional singers' dialect within the traditional register, a geographically defined subset of the pantraditional language employed by *guslari* across the epic territory.

Such witnesses argue the existence of both idiolects and dialects within the traditional register of South Slavic epic,[51] a situation broadly congruent with what N. Postlethwaite (1979) has suggested, after textual analysis, for the ancient Greek *epos*. On the basis of an examination of the singularity of Hymns diction,

---

48. In the original language, respectively: "Cmili [for a period of time]" or "Kako cmili, nevolja mu bila," as against "[name] u tamnici cmili" (with customary translation of the verbs as historical present).

49. On the traditional rules underlying South Slavic epic phraseology, cf. Foley 1990a: chap. 5.

50. One is a four-syllable or first-hemistich phrase, one a whole-line or decasyllabic unit, and the last a six-syllable or second-hemistich phrase.

51. An additional, highly instructive example of idiolectal usage is the divergence in the ways that Kukuruzović and Bajgorić handle the influx of Turkicisms and compositionally related morphs in the South Slavic traditional register. While they both include numerous actual Turkish loan-words in a canonical formulaic phrase, X *učiniti* (X *perform*), where X stands for the loan-word and the phrase as a whole occupies the second colon of the decasyllable, Kukuruzović also inserts non-Turkish words (both nouns and adverbs) into the same formula and position. The X *učiniti* pattern thus characterizes the dialect they share, while in its extension to non-Turkish words Kukuruzović's idiolect is distinctly more innovative than that of Bajgorić. For a complete analysis of this phenomenon, see Foley 1990a: 192–94.

he argues "[that] 'the tradition' was not a type of monolith on which all composers drew according to their requirements, but rather that each composer built up his own 'personal tradition' of favoured formulae."[52] Of course, we cannot establish with certainty the limits of idiolect and dialect in works that survive only in manuscripts, indeed in the case of the *epos* in manuscripts far removed from the fact and time of composition. But just as we can use the perspective of diachrony to account for linguistic innovations of various kinds, so we can summon the concept of synchronic specialization of the register to account for what seem to be compositional options. Thus the poet of the *Hymn to Hermes* consistently employs the nonepic phrase *kudimos Hermês* ("honored Hermes") to name the god in the adonean clausula, while except in rare, ad hoc instances the epic poet(s) do not name him at all in that portion of the hexameter. *Kudimos Hermês* is a feature of the *Hermes* poet's idiolect, an individual reflex governed by traditional rules.[53]

Similarly, the decided preference for *kratus Argeïphontês* ("mighty slayer of Argos") from C1 to line-end over both the Hymns and the epics, with the exceptions again being ad hoc or analogical formations, illustrates at least a dialectal reflex—in that it is shared by both forms of *epos*—and possibly a pantraditional usage. Again, we cannot apply the concepts of idiolect and dialect except by deduction, and certain attribution is well beyond the scope of textual analysis, but in a general way these levels of register help to explain the marshaling of compositional options. Working within traditional rules, different individuals or regions will occasionally develop (and maintain) different responses to the challenge of maintaining a symbiosis of prosody and phraseology.[54]

Such dialectal and idiolectal variance within the pantraditional language not only constitutes a natural and logical complication of theories of traditional phraseology, thus dissolving the romantic reductionism of a single diction for all participants in what would amount to a quite mechanical process; it also provides an opportunity to glimpse how nominal the expressive integers really are in their lexical content. I have argued above, and elsewhere,[55] that formulaic phrases, as well as other features of the traditional register, are much more important for what they connote by traditional fiat than for what they may seem to insist upon in their lexical surfaces. Noun-epithet formulas were thus interpreted as indexical of the characterizations they referenced pars pro toto, rather than as always and everywhere appropriate to their momentary usage within a specific situation. Indeed, it has been suggested that the epithet itself serves

---

52. 1979: 17. Postlethwaite cites Pope 1963 (esp. 8–9) as the first to suggest the existence of idiolectal versions of the traditional poetic language for the *epos*.

53. Cf. Foley 1990a: 188 on the general principle of personal varieties of the poetic register: "Such idiolectal variance amounts to the individual's signature on the unwritten document of oral traditional style."

54. Cf. Nagy's notion of Panhellenic streamlining, discussed in chap. 3, which would amount to a (pretextual) force acting to level such differences. Idiolectal and dialectal variety in the *epos* phraseology will in any case be limited by the metrical homogeneity of genres in the *epos*, as noted above.

55. Cf. Foley 1991, esp. 17–33.

chiefly as a necessary partner to its noun in the cumulative production of a single "word"; to divide this combination, to insist on the situation-specific activity of the epithet, amounts to subdividing the word beyond its ability to signify according to the traditional contract.[56] Such noun-epithet formulas, and to an extent all such components of the traditional performance register, promote a continuity of reception by indexing extrasituational ideas and realities according to a predetermined code.

With the evidence of dialects and idiolects we encounter a further, but still inherently logical, extension of this poetic dynamics. In essence, what constitutes a "word" for one poet may not exist as an indexical element for another poet in the same region or, even more likely, in another region. The first singer may summon the traditional scene of the prisoner lamenting with one phrase, while the second may accomplish exactly the same poetic feat by use of another integer. For the first poet *three* days may consistently describe the period during which said prisoner upsets the social and political order with his shouting, while for his counterpart *two* days will be the canonical interval. Without the linguistic flexibility and specification built into the idiolect-dialect model, we would be forced to understand these and other divergences as systemic modulations on a common stock of generative phrases, a theory that suffers more and more as the formal differences among singers' and regions' usages increase. Wholesale "substitutions" of phraseology or wide "discrepancies" in thematic structure, for example, beg the question of just how universal a generative explanation can be before it becomes more descriptive than explicative. With the idiolect-dialect model, however, grounded as it is in analysis of actual recorded performances whose singers and regions are known, there is no need for overelaborate, unconvincing, universalist models: we can allow the individual and the geographically defined area full license to operate within traditional rules and to establish personal and regional levels of specification within the phraseology and narrative structure.

To put the same matter in terms with which we have been working, we can allow these individuals and regions license to forge their own lexical keys to the invocation of the performance arena, their own points of access to communicative economy. By extension from the nominal character of metonymic phrases, their personal store of phrases—relatively small, after all, in relation to the diction they share with others—must answer only two basic requirements: that it accord with the compositional dictates called traditional rules, and that it be used with the kind of idiomatic consistency that establishes an institutionalized

---

56. Consider an analogy. The constituent sounds of the modern English [bot], "boat," taken together as a morphemic whole, index the idea of "ship, vessel." Taken separately, however, neither [b] nor [o] nor [t] can convey this or any other idea: the signifying code is violated by atomizing the smallest logical unit of meaning. A graphic example of the dampening of the semantics of constituent elements in the interest of a larger "word" is furnished by the South Slavic formula *niz Markovac kleti*. Literally meaning "below accursed Markovac," this apparently derogatory phrase is regularly applied to the birthplace of Marko Kraljević, one of the chief Serbian heroes. The singer's explanation that "it has to be said this way" underlines the traditional indexical function of this otherwise curious noun-epithet combination. See further Foley 1991: 244–46.

relationship between integer and extrasituational meaning. If the requirements of linguistic shape and referential regularity are met, the given phrase can serve as an index to the immanent tradition—whether or not it happens to occur in the performance oeuvre of another poet or another region. To state the principle plainly, then: idiolectal and dialectal forms can and do serve the purpose of word-power, illustrating the fundamentally nominal nature of the lexical content of a register while projecting a complex metonymic resonance that derives from performance tradition.

So it is with *kudimos Hermês* and *kratus Argeïphontês*. The former amounts to a specialization by the *Hymn to Hermes* poet that for whatever reason has not found its way into the surviving epic poems. On this score the Hymns and epics vary almost absolutely: with three eccentric variations, Hermes is never named in the adonean clausula, with this phrase or with any other. Nonetheless, the regularity with which the Hymn poet turns to *kudimos Hermês* constitutes evidence that this phraseological "byte" serves an indexical function, summoning the son of Zeus and Maia to the performance arena and in effect deploying his omnibus mythic history as the interactive background for each of the finite situations in which he is so named.

The poetic strategy is no different with *kratus Argeïphontês*, "mighty slayer of Argos." In this case the name is (at least) dialectal, appearing in both the Hymns and the epics; rather than an individual poet's response to traditional rules that on available evidence gained no wider currency, this second name for Hermes proves to be common coin in the compositional realm of *epos*. It likewise uses a nominal entry-point—this time the specificity of the Argos episode instead of the generalized "honorable" character of the god—to index the whole of the mythologized figure, and once again it is not the decontextualized component parts but rather the whole "word" that matters. Hermes is called *kratus Argeïphontês* not because the poet lacks imagination or finds himself in a fix, nor because the slaying of Argos is pertinent to this or that subsequent (or preceding!) adventure, but because this name indexes his entire personality in the *epos*. There is a degree of Parryan thrift in the deployment of both *kudimos Hermês* and *kratus Argeïphontês*, but this is a feature of their compositional and not their significative function: for the purpose of traditional reference, the fundamental point is that they are licensed, pars pro toto, to make Hermes present via the traditional register. That is their special contribution to communicative economy, and their role in a performance tradition that operates through word-power.

Let us then return to Sargent's complaint that "*kratus Argeïphontês* . . . is hardly appropriate to the newborn Hermes" and her conclusion that "because these incongruities occur usually at the end of a line, I think they can be explained as desperate expedients under stress, and tolerantly overlooked." Epithets can be desperate only when they have no word-power, when they cannot perform the rhetorical function of summoning the named character to narrative present, and so toleration for a poet's unfortunate response to stress is certainly not required here. More important, I would maintain that *kratus Argeïphontês* is indeed fully appropriate to the infant Hermes, or the Hermes of any other moment or adventure. The core of the issue lies in what constitutes appropriateness: as argued above, it is not situational "fit," since to activate the semantics of the epithet alone—as opposed to the larger, indexical "word"—is to misapprehend the word-power inherent in all noun-epithet combinations. Rather, the fit must exist between the nominal signal and its traditional, performance-based meaning, between the integer and its metonymic implication. Another way to say the same thing is to observe that this kind of pars pro toto identification is a primary mode of characterization, or, from a third perspective, to note that there simply is no situation in which the entire mythic identity of Hermes—as a complex, multidimensional figure keyed by one of his "special formulae"—would be *in*appropriate. Within the performance arena there is no contradiction in an infant slayer of Argos.

Narrative Networks in the *Hymn to Demeter*

As we focus more closely on the *Hymn to Demeter,* wherein various features such as Persephone's names ("wise," "prudent," e.g.)[57] and the *epos*-wide integer "he/she did not disobey"[58] index metonymic meaning within the phraseological dimension of the register, let us be particularly aware of the resonance associated with larger, narrative patterns. For just as Hermes' names commanded a certain word-power not wholly derivable from their part-by-part semantics, so there exist scenes and motifs in *Demeter* that likewise project traditional, performance-derived implications. Our charge in decoding such integers, then, is to resist the easy assimilation to textual dynamics and to inquire whether such scenes and

57. Thus we need not share Sargent's concern that "while in some contexts *periphrôn* and *daïphrôn* may describe Persephone very well, they do not describe the young and innocent victim in the hymn to Demeter" (1973: xi), since as metonyms in the traditional register formulaic phrases never simply describe any single situation. Note that *periphrôn* is also well established in the *Odyssey* as a contributing (and thus lexically muted) element in larger "words" that name Penelope (50 times), Eurykleia (3 times), and Arete (once) in widely variant immediate contexts. Additionally, one can explain the *Hymn to Demeter*'s avoidance of the epithet *epainê* ("dread"), employed six times in the *Odyssey* but never in any of the Hymns, as a dialect feature without having to resort to the more generally untenable hypothesis of semantic inappropriateness; theoretically, "dread" would apply to the innocent young victim Persephone as readily as "mighty slayer of Argos" applies to the infant Hermes. Cf. the idiolectal "deep-girdled daughter" *(bathuzônoio thugatros,* gen.), applied to Persephone and used exclusively in *Demeter* (201, 304), and "deep-girdled Metaneira" *(bathuzônôi Metaneirêi,* dat.), also employed only in *Demeter* (161), with the dialectal or pantraditional "deep-girdled women" *(bathuzônous te gunaikas,* acc. pl., at *Il.* 9.594 and *Od.* 3.154, and *bathuzônôn te gunaikôn,* gen. pl., at *Demeter* 95, which show an idiolectal or dialectal distribution according to morphology).

58. This phrase and its near morphological relatives account for fully 25 of the 37 instances of *apitheô* "disobey" in the *epos* (21/29 in the *Iliad,* 2/4 in the *Odyssey,* and 2/4 in the Hymns), and of the remaining 12 many can be understood as reflexes of the same phraseology. The more important point is that this phrase consistently entails action intended to set right an imbalance or relieve an impasse, whether the particular context be Hera's injunction to Athena to stir up the Achaeans (*Il.* 2.166), Odysseus's command to Eurykleia to purify the palace after the slaughter (*Od.* 22.492), Zeus's order to Rhea to inform Demeter of his partial capitulation and order her to release her death grip on the earth (*Dem* 448; she "did not disobey" 22 lines later), or any of the other particular situations informed by this metonym.

motifs serve in some fashion as empowering, enabling metonyms, whether they contribute to the kind of expressive register we have been describing, and whether they therefore participate in (re-)establishing a continuity of reception. To put it gnomically, and with the pun very much intended, is there more to such integers than meets the eye?[59]

We may begin by briefly citing rhetorical reflexes of traditional oral forms that qualify as dialectal, genre-specific features, namely the opening and closing patterns found in so many of the Hymns. For the purposes of establishing the performance arena, or of keying performance, the specific phraseology employed to start the Hymn is less important than the general thrust of initial address to the god or goddess—customarily heavy with (indexical) epithets—together with some notation of singing. Thus *Demeter* opens with

> Δήμητρ' ἠύκομον, σεμνὴν θεόν, ἄρχομ' ἀείδειν,
>
> I begin to sing of fair-haired Demeter, revered goddess,

and within a few lines has also referred to its addressee as "with golden sword" and "bearing beautiful fruit."[60] Similarly, the much shorter second *Hymn to Athena* signals the arena in which the communicative exchange will occur with a variation on the same phrase and an even denser accumulation of epithets (no. 28: 1–4):

> Παλλάδ' Ἀθηναίην, κυδρὴν θεόν, ἄρχομ' ἀείδειν
> γλαυκῶπιν, πολύμητιν, ἀμείλιχον ἦτορ ἔχουσαν,
> παρθένον αἰδοίην, ἐρυσίπτολιν, ἀλκήεσσαν,
> Τριτογενῆ, . . .
>
> I begin to sing of Pallas Athena, renowned goddess,
> bright-eyed, many-counseled, of implacable heart,
> pure virgin, protector of cities, valiant,
> Trito-born, . . .[61]

Even though this second Hymn has no narrative dimension to speak of, only briefly recounting the goddess's miraculous birth, the same compositional strategy is employed, and in the agglomeration of names and initiatory phraseology we glimpse features that promote continuity of reception in genre and register.

Nor is that strategy limited exclusively to the opening phraseology shared by these two examples, although the "I begin to sing" (. . . *archom' aeidein*) formula

---

59. As background to the discussion to follow, cf. Clay's excellent review of prior scholarship on the *Demeter,* included in her comments on the political implications of the Hymn (1989: 202–65).

60. Respectively, *chrusaorou* and *aglaokarpou* (both in *Dem* 4).

61. Among the possible meanings given by Liddell and Scott 1968 for *Tritogeneia* are: born from the lake Tritonis in Libya, from Triton (a torrent in Boeotia), or from a spring in Arcadia; also "head-born" (which accords with what immediately follows as well as with her general mythic history), "born on the third day of the month," the "third child" after Apollo and Artemis, and so forth. Cf. *Il.* 4.515, 8.39, 22.183 and *Od.* 3.378. Once again, the lexical content of the epithet is nominal, and thus subsidiary to its indexical force as a way of summoning Athena traditionally.

is quite common.[62] Other integers can perform the same function, providing alternate pathways to the same performance arena, accompanied as above by a spate of names, as in the second *Hymn to the Dioskouroi* (no. 33: 1–3)—

Ἀμφὶ Διὸς κούρους, ἑλικώπιδες ἔσπετε Μοῦσαι,
Τυνδαρίδας, Λήδης καλλισφύρου ἀγλαὰ τέκνα,
Κάστορά θ' ἱππόδαμον καὶ ἀμώμητον Πολυδεύκεα,

Quick-glancing Muses, tell of the sons of Zeus,
sons of Tyndareos,[63] glorious children of fair-ankled Leda,
Kastor tamer of horses and blameless Polydeukes,

—or even the superficially quite different opening to the *Hymn to Ares* (no. 8: 1–5, 9)—

Ἄρες ὑπερμενέτα, βρισάρματε, χρυσεοπήληξ,
ὀβριμόθυμε, φέρασπι, πολισσόε, χαλκοκορυστά,
καρτερόχειρ, ἀμόγητε, δορυσθενές, ἔρκος Ὀλύμπου,
Νίκης εὐπολέμοιο πάτερ, συναρωγὲ Θέμιστος,
ἀντιβίοισι τύραννε, δικαιοτάτων ἀγὲ φωτῶν . . .
κλῦθι, βροτῶν ἐπίκουρε, δοτὴρ εὐθαλέος ἥβης,

Mighty Ares, golden-helmeted rider of chariots,
stout-hearted, shield-carrying and bronze-geared savior of cities,
strong-handed and unwearying lord of the spear, bulwark of Olympos,
father of fair Victory, and succorer of Themis.
You curb the unruly and lead truly just men, . . .
Hearken, helper of mortals and giver of flourishing youth.

All four passages, and in fact virtually all of the Hymns,[64] share two keying features at their openings. First, one of a selection of formulaic invocations sounds the knell of introduction, resonating against both the genre-specific convention of the Hymn and, more widely in the *epos,* against the rhetoric of beginnings in the *Iliad* and *Odyssey* proems.[65] Second, word-power derives as well from the plethora of epithets—"bytes" of traditional characterization—applied to the subject of the given Hymn.

Inasmuch as these epithets prove standard features of the Hymn genre, constituting a defining and enabling characteristic of the form, we may inquire further about their function. In addition to the obvious praise-poem dynamics, paralleled in many other traditions of panegyric,[66] note that the names and

62. On the introductions to the Hymns, see Janko 1981: 10–11.

63. On the ambivalent lineage of the Dioskouroi, Athanassakis (1976: 107) observes: "The tradition that makes Zeus the father of Kastor and Polydeukes is therefore post-Homeric, and its earliest occurrence must be Hesiod's *Ehoiai* (66 Loeb). The patronymic Tyndaridai refers to their putative father, and it was used in both literature and cult." As with Athena's mysterious epithet "Trito-born," the literal, lexical sense is subsidiary to its metonymic function.

64. Cf. Janko 1981: 23–24.

65. Another such "beginning" is that which introduces the Iliadic Catalog of Ships (2.484–94).

66. See esp. the South African tradition of Xhosa praise poetry (Opland 1975, 1983); cf. the range of brief narratives from the same culture (esp. Scheub 1992).

attributes collectively join each individual poem, and the Hymn genre as a whole, to the rest of the *epos* tradition by mirroring the epic in both style and substance. The same figures celebrated in the Hymns, in other words, are brought to the performance arena in epic via the same communicative strategy: invocation through the traditional, performance-derived register. And not only are many of the actual Hymn phrases shared with the epic register, but the general onomastic style informs both genres. In short, both the particular integers and their systemic mathematics constitute a shared mode of characterization, an aspect of word-power that pervades the *epos* tradition.

We may add that this common mode of characterization is intensified and further specialized in the Hymns, thus developing a genre-specific function that derives from an overall traditional dynamic. Metonymic reference becomes not simply a way to summon a god to poetic presence, as in extended narrative, but a "way of speaking" that harmonizes with the fundamental lyric thrust of the Hymn genre. What better way to praise and show reverence than to index the god's identity through word-power? What more appropriate, more acceptable avenue to divinity than to call him or her by names that bear institutionalized reference? Indeed, one cannot imagine any other onomastic strategy that would serve this purpose, simply because optimal expression and continuity of reception depend upon fluency in the dedicated register. In short, if poets command the word-power to name the god or goddess whom they wish to celebrate, they can summon that divinity with an effectiveness and alacrity of emergence possible only in the highly economical idiom fostered by a performance tradition.

The Hymn genre regularly exhibits a corresponding metonymic signal at the other end of its exposition—in the closure to the praise of the given god.[67] Often that signal emerges from the prayer that forms the body of the Hymn and looks toward a subsequent song, which has been interpreted as either another Hymn or the "main event" of Homeric narrative. The *Hymn to Pan* (no. 19), for example, ends with a formulaic line that marks closure in twelve of the thirty-three Hymns:

αὐτὰρ ἐγὼ καὶ σεῖο καὶ ἄλλης μνήσομ' ἀοιδῆς.

But now I will remember you and another song as well.

Interestingly, not only the shorter Hymns, which might more easily be considered preliminary to a longer narrative performance, but also three of the four longer members of the genre (*Demeter, Apollo,* and *Hermes*) employ this phrase, and the fourth (*Aphrodite*) uses a related line (no. 5: 293):

σεῦ δ' ἐγὼ ἀρξάμενος μεταβήσομαι ἄλλον ἐς ὕμνον.

Having begun with you, I will proceed to another hymn.

---

67. Because this aspect of the Hymns has been so thoroughly studied (cf. esp. Janko 1981 on "salutation, prayer(s), and poet's task"), our comments here will be brief.

Exactly the same formula also ends the first *Hymn to Artemis* (no. 9). But whether a Hymn closes with one of these explicit phrases or with the nonspecific prayer for health and support that may well imply such a generic intention, we can observe that patterns regularly employed to signal the terminus of a Hymn are, like the introductory patterns at its other extremity, a feature of register.[68] Between these two traditional "bookends" is contained the individualized praise of the god or goddess—whether as a momentary panegyric or as a fully developed mythic history—and the poet and audience work within a well-demarcated performance arena. The special communicative economy of the Hymn is enabled through institutionalized rhetorical appeal to performance and institutionalized reference to tradition.

Epos-wide Patterns

The *Hymn to Demeter* depends for its word-power on these generic signals at its periphery, and on numerous other metonymic patterns shared not with other (surviving) Hymns but with the *epos* tradition at large. In this respect the Hymns resonate to some of the same narrative frequencies as do the *Iliad* and *Odyssey,* and this is perhaps the best evidence available of the unified nature of the ancient Greek *epos.* We shall be concentrating on five instances of such intergeneric congruency in *Demeter:* suspicion of "death" and self-defilement, refusal of nourishment, the lying tale, the guest-host pattern, and the (Im)mortal Imperative/embassy of peers.

Suspicion of death and self-defilement. At lines 38–46 the poet describes Demeter's reaction to hearing her daughter Persephone's terrible, but as yet undifferentiated, cry of anguish:[69]

> The peaks of the mountains and the depths of the sea resounded
> with her immortal voice, and her mighty mother heard her.
> A sharp pain gripped her heart, and she tore
> the headband round her divine hair with her own hands.
> From both of her shoulders she cast down her dark veil
> and rushed like a bird over the nourishing land and the sea,
> searching; but none of the gods or mortal men
> wanted to tell her the truth and none
> of the birds of omen came to her as truthful messenger.

In the *Iliad* this pattern occurs twice, involving Achilleus's first word of Patroklos's demise (18.5ff.) and Andromache's incipient news of Hektor's death (22.437ff.). These two epic—and of course decidedly mortal—instances follow

---

68. These genre-dependent signals can also be understood as what Bauman calls an "appeal to tradition" (1977: 21): "a key to performance, a way of signaling the assumption of responsibility for the proper doing of a communicative act," which, as stressed throughout this volume, means a proper *reception* as well as initial expressive act.

69. In this section I will quote the Greek original only when necessary to establish a phraseological link; otherwise the examples will be cited in English translation.

a generalized sequence of (a) initial suspicion, (b) realization, whether by messenger or personal observation, (c) self-abuse, and (d) a lament for the dead.[70]

Because the pattern as it occurs in *Demeter* has allegiance both to the *epos* tradition at large and more immediately to the Hymn genre, and since in *Demeter* it conveys a divine rather than a mortal loss, certain aspects of the epic sequence are retained and others are modified.[71] In both Iliadic cases the first glimmer that the companion or mate has died is indistinct, with Achilleus noting that the tide of battle has turned and Andromache overhearing the sound of mourning inside Priam's palace. Likewise, Persephone's resounding voice alerts her mother to an intimation of dire events, but Demeter must search far and wide, with no initial success, to move beyond intimation to knowledge of the actual predicament. A realization of what has been inexplicitly foreordained will eventually follow, through the agency of Hekate and Helios, but naturally it cannot involve the literal death of an immortal; permanent loss to Hades, the god of the underworld, however, amounts to a mythically equivalent catastrophe on the divine plane.

In the *Iliad* Achilleus and Andromache respond to the revealed certainty of their losses through typical, gendered modes of self-defilement, the man besmirching himself with dust and ashes and tearing at his hair, and the woman casting off the headband or other female accouterment. These two instances of physical self-desecration also echo against other epic moments, outside of the "suspicion of death" pattern, in which Priam, Hekabe, and Briseis express their grief via the same traditional behavior.[72] In her grief Demeter has similarly defiled herself, ripping off her headband (*krêdemnon*), a highly charged symbol associated in various ways with femininity,[73] and casting down her cloak, while she disfigures herself by tearing at her hair (*Dem* 40–43) and, after having had her intimation made a brutal reality by Helios, tearing at her body "for a long time" (94). But while Andromache and Achilleus follow their gendered traditional imperatives with, respectively, a formal woman's lament (22.477–514) and an apparently unstructured man's threnody (18.35) that leads to his mother's appearance and (again typically

---

70. For a fuller discussion of this pattern in the epic, cf. Foley 1991: 157–59; note that the lament has a traditional, performance-derived structure of its own (ibid.: 168–74).

71. "Retention" and "modification" are merely convenient ways to briefly describe a multiform morphology that of course has no hierarchy of archetypal forms and imitations. For that reason, I would resist understanding either the epic or the Hymnic reflexes of these patterns as "primary," and relegating the other(s) to a derivative status.

72. Cf. Foley 1991: 158: "Tearing at himself and rolling in the ashes, Achilleus is by metonymic extension aligning himself with other stricken characters: Priam, both when he first sees his son's body dragged across the Trojan plain (22.408, 414–15) and when Iris finds him still inconsolable two books later (24.163–65); Hekabe (22.405–7), whose actions mirror those of Andromache; and even Briseis (19.282–85), who finds Patroklos fallen on her return to Achilleus' hut." Cf. the possible survival of this characteristic action-pattern in medieval and modern Greek folksong tradition (Sifakis 1992: 145).

73. Cf. Nagler's extended discussion of the traditional network of meanings surrounding *krêdemnon* (1974: 44–63).

the man's) pledge to retributive action,[74] Demeter reacts somewhat differently. She mourns by removing herself from the divine sphere, by entering service as a nurse to a mortal family, and eventually by withdrawing from the world the precious natural sustenance for which she is responsible.[75]

In addition to providing a kind of structural balance in the myth, with the "surrogate child" Demophoön whom she nurses temporarily replacing the daughter she has lost to the death-god Hades, Demeter's self-removal amounts to a suspension of natural processes. Like all instances of pollution in the *epos* tradition,[76] this one will require a compensating purification. From suspicion of death and self-defilement, a metonymic narrative pattern in the shared register of *epos,* has emerged lamentation and a proleptic need for regeneration that accords gracefully with the mythic history of Demeter and Persephone.[77] Within the performance arena circumscribed by the genre-specific opening and closing, the *Demeter* poet has employed a highly resonant integer from the traditional register to enrich this tale of loss and eventual return. From the perspective of word-power, this particular tale is deepened by the metonymic value of the extrasituational pattern, from the moment that Demeter—in traditional terms sister to Andromache and brother to Achilleus—first suspects the fate that has befallen her beloved daughter.

Refusal of nourishment. The next few narrative integers to be treated are in fact contained within the last pattern, the first of these smaller signals consisting of a character's refusal of proffered nourishment in the context of mourning. Such refusal constitutes abrogation of the rite of hospitality in the immediate context, and abridgment of the Feast sequence in a broader perspective.[78] Achilleus in his grief behaves very similarly—on an epic and mortal scale, of course—from the time of his withdrawal from battle in reaction to Agamemnon's insult, but especially from the moment he senses the death of his dear comrade Patroklos. The pattern he overrides right up through the middle of *Iliad* 24 may, as documented elsewhere, be described as

74. In such circumstances men take (often heedless) action; women attempt to weave the dislocation into the larger community fabric, fostering a kind of acceptance (see further Foley 1991, esp. 168–89). Note Achilleus's pledge (18.90–93), parallel to Priam's vow in Book 24: ". . . the spirit within does not drive me / to go on living and be among men, except on condition / that Hektor first be beaten down under my spear, lose his life / and pay the price for stripping Patroklos, the son of Menoitios."

75. This withdrawal integrates with the larger story-pattern underlying the *Hymn to Demeter,* as we shall see below. Note that the expected aural signal of lament, a feature of the Iliadic versions of this pattern, is implied in Helios's explanation and admonition to Demeter (80–83): "But, Goddess, stop your *great wailing [megan goön]*; you mustn't give / yourself to grief so great and fruitless." As for self-exile, the poet says explicitly (91–93): "Afterwards, angered with Kronion, lord of black clouds, / she withdrew from the assembly of the gods and from lofty Olympos / and went through the cities of men and the wealth of their labors. . . ."

76. Cf. the traditional meaning of the verb *aischunô,* "'defile' with the complementary institutionalized association of some purification required to remove that defilement" (Foley 1991: 167).

77. How this meshing relates (or does not relate) to the rituals associated with Eleusis is beyond the scope of the present discussion; see further n. 80 below. Cf. Athanassakis 1976: 73–79 for a running commentary on possible links between the Hymn and the rituals.

78. Cf. Foley 1990a: 265–76 on the structural morphology of the Feast in the *Odyssey;* Foley 1991: 174–89 on the metonymic resonance of Assembly/Lamentation–Purification–Feast–Mediation.

    Assembly or Lamentation
    Purification
    Feast
    Mediation

where an inexorable momentum drives the movement from open and not seldom acrimonious debate or the ravages of mourning to the achieved community epitomized in the breaking of bread and the mediation that follows. It is this traditional momentum that Achilleus holds at bay as he time and again refuses to be washed and denies whatever food and drink are offered him. Only when he and Priam have come to terms, each man accepting the cruel and irreparable loss of a loved one, can the long-deferred feast take place and the mediation of personal peace eventuate.

It is likewise implied in Demeter's traditional mourning, which as we have seen explicitly includes defilement demanding purification, that she eventually rejoin her community after she comes to terms with the loss that has been visited upon her. In the process the poet illustrates the depths of her despair by institutionalized reference to the *Refusal of nourishment* integer, which occurs twice in the Hymn. The first instance metonymically amplifies her searching for the true meaning of Persephone's cry (47–50):

> For nine days then all over the earth mighty Deo
> roamed about with bright torches in her hands,
> and in her sorrow never tasted ambrosia
> or nectar sweet to drink, and never bathed her skin.

The actual foodstuffs differ from those endemic to the human sphere, as they must, but the implications of the goddess's abstention are the same: progress toward community and mediation is being held in check by the acuteness of her sorrow.

The same resolute denial of bodily imperatives—in the *Hymn to Demeter* translated more metonymically than literally to the behavior of a deity who naturally does not "require" nourishment or cleansing and in her divine status is forbidden mortal wine[79]—continues after her realization that Hades has captured Persephone, giving way in her new environment to a partial accommodation (200–201, 206–11):

> And without laughing or tasting food and drink
> she sat pining with longing for her deep-girded daughter . . .
> Metaneira now filled a cup with wine and gave it
> to her, but she refused it; it was not right for her, she said,

79. Cf. Clay 1989: 236; in general, she interprets the Eleusinian episode as "overtly etiological" (233–36). In my own view the metonymic force of the disguised stranger, and all that such a figure implies in the guest-host pattern (see below), overrides the prohibition concerning mortal wine. The situation of Athena as pseudo-Mentes in *Odyssey* 1, a god in mortal disguise who apparently accepts the food and wine put before her and Telemachos, serves as an analogy here. Cf. Richardson 1974: 224, n. to 207.

> to drink red wine. She asked them to give her a drink
> of barley-meal and water mixed with tender pennyroyal.
> She mixed the drink and gave it to the goddess, as she had asked,
> and mighty Deo accepted it, complying with holy custom.

Besides being paradigmatic of the *kukeôn* potion apparently used in Eleusinian rites,[80] this sequence portrays Demeter's initial refusal of nourishment and qualified acceptance of a wineless substitute. Whatever else we understand as encoded in this passage, it is clear that the metonymic signal assists in providing a traditional narrative dimension to the proceedings. It will be this same inability to put aside mourning that before long (302ff.) will result in her suspension of the earth's life-giving fertility.

The Lying tale. Pseudo-autobiographical accounts intended to deceive one's host(s) hardly need any introduction as an integer in the *epos* register; they are of course Odysseus's stock-in-trade, one of his chief stratagems in his quest to survive and ultimately to return. Thus when Demeter, posing as an old woman, resorts to a lying tale, we can interpret her physical and verbal disguise as a traditional preliminary to her own eventual Return. A few lines from her story—which is elicited according to traditional protocol by her "hosts" Kallidike, Kleisidike, Demo, and Kallithoe, daughters of Keleos, lord of Eleusis[81]—will sample the flavor of her dissembling (119–34):

> "Dear children, whoever of ladylike women you are,
> I greet you and will explain; indeed it is fitting
> to tell you the truth, since you are asking.
> Dos is the name which my mighty mother gave me.
> And now from Crete on the broad back of the sea

---

80. Cf. esp. Allen, Halliday, and Sikes 1980: 152–54. Probing the relationship of the Eleusis interlude in the Hymn to what transpired in cult activities at Eleusis presents a knotty methodological problem, forcing an uncomfortable homology between poetic description and other kinds of "evidence." As Clay cautions (1989: 203), "the hunt for clues to the secret rites has, to a certain extent, jeopardized the interpretation of the hymn. Whenever a detail does not appear immediately germane to the narrative, its presence is explained by appeal to ritual practice." As one instance of this dangerous interpretive predilection, she cites Demeter's fasting as purportedly parallel to "a similar period of abstention by the initiates at Eleusis" (Richardson 1974: 165). As we have seen, however, the fasting is a poetic convention with considerable metonymic resonance in the *epos* tradition, and need not be justified with what amounts to an argument *ex silentio*. Cf. further n. 78 above.

81. Cf. Reece 1993: 25–26 on the convention of the host questioning the visitor. It should be noted that the Eleusis episode has proved troublesome for critics who find the *Demeter* lacking in specific motivation for the goddess's sojourn among humankind. As Clay observes (1989: 223–24): "In other versions of the myth, Demeter's stay in Eleusis raises no such problems but is fully integrated into the central narrative. Thus, the goddess comes to Eleusis in the course of her search for Persephone and learns of her daughter's whereabouts from the local inhabitants. In gratitude, Demeter rewards them with the gift of agriculture and, in some cases, the establishment of her Mysteries." One could posit that Demeter's withdrawal and self-exile themselves constitute "motivation" for her stay among mortals (see discussion of the Return pattern below), that learning the details of the abduction from Helios amounts to a morphological variant in the myth (in the Suspicion of death and self-defilement pattern the suspicion is customarily confirmed without much hesitation; cf. Foley 1991: 157–59), and that the gift of the mysteries reflects the Eleusinians' generosity in providing her temporary refuge and surrogate motherhood. This is to say nothing of the more general referential background that must have accompanied any version of the Demeter-Persephone myth.

> I came unwillingly; marauding men by brute force
> carried me off against my will, and later
> they landed their swift ship at Thorikos, where the women
> came out in a body and the men themselves
> prepared a meal by the stern-cables of the ship.
> But my heart had no desire for the evening's sweet meal;
> I eluded them and, rushing through the black land,
> I fled my reckless masters, so that they might not enjoy
> the benefit of my price, since, like thieves, they carried me across the sea.
> So I have wandered to this place and know not at all
> what land this is and what men live in it. . . ."

This tale, reminiscent of Odysseus's Cretan stories in Books 13 and 14,[82] gains the transfigured Demeter admission to the Eleusinian community as Demophoön's nurse. In self-imposed exile from Olympos, she will dwell for a time among humans, raising the child as an immortal, until her superhuman ministrations are discovered and she reveals herself and directs the Eleusinians to build a temple and worship her. But even then, after the lying tale has done its work and she has reassumed her divine form (and her honored position in the temporal realm), the terrible grief of her loss still burns within her, and manifests itself as the suspension of the earth's fecundity. Like Odysseus's lies, Demeter's false representations move her closer to the Return she seeks, but they cannot accomplish it; that final step must await a different kind of verbal transaction.

The Guest-host pattern. The process of introduction into the Eleusinian society entails more than a diverting falsification of identity, precisely because the poet aligns this particular entry of the stranger or guest with all other such episodes through the shared sequence of events prescribed for guest and host.[83] As noted above, Keleos's daughters prompt the "old woman" Demeter by asking after her lineage and place of origin and, as Reece has authoritatively established,[84] this scene takes its place alongside seventeen other instances of the pattern in the *Iliad,* the *Odyssey,* and the *Hymn to Aphrodite.*

The *Demeter* poet both draws on the referential power of the guest-host sequence—that is, of its metonymic, value-added meaning as an integer in the traditional register—and molds the pattern individually or idiolectally for deployment in the Hymn. On the one hand, we notice many of the typical motifs

---

82. 13.256–86, 14.192–359. In their different ways, both of these lead to progress toward the goal of Return, with the former so amusing Athena that she reveals herself and they set about planning the destruction of the suitors, while the latter successfully establishes Eumaios's loyalty and leads to a symbolically important feast in the swineherd's modest hut. As in other instances when a character is about to lie, Odysseus—echoing Demeter across genres but within the *epos* tradition—starts his string of falsehoods to Eumaios (14.192) by explicitly certifying the truth of what is to follow.

83. Cf. Reece 1993 for the definitive study of this pattern in the Homeric poems. He also suggests the possible construal of the Demeter sequence as a theoxeny, that is, a pattern "in which a disguised god comes to the homes of mortals in order to test their hospitality" (182; cf. application on 183).

84. Cf. 1993: 229–30 for his schematic analysis of the "stranger's welcome" in the *Hymn to Demeter.* Much of what follows below in discussion of this scene depends on his morphology of the pattern.

that constitute the scene: the "maiden[s] at the well" (98ff.),[85] the reception (190–91), feasting (206–10), and identification (111–34) are a few of the more prominent and expectable constituents that help to index Demeter's entry into the Eleusinian community as a species of the same action that recurs with considerable frequency throughout the extant texts of the *epos* and appears to have been a narrative staple of the traditional, performance-derived idiom. On the other hand, the motifs line up quite out of customary order, with identification, for example, preceding rather than following the feast. Moreover, the content of the motifs is often eccentric when compared to other instances: most prominently, and here the Refusal of nourishment integer comes into play, the feast is first forestalled as Demeter declines the red wine, and then severely constrained when she accepts only the barley-meal and water. In assessing these shifts within the guest-host pattern, we need not choose between the word-power of metonymic referentiality and the individual play of the imagination.[86] Since the poet's "changes" involve other motifs or integers themselves resonant with traditional implication (e.g., Refusal of nourishment, Lying tale), and since the Guest-host sequence as recorded in the surviving *epos* exhibits a morphology that can accommodate and respond to the needs of many variant situations, we can credit the *Demeter* poet with a compositional achievement that is both creative and deeply traditional.

A small but telltale sign of the scene's debt to word-power may be found in the apparently minor detail of Demeter's seating.[87] On encountering the stranger her daughters have brought to the household, Metaneira reacts in accordance with custom—both social and metonymic—and out of that inchoate mixture of foreboding and dread that mortals often show in the presence of a divinity (190–99):

> Awe, reverence and pale fear seized the mother;
> and she yielded her seat to the goddess and asked her to sit.
> But Demeter, the bringer of seasons and splendid gifts,
> did not want to sit on the lustrous seat;
> she kept silent and cast down her beautiful eyes
> until Iambe, knowing her duties, placed in front of her
> a well-fitted seat and over it she threw a white fleece.
> Demeter sat on it and with her hands she held in front of her a veil,
> remaining on the seat for long, speechless and brooding,
> doing nothing and speaking to nobody.

85. This liminal spot and situation, like many others in the *Odyssey*, is marked by the presence of an olive plant (here *thamnos elaiês*, olive bush, 100). Cf., e.g., the haft of the axe Kalypso gives Odysseus to help fashion his raft (5.236), Kyklops's club (9.378), and Odysseus's and Penelope's bed (23.190ff.), all made of the same material, as well as the intertwining wild and domestic olive trees where Odysseus spends his first night ashore in Phaiakia (5.477) and the olive tree under which Athena and Odysseus plan the suitors' demise (13.372).

86. Compare the postponement of the Feast in *Odyssey* 10, as Odysseus forestalls the usual rhythm until his men are changed back to human form (cf. Foley 1990a: 261).

87. On this motif as a traditional element associated with the Feast scene, cf. Foley 1990a: 268 and 1991: 183–84; Reece (1993, esp. 21–22) counts this element as part of the "stranger's welcome" pattern and preliminary to the Feast.

The offering of a seat to the guest, as inconsequential as it may seem outside of the idiomatic context of the *epos* register, betokens by traditional fiat a feast to follow. As such, the offer constitutes the precondition to the sharing of sustenance and, by a symbolic extension woven into the fabric of Homeric poetry, to a consequent mediation. Thus when in *Iliad* 24 Priam, understandably impatient to retrieve his son and to complete his sad and dangerous errand, at first refuses Achilleus's offer of a seat, he in effect insults his host's honorable hospitality and threatens to derail the mediation toward which they—and the *Iliad*—have so painfully worked.[88] Demeter's initial refusal likewise emphasizes how stricken she is with worry over her dear child, as the Hymn poet momentarily forestalls the expected response to the host's attempted seating of the guest. Utilizing a strategy that depends upon the communicative economy of the *epos* register, and upon our fluency in that special language, the poet emphasizes Demeter's grief by harmonizing this delay with the refusal of nourishment that will immediately follow. Once again we see evidence of a poet who makes creative, situation-specific use of highly resonant traditional forms.

(Im)mortal Imperative/Embassy of Peers. Although Demeter found a degree of solace among humankind in Eleusis, her sadness remained fundamentally unabated, as she "kept on wasting with longing for her deep-girded daughter" (304); eventually this overwhelming grief leads her to impose a terrible sentence of sterility upon the world. Once this abrogation of natural process has occurred, Zeus is forced to consider ameliorative action and dispatches Iris to deliver the following message to the despondent goddess (321–23):

> "Demeter, Zeus the father, whose wisdom never wanes,
> invites you to come among the tribes of the immortal gods.
> But come and let not the word of Zeus be unaccomplished."

Predictably, this unbending command has little effect upon the aggrieved mother, and her nonacquiescence is only amplified by the traditional pattern that structures Iris's message. For this is the first of three occurrences in the *Demeter* of the (Im)mortal Imperative motif that appears so tellingly in the *Iliad*—in connection with Agamemnon's dream (2.23ff.), Thetis's errand to Achilleus (24.128ff.), and Iris's parallel errand to Priam (24.171ff.)—and in the *Odyssey*—Athena's visit to Telemachos (1.96ff.) and Hermes' parallel expedition to Kalypso (5.43ff.).[89]

The (Im)mortal Imperative takes a particular idiolectal or dialectal form in the epics, from which the occurrences in the *Hymn to Demeter* vary somewhat, but not strikingly. In the *Iliad* and *Odyssey* there are usually three steps in delivery of the message from Zeus: "(1) expression of care or concern, (2)

---

88. Cf. Foley 1991: 183: "For Priam to be offered a chair amounts to Achilleus's invitation to share with him the fundamental ceremony of human community from which both of them have absented themselves in their grief, but to which they are now returning." Further, "[Priam's] refusal is a denial of the immanent meaning of that form, and just as surely a violation of the honor and peace that finally give context to death. Small wonder that Achilleus is near erupting into violence; in a sense his measured corrective of Priam's impatience is the truest test yet of his newly won humanity."

89. For detailed discussion of this pattern and its instances in the epics, cf. Foley 1991: 159–63.

self-identification of the messenger, and (3) delivery of the unlikely or forbidding message."[90] The regularity of this pattern, a rhetoricized key to performance, indexes the particular message under the heading of imperatives that cannot be overridden, commands that cannot be disobeyed. Of course, in all of the epic instances the recipient is a mortal, that is, a figure categorically subservient to the deathless gods in general, and especially to Zeus. But even the goddess Demeter, approached and solicited through this metonymic pattern, could reasonably be expected to submit before the combined force of Zeus's divine authority and the register's word-power. That she contests a decree that tradition has marked as automatically to be accepted is a measure both of her own divinity and of the depth and persistence of her grief. The crime perpetrated by Hades, which we should not forget was also originally sanctioned by the chief Olympian himself,[91] will not be so easily brushed aside, even by the kind of metonymic command that as a rule demands unquestioning obedience.

What is more, she continues to resist even when Zeus strengthens the appeal by sending all of the other gods as an embassy of peers, in an action cognate to the Achaeans' attempt in *Iliad* 9 to persuade Achilleus to put away *his* wrath and to return to himself and his much-needed support of the Greeks (325–30):

> So then again the father sent forth all the blessed
> immortal gods. They ran to her, and each in his turn
> summoned her and gave her many beautiful gifts
> and whatever honors she might want to choose among the immortals.
> But no one could persuade the mind and thought
> of the angry goddess who stubbornly spurned their offers.

It is notable not merely that Demeter spurns her peers—one would expect that reaction by now—but specifically that she turns away their compensatory offers of "beautiful gifts and honors" (*perikallea dôra / timas th'*, 327–28), precisely those compensations that Achilleus finds to be inadequate substitutes for the loss he has experienced through Agamemnon's transgression. Zeus has extended the olive branch, first quite imperiously through the (Im)mortal Imperative and then more respectfully via this embassy.[92] But neither approach really gets at

90. The idiolectal (or dialectal) version of (Im)mortal Imperative in the *Hymn to Demeter* departs from the epic model in two minor ways: first, the expression of care or concern is submerged in the message to be delivered; and second, the messenger does not use the "canonical" formulaic line ("I am a messenger to you from Zeus") to identify him- or herself. These are the kinds of idiolectal and dialectal differences that characterize different levels of recurrence in South Slavic narrative patterns; cf. Foley 1990a: chap. 8.

91. *Demeter*, line 3, as charged by the narrator; accused by Persephone herself at 414.

92. Because of the relative rarity of the embassy in the extant *epos* texts, it might possibly be argued that the assemblage of peers in the *Demeter* is more likely a literary imitation of the Iliadic event than another instance of a traditional metonymic pattern. While recognizing the paucity of evidence, I would resist this hypothesis for at least two reasons: (1) the *epos* as we know it, whether composed wholly in writing or not, utilizes as its compositional idiom a register characterized by such traditional multiforms; and (2) the *Demeter* passage is extremely brief, as seems appropriate to the Hymn genre, and is therefore related to the Iliadic occurrence not through a blow-by-blow restatement but rather through a shared structure. On the similarity between Achilleus's self-imposed isolation and that of Demeter, see M. Lord 1967, Sowa 1984: 108–16, and Clay 1989: 249f.

the core problem (just as none of the Achaeans' proposals ever really addresses the *lôbê* ["defilement"] that is the true source of Achilleus's wrath):[93] Demeter's love for and devotion to her child cannot be forcibly voided, nor can her commitment be bought off with wealth and promised honors.

Having failed in his direct approach to the goddess, Zeus now turns to the captor, his own brother Hades, in an attempt to forge a compromise that can move the intransigent Demeter to release her stranglehold on earth's vitality. Once again the "father of gods and people" deploys a messenger, this time Hermes, and once again it is the traditional rhetorical associations of the (Im)mortal Imperative pattern that drive his mission and rhetorically urge the necessity of accepting the terms of the message. As the integer demands, the message itself is "unlikely or forbidding," namely, that Hades must immediately relinquish Persephone to appease her mother, who, as Hermes notes in ending his plea, has now withdrawn from the community of gods. This time, as word-power (always) warrants, the command is obeyed, but with a remarkable (because both unique and traditional) qualification: before Persephone can step into the chariot, Hades momentarily detains her (371–74):

> αὐτὰρ ὅ γ' αὐτὸς
> ῥοιῆς κόκκον ἔδωκε φαγεῖν μελιηδέα λάθρῃ,
> ἀμφὶ ἓ νωμήσας, ἵνα μὴ μένοι ἤματα πάντα
> αὖθι παρ' αἰδοίῃ Δημήτερι κυανοπέπλῳ.

> But Hades himself
> gave her to eat a honey-sweet pomegranate seed,
> contriving secretly about her, so that she might not spend
> all her days again with dark-robed, revered Demeter.

Through this "guest-gift," which may also amount to what Reece (1993: 37) calls the guest's "departure meal," the lord of the underworld craftily establishes *xenia,* a socially and idiomatically approved bond between guest and host, between himself and the young woman. In ironic contrast to the criminal nature of her abduction, this traditionally reverberative action forges an important and permanent link between the unlikely pair of host Hades and guest Persephone, the metonymic significance of which is that Demeter's daughter is free to leave now but will be required to return to her "host" to reciprocate in the future.[94] As is the case with so many passages in the Homeric poems, the lack of this "supplementary" information—made immanent via the traditional pattern of *xenia* for the audience/reader fluent in the performance-derived register—leaves a gap of indeterminacy in the decontextualized text. With this information in hand, however, the full complexity of the episode begins to emerge: Hades has

93. Cf. *Iliad* 9.387. A study of *lôbê* as the root problem and dynamic of the *Iliad* is in preparation.
94. Cf. Athanassakis 1976: 78. As Clay has pointed out (personal communication), "the *xenos* is only obliged to reciprocate on his home turf." I would interpret this exception as an accommodation of the traditional multiform to deployment in the Hymn genre and to an instance of *xenia* involving divine participants. Cf. the accommodation evident in both the Suspicion of death and self-defilement and the Refusal of nourishment patterns.

obeyed the traditional construct of the (Im)mortal Imperative, to be sure, but has attached a condition by inserting another traditional construct into the negotiations. If we follow not simply the nominal actions but also their institutionalized implications, then we glimpse Persephone's fate before she and her mother do.

The third instance of the (Im)mortal Imperative seals that fate by at last bringing to Demeter a command she can and will obey, in accordance with both her prior conditions and the metonymic call for obedience that is embedded in the very form of the command. As mother and daughter rejoice in their reunion, Rhea delivers the message (460–69):

> "Come, child! Far-seeing, loud-thundering Zeus invites you
> to come among the races of the gods and promises to give you
> whatever honors you wish among the immortal gods.
> With a nod of his head he promised you that, as the year revolves,
> your daughter could spend one portion of it in the misty darkness
> and the other two with you and the other immortals.
> With a nod of his head he said it would thus be brought to pass.
> But obey me, my child! Come and do not nurse
> unrelenting anger against Kronion, lord of dark clouds;
> Soon make the life-giving seed grow for men."

The expression of care and concern that is explicit in the epic version of this pattern, but implicit in the two earlier instances in the Hymn, rises nearer the surface here as the messenger identifies the authority behind her words and recounts the compromise that Zeus has forged. With the traditional signal of a nod of the head,[95] he has certified a contract that appeases both Demeter and Hades by allotting mother and mate regular, recurrent divisions of the annual cycle. The "unlikely or forbidding" content of the message consists of a two-part instruction to Demeter: digest your wrath (something she has so far been completely unable to do) and restore the earth's bounty (something she has so far been absolutely unwilling to do).

The combination of Zeus's accession to her demands and the inherent force of the (Im)mortal Imperative pattern then dovetail in producing Demeter's response (470–82):

> Thus Rhea spoke and fair-wreathed Demeter did not disobey,
> but swiftly made the seed sprout out of the fertile fields.
> The whole broad earth teemed with leaves and flowers;
> and she went to the kings who administer the laws,
> Triptolemos and Diokles, smiter of horses, and mighty Eumolpos
> and Keleos, leader of the people, and showed them the
> celebration of the holy rites, and explained to all,

---

95. On the absolute nature of Zeus's commands, cf. his caution to Thetis about the power of his nodding as a signal (*Iliad* 1.524–27).

to Triptolemos, to Polyxeinos and also to Diokles,
the awful mysteries not to be transgressed, violated
or divulged, because the tongue is restrained by reverence for the gods.
Whoever on this earth has seen these is blessed,
but he who has no part in the holy rites has
another lot as he wastes away in dank darkness.

The same patterned, divine directive that had no influence on Demeter at its
first appearance, and which then elicited conditional compliance from Hades,
now gives way to what this traditional integer customarily secures within the
performance arena: obedience without question, and without primary regard to
the superficial narrative logic of the particular situation. The miracle of
Demeter's restoration thus stems in part from the force of the *epos* tradition
itself. We can interpret the earlier failure of the (Im)mortal Imperative to move
the goddess as a traditional emphasis of the extent to which she is suffering over
the loss of her daughter: not even the power of Zeus—as expressed through the
word-power of this pattern—can bring her into line. And if Hades' wordless
acceptance of Hermes' message, couched in the familiar terms of the same
reverberative frame, seems abrupt, we should remember that such "gaps of
indeterminacy" in oral-derived traditional texts are not seldom filled by extratextual, immanent associations. So it is with the third occurrence, which leads
not only to the return of the natural cycle but also to the establishment of a
similarly cyclical event among the Eleusinians; from this point on, and just as
surely as Persephone marks the recurrent change of seasons, the Eleusinians will
punctuate their social and religious existence with recurring rites of Demeter.
To them is granted the privilege of miming the annual round, itself the (re-)cre-
ation of the goddess whom they worship.

Story-Pattern: Demeter's Eternal Return

Given the limited selection of longer Homeric Hymns, that is, those with a
substantial narrative matrix, as well as the lack of a true generic analog in
oral traditions outside ancient Greek, any conclusions about the presence in
this Hymn of the kind of story-pattern that structures the Homeric epics—and
myriad other long narratives[96]—must be considered conditional. But uncertainty about the overall dimensions and morphology of such patterns as they
may or may not exist in the Hymn genre should not prevent us from taking
note of the obvious dedicated signals denoting Return, and in fact that fundamental rhythm as it appears in the *Hymn to Demeter* has already received

96. Cf. the Withdrawal-Devastation-Return pattern in the *Iliad* (e.g., Lord 1960: 186–97; Nagler
1974: 131–66), which may or may not be seen as genetically related to the Return Song pattern that
underlies the *Odyssey*. On the Return pattern, cf. Foley 1990a: chap. 10. The fact that this latter
story-type occurs in ancient Greek, South Slavic, Turkish, English, and other traditions does not
necessitate viewing it as an Indo-European inheritance; it could have been passed from one group to
another by simple contact.

attention.[97] What is at stake in this investigation is of course the identification and empowerment of the largest metonymic integer in the Hymn: if Return can be shown to be participatory in the poetic dynamics of the *Demeter*, not as an epic story-pattern but as a set of cues that activate extratextual contexts by institutionalized appeal to the *epos* register, then we have enriched and complicated our co-creation of the work by furthering the continuity of reception.

At the level of the *Hymn to Demeter* as a whole, I would argue that not just a single- but a double-cycle Return is implied. Such a duplex traditional organization, paralleled as one among many natural morphological variations in the Return epics from South Slavic,[98] begins with the forcible withdrawal of Persephone by Hades. That initial action, leading to the traditionally requisite captivity, begins one strand of the narrative and leads to the expectable devastation—the young girl's desolation as expressed in the highly metonymic (if undifferentiated) cry of mourning that reaches her mother's ears. Through negotiation,[99] the usual mechanism in comparative epic as well, the captor is persuaded to release the prisoner, who then returns and reunites with the loved one—in the epics a spouse or fiancée like Penelope—and the tale comes to a fitting, rebalanced closure.

This much of the story reflects the sort of action through which, for example, Odysseus passes, albeit on the much grander scale appropriate to the different generic species of the *Odyssey*. What may not be so readily apparent is that it also reflects literally hundreds of collected song-texts from the South Slavic tradition, wherein a captured hero cries out in his misery loudly enough to prompt negotiation and (often conditional) release, later returning to his homeland to rout his mate's suitors through ritual or real combat and generally to set matters right through a series of tests and recognitions. That heroic role can, as indicated above, be occupied by not one but two individuals, each of them undergoing the Return pattern, sometimes separately but more often in conjunction. What customarily links the two tracks is a flashback account of the first hero's capture and consequent devastation, just the sort of inserted history

---

97. Cf. M. Lord 1967, the most specific and intensive examination of withdrawal and return in the *Demeter*. She describes the pattern in terms of six themes (241): "(1) the withdrawal of the hero (or heroine), which sometimes takes the form of a long absence; this element is often closely linked with a quarrel and the loss of someone beloved; (2) disguise during the absence or upon the return of the hero, frequently accompanied by a deceitful story; (3) the theme of hospitality to the wandering hero; (4) the recognition of the hero, or at least a fuller revelation of his identity; (5) disaster during or occasioned by his absence; (6) the reconciliation of the hero and return."

98. In the song *Alagić Alija and Velagić Selim* as sung by the Parry-Lord *guslar* Ibro Bašić, for example, as in many similar performances, a newly captured hero, Alagić Alija, meets an old comrade, Velagić Selim, after being thrown into the enemy ban's prison. AA answers VS's questions about homeland, wife, and son, and VS soon strikes a bargain with the wife of his captor for a month's freedom to repair the problems he hears recounted. He sets things straight at home and subsequently keeps his promise to reenter prison. He and AA are then rescued by two (female) substitute heroes: AA's fiancée Fata and a confidante bring them horses and gear, and the double return is accomplished. Cf. further Foley 1990a: 363–69.

99. Via the (Im)mortal Imperative pattern investigated above.

Persephone gives her mother after they are reunited.[100] At any rate, the point is that Return patterns, far from being limited to a simplex, single-cycle sequence, exhibit an extensive morphology, and the double-cycle, two-tiered variety is quite common in the well-collected tradition of South Slavic epic.[101]

Thus our opening perspective on Persephone as a Return "hero(ine)" does not prevent us from viewing Demeter as equally enmeshed in a sequence of Absence or Withdrawal through Return. In the mother's case the withdrawal is more like that of Achilleus in the *Iliad*:[102] both are honored figures pushed beyond their ability to bear the insult, characters with a vital, unique ability and function whose maltreatment causes them to lose touch with community and move into self-exile. Devastation inexorably follows such action,[103] not only at the logical surface of the narrative, where both Demeter and Achilleus are wronged and their respective communities are prima facie likely to suffer from their absence, but also at the traditional, performance-derived level of register. For in both cases word-power concurs with the literal thrust of the narrative, metonymically prescribing that withdrawal must necessarily lead to devastation, and eventually, after many trials and negotiations, to Return. Demeter proceeds through her own pattern, on a parallel track to that of her daughter; the difference between the mother's situation and that of Achilleus is profound and perhaps a measure of genre and myth as well as of divine versus human status. Whereas Demeter will ultimately regain her loved one, at least for the major part of every year, Patroklos is lost to his dear companion forever, and the tragically mortal Achilleus must deal with the irreversibility of that loss in fashioning his own Return to battle and finally to human community.

It may be well to note one additional feature of the two-track structure of Return in the *Demeter*. Since Persephone's abduction and life in the underworld are treated comparatively briefly, it is only too easy to concentrate on the mother's activities—which are portrayed center-stage for much of the Hymn—as the defining sequence for the poem. But here the comparative perspective may shed some additional light. Double-cycle Return songs in South Slavic customarily "feature" one of the two heroes as the tale's main protagonist, the one who will often eventually help to achieve his compatriot's release. Meanwhile, the seemingly inactive member of the pairing undergoes a cognate devastation but, because he remains in captivity, does not receive nearly as much explicit atten-

100. This is true of *Alagić Alija and Velagić Selim* (see n. 98), for example. The flashback is also a common feature of different story-types, in the Christian as well as Moslem traditions; cf. the retrojective episode in one species (many versions) of the *Marko Kraljević Recognizes His Father's Sword* tale (cf. Foley 1991: 100–106).

101. The "song amalgam," or combination of songs A and B to form a composite AB, is also well attested; for an especially clear example in which A, B, and AB all exist within the same singer's repertoire, see Foley 1990a: 369–87. Multiformity at the level of story-pattern is no more or less "natural" than multiformity at the levels of narrative scene or of phraseology: each provides necessary suppleness in the traditional performance register.

102. Cf. n. 96 above.

103. One could compare the action of the hero in the composite Return Song in South Slavic (see n. 101 above): after discovering the Penelope figure's infidelity, he immediately leaves his home and society to join the enemy forces.

tion. This same sort of discrepancy masks the duplex nature of Return in the *Demeter*, but it should not blind us to the complex, subtle structure of the Hymn.

With this overview in hand, let us focus for a moment on three of the smaller narrative integers explicated above and their relation to the Return rhythm. With respect to Suspicion of death and self-defilement, we recall that it is this traditional narrative integer that Homer employs to describe Achilleus's first knowledge of Patroklos's death in *Iliad* 18. Although like most such patterns the Suspicion metonym also has a life of its own, existing outside this combination, its indexical force meshes seamlessly with the pain of a loss so grievous that it will eventually lead to retributive action and return, after confirmation of the loss by a god (Thetis for Achilleus, Helios for Demeter).[104] The same narrative pattern structures Andromache's initial glimmer of Hektor's demise in Book 22, and it will be followed as in the other instances by gender-specific defilement in mourning, but there the narrative thread ends: Andromache's gendered response to her deprivation cannot be retributive action but must be formal, and traditional, lament. The prolepsis generated by the Suspicion metonym thus depends on its assignment, for in the fundamentally paratactic logic of the *epos* register, scenes mean according to two criteria—their traditional implications and their situational environment. In all cases the pattern indexes the truth of the suspicion and the reaction of self-defilement; it also has the potential to participate in the Return paradigm—as it does for Achilleus and Demeter but not for Andromache—as an omen of eventual retribution and return.

Achilleus's Refusal of nourishment retards the momentum of his return, short-circuiting the larger narrative pattern of Assembly/Mourning–Purification–Feast–Mediation, and Demeter's abstention from food and drink accomplishes the same purpose. This particular nexus offers an opportunity to emphasize the rhetorical force of the integer, with a pattern intended primarily, we may logically suppose, for a human protagonist being employed to describe a divine state of mind. For the issue at hand is not whether the immortal goddess really *needs* nourishment, but whether her grief is to be indexed along with that of Achilleus; not whether she can survive without (human) sustenance, but whether her state of mind is that of other traditional figures who suffer in this recognizable, metonymic way. In short, Refusal signals not merely the nominal concern of the given figure's impending starvation but his or her psychological state and, through derailment of the dynamic leading from Feast to Mediation, his or her absolute separation from community.[105] Return is in effect held at bay by this pattern, which acts as a narrative counterweight to the overall story-pattern in both *Demeter* and the *Iliad*.

The Lying tale, on the other hand, amounts to a stratagem used by the hero(ine) to proceed toward his or her goal, and therefore contributes, even if indirectly, to the momentum of the Return. Again the comparative perspective

---

104. Achilleus's withdrawal is of course much more detailed and prolonged than that of Demeter, but elements of the pattern seem to be shared across genres.

105. Also participatory in this sequence is the Guest-host pattern, which both carries a valence of its own, as described above, and dovetails snugly with the Return sequence.

from South Slavic epics offers supporting evidence. Like Odysseus, the heroes of the Moslem return songs engineer their reintroductions through a succession of falsehoods, disguise(s), and tests, a program of quite ruthless examinations that may involve children, mate, father, mother, and even a faithful old nurse.[106] Through the lying tales the South Slavic heroes—customarily disguised as recently released prisoners and beggars—"test the waters" before revealing their true identities, just as Demeter poses as an old woman before revealing herself as the goddess she is. In a traditional paradox, the protagonist's present lying foreordains future disclosure of the truth, coincident in the narrative with a resumption of position. From this coincidence of truth and revelation stems the authority of Demeter's establishment of the Eleusinian rituals and her first stage of Return; her full reemergence among the gods must await the completion of negotiations with Zeus.

In conclusion, word-power prescribes that we participate in a continuity of reception for the oral-derived traditional text of the *Hymn to Demeter* by taking into account those aspects of the oral traditional register of ancient Greek *epos* that survive into the textual medium. In general, the idiom employed by the *Demeter* poet, whether construed in terms of the Parry-Lord integers or Bauman's keys, places the work within what we have called the performance arena. This arena licenses a unique kind of transaction, with the mere use of the appropriate idiom or register opening a channel of communication that offers a focused and highly economical form of expression and reception. In addition to this general effect, the specific metonymic valences of various traditional integers contribute extratextual meaning to the communication, appealing by now-rhetorical convention to an indexed body of immanent signification. Although the objective reality of a unique text amounts to an intersemiotic translation of the face-to-face performance experience, we may still observe that, at one rhetorical remove, performance is the enabling event and tradition is the enabling referent.

And what finally takes place within the performance arena, through the agency of a register that makes possible such communicative economy? Most obviously, there is programmatic praise of the goddess Demeter, conducted through the Hymn genre, an ethnopoetically explicit way of speaking within the *epos* that is devoted solely to this purpose, and which therefore prescribes a dedicated mode of expression and perception. More subtly, and complementarily to the genre-dependent aspects of traditional structure, we have observed integers that resonate within the *epos* tradition at large, lending the idiosyncratic

106. Just as Odysseus and his South Slavic kin arrive in their homelands disguised as beggars or prisoners, so Demeter takes on the form of an old woman who, it is specifically noted (101–104), has passed beyond the time of childbearing and the "gifts of beautiful-garlanded Aphrodite." In other words, the disguised returning hero(ine) is in all cases a figure who has for whatever apparent reason—age or circumstance or both—adopted an extrafamilial, unattached status, from which distanced perspective he or she can observe and plan in secret. As to the series of recognitions, we should add that it is not unknown for a South Slavic returning hero to be identified by a female who recognizes the *beleg* ("scar") on his leg.

figures and moments of the *Demeter* a special, extratextual fullness. We feel the mother's grief the more keenly because it is indexed along with Achilleus's and Andromache's pain; we sense the impending Return the more surely precisely because of the telltale dissembling of Demeter's lying tale and, curiously enough, because of her concomitant postponement of the Feast-to-Mediation rhythm. In short, we understand the *Hymn to Demeter* best when we provide for a continuity of reception, even as its brilliantly innovative and yet deeply traditional poet closes his praise song with a capsule exhortation uniting himself, his immediate and subsequent audiences, the privileged inhabitants of Eleusis, and the eternally returning Demeter and her daughter (490–95):[107]

> But come now, you who dwell in the fragrant town of Eleusis,
> sea-girt Paros and rocky Antron,
> mighty mistress Deo, bringer of seasons and splendid gifts,
> both you and your daughter, beauteous Persephone,
> for my song kindly grant me possessions pleasing the heart,
> and I shall remember you and another song, too.

The time-bound act of hymn composition and the timeless moment of ritual and tradition are effectively a single experience for this singer of tales in performance.

In the next chapter we will be considering how word-power translates to a vernacular saint's life from the Anglo-Saxon period, a work that, like the precious remnants of ancient Greek *epos,* survives only in manuscript and yet shows clear evidence of the rhetorical persistence of traditional forms.

---

107. Even the phraseological structure of these lines mirrors the fusion of tradition and innovation. In addition to their basis in the traditional rules that inform all diction in ancient Greek *epos* (cf. Foley 1990a: chap. 4), we note such features as the ubiquitous rhetorical marker *All' ag'* (490), the common clausula *dêmon echousa* (490; variants in both epics and the Hymns), the dialectal or idiolectal 492 (only in the *Demeter*: 54, 192), and the equally Hymn-specific closure at 494 (cf. *Hymn to Earth* [30].18, *Hymn to Helios* [31].17).

VI

INDEXED TRANSLATION
THE POET'S SELF-INTERRUPTION IN
THE OLD ENGLISH *ANDREAS*

H(w)æt, ic hwile nu   haliges lare
leoðgiddinga,   lof þæs þe worhte,
wordum wemde,   wyrd undyrne.

Lo, for a while now I have told
the story of the holy one in poem-songs,
the praise of what he worked, his unsecret fate.

Andreas 1478–80

Gleawe men sceolon gieddum wrixlan

Wise men shall exchange *gieds*.

Maxims I 4a

Much of the last chapter was devoted to confronting the riddle posed by the rhetorical persistence of traditional forms in an ancient Greek text, the *Homeric Hymn to Demeter*. With those reflections in mind, let us pose the same question to another textual witness, this time from Old English: Why does the poet of the verse hagiography *Andreas,* or any other Anglo-Saxon poet, continue to depend upon traditional forms as the foundation of his or her expressive repertoire?

As I have tried to show for other traditions, a verbal artist uses a given register not for its expediency but for its unique significative capabilities: namely, because it indexes the context in which he or she wants the communication to be received. Thus Homer, or whatever group of poets antiquity was identifying with the name Homer, uses the hexameter diction first and foremost because it establishes the interactive context of ancient Greek *epos* in which the present performance or text is to be placed. Even when Homer or his colleagues turn away from the *Iliad* and *Odyssey* toward the composition of chiefly lyric Hymns, their employment of the hexameter register signals the mythic background against which these prayers and praises are sung. Likewise, the South Slavic epic bards automatically invoke a mythic context for events and characters merely by resorting to the decasyllabic register that is the medium of most of the heroic poetry, while women, bearers and performers of charms and other kinds of poetry, summon a different arena by turning to one of their octosyllabic "ways of speaking."

If the poetic register, that specialized variety of language and narrative patterns tied to situation and social function, is so evocative of context, thus enriching any particular performance with unspoken but still immanent resonance, then why should a poet abandon its unique qualities as an expressive instrument simply because he or she begins to read or write? To phrase the same matter in another way, how can such a poet afford to lose the traditional resonance inherent in such a specially coded language? To forgo the inimitable advantages of the "dedicated" medium is to cut oneself off from a body of implication that is directly accessible in no other way. Small wonder that wordsmiths clung stubbornly to a highly stylized, artificial diction and scenic repertoire; until other stylistic means could be devised that permitted a comparable artistic advantage, what reason could they have had to do otherwise?

Of course, there is another crucial dimension to this situation, one that our only too ready assimilation of Old English poetry to contemporary textuality often shields from view.[1] I speak once again of the audience, or reader, the other bookend to the communicative act whom we ignore or render monolithic at our peril. As discussed in chapter 2, many recent developments in literary theory have aimed at upgrading the audience to full partnership in the making of the work of art, by recognizing that reception is not at all a foregone conclusion but itself a complex, multifaceted process. The school of Receptionalism, pioneered by Hans Robert Jauss and Wolfgang Iser, positions the "work" midway between the text and its perceiver, with a spectrum of "realities" constituted as much by the plethora of readers as by the physical object of the text. As I have attempted to illustrate, this model translates readily to traditional texts and even traditional oral performances, with allowances made for the endemic heterogeneity of the audience on the one hand and the focusing factor of traditional signification on the other. Young and old, female and male, experienced and inexperienced may be present in the same audience, each with his or her own predispositions; in this case, however, the very consistency of register—in both its semantic and metonymic dimensions—will to an extent counteract the centrifugal responses of an otherwise diverse audience, or set of audiences. Within the performance arena defined by the use of a given register—the communicative equivalent of selecting a channel for transmission and reception—the answer to Stanley Fish's famous and often repeated question (1980) is: "Yes, there *is* a 'text' in this class."

To recapitulate the thrust of chapter 3, then, let us think of Old English poetry not as an oral or written phenomenon, but as a poetry in which individual and creative artists employ a traditional, performance-derived register. Second, let

---

1. As Ward Parks (1991: 52) points out, this assimilation is intimately allied with the larger cultural trope: "The textualizing of orality is just one movement, then, in the textualization of the world, a happening to which current critical discourse gives continuing testimony. And all of this is an expression of the collective interests of those controlling the modes of discourse in which discussion of these matters is carried on. Disengaging from this hermeneutical program will not be easy."

us recognize that traditional oral forms persist in manuscripts not because they are merely useful, or charming, or metrically or stylistically correct, but because they continue to encode an immanent context, a referential background that deepens and complicates whatever more particular events occupy the foreground in a given work. And, third, let us not forget the audience, both their demands and their responsibilities as partners in the signifying loop. Without audiences and readers willing and able to listen, the most splendid old oak will make no sound when it falls, and the most densely coded traditional utterance may appear only pedestrian or awkward—Homer or the Old English poet "nodding." All three of these principles ask no more than a reasonable complication of the work of art, paying attention not only to *what* but also to *how* it means.

Placing the *Andreas* Poem

The Old English poetic tale that editors have denominated *Andreas* has always occupied a curious slot in the extant canon. As a versification of the apocryphal story of Andrew and Matthew among the Mermedonians, it qualifies as a hagiography or saint's life, but has limited stylistic affiliation with generic counterparts such as *Elene*, essentially the *inventio crucis* tale, or *Juliana*, based clearly on the Acta Sanctorum for February 16, or *Guthlac A* and *B*, at least the latter part of which stems from Felix of Crowland's *Life of St. Guthlac*.[2] More than any of these other poems, the Andrew narrative presents its hero as a Germanic warrior, a classic hero in the style of *Beowulf*. In fact, it will not be an exaggeration to observe that *Andreas* has often been studied more for its apparent relationship to *Beowulf*—in phraseology and scenic pattern as well as general tone—than on its own merits or for its own sake. Nineteenth-century criticism, debating as it did the matter of authorship on the basis of such correspondences, had a special interest in *Andreas,* and similar concerns have surfaced ever since.[3]

Classing the poem as a heroic hagiography and locating more distant relatives in such Anglo-Saxon works as *The Dream of the Rood*, a dream-vision of the heroic ordeal of crucifixion as related by the cross (Christ's "comrade-in-arms"), does not exhaust the problematic nature of *Andreas*. Critics have argued over its figural or typological structure, for example, as well as over the question of its probable textual source.[4] It is this latter issue that particularly concerns us here.

In 1949 Claes Schaar reached what proved to be an authoritative conclusion: that the Old English poet must have worked from a lost Latin translation of the

2. Cf. Greenfield 1965: 102–23; Greenfield and Calder 1986: 158–83, esp. 159–66 on *Andreas*.

3. As an early example, Sarrazin (1886: 531), who sought to prove "dass Kynewulf und der Verfasser des Beowulf identisch sind." For later opinions on the relationship between *Beowulf* and *Andreas,* cf. esp. Peters 1951, Greenfield 1965: 103–104 (Greenfield and Calder 1986: 159), Hamilton 1975, and Riedinger 1989, 1993. In the latter article Riedinger contends (283) "that the verbal similarities between the two poems are generally not a direct product of either oral tradition or literary convention," but that "the *Andreas*-poet borrowed frequently, and methodically, from *Beowulf*."

4. On the typological structure, cf. the bibliography cited in Biggs 1988: 413, n. 2; for a broad survey of relevant scholarship, cf. Boenig 1991a: 15–19.

Greek Πράξεις Ἀνδρέου καὶ Ματθεία εἰς τὴν πόλιν τῶν ἀνθρωποφάγων [hereafter *Praxeis*].[5] Basing his hypothesis on the fact that the poem corresponds most closely to the Greek text, he also posited a Latin intermediary, arguing that we cannot easily assume a widespread reading knowledge of Greek in Anglo-Saxon England. This compromise position has held sway in most quarters, with Robert Boenig, who conducted the most recent and most thorough examination of all relevant texts, coming to a similar opinion (1991a: 23): "the Greek text is by far the closest in structure and language of any surviving version of the Andreas legend to both *Andreas* and the two Old English prose versions." Although Boenig stresses the possibility that a knowledge of Greek might have provided a direct link between the *Praxeis* and the Anglo-Saxon "translation," he too feels that there was probably some sort of Latin intermediary, itself no longer extant, between the two.[6]

This uncertain situation, in which scholars have located a text that corresponds most closely but must still have recourse to the hypothesis of a "missing link" to establish a realistic path of transmission, makes straightforward text-to-text comparison a dangerous approach to source study. For this reason I favor a modified comparative method that satisfies two conditions: namely, that the Old English phrases or scenes be *both* wholly unprecedented in the *Praxeis* source *and* demonstrably a part of the Anglo-Saxon traditional repertoire. In other words, in order to qualify as a point of divergence, it is not enough that any given Old English integer merely lack an equivalent in the Greek; such inequivalence might as well be the result of omission from an intervening text as the contribution of the Anglo-Saxon poet working within a dedicated idiom. The phrase or scene in question must additionally show some direct evidence of belonging to the poetic register, and thus of keying performance and enabling the special kind of communicative economy possible within the performance arena.

Further, since what we are attempting to illustrate is not a physical mode of composition (actual oral performance) but rather a mode of expression and perception that—now rhetorically—is carried on in texts, the remarks made below most surely do not preclude other avenues of interpretation. The typological studies that have figured so prominently in *Andreas* criticism, to take but one example, should not necessarily clash with the perspective offered here. If, as Boenig contends, the poet was indeed making "doctrinal alterations of the source" (1991a: 109), one can unproblematically envision his doing so within the traditional idiom, using the reverberative language to an individual, focused purpose within a text. Let me stipulate from the start, then, that understanding *Andreas* as an "indexed translation" is theoretically compatible with many other

---

5. 1949: 12–24, esp. 23.

6. For Boenig's extended opinion, cf. pp. 23–29, and note his reference to Robinson 1973 as supporting evidence for the *Andreas* poet's possible knowledge of Greek; cf. also Boenig 1991b: vii–ix. Though he proceeds via a methodology much different from that employed in this volume, the object of Boenig's study is not dissimilar; he is primarily concerned with "the art of such translation and what makes it a different—and more rewarding—activity than the merely accurate reproduction of exact meaning that is the primary meaning of our word *translation*."

approaches to the poem, and is offered not to compete with but to mesh with and to deepen other critical perspectives.[7]

Self-Interruption and Word-Power

The *Andreas* poet proceeds quite a distance—1,477 of 1,722 alliterative lines, to be exact—in his retelling of the apocryphal account of Matthew and Andrew among the Mermedonians before he suddenly interrupts his own performance. He does so in order to vouchsafe his uncertainty about continuing, to question his own capability to carry the tale through to its conclusion. Since this self-imposed intermezzo is unique in the surviving poetry, there exists no ready model or analogy to help us with its interpretation, and we are left to ascribe to this otherwise competent poet an admission of lack of religious learning or poetic ability or a failure of nerve, or to agree with Kenneth Brooks, most recent editor of the poem, that "[the poet] seems to be making a rhetorical disclaimer that he does not know the whole story of St. Andrew, in order to condense his poem" (1961: 112).[8]

What I propose to offer in this chapter is another explanation for the interruption, based fundamentally on the ideas about word-power, performance, and tradition developed earlier in the volume. As a preview, the key to this approach will lie in recognizing that the *Andreas* is indeed a *performance*—not the imagined improvisation of an oral bard, to be sure, but nonetheless a kind of performance in text.[9] From this insight and comparison with the *Praxeis* source according to the stipulations specified above, we will be able to ascertain what the poet means when he quite heavy-handedly puts down his verse-making in order to comment on it, exiting the planned program to construct his own metanarrative. As dislocating as his temporary abandonment of the versified story may seem, it will in fact aid us in more thoroughly understanding the nature of the medium within which he and his counterparts work, and particularly of the way in which that medium fosters a unique combination of traditional resonance and indi-

---

7. Or we may of course construe the other methods or perspectives as deepening the approach through indexed translation.

8. Cf. Biggs (1988), who interprets the passage just before the interruption as "identif[ying] the saint's suffering with Christ's passion" (426), and concludes that the interruption is rhetorically strategic (426–27): "Simply by using this dramatic break beginning with the emphatic, introductory 'hwæt,' the poet calls attention to the finality of the events that immediately precede it. Unlike the legend, which is content to pass from the story of the torture to the story of the conversion, the *Andreas*-poet temporarily halts the narrative to force his audience to reflect on his understanding of the scene's significance." Cf. also Earl (1980), who interprets the interruption in the light of his typological hypothesis (69, his italics): "The poet here expresses a notion that should startle the modern reader: that a man wise in the Law will *already know* this tale in his heart. Strange as it is, the idea that the tale itself can be known through wisdom or piety, even without historical knowledge, is actually a *topos* in medieval hagiography." On what he views as the self-reflecting and political nature of the interruption, cf. Hermann 1989: 140–41.

9. Cf. Doane (1991: 80–81, italics mine): "Whenever scribes who are a part of the oral traditional culture write or copy traditional oral works, they do not merely mechanically hand them down; they rehear them, 'mouth' them, *reperform* them in the act of writing."

vidual craft. In short, the perspective presented here will suggest how to avoid disenfranchising either the traditional oral roots of Old English verse, which now persist as a textual rhetoric, or the peculiar, quite singular genius of the *Andreas* poet.[10]

Adding Traditional Insult to Textual Injury

As a brief example of how this singer of tales in performance uses the traditional register, I summon what may seem at first sight an unlikely witness: the description of Andrew's first of four miserable nights in prison.[11] All day long his faith has been tested by physical torture, and the night only brings a continuation of that scourging in the form of a mental assault. To the expectable notation of his suffering, the poet adds the following (1255b-69a):[12]

	Snaw eorðan band
wintergeworpum;	weder coledon
heardum hægelscurum,	swylce hrim ond forst,
hare hildstapan,	hæleþa eðel
lucon, leoda gesetu.	Land wæron freorig;
cealdum cylegicelum	clang wæteres þrym,
ofer eastreamas	is brycgade,
blæce brimrade.	Bliðheort wunode
eorl unforcuð,	elnes gemyndig,
þrist ond þrohtheard,	in þreanedum
wintercealdan niht.	No on gewitte blon,
acol for þy egesan,	þæs þe he ær ongann,
þæt he a domlicost	dryhten herede,
weorðade wordum,	oððæt wuldres gim
heofontorht onhlad.	

---

10. The argument thus runs counter to reductionist views of the poem such as Shippey's evaluation (1972: 119): "The main point is that [the poem's] local successes and failures often come from the same root, a reluctance or inability to abandon the syntax and vocabulary appropriate for a secular epic." As throughout this volume, our focus remains on the inimitable advantages of the traditional register in providing a dedicated medium of expression and reception. On the contribution of the heroic tradition to characterization, cf. Boenig 1991b: x: "This creation of Andreas-as-Beowulf is a mature and poetically successful response of the *Andreas*-poet to his sources, for it deepens the paradox of the already paradoxical figure of Andrew, the unwilling apostle"; in addition, xxxiii-xxxiv on heroic language. Another perspective is provided by Hermann (1989: 148), who argues that "everything Andreas is said to want to leave is part of the formulaic treasury of warfare handed down in Germanic poetic tradition. In this case, such formulas index the sublation of the glorious Germanic heroic past in the name of the Christian mission." Cf. also Olsen 1984: 129–54; more generally on Cynewulf, Calder 1981, esp. 144–70.

11. For a thorough analysis of the thematic pattern of Scourging that underlies this section of the poem, cf. Foley 1990a: 344–54.

12. Translations from the Old English are my own. These renderings are designed to allow the reader to make precise comparisons between the Anglo-Saxon original and the modern English translation; for that reason I have sometimes sacrificed smoothness and sequence to the goal (almost completely achieved) of half-line to half-line correspondence.

                              Snow bound the earth
in winter-drifts;   the weather cooled
with hard hail-showers,   likewise rime and frost,
gray battle-stalkers,   the heroes' homeland
locked, people's dwellings.   Lands were freezing;
in cold icicles   the water's power shrank,
over river-streams   the ice formed a bridge,
pale sea-roads.   Joyful in heart dwelled
the brave nobleman,   mindful of valor,
bold and enduring,   in great distress
the winter-cold night.   He never ceased in mind,
afraid before the terror,   from what he began before,
so that he most gloriously   praised the lord,
honored him with words,   until glory's jewel
appeared heaven-bright.

There is absolutely no precedent for this passage in the Greek *Praxeis,* and for good reason: it represents an appearance of the ubiquitous and much-discussed "Exile theme" first identified by Stanley Greenfield.[13] As such, it is a decidedly Anglo-Saxon gloss on the Greek narrative, a "traditional translation," if you will. For the *Andreas* poet has done no more (and no less) than to index the idea of psychological torture of the solitary saint by appeal to a ready and resonant analogy—the equally solitary, equally miserable figure of exile whom we encounter throughout the poetic canon. Read outside of this paradigm, the passage seems strange and awkward: we wonder why the poet branches off to such a lyric expostulation, and we may even be curious about the pertinence or believability of such a radical change in the weather. Read against the traditional situation indexed by the Exile pattern, however, that is, against the familiar circumstances of such eremitic figures as the Wanderer, the Seafarer, and their kin,[14] this moment in the story of Andrew appears in a new light, viewed from inside the syncretic poetics of Old English traditional verse.

Before and After: Source and "Translation"

With the idea of a "traditional" or "indexed" translation in mind, that is, with the notion of a target language that offers its own highly developed repertoire of expressive possibilities, let us consider what happens just before and after the

---

13. Cf. *Praxeis,* chap. 26. On the structure and morphology of the Exile pattern, cf. Greenfield's original description (1955); also Rissanen 1969, Renoir 1981, 1988.

14. *The Wanderer* and *The Seafarer,* perhaps the best known of the Old English elegies, describe the fate of individuals disattached from their society who struggle not toward an earthly and transient lord, troop (*comitatus*), and position but rather toward their heavenly, eternal counterparts. In her recent edition of the elegies (1992), Anne Klinck includes, in addition to these two poems, *The Riming Poem, Deor, Wulf and Eadwacer, The Wife's Lament, Resignation, Riddle 60, The Husband's Message,* and *The Ruin.*

poet's self-interruption at 1478–91. First, here is a literal rendering of that portion of the Greek *Praxeis* that corresponds to *Andreas* 1450–77:[15]

> And standing apart [Andrew] spoke: "For I know, O lord, that you have not forsaken me." And when it was evening they took him back and threw him into the prison, having bound his hands behind him. And he was exceedingly exhausted and enfeebled. And the men of the city spoke among themselves: "Perhaps he will die this same night, and we will not find him living tomorrow." For he was exhausted, and his flesh was spent.
>
> And the lord appeared in the prison, and having extended his hand he spoke to Andrew: "Give me your hand, and arise whole." And having looked upon the lord Jesus, he gave his hand to him and arose whole, and falling down he worshipped him and spoke: "I thank you, my lord Jesus Christ."

I now append the twenty-eight-line section from *Andreas,* marking with an asterisk (*) those half-lines that have a direct and unambiguous precedent in the *Praxeis* and with a plus sign (+) those that are formal "variations" on the asterisked half-lines.[16] We will have occasion to comment on some of these verses below.

```
*Ða worde cwæð        wigendra hleo:                        1450
"Sie ðe ðanc ond lof,      *þeoda waldend,
to widan feore      +wuldor on heofenum,
*ðæs ðu me on sare,      +sigedryhten min,
ellþeodigne      *an ne forlæte."
   Swa se dædfruma        dryhten herede                    1455
halgan stefne,      *oððæt hador sig[e]l
*wuldortorht gewat      *under wadu scriðan.
Þa þa folctogan        feorðan siðe,
egle ondsacan,      *æðeling læddon
*to þam carcerne;        woldon cræfta gehygd,               1460
magorædendes        mod oncyrran
on þære deorcan niht.      *Þa com dryhten God
*in þæt hlinræced,      +hæleða wuldor,
ond þa wine synne        wordum grette
*ond frofre gecwæð,      +fæder manncynnes,                 1465
+lifes lareow.      *Heht his lichoman
*hales brucan:      "Ne scealt ðu in henðum a leng
searohæbbendra      sar þrowian."
   *Aras þa mægene rof;      *sægde meotude þanc,
*hal of hæfte      heardra wita.                            1470
Næs him gewemmed wlite,        ne wloh of hrægle
lungre alysed,      ne loc of heafde,
ne ban gebrocen,        ne blodig wund
lic(e) gelenge,      ne laðes dæl
þurh dolgslege        dreore bestemed,                      1475
```

---

15. See *Praxeis,* chap. 25.

16. Variation is a formal mode of apposition that represents one of the most typical stylistic features of Old English verse. For definition, bibliography, and examples, cf. the discussion below, esp. n. 25.

ac wæs eft swa ær   þeah þa æðelan miht
lof lædende,   ond on his lice trum.

*Thus in a word spoke   the protector of warriors: 1450
"Thanks and praise to you,   *ruler of peoples,
forever   +glory in the heavens,
*because you in my misery,   +my victory-lord,
*did not forsake me   in a strange land."
   So the originator of deeds   praised the lord   1455
in a holy voice,   *until the clear sun
*departed glory-bright   *to glide under the waves.
Then the folk-leaders   for the fourth time,
terrible adversaries,   *led the noble one
*to the prison;   they wished the mighty thought[17]   1460
of the counsellor of men,   to pervert his spirit,
in the dark night.   *Then came the lord God
*into the grated building,   +glory of heroes,
and then his friend   greeted with words
*and spoke in comfort,   +father of mankind,   1465
+teacher of life.   *He commanded him his body-covering
*to enjoy unharmed: "You must not in suffering any longer
endure the pain   of armed men."
   *Then the one brave in might arose;   *he said thanks to the
                                                          measurer
*from captivity, unharmed   from grievous torments.   1470
His appearance was not defiled,   nor the hem from his garment
even torn off,   nor a lock of hair from his head,
nor a bone broken,   nor a bloody wound
visible on his body,   nor was any kind of injury
through wounding blows   drenched with gore,   1475
but after as before he was   through the noble power
offering praise,   and was sound in his body.

The pattern of asterisked half-lines indicates, in a kind of gross anatomical sketch, the relationship of the *Praxeis* source to the Old English versification. The *Andreas* poet is essentially retelling the story fairly closely, but hardly slavishly; in the normal manner of the traditional register, the skeleton of the narrative is fleshed out with formal variations as well as augmentations of different sorts, and there is no attempt to provide a literal translation.[18] In addition, there are small insertions into the story that have no basis in the *Praxeis*. Many of these divergences, some of them quite familiar items in the traditional poetic wordhoard of Anglo-Saxon verse, illustrate the poet's individ-

17. I generally follow Brooks (1961: 112, n. to line 1460) in rendering *cræfta gehygd* as "mighty thought" (singular instead of Brooks's plural).
18. Especially in this context of moving from source text to traditional idiom, one might even question whether the concept of "literal translation" has much pertinence. The graphic differences between the two texts—in significative mode as well as superficial content—highlight the intersemiotic shift that to some degree is always entailed in translation, but which we programmatically submerge in practice if not theory.

ual artistry, the deftness with which he molds the target idiom to resonate with stylistic overtones.

At the microcosmic level, the relatively common phrase *wigendra hleo* ("protector of warriors," 1450b), which has no precedent in the source, illustrates the poet's predilections in this special mode of translation. Customarily used in the poetic register to denominate a figure of patently martial and heroic achievement in defense of a people (Beowulf, Hrothgar, and Sigemund in *Beowulf;* Edmund in *Capture of the Five Boroughs*),[19] it can also be applied to God, in his capacity as protector of the human race. The narrator of the *Advent Lyrics* refers to God in this way toward the end of the eleventh lyric, and the *Andreas* poet has Andrew call his as yet unrecognized divine companion "protector of warriors" during their sea journey earlier in the poem.[20] As a traditional phrase, *wigendra hleo* thus refers fundamentally to a heroic figure who has performed bravely for the sake of his people, and this indexical meaning can be transferred, in a cultural move common in the poetry, from the secular protector to the Christian God who defends the larger human flock.

But neither the core assignment of meaning nor its ready transposition to the world of Christian thought and action can explain the last two occurrences of *wigendra hleo,* both of them in *Andreas.* The final one, at 1672b, names the holy man Andrew as "protector of warriors," thus assigning the meek and much-beleaguered saint to the cadre of heroic figures mentioned above. He is given this resonant title by none other than God himself, who is issuing Andrew an order to return to the land of the Mermedonians to secure their incipient conversion (1672–74):

> Wuna in þære winbyrig,   *wigendra hleo,*
> salu sinchroden,   seofon nihta fyrst;
> syððan ðu mid mildse   minre ferest.

> Dwell in that wine-city,   *protector of warriors,*
> in halls decorated with treasure,   for seven nights' space;
> afterwards with my favor   you will journey forth.

He dutifully spends the prescribed seven-day period among the former cannibals, and his ministrations prove effective: in a continuation of the traditional translation, the poet tells us that this *wuldres þegn* ("thane of glory," 1678b)[21] was

---

19. *Bwf* 1972b/2337b, 429b, and 899b, respectively; *CFB* 12b. The abbreviations for Old English poems used throughout this chapter are those employed in the poetic concordance (Bessinger and Smith 1978).

20. *Chr* 409a, *And* 506a; cf. *And* 896b.

21. On this phrase cf. *Gen* 1574b, 2268b; *Mnl* 115b. In the first instance the poet recalls, within the story of Noah's shame and the cursing of Cain, how Adam and Eve were driven from Eden by a *wuldres þegn.* The second "thane of glory" announces Ishmael's impending birth to Agar, serving-woman to Abraham and Sarah. The *Menologium* announces the nativity of the *wuldres þegn* St. John the Baptist. All four usages share a broadly focused "agent" function, with the "thane of glory" carrying out God's work by announcing his message; this metonym is not nearly as focused in extralexical meaning as "protector of warriors," and thus helps to illustrate the spectrum of signification encoded in traditional phrases.

the reason for their growth in faith. Without doubt the indexed characterization of Andrew as *wigendra hleo* harmonizes well with the saint's achievements—for he clearly accomplishes as much in the field of proselytizing as his onomastic confreres do on the field of battle.

Traditional characterization, by implicit reference to the type encoded in the phrase "protector of warriors," also lies behind the occurrence of the formulaic phrase at 1450b, in the passage just before the interruption. At this juncture the holy man, having echoed Christ in asking God "hwæt forlætest ðu me?" ("why did you forsake me?" 1413b) and having received God's pledge of support and corroborating visual symbol of the beautiful groves of trees blooming where he had moments ago shed his blood (1448–49), now addresses his creator with thanks (1450–54, above). One could explain this instance of "protector of warriors" as looking ahead—after the interruption—to the time when Andrew will miraculously loose the destructive waters (1498ff.), or perhaps with more immediate logic to the closing moments of the poem when, as we have seen, Andrew returns to Mermedonia to firm up the Christian conquest. But I believe we more fully understand the expressive method and more readily foster a continuity of reception if we interpret this conferred title as applying to the whole of Andrew's hagiographical existence, that is, to the poem's activities from start to finish. Andrew's actions are heroic, this traditional phrase is telling us, on a par with those of such mythic paragons as Beowulf, Hrothgar, and Sigemund, equal in their way to the political and historical deeds of Edmund, parallel to the saving grace of God himself. Such indexed parity is the fundamental poetic function of *wigendra hleo,* a highly resonant item in the traditional register.

Less specifically metonymic but still traditionally resonant is the three-verse description (1456b–57) of the sun setting, a detail that, strictly speaking, does have a source in the *Praxeis* in the homely phrase "And when it was evening." Instead of selecting a matching phrase, however, one that merely conveys this information, the *Andreas* poet has recourse to what an audience's knowledge of the traditional register would lead them to expect and recognize: the elaborate, metaphorical account of the dying of the light. We may compare this particular description with parallels in *Andreas*—

> oðþæt beorht gewat
> sunne swegeltorht   to sete glidan (1247b–48)

> until bright departed
> the sun shining in the sky   gliding to its setting

and

> oþðæt sunne gewat   to sete glidan
> under niflan næs. (1304–5a)

> until the sun departed   gliding to its setting
> under the steep headland.

—or we may journey farther afield, for example to *The Battle of Brunanburh*, where the carnage continues all day long (13b-17a):

> siðþan sunne up
> on morgentid,   mære tungol,
> glad ofer grundas,   godes condel beorht,
> eces drihtnes,   oð sio æþele gesceaft
> sah to setle.

> after the sun up
> in morning-time,   illustrious star,
> glided over the depths,   bright candle of God,
> of the eternal lord,   until the noble creature
> sank to its setting.

At the very least this sort of finely crafted, lyrical moment indexes a dramatic division between what has gone before and what is to come; in addition to simply marking a diurnal boundary, in other words, it marks a portentous division—in *Andreas* between one day's bloody trial and the next, in *Brunanburh* between the day-long battle and the gory scene that is its aftermath. It may also be associated with the fact of heroic battle per se, either the clashing armies in *Brunanburh* or the saint's (similarly described) torture by the heathen in *Andreas*. While not as closely focused as the "protector of warriors" phrase, the variant lines on the sun's setting reveal a more-than-lexical innuendo: with the end of the day, something is finished and something else is started.[22]

A third feature apparently added by the poet to the lines preceding his self-interruption illustrates an interesting echo of earlier passages. This is the brief "catalogue of healing" (1471–77) that expands upon the saint's miraculous restoration. First come the two lines that correspond straightforwardly enough to the source (*Praxeis,* chapter 29; *Andreas,* 1469–70):

> And having looked upon the lord Jesus, he gave his hand to him and arose whole, and falling down he worshipped him and spoke: "I thank you, my lord Jesus Christ."

> *Aras þa mægene rof;   *sægde meotude þanc,
> *hal of hæfte   heardra wita.

> *Then the one brave in might arose;   *he said thanks to the
>   measurer
> *from captivity, unharmed   from grievous torments.

We then hear an extrapolation on the holy man's transfiguration, presented as a rhetorical series of negatives that have no precedent in the Greek: we learn now that the Old English saint's countenance was not defiled, nor was the hem

---

22. Note that the "end of day" pattern is not restricted to expression through one or a few particular formulaic phrases. It is in the nature of Old English narrative patterns of various sizes that the relationship of idea to expression is not one to one, but one to many; cf. further Foley 1990a: 354–58.

of his garment torn off, nor a lock of hair lost from his head, nor a bone broken, nor a bloody wound visible on his body, nor any part of his body drenched with blood because of a cruel wound. The poet emphasizes, iteratively and seriatim, that through God's agency he became once again as he was before.

This enumeration echoes three earlier passages in the *Andreas* that likewise have no precedent in the *Praxeis,* namely the three descriptions of the wounds inflicted on the prisoner, one description during each of the three days of torture. Of course, these prior catalogues are presented not as negative series emphasizing the saint's restoration, but as horrifying accounts of the severity of his ordeal. I quote a short selection from each of them:

Wæs þæs halgan lic
sarbennum soden,   swate bestemed,
banhus abrocen;   blod yðum weoll,
haton heolfre. (1238b-41a)

The holy one's body was
afflicted with pain-wounds,   drenched with blood,
the bone-house broken;   blood surged in waves,
with hot gore.

Swat yðum weoll
þurh bancofan,   blod lifrum swealg,
hatan heolfre;   hra weorces ne sann
wundum werig. (1275b-78a)

Blood surged in waves
through his bone-chamber,   blood poured in thick streams,
with hot gore;   the body did not rest from the work,
weary with wounds.

wæs se halga wer
sare geswungen,   searwum gebunden,
dolgbennum þurhdrifen,   ðendon dæg lihte. (1395b-97)

the holy man was
painfully scourged,   cunningly bound,
pierced through with deep wounds,   while day shone.

More than mere textual correspondence, however, these lexical and narrative echoes call attention to the poet's use of the traditional poetic register. For the first three passages represent realizations of a constituent element—"The prisoner's wounds are described"—within a thrice-repeated pattern that has been identified as the "Scourging theme" in *Andreas,* a recurrent pattern that, significantly, has no basis in the Greek source.[23] Alerted to this narrative matrix, we may "reread" the transfiguration of the saint in a different light. The third day of torture, like the first two, has involved

---

23. Cf. Foley 1990a: 344–54.

1. The enemy arriving with a large troop,
2. Leading the prisoner out and dragging him around the city,
3. A description of his wounds,
4. Leading the prisoner back to his cell, and
5. The prisoner confronting night and mental torture.

Although the *Praxeis* typically makes no mention of the final element on this third day, the heathens in *Andreas* are pictured as practicing their evil psychological designs anyway (1460b-62a):

> woldon cræfta gehygd,
> magorædendes   mod oncyrran
> on þære deorcan niht.
>
> they wished the mighty thought
> of the counsellor of men,   to pervert his spirit,
> in the dark night.

Then, in opposition to their machinations, as well as to both the Exile theme we noted above during the first night and the attack of the *atol æglæca*[24] and his troop during the second night (1311f.), God enters Andrew's cell. What is more, he comes not to test but to reward Andrew for his perseverance, and the poet underlines the reversal idiomatically and through the poetic register by, in effect, subtracting the afflictions that were thematically added to the saint's misery in earlier passages, enumerating them as we have seen in a catalogue. It is as if the *Andreas* poet were balancing the terrible afflictions visited upon the holy man with a point-by-point dismissal of his physical suffering. In a rhetorical tour de force that is thus *both* traditional *and* individual, the poet deepens the "translation" by a personalized selection from the wordhoard.

Another aspect of the *Andreas* poet's art, and one that likewise reflects both a traditional and an individual contribution, lies in the deployment of phrases constituting "variation." Defined by Fred C. Robinson (1979: 129) as "syntactically parallel words or word-groups which share a common referent and which occur within a single clause," this most typical of Old English stylistic figures embodies paratactic expression in each of its very frequent occurrences.[25] Such appositive verses, marked in the passage reproduced earlier by plus (+) signs,

---

24. In addition to the three occurrences of this formula in *Beowulf* to describe the monster Grendel (592a, 732a, 816a), note the application to Satan in *Christ and Satan* (160a). Evaluation of the metonymic meaning of the phrase should also include consideration of the seven instances of the formulaic variant *earm(e) æglæca(n)*: *XSt* 73a, 446a, 578a, 712a, *Glc* 575a, *Jln* 430a, *Phx* 442a. In accordance with the traditional rules for the Anglo-Saxon poetic register, the semantic force of the adjectives *atol* ("horrible, harmful") and *earm* ("miserable, wretched")—relatively close in lexical meaning at any rate—is muted in favor of the indexical force of the half-line phrase as a whole "word."

25. Cf. also Robinson's investigation of variation in *Beowulf* (1985). The earliest authoritative study of variation as a literary figure is Brodeur (1959: 39–70), who defines it as "a double or multiple statement of the same concept or idea in different words, with a more or less perceptible shift in stress: one member of a variation may state the thought either more generally or more specifically than the other; or the second member, while restating essentially the same concept or idea, may do so in a manner which emphasizes a somewhat different aspect of it" (40). With particular reference to *Andreas*, cf. Boenig 1991b: xxxi-xxxiii.

have sometimes been thought to be compositional aids, that is, alliterative bridges that, supernumerary in respect to the core content of the given passage, allow the poet a flexibility in constructing his lines by providing ready fillers to eke out more crucial half-lines. Not unlike some mechanistic views of Homeric diction, this perspective reduces variation to primarily a species of *metri causa*. At the other end of the spectrum, we find critics who, once again reflecting the mechanism-versus-aesthetics dichotomy, strain to justify the usage of each variational member on the sole or at least principal basis of its appropriateness to local context. For these critics, the worth of a poem depends to no small extent on how carefully its author selects each appositional phrase to produce ever finer nuances of situational meaning.[26]

In helping to define the Old English poetic register, variation participates fundamentally in the establishment of the performance arena, and thus in the negotiation of meaning that takes place under the aegis of communicative economy. Like any such expressive and receptive strategy, it operates first at the level of a generic stylistic index and then at the level of the content of individual items. In other words, the very fact of variation—the typical texture of appositive, paratactic structure—constitutes a key to performance, a signal designating the channel in which the message is to be sent and received.[27] Now transformed into a textual rhetoric, this signal is indexical of the Anglo-Saxon idiom: its traditional message is, most generally, that the given communication is to be coded in the language of word-power. Within this performance arena, circumscribed by the stylistic principle of variation, individual instances of apposition will both secure the general strategy and provide value-added meanings of their own. In some cases, as we shall see below, those metonymic valences are quite focused; in others, it is the overall structure of variation as a key to performance that, on available evidence, seems more important.

The passage examined here offers us an opportunity to watch the *Andreas* poet at work, and to judge the nature of his practice, both as a poetic strategy that assists in establishing the performance arena and as a collation of individual items with varying kinds and degrees of indexical signification. In apparent response to the source clause, "And the lord appeared in the prison" (Ο δὲ κύριος παρεγένετο ἐν τῇ φυλακῇ, chapter 29), he translates "Then came the

26. In keeping with this volume's plea for a syncretic poetics, the traditional oral side of which is necessarily emphasized in these pages, I would add that studies such as Robinson 1985, concerned almost entirely with the textual implications of variation, make an important contribution to our overall understanding of the register. As I hope the examples below will indicate, however, we read the poetry most articulately when we foster a continuity of reception by attending to the traditional, performance-derived mode of signification as well.

27. This quality of generalized metonymic effect as a background to the contribution of individual items within the larger structure is reflected in many other patterns in traditional narrative. One example is the "negative comparison" in South Slavic epic (cf. Foley 1991: 75–83, 111–15), which consists of a series of questions, all of them answered negatively before appending the "real" reason for a given situation or instance of behavior. As the questions are addressed one after the next, the metonymic force of the pattern frames the discourse and points toward the revelation that a knowledge of the traditional figure leads one to expect. In addition to the cumulative thrust of the pattern, each item in the series also bears some kind of immanent implication.

lord God" (þa com dryhten god, 1462b). So far, so literal, or nearly literal. But the translation continues by augmenting this verse with three variations: *hæleða wuldor* ("glory of heroes," 1463b), *fæder manncynnes* ("father of mankind," 1465b), and *lifes lareow* ("teacher of life," 1466a). None of these is in any way stimulated by the source, and each has a traditional background in the poetic wordhoard. As a group these four "namings" furnish a collective signal to the reader/audience that God is being described not just by a small collection of Anglo-Saxon terms, but with the full implications of the Anglo-Saxon traditional register. Even on this more general level, they are in no way simply inessential fillers, supporting the poet in metrically assembling the translation, nor is each of them summoned to this narrative nexus merely for a textually explicit effect. The four namings constitute a fundamental trope in the register, promoting a continuity of reception for the passage and poem as larger wholes, while, in addition, each one contributes a poetic resonance of its own.

To start with "lord God" itself, we can shed some light on the situation by noting that not even its transparent debt to the *kurios* of the *Praxeis* can entirely explain its occurrence in the Old English text. Apart from phrases with superficial semantic resemblance,[28] the combination "lord God" (*dryhten god* or its reversal *god dryhten*) appears eleven times in the surviving poetry, many more if one includes the somewhat specialized case of the metrical psalms.[29] Undoubtedly this pairing was originally sparked by Latin models, but just as surely its ubiquity reflects its status as a formulaic integer and a focus for word-power. Because the "lord God" phrase constitutes less than a full verse unit, however, it cannot stand alone metrically, and the half-line is typically completed with a predicate, a relative construction, or more rarely some other form.[30] In short, even the so-called "literal" element in the ongoing translation of "Then came the lord God" is embedded in an inescapable and resonant web of traditional implication, one that happens to be more pliable compositionally than variations that occupy an entire verse.

As "lord God" echoes rhetorically through the experience of the suitably prepared audience, so the three verses of variation complement the opening strains of the traditional, indexed translation. The first of the triad, "glory of heroes" (*hæleða wuldor*), is itself unique in the surviving poetic canon, adum-

---

28. E.g., þæt þær drihten cwom ("that there the lord came," *Exo* 91b), which depends more on the sorting supported by traditional rules for Old English verse composition than on a formulaic resemblance to the half-line under consideration (cf. Foley 1990a, esp. 237–38 on word-type placement).

29. As Diamond pointed out long ago (1963), the diction of the Psalms is among the most mechanical phraseology in the poetic canon. When one adds to this qualification their frequent metrical irregularity and extreme narrowness of genre, the comparanda they present bear reduced weight. This is not to say that the Psalms would not make a fascinating subject for investigation of what seems to be a late composition by one or more authors in imperfect control of the traditional register.

30. Another facet of the compositional pliability of this phrase is its reversibility. Two instances from the *Kentish Hymn* conveniently illustrate its alliterative bivalency: "ðe ðu, god dryhten,   gastes mæhtum" ("which you, God lord, through the spirit's powers," 12) versus "Ðu, dryhten god,   on dreamum wunast" ("You, Lord god, dwell in joys," 18).

brating the poet's individuality or creativity. At the same time, however, two parallel families of diction, each of them extremely well populated, reveal that traditional rules and rule-based compositional processes lie behind the poet's apparent coinage. Four times in *Andreas,* and many more times elsewhere, we find phrases that correspond to the pattern X *wuldor,* where X designates a noun in the genitive plural. In addition to "glory of X," one could also cite the even more generative pattern *hæleða* Y, where Y stands for a singular noun in any grammatical case. We may more profitably relate "glory of heroes" to the former, more restricted paradigm, whose resonance deepens the initial invocation of "lord God" by adding a heroic overtone to God's visit to the prisoner. It is to the poet's credit as an artist that, playing as it were within the rules of the compositional and significative game, he has managed to use the performance-derived register in a way that engages both traditional context and the specifics of the situation.

The same is true, in varying degrees, of the impact of the other two variations. Naming God "father of mankind" (*fæder manncynnes*) hardly represents an unusual compositional act; the same phrase occurs in *Christ and Satan* (twice), *Fates of the Apostles, The Lord's Prayer III, Resignation* (twice), and the Psalms, in addition to another instance in *Andreas*.[31] Rather than simply filling out a whole alliterative line based on the paired verse—"and spoke in comfort" (ond *frofre gecwæð*), which has a clear precedent in the *Praxeis*—this familiar phrase adds to the characterization of the God who comes to Andreas's aid in one of the darkest moments of his captivity. It does so not solely or even principally through the specialized semantic surface of the phrase, but most tellingly through the institutionalized associations of "father of mankind" as a traditional, metonymic phrase. The final integer in this additive series, "teacher of life" (*lifes lareow*), can be derived from the generic system X *lareow,* where X designates a noun in the genitive plural, but is more closely compared to such phrases as "guide of life" (*lifes latteow*) in both sound and sense.[32] Together these last two elements further flesh out the overall characterization, expanding the initial conception of the "lord God," itself resonant with meaning, in partnership with the "glory of heroes."

We should emphasize that all three variations are wholly without precedent in the source, that they appear to be entirely unmotivated by the *Praxeis* text per se. But in deploying them in this way, the *Andreas* poet is able not only to address the heroic, paternal, and guiding aspects of God, but also to engage the traditional implications of these variously indexical phrases and to reconceive the God of the apocryphal gospel within the Anglo-Saxon poetic register. Far from being supernumerary or (only) textually nuanced, these variations fulfill the poetic imperative of word-power and promote a continuity of reception.

31. *XSt* 309b, 358b, *FAp* 29b, *LP3* 1a, *Rsg* 41b, 62b, *P50* 110b, *And* 846b.
32. For the pattern X *lareow,* cf. *R67* 10a, *Mnl* 135b, and *GlI* 12b; for *lifes latteow* in various spellings, cf. *GlI* 9a, *Ele* 520a, 898a, and *Exo* 104a. Cf. also the very common *lifes leohtfruma(n),* which occurs thirteen times in the poetic corpus.

The same general strategy of "indexed translation" informs *Andreas* after the poet's self-interruption. Immediately below are, first, the *Praxeis* passage (chapter 29) that corresponds to *Andreas* 1492–1508a, and, second, the Old English poetic excerpt itself. As before, I have marked with an asterisk (*) those verses with a direct precedent in the *Praxeis,* and with a plus sign (+) those that constitute variations on such lines:

> And Andreas, having looked into the middle of the prison, saw a pillar standing and an alabaster statue lying on the pillar. Andrew unfolded his hands seven times and spoke to the pillar and the statue upon it: "Fear the sign of the cross, which the heavens and the earth dread, and let the statue on the pillar bring up much water through its mouth as a purge, so that those in this very city may be punished."

```
*He be wealle geseah        wundrum fæste
under sælwage        *sweras unlytle,
*stapulas standan        storme bedrifene,
+eald enta geweorc;        *he wið anne þæra,              1495
+mihtig ond modrof,        *mæðel gehede,
+wis, wundrum gleaw,        +word stunde ahof:
"Geher ðu, marmanstan,        meotudes rædum,
*fore þæs onsyne        ealle gesceafte
*forhte geweorðað,        þonne hie fæder geseoð          1500
heofonas ond eorðan        herigea mæste
on middangeard        mancynn secan!
*Læt nu of þinum staþole        *streamas weallan,
+ea inflede,        nu ðe ælmihtig
hateð, heofona cyning,        þæt ðu hrædlice              1505
on þis fræte folc        forð onsende
wæter widrynig        *to wera cwealme,
+geafon geotende."
```

```
*He saw by the wall        wondrously firm
within the building's walls        *great pillars,
*columns standing        beaten upon by storm,
+old work of giants;        *he with one of them,           1495
+mighty and brave-spirited,        *held speech,
+prudent, wondrously wise,        +at once raised a word:
"Obey, O marble,        the measurer's commands,
*before whose face        all creatures
*become afraid,        when they see the father             1500
of heaven and earth        with the greatest of armies
in middle-earth        seeking mankind!
*Let now from your column        *streams surge,
+a flowing river,        now the almighty
orders you, king of the heavens,        that you quickly     1505
onto this obstinate people        send forth
far-running water        *for the destruction of men,
+a surging sea."
```

Two half-lines in this passage stand out as especially familiar and obviously traditional, although unmotivated by the source: *storme bedrifene* at 1494b and *eald enta geweorc* in the very next verse. The first of these finds numerous structural and lexical echoes throughout the Anglo-Saxon poetic corpus, perhaps none closer—in metonymic as well as lexical content—than the exile-linked occurrence in *The Wife's Lament*, where "min freond siteð / under stanhliþe   storme behrimed" ("my friend sits / under a stone-cliff   *covered with frost by storm*" [47b–48]). The second phrase, either as constituted here, or as *enta ærgeweorc*, or as the metrically shorter *enta geweorc*, likewise resonates throughout the canon, occurring in *The Wanderer, The Ruin, Maxims 2,* and of course *Beowulf,* as well as earlier in *Andreas.*[33] The immediate contexts for the "old work(s) of giants" in these poems range from a meditation on the transience of the world to the great age of cities to the hilt of the magic sword that Beowulf presents to Hrothgar, and on to the pillars of the dragon's horde; the earlier instance in *Andreas* applies to the streets and byways through which the saint was dragged as the Mermedonians tortured him. What these usages share, however, is not the particular circumstances in which they appear, or any literal relationship to giants and their works, but rather the idiomatic value of retrojection into the deep past. By employing *eald enta geweorc* or its phraseological kin, the poets index the subject of their immediate concern among other objects or structures consigned to the same category. Thus the *Andreas* poet employs the phrase a second time in order to render the columns, soon to produce the miraculous purging flood, metonymically ancient and therefore suitably mysterious and powerful.[34]

Given that neither "beaten upon by storm" nor "old work(s) of giants" has any precedent in the *Praxeis,* and that both are traditional and thus bear extrasemantic associations (exile and age/mystery, respectively), we may use their example to propose an underlying poetic strategy more pervasive and systemic than the particular phrases alone can suggest. Scholars have often remarked on the plasticity of the Old English poetic language, and on the necessity of that flexibility for success in satisfying metrical requirements, especially the alliterative constraint. Even when the matter of oral tradition is not brought explicitly into the equation, the specter of mechanism—of compounding elements that seem not to enter into the core meaning of the ongoing narrative, for instance, and may even be considered extraneous—looms threateningly close to the discussion. I would propose an alternative to this way of thinking, and also to the idea of "mere" stylistic devices or a purely textual logic, by arguing that it is precisely in such "throwaway" verses, which may at first sight seem accommodating but somehow supernumerary, that the excellent poet shows his or her true command of the poetic art. Because the *Beowulf* poet can index the sword-hilt—with all of its endemic mystery—in a ready traditional category of objects

33. *Wdr* 87a, *Ruin* 2b, *Mx2* 2a, *Bwf* 1679a, 2717b, 2774a, *And* 1235a.
34. Cf. Foley 1991: 210–14 on the certifying and indexical phrase *þæt wæs god cyning* ("that was an excellent king") and its variants, which serve metonymically to guarantee the designated figure's regal credentials.

and structures of great age and indeterminate provenance, he reveals an ability to compose the poem not *in spite of* the traditional idiom but rather *through its unique agency*. Similarly, phrases such as the two examined here allow the *Andreas* poet to harness the metonymic power of the register in service of his indexed translation, in which the story told in the *Praxeis* (or a close relative) becomes a work of identifiably and authentically Anglo-Saxon verbal art.

As in the passage just before the interruption, the poet also "adds" verses of variation that have no precedent in the source text. The most basic and important function of these appositive phrases is to key performance: once again, it is the very fact of variation as a metonymic structure that helps to prescribe the special mode of expression and perception in which this communicative exchange will take place. Indeed, the generic valence of the strategy as a whole moves into the foreground in the passage that follows the interruption, as the poet supplements the simple "he" of 1495b—which corresponds to the implied subject of *eipen* "[he] spoke" in the *Praxeis*—with two half-lines: "mighty and brave-spirited" (*mihtig ond modrof*, 1496a) and "prudent, wondrously wise" (*wis, wundrum gleaw*, 1497a). Neither of these verses, which I would nonetheless take as part of the translation, can be traced to the Greek source. And while they both conform to the traditional compositional rules for Anglo-Saxon poetic phrase-ology, neither has a specifically formulaic context in the surviving canon.[35] In other words, by working within the register, the *Andreas* poet has indexed his translation through the variation paradigm; although the phrases that serve as the nodes of this verbal architecture seem to have little or no specific metonymic implications, the structure as a whole resonates with the word-power of the overall figure.

For a final example of how the Old English composer adapts the tale of St. Andrew to his own communicative medium—the register through which he speaks and his audience (including, to an extent, modern readers) receives the story—I turn to lines 1500b-2:

> þonne his fæder geseoð
> heofonas ond eorðan   herigea mæste
> on middangeard   mancynn secan!

> when they see the father
> of heaven and earth   with the greatest of armies
> in middle-earth   seeking mankind!

Here the issue is not phraseology per se so much as the *Andreas* poet's departure from the overall thrust of this scene. Just before these few verses both the *Praxeis*

---

35. On traditional rules, cf. Foley 1990a, esp. 237–39. Line 1496a may resonate on the basis of the collocation between *mod-* ("brave") and *mæðel-* ("council, speech"); cf. *Exo* 255a, *Bwf* 1876a, *GfM* 41, *R86* 2, and especially (with idiolectal focus?) *And* 1049 and 1096. The closest comparand to 1497a is *R32* 14a: "wis worda gleaw." It is important to remember in this regard that the stress-based Old English alliterative line fosters many fewer exact and close repetitions than more encapsulating prosodies such as the Homeric hexameter or South Slavic decasyllable; on this aspect of tradition-dependence, cf. Foley 1990a: 201–39.

and the Old English poem begin Andrew's commandment to the statue or pillar by ordering it to fear (φοβήθητι/forhte geweorðað) what the Greek source identifies as "the sign of the cross" (τὸν τύπον τοῦ σταυροῦ) but the poem leaves designated as simply *þæs onsyne* ("this sight"). From that point on, the *Andreas* poet is on his own up through the lines quoted above, the only lexical correspondence being the apparently circumstantial one involving "heaven and earth," each instance actually being used quite differently. Why does the poet extrapolate the fear from simple reverence of God to the specific event of the deity's incursion into the world on what appears to be a fearsome errand? Clearly this portrayal of God's threatened advent, once again wholly unprecedented in the *Praxeis,* is a further elaboration, but for what reason?

We can suggest one possible answer by recalling what Hugh Keenan has demonstrated about the typically Anglo-Saxon preoccupation with the Apocalypse and, in particular, the typological connection of that much-anticipated event with the original Flood.[36] The God who is seeking mankind in this episode from *Andreas* can then also be understood as the Christ of Domesdæg and Revelations, the avenging Christ whom many will indeed have cause to fear, together with the paradigmatic event that echoes throughout the Old English canon and the Anglo-Saxon Chronicle. The purging flood about to be set loose by God's agent Andrew is linked typologically to the Last Judgment; just as the original Flood prefigured the end of the world, so this Mermedonian cataclysm stands in a cognate relationship to the final day. In the case of these few lines, like the other features examined above ostensibly the personal and yet thoroughly traditional contribution of the Old English "translator," it is once again an extratextual, metonymic meaning that solves the riddle of their role in the poem. Far from being extraneous embroidery, the Apocalyptic gloss adds another dimension to God's punishment of the Mermedonians, and not incidentally to Andrew's stature as a type of Christ.

Performance and Performance Anxiety

Now that we have some idea of the extent to which the *Andreas* poet has indexed his translation by including phrases and patterns unprecedented in his source and drawn from the traditional compositional register, we may attempt to place his self-interruption in a fresh context. Let us begin by quoting the passage in full (1478–91):

> H(w)æt, ic hwile nu   haliges lare
> leoðgiddinga,   lof þæs þe worhte,
> wordum wemde,   wyrd undyrne.   1480

36. For the first explicit description of the typological link in Old English poetry, see Keenan 1968: 188–89. As an illustration of how the perspectives from word-power and typology can mesh and deepen one another, consider the Apocalypse-Flood link projected by the passage and T. Hill's comments (1969) on the *Andreas* flood as baptismal.

Ofer min gemet   mycel is to secganne,
langsum leornung,   þæt he in life adreag,
eall æfter orde;   þæt scell æglæwra
mann on moldan   þonne ic me tælige
findan on ferðe,   þæt fram fruman cunne   1485
eall þa earfeðo   þe he mid elne adreah
grimra guða.   Hwæðre git sceolon
lytlum sticcum   leoðworda dæl
furður reccan;   þæt is fyrnsægen,
hu he weorna feala   wita geðolode,   1490
heardra hilda,   in þære hæðenan byrig.

Lo, I for a while now   the story of the holy one
in poem-songs,   the praise of what he worked,
have told in words,   his unsecret fate.   1480
Beyond my measure   great it is to say,
long-lasting learning,   what he endured in life,
all from the beginning;   that must a wiser
man on earth   than I count myself
find in his heart,   so that he knows from the origin   1485
all the hardships   that [Andrew] endured with courage,
the grim battles.   Yet nevertheless we must
in little pieces   a share of song-words
relate further;   that is said of old,
how he a great many   torments suffered,   1490
severe combats,   in that heathen city.

If performance amounts, in Richard Bauman's words, to "the nexus of tradition, practice, and emergence in verbal art" (1977: 48), then what we have
learned about the Old English poeticizing of the Andrew story qualifies it as a
kind of performed work. It is also a performance in the sense advocated by
Receptionalist critics such as Jauss and Iser, who envision the work of verbal
art as an emergent co-creation by author and reader/audience. In the latter sense
there exist gaps of indeterminacy—like the questions of the significative thrust
of *eald enta geweorc* or of the Apocalyptic extrapolation examined above—that
can be bridged only by the reader's or audience's bringing to bear certain
knowledge that, strictly speaking, cannot be "found" in or projected from the
given text in the usual way. Whether we are considering a modern novel or an
early medieval poem, then, all experiences of texts can be understood as (inevitably idiosyncratic) performances.

The *Andreas* poet, for his part, is performing the Andrew story both within
the limits and with the aid of the traditional poetic register. His is, as we have
remarked, a kind of indexed translation, with the narrative rendered idiomatically in a target language itself redolent of meaning on its own terms and within
its own categories. At one point during the performance—to be precise, just after
completion of the third of the three Scourging episodes—the poet acknowledges
a degree of what we may call "performance anxiety," exiting the story-line for
a moment to detail what he sees as his own shortcomings as an interpreter of

the tale in Old English. Observing that his account has already been extensive, the poet stresses that it is far beyond his ability to describe the saint's suffering from beginning to end, that such an immense task should be left to someone *æglæwra* ("wiser"; literally, "more learned in the law") than he, by which comment he presumably means, according to Brooks (1961: s.v. *ægleaw*), a person better schooled in the scriptures.

While this is a logical enough opinion on the poet's quandary, in that it posits an impediment that would seem sufficiently debilitating to cause anxiety and perhaps the resultant interruption, it oversimplifies a complex situation. We can understand the quandary and motivation for the break in more depth if we start by recognizing that the *Andreas* poet is actually performing at two levels: (a) he is re-creating the *Praxeis* story, and (b) he is employing the traditional register for that re-creation. When he interrupts himself and recounts the problems that stand in the way of continuing, the poet exits the first of these levels of performance—the actual story of Andrew—but not the second. That is, he continues to employ the traditional idiom even as he describes how difficult his task is, and how unprepared he is to go on. An analysis of the phraseology employed during the intermezzo confirms this impression: of the twenty-eight half-lines that the passage comprises, only a single one (1479b) is unparalleled in the rest of the poetic corpus.[37]

Composing within the poetic register, as we have discovered, necessarily means employing a dedicated way of speaking, establishing the performance arena, and prescribing a channel that enables highly economical communication. Thus the phraseology of the interruption does much more than simply meet an idiomatic standard; it continues to key performance and, in some of its aspects, adds a metonymic resonance to the ongoing transaction of expression and reception. To illustrate this last dimension of word-power, that of the value-added meaning traditionally associated with individual phrases, let us briefly consider a few of the particularly reverberative elements within this twenty-four-line passage.

---

37. What follows is a listing of comparanda (normally limited to one example each) for the individual verses that constitute the interruption. It will be noticed that the relationship between the *Andreas* half-lines and their comparanda describes a spectrum, and may amount to an exact repetition, a "formulaic" variation, or a more distant form of kinship. I would emphasize (a) that traditional rules govern all of these verses, including the superficially unparalleled 1479b; and (b) that the symbiosis of prosody and phraseology in Old English is such that, as remarked above, one expects many fewer exact repetitions and formulaic correspondences than in ancient Greek and South Slavic epic (on both of these points, cf. further Foley 1990a: 210–39). Example parallels include: 1478a (Hwæt! þu worn fela, *Bwf* 530a); 1478b (haliges lare, *Exo* 307b); 1479a (leoðgiddunga, *FAp* 97b); 1480a (wordum wemde, *And* 740a); 1480b (wurd undyrne, *FAp* 42b); 1481a (ofer min gemet, *Bwf* 2879a); 1481b (Long is to secganne, *R39* 22b); 1482a (langsum geþuht, *Run* 63b); 1482b (þæt he on elne adreag, *Glc* 532b); 1483a (eall æfter orde, *Ele* 1154a); 1483b (þær sceal forht monig, *Chr* 801b); 1484a (mann on moldan, *P127.5* 2a); 1484b (þæs þe ic soð talige, *And* 1563b); 1485a (findan on fyrhðe, *Ele* 641a); 1485b (cf. 1482b); 1486a (eal þa earfeþu, *Jln* 496a); 1486b (cf. 1482b); 1487a (grimre guðe, *Bwf* 527a); 1487b (Hwæþre eft cymeð, *Phx* 366b); 1488a (lytle hwile, *Gen* 486a); 1488b (weorðmynda dæl, *Bwf* 1752b); 1489a (furþur feran, *Bwf* 254a; cf. secgan furður, *Gen* 2014a); 1489b (þæt ys sio fæhðo, *Bwf* 2999a); 1490a (þær he worna fela, *Bwf* 2003b); 1490b (þrage geþolode, *Bwf* 87b); 1491a (heardra hilda, *Fnb* 26a); 1491b (in þas hæðenan burg, *And* 111b).

The first of these elements is the stylized opening to the interruption, or what has elsewhere been called the "*Hwæt* paradigm."[38] This rhetoric of beginnings, which starts no fewer than nine poems in the Anglo-Saxon corpus (*Beowulf, Andreas, Fates of the Apostles, Exodus, Dream of the Rood, Juliana, Vainglory, Solomon and Saturn, Judgment Day II*), consists of the interjection *hwæt* ("lo!") accompanied by a predicate of speaking or hearing (here *wordum wemde*), and identification of the speaker as "we" or "I." By rhetorical convention this combination of textual cues

> amounts to the announcement of the onset of heroic narrative, including institu-
> tionalized reference to the audience's experience of other such stories, the keying
> of expectation, and within the Christian poems, a "rereading" of the newer stories
> (saint's lives or other forms) through the heroic idiom of native Germanic diction,
> narrative patterns, and so forth. The signals that make up the *Hwæt* paradigm
> open the word-hoard, as it were, situating what is to follow in an arena with which
> the audience is assumed to be familiar, the context of immanent art.[39]

The *Andreas* poet is "re-beginning" his tale, or starting a new tale, and marking a change of direction in his performance. At the same time, it is a tale, and a direction, rendered familiar to the reader/audience by the invocation of word-power that is implicit in the *Hwæt* paradigm.

The next two phraseological features resonate in harmony with the opening, emphasizing the traditional, performance-derived nature of the story that has temporarily been suspended. The only other occurrence of *leoðgiddinga* ("in poem-songs," 1479a) is at *Fates of the Apostles* 97b, where it again marks a departure from the main business of the narrative—an account of the different disciples' responses to Christ's injunction to "Go and teach all nations"; but this time it also introduces the famous runic signature of the apparent author, Cynewulf. This phrase, possibly an idiolectal item in the traditional wordhoard, participates in a riddling prelude to the runes that, when properly arranged, spell out Cynewulf's name.[40] As in *Andreas,* the departure invokes a knowledge of tradition as the interpretive matrix necessary to what we have been calling a continuity of reception (*FAp* 96–98a):

---

38. For an extended discussion with examples, cf. Foley 1991: 214–23.

39. Foley 1991: 223.

40. I refer here to the common (but hardly incontestable) critical assumption that the four Old English poems bearing the encoded "signature" of a certain Cynewulf (*Elene, Juliana, Christ II,* and *Fates of the Apostles*) are in fact to be attributed to the same author. If, further, the *Fates of the Apostles,* which immediately follows *Andreas* in the Vercelli Book manuscript and also concerns exploits of the apostles in a general way, is taken as continuous with *Andreas,* then one can interpret the Cynewulfian signature as denoting authorship of a two-poem composite. As for the riddling tone of the *Fates* passage, both the injunction to be clever in analysis (96–98a) and the coda implying that a secret has been revealed (105b-6) echo the phraseology and general style of the Exeter Book riddles. This kind of subgeneric signal is relatively common in the poetry (a particularly striking example is the enigma of God's origin as expressed in riddling language in the eighth Advent Lyric [*Christ I* 241f.]), and relies upon the traditional nature of the poetic register dedicated to the Riddle genre.

> Her mæg findan   for(e)þances gleaw,
> se ðe hine lysteð   *leoðgiddunga,*
> hwa þas fitte fegde.

> Here [one] can find,   a person wise in perception,
> one who delights   *in poem-songs,*
> who made this song.

The simplex *-gi(e)d-*, which lies at the basis of *leoðgiddunga,* encodes part of this metonymic meaning by itself: whether describing Judas's special knowledge of the location of the cross in *Elene,* the (textualized) song consumed by the moth in *Riddle 47,* Hrothgar's own conception of his "sermon" in *Beowulf,* or other moments and situations in the poetic canon,[41] this word signals the nexus of song and wisdom, that is, of performance and tradition. The poet of *Maxims 1* seems to speak for many when he affirms in introducing his collection of proverbs that "Gleawe men sceolon gieddum wrixlan" ("Wise men shall exchange *gied*s," 4).[42]

Such fluency in the register, in the "way of speaking" that constitutes the vehicle of Old English poetry, is all the more remarkable when we consider that the interruption must represent undiscovered generic territory for the poet: on available evidence, this is a unique "genre," wholly without a model or rules, and yet he carries on idiomatically and without discernible hesitation. In this fluency the *Andreas* poet is not unlike many traditional artists in other cultures—some of whom use literacy for some purposes—who know their compositional registers so thoroughly that they can create "new" kinds of discourse within the idiom.

We may recall from chapter 4 the description of just such an event, recorded by our fieldwork team in central Serbia in 1975, from an epic bard named Milutin Milojević in the village of Velika Ivanča. Milojević had just finished a performance of a long narrative and a poetic recitation of the members of his army battalion (another new genre!) when we asked whether we could take his photograph for our records. In response he spontaneously composed the following four lines:

> Ja od Boga imam dobrog dara,
> Evo mene mojega slikara;
> Kogod 'oće, ko me lepo čuje,
> On mene lepo nek slikuje.

---

41. Respectively, *Ele* 418a (etc.), *R47* 3b, *Bwf* 1723b.

42. Among other traditional phrases pointing in the same direction, cf. esp. 1488–89. The hapax legomenon *fyrnsægen* ("said of old," 1489b) contrasts interestingly with *fyrngewrito/-u* ("old writings"), which occurs six times in the Anglo-Saxon poetic corpus, four in *Elene* (155a, 373b, 431a, 560b; all describing in general terms the source of wisdom to which the Hebrews will turn to locate the cross), and two in *Precepts* (67b, 73a; designating the codes that the father admonishes his son to keep). It should also be noted that *leoðworda dæl* ("a share of song-words," 1488b) and *lytlum sticcum* ("in little pieces," 1488a) seem to amount to an emic, or ethnic, appraisal of the poet's compositional process. Cf. further n. 37.

> Yes, from God I have a fine gift,
> Here comes my photographer;
> Whoever wishes, whoever hears me well,
> Let him take my picture well.

Milojević had never had his picture taken before, so we may be sure that these were "new" lines. But they were at the same time also highly traditional lines, in the sense of having innumerable parallels in the South Slavic epic register.[43] This poet was memorializing a unique event not in the unmarked conversational prose we presume as a norm for such activities, but wholly within the epic "way of speaking."

Of course I will not claim that the *Andreas* "translator" was an oral poet whose methods were in every respect congruent with those of Milutin Milojević, whose novel composition is cited here only to illustrate how dynamic and pliable an instrument a traditional register really is. But I will claim that the Old English poet is, in an important sense, a singer of tales in performance. For it is such a register, which can support a tremendous range of composition from the most "canonical" to the most occasional forms, that the presumably learned and literate Old English poet also seems to be able to employ,[44] even to the extent of conveying his doubts about continuing the translation in progress. What does it mean, then, when he calls for a person *æglæwra* than he to complete the translation?

Clearly he is not describing his ability to use the dedicated "way of speaking," since he seems to be able to compose quite fluently even in an unknown genre. Just as clearly, access to the raw data of the story of Andrew cannot be the problem: his general fidelity to the sequence and detail of the *Praxeis,* broken chiefly by traditional glosses that index his translation, argues strongly for the presence of a text that he himself can consult, probably a lost Latin intermediary of the Greek story. What I suspect the *Andreas* poet may be longing for is neither the one nor the other of these desiderata, but rather their combination or "fit."[45] In other words, a person "wiser in the law" would be a poet who could more easily adapt his fluency to this particular compositional task, who could match register and source text with what he may feel is more success or authority. It is perhaps only sensible to suspend judgment on whether the poet "truly" considers himself inadequate or whether this is an Anglo-Saxon avatar of the modesty topos, but in either case I believe it is in short a syncretic poetics that he longs for.

43. Cf. n. 29 in chap. 4.
44. Cf. chap. 3 above, and esp. Doane 1991, 1994.
45. This particular kind of skill coincides with the confluence of wisdom and song that we have seen imaged in the morph *-gi(e)d-*. Equally instructive are the various occurrences of *-gleaw-*: cf. the instances in connection with riddling language (e.g., *And* 557a); in reference to the pursuit of traditional knowledge (e.g., *Ele* 805a, with Judas becoming *ægleaw* just after he receives God's sacred revelation); or in indexed elaboration on a source (e.g., *And* 817b, with *hygeþances gleaw* ("[though] wise in mind-thought") augmenting the *Praxeis* clause, *ou dunêsêi auta hupenegkein,* "you will not be able to bear [the tales of Christ's miracles]").

Could the particular episode on which he is soon to embark—Andrew's summoning the retributive flood from the statue's mouth—have stimulated his hesitation at precisely this point? Having just finished the three Scourging episodes, for which he has successfully fashioned a traditionally indexed rendering, did he sense an especially acute problem in the impending lack of fit between his traditional idiom and the next episode (the destructive flood)? Did the translation of this structured narrative event—based on a text, we must keep in mind—match poorly with the scenic contents of his repertoire? (We need to remember here that the interruption placed no narrative demands on that repertoire, and that its source was as far as can be determined not a preexistent text but the "whole cloth" of his own thoughts and reactions.)

For now, perhaps it is enough to say that the *Andreas* poet's self-interruption, taken in the context of the surrounding "indexed translation," offers us a unique perspective on the craft of poetry in Anglo-Saxon England. Without recourse to untenable and exclusivist typologies, we can take account of the traditional oral register used by this presumably literate and highly individual artist. Perhaps we can also understand how a syncretic poetics—a poetics that acknowledges the contributions of both text-based strategies such as typology and the rhetorically persistent dimension of word-power—helps us toward a continuity of reception and toward a better appreciation of the remarkable performance by this singer of tales, both its undeniable creativity and its patently traditional resonance.

CONCLUSION

"πᾶσι γὰρ ἀνθρώποισιν ἐπιχθονίοισιν ἀοιδοὶ
τιμῆς ἔμμοροί εἰσι καὶ αἰδοῦς, οὕνεκ' ἄρα σφέας
οἴμας Μοῦσ' ἐδίδαξε, φίλησε δὲ φῦλον ἀοιδῶν."

For all of the peoples on the earth the singers' share
is honor and reverence, because it is they whom the Muse
has shown her paths, for she loves the tribe of singers.

Odyssey 8.479–81

Što, ovaj, upamtim, ja upamtim;
Što ne upamtim ja sasnim noći.

Well, what I remember, I remember;
What I don't remember I dream at night.

Desanka Matijašević, *bajalica*

The fundamental argument of this volume can be encapsulated proverbially in the following premise: *word-power derives from the enabling event of performance and the enabling referent of tradition.* For its part, performance constitutes the condition for bringing into play the special significative force associated with emergence. Words come to mean immensely more, and differently, than the semiotically narrowed transcriptions into which performances are subsequently reduced, and we mis-"read" performances when we simply assimilate them to our own culturally privileged medium of text. Complementarily, tradition describes that body of implication, itself ever changing within limits, to which a performed work of verbal art institutionally appeals. It is the context, the understanding, the set of assumptions and reactions that fills out the processual nature of the event, providing a wholeness that, strictly speaking, cannot be located in or projected from the decontextualized text alone.

In the composite theory of the singer of tales in performance, I believe we can perceive the common ground shared by three powerful approaches to traditional oral works. The Ethnography of Speaking, in particular the "performance" school, holds that "there is something going on in the communicative interchange which says to the auditor, 'interpret what I say in some special sense;

do not take it to mean what the words alone, taken literally, would convey'" (Bauman 1977: 9). By becoming aware of the many other, non-"textual" channels through which the transaction is taking place, the audience can learn what that "special sense" is—and perhaps avoid making the blunders for which the splendidly literal Pelt Kid of Zuni legend is chastised by his grandmother.

Just as the ability to decode "keys to performance" proves a prerequisite to wielding word-power, so an active consideration of what Dell Hymes has called the rhetorical structure of Native American narrative is necessary to its fuller, more nuanced understanding. Whether at the microcosmic level of the line, versicle, and verse or at the upper strata of stanza, scene, act, and part, our failure to grasp the expressive rules for this "way of speaking" will compromise our participation in the overall continuity of reception. Another advocate of the Ethnopoetic approach, Dennis Tedlock, has stressed the importance of performance dimensions by scoring his translated libretti for oral realization by readers. In redirecting our attention to pause, loudness, pitch, and other aspects of enactment, he has helped us to recognize myopic overdependence on muted texts alone. Whatever the particular brand or methodology, Ethnopoetics likewise moves us toward a greater awareness of word-power—the kind of associative meaning traditionally encoded in that unlikeliest of South Slavic heroes, Tale of Orašac.

Third among the approaches brought together under the theoretical umbrella of word-power has been Oral-Formulaic Theory, specifically as extended to Immanent Art. From the very beginning of his revolutionary work, Milman Parry was concerned with the role of the ancient Greek poetic tradition, and he and Albert Lord sought to understand that inferred tradition by field investigation in the South Slavic lands. What I have tried to add to their study of the integers of traditional oral expression is a mathematics of signification, a perspective that sheds some light on how this way of speaking is also and vitally a "way of meaning," and on how a performance tradition is at root an immanent art. In chapter 1 I defined the quality of immanence as "the set of metonymic, associative meanings institutionally delivered and received through a dedicated idiom or register either during or on the authority of traditional oral performance." This perspective shares the Ethnography of Speaking's concern with the "special sense" in which a communication is to be interpreted, as well as the commitment of Ethnopoetics to presentation and understanding of traditional oral art on its own terms.

In explicating the overall theory of the singer of tales in performance, it proved heuristically convenient to denominate three aspects for individual consideration. The *performance arena,* defined as "the locus where the event of performance takes place, where words are invested with their special power," only secondarily refers to a physically determinate location. More basically, it is an abstract site or recurrent forum for a specific verbal activity, a place (defined abstractly and ritualistically rather than empirically) where participants go to transact the business of performance. Within that arena they speak not in the unmarked idiom of everyday discourse, or in a standard textual variety of the language, but rather in a dedicated *register* whose sole reason for existence is to serve as the vehicle for performance. This register, as the Ethnography of Speaking and Ethnopoetics teach us, comprises not only the set of expressive features that can be assimilated to a textual model, but also all those channels (gestures, paralinguistic cues, and so forth) that translate to textual representation only partially or not at all. If the performer and audience can enter the arena and speak the dedicated register fluently—at the levels of both phraseology and larger patterns as required by the individual tradition or genre—then the verbal transaction proceeds with a unique *communicative economy*. Since the channel maximizes efficiency by licensing only a relatively narrow spectrum of discourse while at the same time encoding its meaning densely and metonymically, it permits very substantial exchange with relatively few signals. Meeting these conditions—entering the performance arena and employing the appropriate register—enables communicative economy by direct engagement of what is immanent to the act and fact of traditional performance.

Essential to this heightened exchange and intelligibility is at least a working fluency on the part of not only the performer, but also and crucially the audience and then reader. Unless all parties to the exchange have a base-level command of the register—its implied meanings as well as its rules for phraseology, narrative pattern, and the like—even the most carefully coded message will go unreceived or, potentially even worse, will be distorted. To maintain what I have called a continuity of reception requires an audience trained to decode signals and, in terms of the Receptionalist perspective offered in chapter 2, to bridge gaps of indeterminacy. Does this process entail a lockstep procedure that involves only one "right" interpretation for each integer? Of course not: any reception of a work of art will depend in part on the individuality of the audience member, as well as on his or her cultural and historical predispositions. As in most human endeavors, it will always be a matter of balance and of endemic pluralism, with contributions from the original performance tradition, from the contemporary cultural context, and from individual experience. This volume merely argues for increased attention to the traditional contribution, that is, in favor of a tutorial in the register through whose dedicated idiom we encounter the given work. Naturally, no matter how assiduous the lessons, we can never wholly become the original audience; but, as I hope the later chapters of the present volume have illustrated, we can achieve a finite if partial gain in our understanding of the mode of delivery and the message conveyed.

That gain may be especially precious in our study of those singers of tales in performance whose works survive only as texts. In recent years scholars have effectively dismantled the once-doctrinal Great Divide theory, proving through fieldwork and analytical procedures that the binary model of orality versus literacy is far too simplistic to address the complexity of the world's verbal arts. In this volume I have advocated a spectrum model for oral traditional works, from the now rare situations in which writing has played no part whatsoever through the myriad intermediate cases where oral tradition and literacy intertwine in fascinating ways and on to the works composed by literate authors that nonetheless owe some debt to an originative oral tradition. I would emphasize that this is in no way to be taken as an evolutionary model; for one thing, the phenomenon of different registers within a given culture's (and person's) expressive repertoire precludes any such leveling hypothesis. Indeed, we must make every effort to avoid such crippling, reductive generalizations; it is for the same reason that I have tried to proceed with due respect for the tradition-, genre-, and medium-dependence of each work investigated.

With these calibrations in mind, I have attempted in chapter 3 to provide a theoretical basis for what has historically been bracketed by most investigators: the puzzling, even stubborn recurrence of traditional oral integers in unambiguously textual works, that is, in verbal art that we have every reason to believe was composed in writing by an author physically far removed from the act and experience of oral tradition. What happens, in other words, when the audience is, from the start, listening to (or even reading) an author's *text*? I believe the answer to this troubling question lies in understanding the relative weight of the two terms in "oral tradition" and the continuity of reception that smooths the significative ground between the power of spoken and written words.

Just as Milman Parry's initial emphasis on tradition drove the development of Oral-Formulaic Theory and Immanent Art, and just as many of Richard Bauman's keys to performance and Dell Hymes's poetic structures can resurface (with translation) in a written format, so the word-power that originates in oral performance survives in texts. Traditional, performance-derived registers cannot manage apotheosis in the same form, of course, but they do beget dynamic and empowering progeny that reflect their lineage through what I have called a rhetorical persistence of traditional forms. But for the text, the performance arena is purely a signal entirely without physical reality, and the register consists only of those integers and keys that can be deployed in the textual medium. And we should add, in concert with the syncretic poetics advocated throughout this volume, that traditional oral strategies for expression and reception must to varying degrees share center stage with specifically textual and intertextual strategies. But to ignore the array of meanings attached to traditional registers on the grounds that one is dealing with written records rather than oral performances amounts to a species of the Great Divide typology; we need to realize that the "way of speaking" persists, albeit in modified form, in the new medium.

To anticipate one possible objection, let us consider the following line of questioning: How, one might ask, does the composite view represented by the singer of tales in performance differ from more conventional assumptions about literature? After all, one might respond, verbal art of every stripe assumes a variety of extratextual contexts and necessarily makes reference to worlds of implication outside the confines of the text. How then do traditional oral works, especially those that involve texts in some fashion, qualify as a special category, as something different?

The first and broadest answer is that no hard and fast, exclusive distinction can be supported as long as we respect the natural variety of the world's oral traditions and the heterogeneity of interactions between oral traditions and texts that have survived to us. All verbal art projects meaning from coded signals, makes explicit what is implicit, bridges gaps of indeterminacy. All verbal art requires that the audience or reader bring something to the co-creation of the work. The issue to be raised is thus not whether but to what degree the performance or work is dependent for its intelligibility and artistic excellence on the "special sense" in which it must be taken, on the way of speaking it represents, on the formulaic and narrative idiom it employs. Are the features of performance arena and register merely traces of an idiom no longer essential to expression and reception, or are they to some extent constitutive of coherence and art? Realistically, there must be innumerable points along the spectrum from constitutive to inessential, with even the most "literary" of forms preserving this or that dynamic as an inheritance from oral tradition. Our responsibility is thus not to fracture that spectrum into artificial sections, suppressing its natural heterogeneity in a pyrrhic search for airtight categories. It is rather to apply an appropriately calibrated version of the syncretic poetics that has been advocated throughout this volume.

The second, more specific answer goes as follows. We should not be surprised that works from very disparate points on the spectrum still have some features in common. Of course, many of the traditional oral characteristics can be found in highly literate texts; how could it be otherwise, simply from a genetic point of view? Traditions will differ among themselves, and from one genre to another, but at the same time some features that drive the expression and reception of traditional oral works will also modulate into specifically textual strategies. Exploration of that modulation is well beyond the scope of the present volume, in that it entails not transcriptions or authored texts with roots in oral tradition that still depend on the kind of word-power we have been examining, but rather fully textualized works from which the dimensions of performance arena, register, and communicative economy have effectively disappeared. To repeat, however, within the sphere of verbal art in which word-power is operative, we should begin by asking what version of the syncretic poetics is pertinent and useful for the work under consideration.

In chapters 4 through 6 I have tried to show how such a poetics might be applied to actual performances and texts, selecting for illustration genres and particular works that have enjoyed little if any attention in prior investigations of oral tradition. The first of these, *bajanje* or charms from rural Serbia, represents an ongoing but sparsely studied tradition; its discussion in chapter 4 was based entirely on our fieldwork team's firsthand experience with a variety of informants in the village of Orašac in the region of Šumadija. Chapters 5 and 6 took as their subjects the largely neglected Homeric Hymns from ancient Greek and the verse hagiography *Andreas* from Anglo-Saxon, both of which are oral-derived texts in which traditional forms have maintained a measure of their word-power as affective rhetoric. The *Hymn to Demeter* offered the opportunity to move outside the epic hegemony in archaic Greek *epos:* to study a genre with its own rules and definition but, significantly, with some points of connection to the phraseology and narrative patterning of the *Iliad* and *Odyssey.*

The Old English *Andreas,* on the other hand, revealed itself to be an "indexed translation" of a Greek or Latin source, and provided an example of how a highly individual, presumably literate poet can work pen in hand but still very much within the traditional register or idiom.

To close by means of the kind of ring-structure deeply rooted in many traditional oral idioms, let me reaffirm what was offered as a proverbial summation in the opening sentence of this conclusion: *word-power derives from the enabling event of performance and the enabling referent of tradition.* Even when performance modulates into transcription or authored text, the empowering use of register and (now rhetorical) entry of the performance arena can lead to some degree of communicative economy, assuming that the audience or reader is sufficiently fluent in that register and able to join the performer or author in that arena. Most fundamentally, the singer of tales in performance selects and uses a "way of speaking" not *metri causa* but *artis causa.*

BIBLIOGRAPHY

Abrahams, Roger D. 1977. "Toward an Enactment-Centered Theory of Folklore." In *Frontiers of Folklore,* ed. William R. Bascom, pp. 79–117. Boulder, Colo.: Westview Press.

———. 1983. *The Man-of-Words in the West Indies: Performance and the Emergence of Creole Culture.* Baltimore: Johns Hopkins University Press.

Allen, T. W.; W. R. Halliday; and E. E. Sikes. 1980. Eds., *The Homeric Hymns.* Rpt. of 1936 ed. Amsterdam: Adolf M. Hakkert.

Amodio, Mark C. 1994. Ed., *Oral Poetics in Middle English Poetry.* New York: Garland.

Arewa, E. Ojo, and Alan Dundes. 1964. "Proverbs and the Ethnography of Speaking Folklore." *American Anthropologist* 66: 70–85.

Athanassakis, Apostolos N. 1976. Trans., *The Homeric Hymns.* Baltimore: Johns Hopkins University Press.

Austerlitz, Robert. 1958. *Ob-Ugric Metrics: The Metrical Structure of Ostyak and Vogul Folk-Poetry.* Folklore Fellows Communications 174. Helsinki: Suomalainen Tiedeakatemia.

Austin, J. L. 1962. *How to Do Things with Words.* Oxford: Clarendon Press.

Bakhtin, Mikhail. 1981. *The Dialogic Imagination: Four Essays.* Trans. Caryl Emerson and Michael Holquist. Austin: University of Texas Press.

Bakker, Egbert. 1993. "Information, Activation, Preservation: The Interdependence of Text and Performance in an Oral Tradition." *Oral Tradition* 8: 5–20.

Bassett, Samuel E. 1919. "The Theory of the Homeric Caesura According to the Extant Remains of the Ancient Doctrine." *American Journal of Philology* 40: 343–72.

Basso, Ellen B. 1985. *A Musical View of the Universe.* Philadelphia: University of Pennsylvania Press.

———. 1990. "The Last Cannibal." *Journal of Folklore Research* 27: 133–73.

Basso, Keith H. 1984. "'Stalking with Stories': Names, Places, and Moral Narratives among the Western Apache." In *Text, Play, and Story: The Construction and Reconstruction of Self and Society (1983 Proceedings of the American Ethnological Society),* ed. Stuart Plattner and Edward Bruner, pp. 19–55. Washington: American Ethnological Society. Rpt. in K. Basso 1990: 99–137.

———. 1988. "'Speaking with Names': Language and Landscape among the Western Apache." *Cultural Anthropology* 3: 99–130. Rpt. in K. Basso 1990: 138–73.

———. 1990. *Western Apache Language and Culture: Essays in Linguistic Anthropology.* Tucson: University of Arizona Press.

Bauman, Richard. 1977. *Verbal Art as Performance.* Prospect Heights, Ill.: Waveland Press.

———. 1982. "Conceptions of Folklore in the Development of Literary Semiotics." *Semiotica* 39: 1–20.

———. 1986. *Story, Performance, and Event: Contextual Studies of Oral Narrative.* Cambridge: Cambridge University Press.

Bauman, Richard, and Charles L. Briggs. 1990. "Poetics and Performance as Critical Perspectives on Language and Social Life." *Annual Review of Anthropology* 19: 59–88.

Bauman, Richard, and Joel Sherzer. 1989. Eds., *Explorations in the Ethnography of Speaking.* 2nd ed. Cambridge: Cambridge University Press.

Bäuml, Franz H. 1980. "Varieties and Consequences of Medieval Literacy and Illiteracy." *Speculum* 55: 237–65.

———. 1984–85. "Medieval Texts and the Two Theories of Oral-Formulaic Composition: A Proposal for a Third Theory." *New Literary History* 16: 31–49.

Ben-Amos, Dan. 1969. "Analytical Categories and Ethnic Genres." *Genre* 2: 275–301.

———. 1971. "Toward a Definition of Folklore in Context." *Journal of American Folklore* 84: 3–15.

———. 1979. "The Ceremony of Innocence." *Western Folklore* 38: 47–52.

———. 1984. "The Seven Strands of *Tradition*: Varieties in Its Meaning in American Folklore Studies." *Journal of Folklore Research* 21: 97–131.

Ben-Amos, Dan, and Kenneth S. Goldstein. 1975. Eds., *Folklore: Performance and Communication*. The Hague: Mouton.

Benson, Larry D. 1966. "The Literary Character of Anglo-Saxon Formulaic Poetry." *Publications of the Modern Language Association* 81: 334–41.

Benson, Morton. 1984. *Serbocroatian-English Dictionary* (*Srpskohrvatski-engleski rečnik*). 2nd rev. ed. Belgrade: Prosveta.

Besnier, Niko. 1988. "The Linguistic Relationships of Spoken and Written Nukulaelae Registers." *Language* 64: 707–36.

Bessinger, Jess B. Jr., and Philip H. Smith. 1978. Ed. and progr., *A Concordance to the Anglo-Saxon Poetic Records*. Ithaca: Cornell University Press.

Biggs, Frederick M. 1988. "The Passion of Andreas: *Andreas* 1398–1491." *Studies in Philology* 85: 413–27.

Boenig, Robert. 1991a. *Saint and Hero:* Andreas *and Medieval Doctrine*. Lewisburg, Pa.: Bucknell University Press.

———. 1991b. Trans., *The Acts of Andrew in the Country of the Cannibals: Translations from the Greek, Latin, and Old English*. New York: Garland.

Boyarin, Jonathan. 1993. Ed., *The Ethnography of Reading*. Berkeley: University of California Press.

Briggs, Charles L. 1988. *Competence in Performance: The Creativity of Tradition in Mexicano Verbal Art*. Philadelphia: University of Pennsylvania Press.

———. 1990. Ed. with Julián Josué Vigil. *The Lost Gold Mine of Juan Mondragón: A Legend from New Mexico Performed by Melaquías Romero*. Tucson: University of Arizona Press.

Bright, William. 1979. "A Karok Myth in 'Measured Verse': The Translation of a Performance." *Journal of California and Great Basin Anthropology* 1: 117–23.

Brodeur, Arthur G. 1959. *The Art of Beowulf*. Berkeley: University of California Press.

Bronner, Simon J. 1986. *American Folklore Studies: An Intellectual History*. Lawrence: University Press of Kansas.

———. 1988. "Art, Performance, and Praxis: The Rhetoric of Contemporary Folklore Studies." *Western Folklore* 47: 75–101.

Brooks, Kenneth R. 1961. Ed., *Andreas and the Fates of the Apostles*. Oxford: Clarendon Press.

Buonanno, Michael. 1990. "The Palermitan Epic: Dialogism and the Inscription of Social Relations." *Journal of American Folklore* 103: 324–33.

Bynum, David E. 1979. "The Singing." In Bynum, ed., *Bihaćka krajina: Epics from Bihać, Cazin, and Kulen Vakuf*. *SCHS* 14: 14–43.

———. 1986. "The Collection and Analysis of Oral Epic Tradition in South Slavic: An Instance." *Oral Tradition* 1: 302–43.

Calder, Daniel G. 1981. *Cynewulf*. Boston: G. K. Hall.

Calhoun, George M. 1935. "The Art of Formula in Homer—ΕΠΕΑ ΠΤΕΡΟΕΝΤΑ." *Classical Philology* 30: 215–27.

Caraveli, Anna. 1982. "The Song beyond the Song: Aesthetics and Social Interaction in Greek Folksong." *Journal of American Folklore* 95: 129–58.

Carrier, James, and Achsah Carrier. 1990. "Every Picture Tells a Story: Visual Alternatives to Oral Tradition in Ponam Society." *Oral Tradition* 5: 354–75.

Chase, Colin. 1981. Ed., *The Dating of Beowulf.* Toronto: University of Toronto Press.

Clay, Jenny Strauss. 1989. *The Politics of Olympus: Form and Meaning in the Major Homeric Hymns.* Princeton: Princeton University Press.

Clifford, James, and George E. Marcus. 1986. *Writing Culture: The Poetics and Politics of Ethnography.* Berkeley: University of California Press.

Cockayne, Oswald. 1965. *Leechdoms, Wortcunning, and Starcraft of Early England.* 3 vols. Wiesbaden: Kraus. Orig. pub. 1864–66.

Combellack, Frederick M. 1950. "Words That Die." *Classical Journal* 46: 21–26.

Coote, Mary P. 1977. "Women's Songs in Serbo-Croatian." *Journal of American Folklore* 90: 331–38.

———. 1978. "Serbocroatian Heroic Songs." In Oinas 1978: 257–85.

———. 1981. "Lying in Passages." *Canadian-American Slavic Studies* 15: 5–23.

———. 1992. "On the Composition of Women's Songs." *Oral Tradition* 7: 332–48.

Curtius, Ernst Robert. 1953. *European Literature and the Latin Middle Ages.* Princeton: Princeton University Press.

de Hoz, J. 1964. "Poesia oral independiente de Homero en Hesíodo y los himnos homéricos." *Emerita* 32: 263–98.

Diamond, Robert E. 1963. *The Diction of the Anglo-Saxon Metrical Psalms.* The Hague: Mouton.

Doane, A. N. 1991. "Oral Texts, Intertexts, and Intratexts: Editing Old English." In *Influence and Intertextuality in Literary History,* ed. Jay Clayton and Eric Rothstein, pp. 75–113. Madison: University of Wisconsin Press.

———. 1994. "Performance as a Constitutive Category in the Editing of Anglo-Saxon Poetic Texts." *Oral Tradition* 9: 420–39.

Doane, A. N., and Carol Braun Pasternack. 1991. Eds., *Vox intexta: Orality and Textuality in the Middle Ages.* Madison: University of Wisconsin Press.

Douglas, Mary. 1966. *Purity and Danger.* London: Routledge and Kegan Paul.

DuBois, Thomas. 1993. "From Maria to Marjatta: The Transformation of an Oral Poem in Elias Lönnrot's *Kalevala.*" *Oral Tradition* 8: 247–88.

Earl, James W. 1980. "The Typological Structure of *Andreas.*" In *Old English Literature in Context: Ten Essays,* ed. John D. Niles, pp. 66–89. Woodbridge and Totowa, N. J.: Boydell and Brewer.

Edwards, G. P. 1971. *The Language of Hesiod in Its Traditional Context.* Oxford: Basil Blackwell.

Edwards, Mark W. 1986. "Homer and Oral Tradition: The Formula, Part I." *Oral Tradition* 1: 171–230.

———. 1988. "Homer and Oral Tradition: The Formula, Part II." *Oral Tradition* 3: 11–60.

———. 1991. *The Iliad: A Commentary. Volume V: Books 17–20.* Cambridge: Cambridge University Press.

———. 1992. "Homer and Oral Tradition: The Type-Scene." *Oral Tradition* 7: 284–330.

Ellis, John M. 1983. *One Fairy Story Too Many: The Brothers Grimm and Their Tales.* Chicago: University of Chicago Press.

Feld, Steven. 1982. *Sound and Sentiment: Birds, Weeping, Poetics, and Song in Kaluli Expression.* Philadelphia: University of Pennsylvania Press.

Fine, Elizabeth C. 1984. *The Folklore Text: From Performance to Print.* Bloomington: Indiana University Press.

Finnegan, Ruth. 1970. *Oral Literature in Africa.* Oxford: Clarendon Press.

———. 1977. *Oral Poetry: Its Nature, Significance, and Social Context.* Cambridge: Cambridge University Press.

———. 1988. *Literacy and Orality: Studies in the Technology of Communication.* Oxford: Basil Blackwell.

————. 1991. "Tradition, But What Tradition and for Whom?" (1990 Milman Parry Lecture on Oral Tradition). *Oral Tradition* 6: 104–24.

Fish, Stanley. 1980. *Is There a Text in This Class? The Authority of Interpretive Communities.* Cambridge, Mass.: Harvard University Press.

Fleischman, Suzanne. 1989. "A Linguistic Perspective on the *Laisses similaires:* Orality and the Pragmatics of Narrative Discourse." *Romance Philology* 43: 70–89.

————. 1990. "Philology, Linguistics, and the Discourse of the Medieval Text." *Speculum* 65: 19–37.

Foley, Anne-Marie C. 1992. "Charles Dickens's Victorian Picaresque." Ph.D. dissertation, University of Missouri–Columbia.

Foley, John Miles. 1980a. "Epic and Charm in Old English and Serbo-Croatian Oral Poetry." *Comparative Criticism* 2: 71–92.

————. 1980b. "Hybrid Prosody: Single Half-lines in Old English and Serbo-Croatian Prosody." *Neophilologus* 64: 284–89.

————. 1981. "*Lǽcdom* and *Bajanje:* A Comparative Study of Old English and Serbo-Croatian Charms." *Centerpoint* 4: 33–40.

————. 1982. "Field Research on Oral Literature and Culture in Serbia." In *Oral and Traditional Literatures,* ed. Norman Simms, a special issue of *Pacific Quarterly Moana,* 7, ii: 47–59.

————. 1983. "Literary Art and Oral Tradition in Old English and Serbian Poetry." *Anglo-Saxon England* 12: 183–214.

————. 1984. "Editing Oral Epic Texts: Theory and Practice." *Text: Transactions of the Society for Textual Scholarship* 1: 75–94.

————. 1985. *Oral-Formulaic Theory and Research: An Introduction and Annotated Bibliography.* New York: Garland.

————. 1987. "Reading the Oral Traditional Text: Aesthetics of Creation and Response." In *Comparative Research on Oral Traditions: A Memorial for Milman Parry,* ed. John Miles Foley, pp. 185–212. Columbus, Ohio: Slavica.

————. 1988. *The Theory of Oral Composition: History and Methodology.* Bloomington: Indiana University Press. Rpt. 1992.

————. 1990a. *Traditional Oral Epic: The* Odyssey, Beowulf, *and the Serbo-Croatian Return Song.* Berkeley: University of California Press. Rpt. 1993.

————. 1990b. Ed., *Oral-Formulaic Theory: A Casebook.* New York: Garland.

————. 1991. *Immanent Art: From Structure to Meaning in Traditional Oral Epic.* Bloomington: Indiana University Press.

————. 1992. "Synthetic Kinship in Serbo-Croatian Epic." In *De Gustibus: Essays for Alain Renoir,* ed. John Miles Foley, pp. 201–15. New York: Garland.

————. 1994. "Sixteen Moments of Silence in Homer." *Quaderni Urbinati di Cultura Classica* 33.

————. In press. "Scholarly Editing in Folk Literature." In *Scholarly Editing: An Introductory Guide to Research,* ed. David Greetham. New York: Modern Language Association.

Foley, John Miles, and Barbara Kerewsky-Halpern. 1976. "*Udovica Jana:* A Case Study of an Oral Performance." *Slavonic and East European Review* 54: 11–23.

Forth, Gregory. 1988. "Fashioned Speech, Full Communication: Aspects of Eastern Sumbanese Ritual Language." In Fox 1988b: 129–60.

Fournier, H. 1946. "Formules homériques de référence avec verbe 'dire.'" *Revue de philologie, de littérature, et d'histoire anciennes,* 3rd ser., 20: 29–68.

Fox, James J. 1988a. "Manu Kama's Road, Tepa Nilu's Path: Theme, Narrative, and Formula in Rotinese Rital Language." In Fox 1988b: 161–201.

————. 1988b. Ed., *To Speak in Pairs: Essays on the Ritual Languages of Eastern Indonesia.* Cambridge: Cambridge University Press.

Friedrich, Paul. 1986. *The Language Parallax: Linguistic Relativism and Poetic Indeterminacy.* Chicago: University of Chicago Press.

Gellrich, Jesse. 1985. *The Idea of the Book in the Middle Ages: Language Theory, Mythology, and Fiction.* Ithaca: Cornell University Press.

Gentili, Bruno. 1988. *Poetry and Its Public in Ancient Greece: From Homer to the Fifth Century.* Baltimore: Johns Hopkins University Press.

George, Kenneth M. 1990. "Felling a Song with a New Ax: Writing and the Reshaping of Ritual Song Performance in Upland Sulawesi." *Journal of American Folklore* 103: 3–23.

Georges, Robert A. 1969. "Toward an Understanding of Storytelling Events." *Journal of American Folklore* 82: 313–28.

———. 1980. "Toward a Resolution of the Text/Context Controversy." *Western Folklore* 39: 34–40.

———. 1986. "The Folklorist as Comparatist." *Western Folklore* 45: 1–20.

Glassie, Henry. 1982. *Passing the Time in Ballymenone: Culture and History of an Ulster Community.* Philadelphia: University of Pennsylvania Press.

Gombrich, E. H. 1972a. *Art and Illusion: A Study in the Psychology of Pictorial Representation.* 4th ed. London: Phaidon Press.

———. 1972b. "The Mask and the Face: The Perception of Physiognomic Likeness in Life and Art." In *Art, Perception, and Reality,* ed. Maurice Mandelbaum, pp. 1–46. Baltimore: Johns Hopkins University Press.

Goody, John R. 1986. *The Logic of Writing and the Organization of Society.* Cambridge: Cambridge University Press.

———. 1987. *The Interface between the Written and the Oral.* Cambridge: Cambridge University Press.

Gossen, Gary H. 1971. "Chamula Genres of Verbal Behavior." *Journal of American Folklore* 84: 145–67.

———. 1974. *Chamulas in the World of the Sun: Time and Space in a Maya Oral Tradition.* Rpt. Prospect Heights, Ill.: Waveland Press, 1984.

Greenfield, Stanley B. 1955. "The Formulaic Expression of the Theme of 'Exile' in Anglo-Saxon Poetry." *Speculum* 30: 200–206.

———. 1965. *A Critical History of Old English Literature.* New York: New York University Press.

Greenfield, Stanley B., and Daniel G. Calder. 1986. *A New Critical History of Old English Literature.* New York: New York University Press.

Grendon, Felix J. 1909. "The Anglo-Saxon Charms." *Journal of American Folklore* 22: 105–237.

Griffin, Jasper. 1980. *Homer on Life and Death.* Oxford: Clarendon Press.

Gunner, Elizabeth. 1986. "The Word, the Book and the Zulu Church of Nazareth." In *Oral Tradition and Literacy: Changing Visions of the World,* ed. R. A. Whitaker and E. R. Sienaert, pp. 179–88. Durban: Natal University Oral Documentation and Research Centre.

———. 1991. "Mixing the Discourses: Genre Boundary Jumping in Popular Song." In *Oral Tradition and Innovation: New Wine in Old Bottles?* ed. E. R. Sienaert, A. N. Bell, and M. Lewis, pp. 68–75. Durban: Natal University Oral Documentation and Research Centre.

Halliday, M. A. K. 1964. With Angus McIntosh and Peter Strevens. *The Linguistic Sciences and Language Teaching.* London: Longmans.

———. 1976. *Halliday: System and Function in Language.* Ed. G. R. Kress. London: Oxford University Press.

———. 1978. *Language as Social Semiotic: The Social Interpretation of Language and Meaning.* London: Edward Arnold, and Baltimore, Md.: University Park Press.

Halpern, Joel M. 1967. *A Serbian Village.* Rev. ed. New York: Harper and Row.

Halpern, Joel M., and Barbara Kerewsky-Halpern. 1972. *A Serbian Village in Historical Perspective.* New York: Holt, Rinehart, and Winston.

Hamilton, David. 1975. "*Andreas* and *Beowulf*: Placing the Hero." In *Anglo-Saxon Po-*

etry: Essays in Appreciation for John C. McGalliard, ed. Lewis Nicholson and Dolores W. Frese, pp. 81–98. Notre Dame: University of Notre Dame Press.

Hammond, N. G. L., and H. H. Scullard. 1970. Eds., *The Oxford Classical Dictionary*. Oxford: Clarendon Press.

Hanks, W. F. 1987. "Discourse Genres in a Theory of Practice." *American Ethnologist* 14: 668–92.

———. 1989. "Text and Textuality." *Annual Review of Anthropology* 18: 95–127.

Harrell, Sarah E. 1991. "Apollo's Fraternal Threats: Language of Succession and Domination in the *Homeric Hymn to Hermes*." *Greek, Roman, and Byzantine Studies* 32: 307–29.

Harris, William V. 1989. *Ancient Literacy*. Cambridge, Mass.: Harvard University Press.

Hendricks, Janet Wall. 1990. "Manipulating Time in an Amazonian Society: Genre and Event among the Shuar." *Journal of Folklore Research* 27: 11–28.

Hermann, John P. 1989. *Allegories of War: Language and Violence in Old English Poetry*. Ann Arbor: University of Michigan Press.

Herzog, George. 1951. "The Music of Yugoslav Heroic Epic Folk Poetry." *Journal of the International Folk Music Council* 3: 62–64.

Heubeck, Alfred, and Arie Hoekstra. 1989. *A Commentary on Homer's Odyssey, Volume II, Books IX-XVI*. Oxford: Clarendon Press.

Heubeck, Alfred; Stephanie West; and J. B. Hainsworth. 1988. *A Commentary on Homer's Odyssey, Volume I, Books I-VIII*. Oxford: Clarendon Press.

Hill, Jane H. 1990. "Weeping as a Meta-Signal in a Mexicano Women's Narrative." *Journal of Folklore Research* 27: 29–49.

Hill, Jonathan D. 1990. "Myth, Music, and History: Poetic Transformations of Narrative Discourse in an Amazonian Society." *Journal of Folklore Research* 27: 115–31.

Hill, Thomas D. 1969. "Figural Narrative in *Andreas*: The Conversion of the Mermedonians." *Neuphilologische Mitteilungen* 70: 261–73.

Hobsbawm, Eric, and Terence Ranger. 1983. Eds., *The Invention of Tradition*. Cambridge: Cambridge University Press.

Hoekstra, A. 1964. *Homeric Modifications of Formulaic Prototypes: Studies in the Development of Greek Epic Diction*. Amsterdam: Noord-Uitgevers Maatschappij.

———. 1969. *The Sub-Epic Stage of the Formulaic Tradition: Studies in the Homeric Hymns to Apollo, to Aphrodite and to Demeter*. Amsterdam: Noord-Uitgevers Maatschappij.

Holoka, James P. 1983. "'Looking Darkly' (ΥΠΟΔΡΑ ΙΔΩΝ): Reflections on Status and Decorum in Homer." *Transactions of the American Philological Association* 113: 1–6.

Hymes, Dell. 1962. "The Ethnography of Speaking." In *Anthropology and Human Behavior*, pp. 13–53. Washington, D.C.: The Anthropological Society of Washington.

———. 1965. "Some North Pacific Coast Poems: A Problem in Anthropological Philology." *American Anthropologist* 67: 316–41. Rpt. with "Postscript" in Hymes 1981: 35–64.

———. 1975a. "Breakthrough into Performance." In Ben-Amos and Goldstein 1975: 11–74. Rpt. with "Appendix" and "Postscript" in Hymes 1981: 79–141.

———. 1975b. "Folklore's Nature and the Sun's Myth." *Journal of American Folklore* 88: 345–69.

———. 1977. "Discovering Oral Performance and Measured Verse in American Indian Narrative." *New Literary History* 7: 431–57. Rev. in Hymes 1981: 309–41.

———. 1981. *"In vain I tried to tell you": Essays in Native American Ethnopoetics*. Philadelphia: University of Pennsylvania Press.

———. 1983. "Victoria Howard's 'Gitskux and His Older Brother': A Clackamas Chinook Myth." In *Smoothing the Ground: Essays on Native American Oral Literature*, ed. Brian Swann, pp. 129–70. Berkeley: University of California Press.

――――. 1985. "Language, Memory, and Selective Performance: Cultee's 'Salmon's Myth' as Told to Boas." *Journal of American Folklore* 98: 391–434.

――――. 1987a. "Anthologies and Narrators." In *Recovering the Word: Essays on Native American Literature,* ed. Brian Swann and Arnold Krupat, pp. 41–84. Berkeley: University of California Press.

――――. 1987b. "Tonkawa Poetics: John Rush Buffalo's 'Coyote and Eagle's Daughter.'" In Sherzer and Woodbury 1987a: 17–61.

――――. 1989a. "Ways of Speaking." In Bauman and Sherzer 1989: 433–51, 473–74.

――――. 1989b. "Tlingit Poetics." *Journal of Folklore Research* 26: 236–48.

――――. 1991. "Custer and Linguistic Anthropology." *Journal of Linguistic Anthropology* 1: 5–11.

――――. 1994. "Ethnopoetics, Oral-Formulaic Theory, and Editing Texts." *Oral Tradition* 9: 330–70.

Iser, Wolfgang. 1974. *The Implied Reader: Patterns of Communication in Prose Fiction from Bunyan to Beckett.* Baltimore: Johns Hopkins University Press.

――――. 1978. *The Act of Reading: A Theory of Aesthetic Response.* Baltimore: Johns Hopkins University Press.

――――. 1989. *Prospecting: From Reader Response to Literary Anthropology.* Baltimore: Johns Hopkins University Press.

Jakobson, Roman. 1952. "Studies in Comparative Slavic Metrics." *Oxford Slavonic Papers* 3: 21–66.

Janko, Richard. 1981. "The Structure of the Homeric Hymns: A Study in Genre." *Hermes* 109: 9–24.

――――. 1982. *Homer, Hesiod, and the Hymns: Diachronic Development in Epic Diction.* Cambridge: Cambridge University Press.

――――. 1990. "The *Iliad* and Its Editors: Dictation and Redaction." *Classical Antiquity* 9: 326–34.

――――. 1992. *The Iliad: A Commentary. Volume IV: Books 13–16.* Cambridge: Cambridge University Press.

Jauss, Hans Robert. 1974. "Literary History as a Challenge to Literary Theory." Trans. Elizabeth Benzinger, from chaps. 5–7 of *Literaturgeschichte als Provokation der Literaturwissenschaft,* 1967. In *New Directions in Literary History,* ed. Ralph Cohen, pp. 11–41. Baltimore: Johns Hopkins University Press.

――――. 1982. *Toward an Aesthetic of Reception.* Trans. Timothy Rahti. Theory and History of Literature, 2. Minneapolis: University of Minnesota Press.

――――. 1985. "The Identity of the Poetic Text in the Changing Horizon of Understanding." In *Identity of the Literary Text,* ed. Mario J. Valdés and Owen Miller, pp. 146–74. Toronto: University of Toronto Press.

Johnson, Barbara. 1980. *The Critical Difference: Essays in the Contemporary Rhetoric of Reading.* Baltimore: Johns Hopkins University Press.

Jones, Steven. 1979a. "Slouching toward Ethnography: The Text/Context Controversy Revisited." *Western Folklore* 38: 42–47.

――――. 1979b. "Dogmatism in the Contextual Revolution." *Western Folklore* 38: 52–55.

Joyner, Charles W. 1975. "A Model for the Analysis of Folklore Performance in Historical Context." *Journal of American Folklore* 88: 254–65.

Karadžić, Vuk Stefanović. 1852. *Srpski rječnik.* Rpt. 1975. Belgrade: Nolit.

Keenan, Hugh T. 1968. "The Apocalyptic Vision in Old English Poetry." Ph.D. dissertation, University of Tennessee.

Kekez, Josip. 1991. "*Bugaršćice:* A Unique Type of Archaic Oral Poetry." *Oral Tradition* 7: 200–24.

Kelly, Susan. 1990. "Anglo-Saxon Lay Society and the Written Word." In *The Uses of Literacy in Early Mediaeval Europe,* ed. Rosamond McKitterick, pp. 36–62. Cambridge: Cambridge University Press.

Kemp, P. 1935. *Healing Ritual: Studies in the Technique and Tradition of the Southern Slavs.* London: Faber and Faber.

Kerewsky-Halpern, Barbara. 1981a. "Genealogy as Genre in a Serbian Village." in *Oral Traditional Literature: A Festschrift for Albert Bates Lord,* ed. John Miles Foley, pp. 301–21. Columbus, Ohio: Slavica.

———. 1981b. "Text and Context in Serbian Ritual Lament." *Canadian-American Slavic Studies* 15: 52–60.

———. 1985. "Trust, Talk, and Touch in Balkan Folk Healing." *Social Science and Medicine* 21: 319–25.

———. 1986. "The Complementarity of Women's Ritual Roles in a Patriarchal Society." In *Papers on a Serbian Village,* ed. Barbara Kerewsky-Halpern and Joel M. Halpern, pp. 42–62. Amherst: University of Massachusetts Anthropology Department.

Kerewsky-Halpern, Barbara, and John Miles Foley. 1978a. "The Power of the Word: Healing Charms as an Oral Genre." *Journal of American Folklore* 91: 903–24.

———. 1978b. "*Bajanje:* Healing Magic in Rural Serbia." In *Culture and Curing,* ed. Peter Morley and Roy Wallis, pp. 40–56. London: Peter Owen, and Pittsburgh: University of Pittsburgh Press.

Kirk, Geoffrey S. 1985. *The Iliad: A Commentary, Volume I: Books 1–4.* Cambridge: Cambridge University Press.

———. 1990. *The Iliad: A Commentary, Volume II: Books 5–8.* Cambridge: Cambridge University Press.

Kirshenblatt-Gimblett, Barbara. 1975. "A Parable in Context: A Social Interactional Analysis of Storytelling Performance." In Ben-Amos and Goldstein 1975: 105–30.

Klaeber, Fr. 1950. Ed., *Beowulf and the Fight at Finnsburg.* 3rd ed. with 1st and 2nd supplements. Boston: D. C. Heath.

Klinck, Anne. 1992. Ed., *The Old English Elegies: A Critical Edition and Study.* Montreal and Kingston: McGill–Queen's University Press.

Knežević, S., and A. Jovanović. 1958. *Jarmenovci.* Belgrade: Srpska Akademija Nauka.

Koljević, Svetozar. 1980. *The Epic in the Making.* Oxford: Clarendon Press.

———. 1992. "Repetition as Invention in the Songs of Vuk Karadžić." *Oral Tradition* 7: 349–64.

Kratz, Corinne A. 1990. "Persuasive Suggestions and Reassuring Promises: Emergent Parallelism and Dialogic Encouragement in Song." *Journal of American Folklore* 103: 42–67.

Langen, Toby C. S. 1989. "Estoy-eh-muut and the Morphologists." *Studies in American Indian Literatures,* 2nd ser., 1, i: 1–12.

———. 1989–90. "The Organization of Thought in Lushootseed (Puget Salish) Literature: Martha Lamont's 'Mink and Changer.'" *Melus* 16, i: 77–93.

Lattimore, Richmond. 1951. Trans., *The Iliad of Homer.* Chicago: University of Chicago Press.

Lawless, Elaine J. 1988. *Handmaidens of the Lord: Women Preachers and Traditional Religion.* Philadelphia: University of Pennsylvania Press.

Leaf, Walter, and M. A. Bayfield. 1965. *The Iliad of Homer.* 2 vols. London: Macmillan, and New York: St. Martin's Press.

Liddell, Henry George, and Robert Scott. 1968. *A Greek-English Lexicon.* Rev. by Henry Stuart Jones. With supplement. Oxford: Clarendon Press.

Lord, Albert B. 1936. "Homer and Huso I: The Singer's Rests in Greek and Southslavic Heroic Song." *Transactions of the American Philological Association* 67: 106–13.

———. 1956. "Avdo Medjedović, *Guslar.*" *Journal of American Folklore* 69: 320–30. Rpt. in Lord 1991: 57–71.

———. 1960. *The Singer of Tales.* Cambridge, Mass.: Harvard University Press. Rpt. New York: Atheneum, 1965 et seq.

———. 1969. "The Theme of the Withdrawn Hero in Serbo-Croatian Oral Epic." *Prilozi za književnost, jezik, istoriju i folklor* 35: 18–30.

———. 1970. "Tradition and the Oral Poet: Homer, Huso, and Avdo Medjedović." In *Atti del Convegno Internazionale sul Tema: La Poesia epica e la sua formazione,* ed. Enrico Cerulli et al., pp. 13–28. Rome: Accademia Nazionale dei Lincei.

———. 1986a. "Perspectives on Recent Work on the Oral Traditional Formula." *Oral Tradition* 1: 467–503.

———. 1986b. "The Merging of Two Worlds: Oral and Written Poetry as Carriers of Ancient Values." In *Oral Tradition in Literature: Interpretation in Context,* ed. John Miles Foley, pp. 19–64. Columbia: University of Missouri Press.

———. 1991. *Epic Singers and Oral Tradition.* Ithaca, N.Y.: Cornell University Press.

Lord, Albert B., and Béla Bartók. 1951. Eds. and trans., *Serbo-Croatian Folk Songs.* New York: Columbia University Press.

Lord, Mary Louise. 1967. "Withdrawal and Return: An Epic Story Pattern in the *Homeric Hymn to Demeter* and in the Homeric Poems." *Classical Journal* 62: 241–48.

LSJ. Henry George Liddell, Robert Scott, and Henry Stuart Jones. *A Greek-English Lexicon.* Oxford: Clarendon Press. With a supplement, 1968.

Machan, Tim William. 1991. "Editing, Orality, and Late Middle English Texts." In Doane and Pasternack 1991: 229–45.

Magoun, Francis P., Jr. 1953. "The Oral-Formulaic Character of Anglo-Saxon Narrative Poetry." *Speculum* 28: 446–67.

Martin, Richard P. 1989. *The Language of Heroes: Speech and Performance in the* Iliad. Ithaca: Cornell University Press.

McDowell, John H. 1983. "The Semiotic Constitution of Kamsá Ritual Language." *Language in Society* 13: 23–46.

———. 1990. "The Community-Building Mission of Kamsá Ritual Language." *Journal of Folklore Research* 27: 67–84.

McLendon, Sally. 1981. "Meaning, Rhetorical Structure, and Discourse Organization in Myth." In *Analyzing Discourse: Text and Talk,* ed. Deborah Tannen, pp. 284–305. Washington, D.C.: Georgetown University Press.

Miletich, John S. 1990. Ed., *The Bugarštica: A Bilingual Anthology of the Earliest Extant South Slavic Folk Narrative Song.* Urbana: University of Illinois Press.

Miller, Andrew M. 1986. *From Delos to Delphi: A Literary Study of the Homeric Hymn to Apollo.* Leiden: E. J. Brill.

Minton, William W. 1962. "Invocation and Catalogue in Hesiod and Homer." *Transactions of the American Philological Association* 93: 188–212.

———. 1970. "The Proem-Hymn of Hesiod's *Theogony.*" *Transactions of the American Philological Association* 101: 357–77.

Mitchell, David. 1988. "Method in the Metaphor: Yje Ritual Language of Wanukaka." In Fox 1988b: 64–86.

Mladenović, Živomir. 1973. "Rukopisi narodnih pesama Vukove zbirke i njihovo izdanje." In *Srpske narodne pesme iz neobavljenih rukopisa Vuka Stef. Karadžića,* ed. with Vladan Nedić, vol. 1, pp. i–cclxxix. Belgrade: Srpska Akademija Nauka.

Morford, Mark P. O., and Robert J. Lenardon. 1991. *Classical Mythology.* 4th ed. New York: Longman.

Muellner, Leonard C. 1976. *The Meaning of Homeric* euchomai *through Its Formulas.* Innsbruck: Institut für Sprachwissenschaft, Universität Innsbruck.

Murko, Matija. 1929/1990. "The Singers and Their Epic Songs." Trans. John Miles Foley. *Oral Tradition* 5: 107–30.

———. 1951. *Tragom srpsko-hrvatske narodne epike: Putovanja u godinama 1930–32.* 2 vols. Zagreb: Jugoslavenska Akademija Znanosti i Umjetnosti.

Nagler, Michael N. 1974. *Spontaneity and Tradition: A Study in the Oral Art of Homer.* Berkeley: University of California Press.

Nagy, Gregory. 1974. *Comparative Studies in Greek and Indic Meter.* Cambridge, Mass.: Harvard University Press.

———. 1979. *The Best of the Achaeans: Concepts of the Hero in Archaic Greek Poetry.* Baltimore: Johns Hopkins University Press.

———. 1990. *Pindar's Homer: The Lyric Possession of an Epic Past.* Baltimore: Johns Hopkins University Press.

———. 1992. "Homeric Questions." *Transactions of the American Philological Association* 122: 17–60.

Nichols, Stephen G. 1990. "Introduction: Philology in a Manuscript Culture." *Speculum* 65: 1–10.

Niles, John D. 1983. *Beowulf: The Poem and Its Tradition.* Cambridge, Mass.: Harvard University Press.

———. 1994. "Editing *Beowulf:* What Can Study of the Ballads Tell Us?" *Oral Tradition* 9: 440–67.

Notopoulos, James A. 1949. "Parataxis in Homer." *Transactions of the American Philological Association* 80: 1–23.

———. 1962. "The Homeric Hymns as Oral Poetry: A Study of the Post-Homeric Oral Tradition." *American Journal of Philology* 83: 337–68.

Obiechina, Emmanuel. 1992. "Narrative Proverbs in the African Novel." *Oral Tradition* 7: 197–230.

O'Brien O'Keeffe, Katherine. 1990. *Visible Song: Transitional Literacy in Old English Verse.* Cambridge: Cambridge University Press.

Oinas, Felix J. 1978. Ed., *Heroic Epic and Saga: An Introduction to the World's Great Folk-Epics.* Bloomington: Indiana University Press.

Olsen, Alexandra Hennessey. 1984. *Speech, Song, and Poetic Craft: The Artistry of the Cynewulf Canon.* New York and Bern: Peter Lang.

O'Neill, Eugene, Jr. 1942. "The Localization of Metrical Word-Types in the Greek Hexameter." *Yale Classical Studies* 8: 103–78.

Ong, Walter J. 1977. "African Talking Drums and Oral Noetics." *New Literary History* 8: 411–29. Rpt. in Ong, *Interfaces of the Word: Studies in the Evolution of Consciousness and Culture,* pp. 92–120. Ithaca: Cornell University Press.

———. 1982. *Orality and Literacy: The Technologizing of the Word.* London: Methuen.

———. 1986. "Text as Interpretation: Mark and After." In *Oral Tradition in Literature: Interpretation in Context,* ed. John Miles Foley, pp. 147–69. Columbia: University of Missouri Press.

Opland, Jeff. 1975. "*Imbongi nezibongo:* The Xhosa Tribal Poet and the Contemporary Poetic Tradition." *Publications of the Modern Language Association* 90: 185–208.

———. 1980. *Anglo-Saxon Oral Poetry: A Study of the Traditions.* New Haven: Yale University Press.

———. 1983. *Xhosa Oral Poetry: Aspects of a Black South African Tradition.* Cambridge: Cambridge University Press.

Parks, Ward. 1989. "Interperformativity and *Beowulf.*" *Narodna umjetnost* 26: 25–35.

———. 1991. "The Textualization of Orality in Literary Criticism." In Doane and Pasternack 1991: 46–61.

Parry, Milman. 1928a. *L'Epithète traditionnelle dans Homère: Essai sur un problème de style homérique.* Paris: Société Editrice "Les Belles Lettres." Rpt. in Parry 1971: 1–190.

———. 1928b. *Les Formules et la métrique d'Homère.* Paris: Société Editrice "Les Belles Lettres." Rpt. in Parry 1971: 191–239.

———. 1930. "Studies in the Epic Technique of Oral Verse-Making. I. Homer and Homeric Style." *Harvard Studies in Classical Philology* 41: 73–147. Rpt. in Parry 1971: 266–324.

———. 1932. "Studies in the Epic Technique of Oral Verse-Making. II. The Homeric

Language as the Language of an Oral Poetry." *Harvard Studies in Classical Philology* 43: 1–50. Rpt. in Parry 1971: 325–64.

————. 1933–35. "Ćor Huso: A Study of Southslavic Song." Field notes, expedition to Yugoslavia. Extracts published in Parry 1971: 437–64.

————. 1937. "About Winged Words." *Classical Philology* 32: 59–63. Rpt. in Parry 1971: 414–18.

————. 1971. *The Making of Homeric Verse: The Collected Papers of Milman Parry.* Oxford: Clarendon Press, 1971.

Pavlović, J. M. 1921. *Život i običaji narodni u kragujevačkoj Jasenici u Šumadiji.* Belgrade: Srpska Kraljevska Akademija.

Peabody, Berkley. 1975. *The Winged Word: A Study in the Technique of Ancient Greek Oral Composition as Seen Principally through Hesiod's "Works and Days."* Albany: State University of New York Press.

Peters, Leonard J. 1951. "The Relationship of the Old English *Andreas* to *Beowulf.*" *Publications of the Modern Language Association* 66: 844–63.

Petrović, A. 1939. *Rakovica: socijalno-zdravstvene i higijenske prilike.* Belgrade: Biblioteka Centralnog Higijenskog Zavoda.

Petrović, P. Ž. 1948. *Život i običaji narodni u Gruži.* Belgrade: Srpska Akademija Nauka.

Pokorny, Julius. 1959/1969. *Indogermanisches etymologisches Wörterbuch.* 2 vols. Bern and Munich: A. Francke.

Pond, Wendy. 1990. "Wry Comment from the Outback: Songs of Protest from the Niua Islands, Tonga." *Oral Tradition* 5: 205–18.

Pope, M. W. M. 1963. "The Parry-Lord Theory of Homeric Composition." *Acta Classica* 6: 1–21.

Postlethwaite, N. 1979. "Formula and Formulaic: Some Evidence from the Homeric Hymns." *Phoenix* 33: 1–18.

Powell, Barry B. 1991. *Homer and the Origin of the Greek Alphabet.* Cambridge: Cambridge University Press.

Praxeis. 1898. M. Bonnet, ed. *Praxeis Andreou kai Mattheia. . . .* In *Acta Apostolorum Apocrypha . . . ,* vol. 2, pt. 1. Leipzig: Hermann Mendelssohn.

Race, William H. 1982. "Aspects of Rhetoric and Form in Greek Hymns." *Greek, Roman, and Byzantine Studies* 23: 5–14.

Radenković, Ljubinko. 1982. *Narodne basme i bajanja.* Niš: Gradina.

Reece, Steve. 1993. *The Stranger's Welcome: Oral Theory and the Aesthetics of the Homeric Hospitality Scene.* Ann Arbor: University of Michigan Press.

Renoir, Alain. 1981. "The Least Elegiac of the Elegies: A Contextual Glance at *The Husband's Message.*" *Studia Neophilologia* 53: 69–76.

————. 1988. *A Key to Old Poems: The Oral-Formulaic Approach to the Interpretation of West-Germanic Verse.* University Park: Pennsylvania State University Press.

Richardson, N. J. 1974. Ed., *The Homeric Hymn to Demeter.* Oxford: Clarendon Press.

Richman, Paula. 1991. Ed., *Many Ramayanas: The Diversity of a Narrative Tradition in South Asia.* Berkeley: University of California Press.

Riedinger, Anita. 1989. "*Andreas* and the Formula in Transition." In *Hermeneutics and Medieval Culture,* ed. Patrick J. Gallacher and Helen Damico, pp. 183–91. Albany: State University of New York Press.

————. 1993. "The Formulaic Relationship between *Beowulf* and *Andreas.*" In *Heroic Poetry in the Anglo-Saxon Period: Studies in Honor of Jess B. Bessinger, Jr.,* ed. Helen Damico and John Leyerle, pp. 283–312. Kalamazoo, Mich.: Medieval Institute.

Rissanen, Matti. 1969. "The Theme of 'Exile' in *The Wife's Lament.*" *Neuphilologische Mitteilungen* 70: 90–104.

Robinson, Fred C. 1973. "Anglo-Saxon Onomastics in the Old English *Andreas.*" *Names* 21: 133–36.

——. 1979. "Two Aspects of Variation in Old English Poetry." In *Old English Poetry: Essays on Style,* ed. Daniel G. Calder, pp. 127–45. Berkeley: University of California Press.

——. 1985. *Beowulf and the Appositive Style.* Knoxville: University of Tennessee Press.

Rosaldo, Michelle Z. 1982. "The Things We Do with Words: Ilongot Speech Acts and Speech Act Theory in Philosophy." *Language in Society* 11: 203–37.

Rosenberg, Bruce A. 1970. *The Art of the American Folk Preacher.* New York: Oxford University Press.

——. 1986. "The Message of the American Folk Sermon." *Oral Tradition* 1: 695–727.

Ruby, Jay. 1982. Ed., *A Crack in the Mirror: Reflexive Perspectives in Anthropology.* Philadelphia: University of Pennsylvania Press.

Russo, Joseph. 1994. "Homer's Style: Nonformulaic Features of an Oral Aesthetic." *Oral Tradition* 9: 371–89.

Sale, William. 1993. "Homer and *Roland*: The Shared Formular Technique." *Oral Tradition* 8: 87–142; 381–412.

SAN. 1959–. *Rečnik srpskohrvatskog književnog i narodnog jezika.* Belgrade: Institut za srpskohrvatski jezik, Srpska Akademija Nauka.

Sargent, Thelma. 1973. *The Homeric Hymns: A Verse Translation.* New York: W. W. Norton.

Sarrazin, Gregor. 1886. "Beowulf und Kynewulf." *Anglia* 9: 515–50.

Schaar, Claes. 1949. *Critical Studies in the Cynewulf Group.* Rpt. New York: Haskell House, 1967.

Schaefer, Ursula. 1991. "Hearing from Books: The Rise of Fictionality in Old English Poetry." In Doane and Pasternack 1991: 117–36.

Scheub, Harold. 1992. Ed., *The World and the Word: Tales and Observations from the Xhosa Oral Tradition.* By Nongenile Masithathu Zenani. Madison: University of Wisconsin Press.

SCHS. 1953–. *Serbocroatian Heroic Songs (Srpskohrvatske junačke pjesme).* Coll., trans., and ed. Milman Parry, Albert B. Lord, and David E. Bynum. Cambridge, Mass., and Belgrade: Harvard University Press and the Serbian Academy of Sciences.

Seeger, Anthony. 1986. "Oratory Is Spoken, Myth Is Told, and Song Is Sung, but They Are All Music to My Ears." In Sherzer and Urban 1986: 60–82.

Segal, Charles. 1992. "Bard and Audience in Homer." In *Homer's Ancient Readers: The Hermeneutics of Greek Epic's Earliest Exegetes,* pp. 3–29. Princeton: Princeton University Press.

Sherzer, Joel. 1983. *Kuna Ways of Speaking: An Ethnographic Perspective.* Austin: University of Texas Press.

——. 1987. "Poetic Structuring of Kuna Discourse: The Line." In Sherzer and Woodbury 1987a: 103–39.

——. 1992. "Modes of Representation and Translation of Native American Discourse: Examples from the San Blas Kuna." In *On the Translation of Native American Literatures,* ed. Brian Swann, pp. 426–40. Washington, D.C.: Smithsonian Institution.

Sherzer, Joel, and Greg Urban. 1986. Eds., *Native South American Discourse.* Berlin: Mouton de Gruyter.

Sherzer, Joel, and Sammie Ann Wicks. 1982. "The Intersection of Music and Language in Kuna Discourse." *Latin American Music Review* 3: 147–64.

Sherzer, Joel, and Anthony Woodbury. 1987a. Eds., *Native American Discourse: Poetics and Rhetoric.* Cambridge: Cambridge University Press.

——. 1987b. "Introduction" to 1987a: 1–16.

Shippey, Thomas. 1972. *Old English Verse.* London: Hutchinson.

Sifakis, G. M. 1992. "Homeric Survivals in the Medieval and Modern Greek Folksong Tradition?" *Greece & Rome,* 2nd ser. 39: 139–54.

Slyomovics, Susan. 1994. "Performing *A Thousand and One Nights* in Egypt." *Oral Tradition* 9: 390–419.

Smith, John D. 1991. *The Epic of Pabuji: A Study, Transcription, and Translation.* Cambridge: Cambridge University Press.

Sowa, Cora Angier. 1984. *Traditional Themes and the Homeric Hymns.* Chicago: Bolchazy-Carducci Publishers.

Spiegel, Gabrielle M. 1990. "History, Historicism, and the Social Logic of the Text in the Middle Ages." *Speculum* 65: 59–86.

Stevanović, Mihailo, et al. 1967. Eds., *Rečnik srpskohrvatskoga književnog jezika.* 6 vols. Novi Sad and Zagreb: Matica Srpska and Matica Hrvatska.

Stock, Brian. 1983. *The Implications of Literacy: Written Language and Models of Interpretation in the Eleventh and Twelfth Centuries.* Princeton: Princeton University Press.

———. 1990. *Listening for the Text: On the Uses of the Past.* Baltimore: Johns Hopkins University Press.

Stolz, Benjamin A. 1969. "On Two Serbo-Croatian Oral Epic Verses: The *Bugarštica* and the *Deseterac.*" In *Poetic Theory/Poetic Practice,* ed. Robert Scholes, pp. 155–64. Iowa City: Midwest Modern Language Association.

Street, Brian V. 1984. *Literacy in Theory and Practice.* Cambridge: Cambridge University Press.

Sweeney, Amin. 1987. *A Full Hearing: Orality and Literacy in the Malay World.* Berkeley: University of California Press.

Škaljić, Abdulah. 1979. *Turcizmi u srpskohrvatskom jeziku.* 4th ed. Sarajevo: Svjetlost.

Tedlock, Dennis. 1971. "On the Translation of Style in Oral Narrative." *Journal of American Folklore* 84: 114–33. Rpt. with "Epilogue" in Tedlock 1983: 31–61.

———. 1972a. *Finding the Center: Narrative Poetry of the Zuni Indians.* New York: Dial Press. Rpt. Lincoln: University of Nebraska Press, 1978.

———. 1972b. "Pueblo Literature: Style and Verisimilitude." In *New Perspectives on the Pueblos,* ed. Alfonso Ortiz, pp. 219–42. Albuquerque: University of New Mexico Press.

———. 1977. "Toward an Oral Poetics." *New Literary History* 8: 507–19.

———. 1983. *The Spoken Word and the Work of Interpretation.* Philadelphia: University of Pennsylvania Press.

———. 1985. *Popol Vuh: The Mayan Book of the Dawn of Life and the Glories of Gods and Kings.* New York: Simon and Schuster.

———. 1987. "Hearing a Voice in an Ancient Text: Quiché Maya Poetics in Performance." In Sherzer and Woodbury 1987a: 140–75.

———. 1990. "From Voice and Ear to Hand and Eye." *Journal of American Folklore* 103: 133–56.

Thomas, Rosalind. 1989. *Oral Tradition and Written Record in Classical Athens.* Cambridge: Cambridge University Press.

Toelken, J. Barre. 1969. "The 'Pretty Language' of Yellowman: Genre, Mode, and Texture in Navaho Coyote Performances." *Genre* 2: 211–35.

———. 1987. "Life and Death in the Navaho Coyote Tales." In *Recovering the Word: Essays on Native American Literature,* ed. Brian Swann and Arnold Krupat, pp. 388–401. Berkeley: University of California Press.

Toelken, J. Barre, and Tacheeni Scott. 1981. "Poetic Retranslation and the 'Pretty Languages' of Yellowman." In *Traditional Literatures of the American Indian: Texts and Interpretations,* ed. Karl Kroeber, pp. 65–116. Lincoln: University of Nebraska Press.

Tyler, Stephen A. 1987. *The Unspeakable: Discourse, Dialogue, and Rhetoric in the Postmodern World.* Madison: University of Wisconsin Press.

Urban, Greg. 1986. "Ceremonial Dialogues in South America." *American Anthropologist* 88: 371–86.

———. 1988. "Ritual Wailing in Amerindian Brazil." *American Anthropologist* 90: 385–400.

Urban, Greg, and Joel Sherzer. 1988. "The Linguistic Anthropology of Native South America." *Annual Review of Anthropology* 17: 283–307.

Vigorita, John F. 1976. "The Antiquity of Serbo-Croatian Verse." *Južnoslovenski filolog* 32: 205–11.

Vivante, Paolo. 1975. "On Homer's Winged Words." *Classical Quarterly,* n.s., 25: 1–12.

———. 1979. "Rosy-fingered Dawn and the Idea of Time." *Ramus* 8: 125–36.

———. 1982. *The Epithets in Homer: A Study in Poetic Values.* New Haven: Yale University Press.

Watkins, Calvert. 1976. "Response." In *Oral Literature and the Formula,* ed. Benjamin A. Stolz and Richard S. Shannon, pp. 107–11. Ann Arbor: Center for the Coordination of Ancient and Modern Studies.

Wilgus, D. K. 1973. "'The Text Is the Thing.'" *Journal of American Folklore* 86: 241–52.

Wilson, Duncan. 1970. *The Life and Times of Vuk Stefanović Karadžić, 1878–1864.* Oxford: Clarendon Press.

Wolf, Friedrich A. 1985. *Prolegomena to Homer.* Trans. from the 1795 Latin ed. by Anthony Grafton, Glenn W. Most, and James E. G. Zetzel. Princeton: Princeton University Press.

Woodbury, Anthony C. 1985. "The Functions of Rhetorical Structure: A Study of Central Alaskan Yupik Eskimo Discourse." *Language in Society* 14: 153–90.

———. 1987. "Rhetorical Structure in a Central Alaskan Yupik Eskimo Traditional Narrative." In Sherzer and Woodbury 1987a: 176–239.

Zan, Yigal. 1982. "The Text/Context Controversy: An Explanatory Perspective." *Western Folklore* 41: 1–27.

Zumthor, Paul. 1990. *Oral Poetry: An Introduction.* Trans. Kathryn Murphy-Judy. Minneapolis: University of Minnesota Press. Orig. pub. as *Introduction à la poésie orale* (Paris: Editions du Seuil, 1983).

Zumwalt, Rosemary Lévy. 1988. *American Folklore Scholarship: A Dialogue of Dissent.* Bloomington: Indiana University Press.

Zurbuchen, Mary Sabina. 1987. *The Language of Balinese Shadow Theater.* Princeton: Princeton University Press.

JOHN MILES FOLEY is William H. Byler Distinguished Professor of English and Classical Studies at the University of Missouri–Columbia, where he also directs the Center for Studies in Oral Tradition. The founding editor of the journal *Oral Tradition*, he is also author of *The Theory of Oral Composition, Traditional Oral Epic*, and *Immanent Art: From Structure to Meaning in Traditional Oral Epic*.